ESSAYS AND LECTURES
ON THE
RELIGIONS OF THE HINDUS

ESSAYS AND LECTURES
ON THE
RELIGIONS OF THE HINDUS

BY

H. H. WILSON, M. A. F.R.S.
LATE BODEN PROFESSOR OF SANSKRIT IN THE
UNIVERSITY OF OXFORD

COLLECTED AND EDITED BY

REINHOLD ROST, PH. D.

IN TWO VOLUMES.

VOL. I
SKETCH OF THE RELIGIOUS SECTS OF THE HINDUS.

GYAN

Published by

GYAN

Gyan Publishing House
5, Ansari Road
Daryaganj, New Delhi-110002
Phone: 011-47034999, 9811692060
E-mail: books@gyanbooks.com

Distribution Network
gyanbooks.com
India, USA, Canada, UK, Australia, France

ISBN : 978-81-212-3356-9 (Set)
ISBN : 978-81-212-4833-4 (HB)
First Published, London, 1861

2nd Impression 2020

Printed at: Gyan Press, Delhi.

**Essays and Lectures
on the
Religions of the Hindus**
Author: H. H. Wilson

ESSAYS AND LECTURES

ON THE

RELIGIONS OF THE HINDUS.

BY

H. H. WILSON, M.A., F.R.S.,

LATE BODEN PROFESSOR OF SANSKRIT IN THE UNIVERSITY OF OXFORD.

COLLECTED AND EDITED BY

REINHOLD ROST, PH. D.

IN TWO VOLUMES.

VOL. I.

SKETCH OF THE RELIGIOUS SECTS OF THE HINDUS.

LONDON:

TRÜBNER & CO. 60, PATERNOSTER ROW.

1861.

SKETCH

ON THE

RELIGIOUS SECTS OF THE HINDUS.

BY

H. H. WILSON, M.A., F.R.S.,

LATE BODEN PROFESSOR OF SANSKRIT IN THE UNIVERSITY OF OXFORD.

A NEW EDITION, SUPERINTENDED

BY

REINHOLD ROST, PH. D.

LONDON:

TRÜBNER & CO. 60, PATERNOSTER ROW.

1861.

PREFACE.

ABOVE forty-eight years have elapsed since Professor H. H. WILSON, then Assistant Surgeon in the service of the East India Company, published his translation of the Meghadúta, the first fruits of his literary labours in the mine of Sanskrit Literature. During the nineteen following years, while engaged in various official capacities, chiefly at Calcutta and Benares, and from the time of his return to England in 1832 till his death (on the 8th of May 1860) he continued to pursue his studies and researches on the literature, history, antiquities and religious systems of the Hindus with indefatigable industry. Ever zealously availing himself of the opportunities which were afforded him by his long residence in India and subsequently by his easy access to the rich stores of Manuscripts, accumulated both at the East India House and the Bodleian Library, for extending, deepening, and consolidating his investigations in Indian lore, he produced a large number of works of various extent, which for usefulness, depth of learning, and wide range of research show him to have been the worthy successor of Sir W. JONES and H. T. COLEBROOKE. The just appreciation of his merits, contained in the sketches of his life, character and labours, in the "Annual Report" of the R. Asiat. Soc. for 1860, and in the "Rapport" of the Société Asiatique for the same year, re-echoes but the meed of admiration and gratitude with which every student of Sanskrit acknowledges the obligations he owes to Professor WILSON's works. Many of these however, ranging as they do over a period of nearly half a century, were originally published in periodicals and transactions of oriental Societies not generally accessible, or have otherwise become scarce, while they still are the standard, and in some instances the only, authority on the various topics of which they treat. Every credit, therefore, is due to the publishers of the series of volumes, of which the present is the first instalment, for the spirit and zeal with which they formed, and at once took measures to carry out, the plan of reprinting a selection of his writings. Of the six divisions, in which these are to appear, the one containing Essays and Lectures on subjects connected with the religions of the Hindus, was proposed to come out first, and at the publishers' request the undersigned undertook to carry it through the press. As it was found expedient to adhere in each division, as far as practicable, to the chronological order in which the several essays intended for it were originally published, the commencement was made with the celebrated "Sketch of the Religious Sects of the Hindus", the first portion of which appeared in the Asiatic Researches for 1828, and the second (from p. 188 of the present edition) in the volume for 1832. The remaining eight Essays and Lectures selected for this division will form the second volume, which is in the press.

On account of the variety of manuscript sources in Persian, Sanskrit, Bengali and different dialects of Hindi, from which the author gleaned the materials for his "Sketch of the Religious Sects of the Hindus", thorough consistency and uniformity in the transliteration of Indian names would have been beyond what could be expected by anyone ever so slightly acquainted with the various graphical, and still more phonetical, changes to which Sanskrit words are liable when passing into the vernacular idioms of modern India. No improvement in this respect was aimed at in the reprint of this work which appeared at Calcutta in the year 1846 (pp. 238 in 8vo), and in which even the most obvious misprints of the original edition have been reproduced with scrupulous fidelity. Some care has, therefore, been bestowed in the present edition upon introducing such accuracy in the spelling of Indian words, both ancient and modern, as shall enable the student to trace without difficulty their original forms. In cases of slight, but unavoidable discrepancies, occasioned, it is feared, in not a few instances by the want of ready communication between the editor and the printer, the reader is referred to the Index. However desirable, too, it would have been to verify the many quotations contained in the Notes, this has been found practicable only so far as some access to the printed literature of India enabled the editor to trace them. With regard to those of them which he has failed to verify he must plead as his excuse that he undertook and carried on the work of editing with but little time to spare from his other avocations. The verifications which he has succeeded in tracing, and the references and few other additions he has thought necessary to make, are enclosed in brackets []; and he hopes that the volume, in the attractive garb, which publishers and printer have combined to give it, may not be the less welcome both to the student of Hindu literature and antiquities, and to everyone to whom the improvement of the religious condition of the Hindus is at heart.

St. Augustine's College, Canterbury;
Oct. 18, 1861.

R. R.

TABLE OF CONTENTS.

A SKETCH

OF THE

RELIGIOUS SECTS OF THE HINDUS.

From the Asiatic Researches, Vols. XVI, Calc. 1828, p. 1–136, and XVII, Calc. 1832, p. 169–314.

SECTION I.

INTRODUCTORY OBSERVATIONS.

THE Hindu religion is a term, that has been hitherto employed in a collective sense, to designate a faith and worship of an almost endlessly diversified description: to trace some of its varieties is the object of the present enquiry.

An early division of the Hindu system, and one conformable to the genius of all Polytheism, separated the practical and popular belief, from the speculative or philosophical doctrines. Whilst the common people addressed their hopes and fears to stocks and stones, and multiplied by their credulity and superstition the grotesque objects of their veneration, some few, of deeper thought and wider contemplation, plunged into the mysteries of man and nature, and endeavoured assiduously, if not successfully, to obtain just notions of the cause, the character and consequence of existence. This distinction prevails even in the *Vedas*, which have their *Karma Káńda* and *Jnána Káńda*, or Ritual and Theology.

The worship of the populace being addressed to different divinities, the followers of the several gods naturally separated into different associations, and the adorers of Brahmá, Vishńu, and Śiva or other phantoms of their faith, became distinct and insulated bodies, in the general aggregate: the conflict of opinion on subjects, on which human reason has never yet agreed, led to similar differences in the philosophical class, and resolved itself into the several *Darśanas*, or schools of philosophy.

It may be supposed, that some time elapsed before the practical worship of any deity was more thán a simple preference, or involved the assertion of the supremacy of the object of its adoration, to the degradation or exclusion of the other gods[1]: in like manner also, the conflicting opinions were matters rather of curiosity than faith, and were neither regarded as subversive of each other, nor as incompatible with the public worship: and hence, notwithstanding the sources of difference that existed in the parts, the unity of the whole remained undisturbed: in this condition, indeed, the apparent mass of the

[1] One division of some antiquity is the preferential appropriation of the four chief divinities to the four original casts; thus Śiva is the *Ádideva* of the *Brahmans*, Vishńu of the *Kshattriyas*, Brahmá of the *Vaiśyas*, and Gańeśa of the *Śúdras*:

विप्राणां दैवतं शम्भुः क्षत्त्रियाणां तु माधवः ।
वैश्यानां तु भवेद्ब्रह्मा शूद्राणां गणनायकः ॥ इति मनुः ॥

Brahmanical order at least, still continues: professing alike to recognise implicitly the authority of the *Vedas*, the worshippers of Śiva, or of Vishńu, and the maintainers of the *Sánkhya* or *Nyáya* doctrines, consider themselves, and even each other, as orthodox members of the Hindu community.

To the internal incongruities of the system, which did not affect its integral existence, others were, in time, superadded, that threatened to dissolve or destroy the whole: of this nature was the exclusive adoration of the old deities, or of new forms of them; and even it may be presumed, the introduction of new divinities. In all these respects, the *Puráńas* and *Tantras* were especially instrumental, and they not only taught their followers to assert the unapproachable superiority of the gods they worshipped, but inspired them with feelings[1] of animosity towards those

[1] Thus in the Bhágavat:

भवव्रतधरा ये च ये च तान्समनुव्रताः ।
पाषण्डिनस्ते भवन्तु सच्छास्त्रपरिपन्थिनः ॥

Those who profess the worship of Bhava, (Śiva,) and those who follow their doctrines, are heretics and enemies of the sacred *Śástras,*—Again:

मुमुक्षवो घोररूपान्हित्वा भूतपतीनथ ।
नारायणकलाः शान्ता भजन्ति ह्यनसूयवः ॥

Those desirous of final emancipation, abandoning the hideous gods of the devils, pursue their devotions, calm, blameless, and being parts of Náráyańa.

The *Padma Puráńa* is more personal towards Vishńu:

विष्णुदर्शनमात्रेण शिवद्रोहः प्रजायते ॥
शिवद्रोहान्न सन्देहो नरकं याति दारुणम् ।
तस्मान्न विष्णुनामाऽपि न वक्तव्यं कदाचन ॥

who presumed to dispute that supremacy: in this conflict the worship of BRAHMÁ has disappeared[1], as well as, indeed, that of the whole pantheon, except VISHṄU, ŚIVA and ŚAKTI, or their modifications; with respect to the two former, in fact, the representatives have borne away the palm from the prototypes, and KṘISHṄA, RÁMA, or the *Linga*, are almost the only forms

From even looking at VISHṄU, the wrath of ŚIVA is kindled, and from his wrath, we fall assuredly into a horrible hell; let not, therefore, the name of VISHṄU ever be pronounced.

The same work is, however, cited by the VAISHṄAVAS, for a very opposite doctrine.

वासुदेवं परित्यज्य यो ऽन्यदेवमुपासते ।
तृषितो जाह्नवीतीरे कूपं खनति दुर्मतिः ॥

He who abandons VÁSUDEVA and worships any other god, is like the fool, who being thirsty, sinks a well in the bank of the Ganges.

The principle goes still further, and those who are inimical to the followers of a Deity, are stigmatised as his personal foes —thus in the *Ádi Puráṅa,* VISHṄU says:

मद्भक्तो वल्लभो यस्य स एव मम वल्लभः ।
तत्परो वल्लभो नास्ति सत्यं सत्यं धनञ्जय ॥

He to whom my votary is a friend, is my friend—he who is opposed to him, is no friend of mine—be assured, *Dhananjaya,* of this.

[1] ŚIVA himself, in the form of KÁLA BHAIRAVA, tore off BRAHMÁ's fifth head, for presuming to say, that he was BRAHMA, the eternal and omnipotent cause of the world, and even the creator of ŚIVA, notwithstanding the four VEDAS and the personified *Omkára*, had all given evidence, that this great, true and indescribable deity was ŚIVA himself. The whole story occurs in the *Káśí Khaṅd* [c. 31] of the *Skanda Puráṅa,* and its real signification is sufficiently obvious.

under which VISHŃU and ŚIVA are now adored in most parts of India[1].

The varieties of opinion kept pace with those of practice, and six heretical schools of philosophy disputed the pre-eminence with their orthodox brethren: we have little or no knowledge of these systems, and even their names are not satisfactorily stated: they seem, however, to be the *Saugata* or *Bauddha*, *Árhata*, or *Jaina*, and *Várhaspatya*, or Atheistical, with their several subdivisions[2].

Had the difference of doctrine taught in the heretical schools been confined to tenets of a merely speculative nature, they would, probably, have encountered little opposition, and excited little enmity among the Brah-

---

[1] The great text-book of the *Vaishńavas* is the *Bhágavat*, with which it may be supposed the present worship, in a great measure, originated, although the Mahábhárat and other older works had previously introduced this divinity. The worship of the *Linga* is, no doubt, very ancient, although it has received, within a few centuries, its present degree of popularity: the *Káśi Khańd* was evidently written to enforce it, and at Benares, its worship entirely overshadows every other ritual.

[2] In a work written by the celebrated *Mádhava*, describing the different ssets as they existed in his day, entitled the *Sarva Darśana*, the *Várhaspatyas*, *Lokáyatas*, and *Chárvákas* are identified, and are really advocates of an atheistical doctrine, denying the existence of a God, or a future state, and referring creation to the aggregation of but four elements. The *Bauddhas*, according to the same authority, admit of four subdivisions, the *Madhyámikas*, *Yogáchàras*, *Sautrántikas* and *Vaibháshikas*. The Jains or Arhats, as still one of the popular divisions, we shall have occasion to notice in the text.

manical class, of which latitude of opinion is a very common characteristic. The founder of the Atheistical school, however, VṚIHASPATI, attacks both the *Vedas* and the *Brahmans*, and asserts that the whole of the Hindu system is a contrivance of the Priesthood, to secure a means of livelihood for themselves[1], whilst the *Bauddhas* and *Jainas*, equally disregarding the *Vedas* and the *Brahmans*, the practice and opinions of the Hindus, invented a set of gods for themselves, and deposed the ancient pantheon: these aggressions provoked resentment: the writings of these sects are alluded to with every epithet of anger and contempt, and they are all anathematised as heretical and atheistical; more active measures than anathemas, it may be presumed, were had recourse to: the followers of

---

[1] Vṛihaspati has the following texts to this effect, [quoted in the Sarva Darśana, Calcutta edition, pp. 3 and 6, and with a v. l. Prabodhach. ed. Brockhaus, p. 30]:

अग्निहोत्रं त्रयो वेदास्त्रिदण्डं भस्मगुण्ठनम् ।
बुद्धिपौरुषहीनानां जीविकेति बृहस्पतिः ॥

"The Agnihotra, the three Vedas, the Tridańda, the smearing of ashes, are only the livelihood of those who have neither intellect nor spirit." After ridiculing the Śráddha, shrewdly enough, he says:

ततश्च जीवनोपायो ब्राह्मणैर्विहितस्त्विह ।
मृतानां प्रेतकार्याणि न त्वन्यद्विद्यते क्वचित् ॥

Hence it is evident, that it was a mere contrivance of the Brahmans to gain a livelihood, to ordain such ceremonies for the dead, and no other reason can be given for them. Of the *Vedas*, he says: त्रयो वेदस्य कर्तारो भण्डधूर्त्तनिशाचराः ॥

The three Authors of the *Vedas* were Buffoons, Rogues, and Fiends—and cites texts in proof of this assertion.

VṚIHASPATI, having no worship at all, easily eluded the storm, but the *Bauddhas* of Hindustan were annihilated by its fury, and the *Jainas* apparently evaded it with difficulty, although they have undoubtedly survived its terrors, and may now defy its force.

The varieties thus arising from innovations in practice and belief, have differed, it may be concluded, at different eras of the Hindu worship. To trace the character of those which have latterly disappeared, or to investigate the remote history of some which still remain and are apparently of ancient date, are tasks for which we are far from being yet prepared: the enquiry is, in itself so vast, and so little progress has been made in the studies necessary to its elucidation, that it must yet remain in the obscurity in which it has hitherto been enveloped; so ambitious a project as that of piercing the impenetrable gloom has not instigated the present attempt, nor has it been proposed to undertake so arduous a labour, as the investigation and comparison of the abstruse notions of the philosophical sects[1]. The humbler aim of these researches has been that of ascertaining the actual condition of the popular religion of the inhabitants of some of the provinces subject to the Bengal Govern-

[1] Something of this has been very well done by *Mr. Ward*, in his account of the Hindus: and since this Essay was read before the Society, the account given by H. T. Colebrooke, Esq. in the first part of the Transactions of the Royal Asiatic Society, of the Sánkhya and Nyáya Systems, has left little more necessary on this subject.

ment; and as a very great variety prevails in that religion, the subject may be considered as not devoid of curiosity and interest, especially as it has been left little better than a blank, in the voluminous compositions or compilations, professing to give an account of the native country of the Hindus.

The description of the different sects of the Hindus, which I propose to offer, is necessarily superficial: it would, indeed, have been impossible to have adopted the only unexceptionable method of acquiring an accurate knowledge of their tenets and observances, or of studying the numerous works in Sanskrit, Persian, or the provincial dialects of Hindi, on which they are founded. I have been obliged to content myself, therefore, with a cursory inspection of a few of those compositions, and to depend for much of my information on oral report, filling up or correcting from these two sources the errors and omissions of two works, on this subject professedly, from which I have derived the ground work of the whole account.

The works alluded to are in the Persian language, though both were written by Hindu authors; the first was compiled by Sítal Sinh, Múnshí to the *Rájá* of Benares; the second by Mathurá Náth, late librarian of the Hindu College, at the same city, a man of great personal respectability and eminent acquirements: these works contain a short history of the origin of the various sects, and descriptions of the appearance, and observances, and present condition of their followers: they comprise all the known varieties, with one or two exceptions, and, indeed, at no one place in India could the enquiry be so well prosecuted as at Benares[1]. The work of MATHURÁ NÁTH is the fullest and most satisfactory, though it leaves much to be desired, and much more than I have been able to supply. In addition to these sources of information, I have had frequent recourse to a work of great popularity and extensive circulation, which embodies the legendary history of all the most celebrated *Bhaktas* or devotees of the Vaishńava order. This work is entitled the *Bhakta Málá*. The original, in a difficult dialect of Hindi, was composed by NÁBHÁJI, about 250 years ago[2], and is little more than a catalogue, with brief and obscure references to some leading circumstances connected with the life of each individual, and from the inexplicit nature of its allusions, as well as the difficulty of its style, is far from intelligible to the generality even of the natives. The work, in its present form, has received some modifications, and obvious additions from a later teacher, NÁRÁYAŃ DÁS, whose share in the composition is, no doubt,

---

[1] The acknowledged resort of all the vagabonds of India, and all who have no where else to repair to: so, the *Káśí Khańd*:

श्रुतिस्मृतिविहीनानां ये शौचाचारविवर्जिताः ।
येषां क्वापि गतिर्नास्ति तेषां वाराणसी गतिः ॥

"To those who are strangers to the *Śruti* and *Smŕiti* (Religion and Law); to those who have never known the observance of pure and indispensable rites; to those who have no other place to repair to; to those, is Benares an asylum." [Compare Prabodhach. ed. Brockhaus, p. 19.]

[2] [Journ. As. Soc. Bombay, Vol. III, p. 4.]

considerable, but cannot be discriminated from NÁBHÁJI's own, beyond the evidence furnished by the specificaction of persons unquestionably subsequent to his time.—NÁRÁYAŃ DÁS probably wrote in the reign of SHÁH JEHÁN. The brevity and obscurity of the original work pervade the additional matter, and to remedy these defects, the original text, or *Múla,* has been take as a guide for an amplified notice of its subjects, or the *Ťíká* of KŔISHŃA DÁS; and the work, as usually met with, always consists of these two divisions. The *Ťíká* is dated *Samvat,* 1769 or A. D. 1713. Besides these, a translation of the *Ťíká*, or a version of it in the more ordinary dialect of Hindustan, has been made by an anonymous author, and a copy of this work, as well as of the original, has furnished me with materials for the following account. The character of the *Bhakta Málá* will best appear from the extracts of translations from it to be hereafter introduced: it may be sufficient here to observe, that it is much less of a historical than legendary description, and that the legends are generally insipid and extravagant: such as it is, however, it exercises a powerful influence, in Upper India, on popular belief, and holds a similar place in the superstitions of this country, as that which was occupied in the darkest ages of the Roman Catholic faith, by the Golden Legend and Acts of the Saints[1].

---

[1] In further illustration of our text, with regard to the instrumentality of the *Puráńas* in generating religious distinctions amongst the Hindus, and as affording a view of the *Vaishńava*

SECTION II.

STATE OF THE HINDU RELIGION, ANTERIOR TO ITS PRESENT CONDITION.

Although I have neither the purpose nor the power to enter into any detail of the remote condition of the

---

feelings on this subject, we may appeal to the *Padma Puráńa*. In the *Uttara Khańda*, or last portion of this work, towards the end of it, several sections are occupied with a dialogue between Śiva and Párvatí, in which the former teaches the latter the leading principles of the *Vaishńava* faith. Two short sections are devoted to the explanation of who are heretics, and which are the heretical works. All are *Páshańdas*, Śiva says, who adore other gods than Vishńu, or who hold, that other deities are his equals, and all Brahmans who are not *Vaishńavas*, are not to be looked at, touched, nor spoken to:—

ये अन्यं देवं परत्वेन वदन्त्यज्ञानमोहिताः ।
नारायणाज्जगन्नाथात्ते वै पाषण्डिनः स्मृताः ॥
यस्तु नारायणं देवं ब्रह्मरुद्रादिदैवतैः ॥
सममन्यैर्निरीक्षेत स पाषण्डी भवेत्सदा ॥
किमत्र बहुनोक्तेन ब्राह्मणा ये ऽप्यवैष्णवाः ।
न स्प्रष्टव्या न वक्तव्या न द्रष्टव्याः कदाचन ॥

Śiva, in acknowledging that the distinguishing marks of his votaries, the skull, tiger's skin, and ashes, are reprobated by the Vedas (Śrutigarhitam) states, that he was directed by Vishńu to inculcate their adoption, purposely to lead those who assumed them into error.—Namuchi and other *Daityas* had become so powerful by the purity of their devotions, that Indra and the other gods were unable to oppose them. The gods had recourse to Vishńu, who, in consequence, ordered Śiva to introduce the *Śaiva* tenets and practices, by which the *Daityas* were beguiled, and rendered "wicked, and thence weak."

In order to assist Śiva in this work, ten great Sages were imbued with the *Támasa* property, or property of darkness and

Hindu faith, yet as its present state is of comparatively very recent origin, it may form a not unnecessary, nor

---

ignorance, and by them such writings were put forth as were calculated to disseminate unrighteous and heretical doctrines, these were KAŃÁDA, GAUTAMA, ŚAKTI, UPAMANYU, JAIMINI, KAPILA, DURVÁSAS, MŔIKAŃDA, VŔIHASPATI, and BHÁRGAVA.

By ŚIVA himself, the *Páśupata* writings were composed; KAŃÁDA is the author of the *Vaiśeshika* Philosophy. The *Nyáya* originates with GAUTAMA. KAPILA, is the founder of the *Sánkhya* School, and VŔIHASPATI of the *Chárváka.* JAIMINI, by ŚIVA's orders, composed the *Mímánsá,* which is heretical, in as far as it inculcates works in preference to faith, and ŚIVA himself, in the disguise of a Brahman, or as VYÁSA, promulgated the Vedánta, which is heterodox in *Vaishńava* estimation, by denying the sensible attributes of the deity. VISHŃU, as BUDDHA, taught the *Bauddha Śástra,* and the practices of going naked, or wearing blue garments, meaning, consequently, not the *Bauddhas,* but the *Jainas,* (बौद्धशास्त्रमसत्प्रोक्तं नग्ननीलपटादिकं). The *Puráńas* were partly instrumental in this business of blinding mankind, and they are thus distinguished by our authority and all the *Vaishńava* works.

The *Mátsya, Kaurma, Lainga, Śaiva, Skánda* and *Agneya,* are *Támasa,* or the works of darkness, having more or less of a *Śaiva* bias.

The *Vishńu, Náradíya, Bhágavat, Gáruda, Pádma* and *Váráha,* are *Sáttwika,* pure and true; being in fact, *Vaishńava* text books.

The *Brahmáńda, Brahma Vaivartta, Márkańdeya, Bhavishya, Vámana* and *Brahmá,* are of the *Rájasa* cast, emanating from the quality of passion. As far as I am acquainted with them, they lean to the *Śákta* division of the Hindus, or the worship of the female principle. The *Márkańdeya* does so notoriously, containing the famous *Chańdí Pátha,* or *Durgá Máhátmya,* which is read at the *Durgá Pújá;* the *Brahma Vaivartta,* is especially dedicated to KŔISHŃA as GOVINDA, and is principally occupied by him and his mistress RÁDHÁ. It is also full on the subject of *Prakŕiti* or personified nature.

uninteresting preliminary branch of the enquiry, to endeavour to determine its existing modifications, at the period immediately preceding the few centuries, which have sufficed to bestow upon it its actual form:

A similar distinction is made even with the *Smṙitis*, or works on law. The codes of VASISHṪHA, HÁRÍTA, VYÁSA, PARÁŚARA, BHARADWÁJA and KAŚYAPA, are of the pure order. Those of YÁJNAVALKYA, ATRI, TITTIRI, DAKSHA, KÁTYÁYANA and VISHṄU of the *Rájasa* class, and those of GAUTAMA, VṘIHASPATI, SAMVARTTA, YAMA, ŚANKHA and UŚANAS, are of the *Támasa* order.

The study of the Puráṅas and Smṙitis of the *Sáttwika* class, secures *Mukti*, or final emancipation, that of those of the *Rájasa* obtains *Swarga*, or Paradise; whilst that of the *Támasa* condemns a person to hell, and a wise man will avoid them.

किमत्र बहुनोक्तेन पुराणेषु स्मृतिष्वपि ।
तामसा नरकायैव वर्ज्जयेत्तान्विचक्षणः ॥

The Vaishṅava writers endeavour to enlist the *Vedas* in their cause, and the following texts are quoted by the Tátparya Nirṅaya:

एको नारायण आसीन्न ब्रह्मा न च शंकरः ।

NÁRÁYAṄA alone was, not BRAHMÁ nor ŚANKARA.

वासुदेवो वा इदमग्र आसीन्न ब्रह्मा न च शंकरः ।

Or VÁSUDEVA was before this (universe,) not BRAHMÁ nor ŚANKARA.

The Śaivas cite the Vedas too, as

सर्वव्यापी स भगवांस्तस्मात्सर्वगतः शिवः ॥

The Lord who pervades all things, is thence termed the omnipresent Śiva.

Rudra is but one, and has no second—

एको ऽपि रुद्रो न द्वितीयः ॥

These citations would scarcely have been made, if not authentic; they probably do occur in the Vedas, but the terms *Náráyaṅa* and *Vásudeva*, or *Śiva* and *Rudra*, are not to be taken in the restricted sense, probably, which their respective followers would assign them.

it happens, also, that some controversial works exist, which throw considerable light upon the subject, and of which the proximity of their date, to the matters of which they treat, may be conjectured with probability or positively ascertained. Of these, the two principal works, and from which I shall derive such scanty information as is attainable, are the *Śankara Digvijaya* of ÁNANDA GIRI, and the *Sarva Darśana Sangraha* of MÁDHAVÁCHÁRYA, the former a reputed disciple of ŚANKARA himself, and the latter a well known and able writer, who lived in the commencement of the 14th century.

The authenticity of the latter of these two works, there is no room to question; and there is but little reason to attach any doubt to the former. Some of the marvels it records of ŚANKARA, which the author professes to have seen, may be thought to affect its credibility, if not its authenticity, and either ÁNANDA GIRI must be an unblushing liar, or the book is not his own: it is, however, of little consequence, as even, if the work be not that of ÁNANDA GIRI himself, it bears internal and indisputable evidence of being the composition of a period, not far removed from that at which he may be supposed to have flourished, and we may, therefore, follow it as a very safe guide, in our enquiries into the actual state of the Hindu Religion about eight or nine centuries ago.

The various sectaries of the Hindu Religion then existing, are all introduced to be combated, and, of course, conquered, by ŚANKARA: the list is rather a long one, but it will be necessary to go through the whole, to ascertain the character of the national faith of those days, and its present modifications, noticing, as we proceed, some of the points of difference or resemblance between the forms of worship which then prevailed, and which now exist. The two great divisions of *Vaishńavas* and *Śaivas* were both in a flourishing condition, and each embraced six principal subdivisions: we shall begin with the former, who are termed; *Bháktas, Bhágavatas, Vaishńavas, Chakrińas,* or *Pancharátrakas*, *Vaikhánasas* and *Karmahínas.*

But as each of these was subdivided into a practical and speculative, or *Karma* and *Jnána* portion, they formed, in fact, twelve classes of the followers of VISHŃU, as the sole and supreme deity.

The *Bháktas* worshipped VISHŃU as VÁSUDEVA, and wore no characteristic marks. The *Bhágavatas* worshipped the same deity as BHÁGAVAT, and impressed upon their persons the usual *Vaishńava* insignia, representing the discus, club, &c. of that divinity; they likewise reverenced the *Sálagrám* stone, and *Tulasi* plant, and in several of their doctrinal notions, as well as in these respects, approach to the present followers of RÁMÁNUJA, although they cannot be regarded as exactly the same. The authorities of these three sects were the *Upanishads* and *Bhagavad Gítá.* The names of both the sects still remain, but they are scarcely applicable to any particular class of *Vaishńavas:* the terms *Bhakta*, or *Bhagat*, usually indicate any individual who pretends to a more rigid devotion than his neighbours, and who especially occupies his mind with spiritual considerations: the *Bhágavat* is one who follows particularly the authority of the *Śrí Bhágavat Puráńa.*

The *Vaishńavas* adored VISHŃU as NÁRÁYAŃA, they wore the usual marks, and promised themselves a sort of sensual paradise after death, in *Vaikuńtha*, or VISHŃU's heaven; their tenets are still current, but they can scarcely be considered to belong to any separate sect.

The *Chakrińas*, or *Pancharátrakas* were, in fact, *Śáktas* of the *Vaishńava* class, worshipping the female personifications of VISHŃU, and observing the ritual of the *Pancharátra Tantra:* they still remain, but scarcely individualised, being confounded with the worshippers of KŔISHŃA and RÁMA on the one hand, and those of *Śakti* or *Deví* on the other.

The *Vaikhánasas* appear to have been but little different from the *Vaishńavas* especially so called; at least ÁNANDA GIRI has not particularised the difference; they worshipped NÁRÁYAŃA as supreme god, and wore his marks. The *Karmahínas* abstained, as the name implies, from all ritual observances, and professed to know *Vishńu* as the sole source and sum of the universe, सर्वं विष्णुमयं जगत्; they can scarcely be considered as an existent sect, though a few individuals of the *Rámánujíya* and *Rámánandí Vaishńavas* may profess the leading doctrines.

The *Vaishńava* forms of the Hindu faith are still, as we shall hereafter see, sufficiently numerous; but we can scarcely identify any one of them with those which seem to have prevailed when the *Śankara Vijaya* of Ánanda Giri was composed. The great divisions, of Rámánuja and Rámánand—the former of which originated, we know, in the course of the 11th century, are unnoticed, and it is also worth while to observe, that neither in this, nor in any other portion of the *Śankara Vijaya*, is any allusion made to the separate worship of Kŕishńa, either in his own person, or that of the infantine forms in which he is now so pre-eminently venerated in many parts of India, nor are the names of Ráma and Sítá, of Lakshmańa or Hanumán, once particularised, as enjoying any portion of distinct and specific adoration.

The *Śaiva* sects are the *Śaivas*, *Raudras*, *Ugras*, *Bháktas*, *Jangamas*, and *Páśupatas*. Their tenets are so blended in the discussion, that it is not possible to separate them, beyond the conjectural discrimination which may be derived from their appellations: the text specifies merely their characteristic marks: thus the *Śaivas* wore the impression of the *Linga* on both arms; the *Raudras* had a *Triśúla*, or trident, stamped on the forehead; the *Ugras* had the *Ḍamaru*, or drum of *Śiva* on their arms, and the *Bháktas* an impression of the *Linga* on the forehead—the *Jangamas* carried a figure of the *Linga* on the head, and the *Páśupatas* inprinted the same object on the forehead, breast, navel, and arms. Of these sects, the *Śaivas* are not now any one particular class—nor are the *Raudras*, *Ugras*, or *Bháktas*, any longer distinct societies: the *Jangamas* remain, but they are chiefly confined to the south of India, and although a *Páśupata*, or worshipper of ŚIVA as PAŚUPATI, may be occasionally encountered, yet this has merged into other sects, and particularly into that of the *Kánphátá Jogis:* the authorities cited bey these sects, according to ÁNANDA GIRI, were the *Śiva Gítá*, *Śiva Sanhitá*, *Śiva Ráhasya* and *Rudra Yámala Tantra:* the various classes of *Jogis* are never alluded to, and the work asserts, what is generally admitted as a fact, that the *Dańdis*, and *Daśnámí Gosains* originated with ŚANKARA ÁCHÁRYA.

Worshippers of BRAHMÁ, or HIRAŃYAGARBHA, are also introduced by ÁNANDA GIRI, whom now it might be difficult to meet with: exclusive adorers of this deity, and temples dedicated to him, do not now occur perhaps in any part of India; at the same time it is an error to suppose that public homage is never paid to him. BRAHMÁ is particularly reverenced at *Pokher* in *Ajmír*, also at *Bithúr*, in the *Doab*, where, at the principal Ghát, denominated *Brahmávartta Ghát*, he is said to have offered an *Aśwamedha* on completing the act of creation: the pin of his slipper left behind him on the occasion, and now fixed in one of the steps of the Ghát, is still worshipped there, and on the full moon of Agrahávana (Nov.-Dec.) a very numerously attended *Melá*, or meeting, that mixes piety with profit, is annually held at that place.

The worshippers of AGNI no longer form a distinct class, a few *Agnihotra Brahmans*, who preserve the family fire, may be met with, but in all other respects they conform to some mode of popular devotion.

The next opponents of Śankara Áchárya were the *Sauras*, or worshippers of the sun, as the creator and cause of the world: a few *Sauras*, chiefly *Brahmans*, still exist as a sect, as will be hereafter noticed; but the divisions enumerated by Ánanda Giri, are now, it is believed, unknown: he distinguishes them into the following six classes.

Those who adored the rising sun, regarding it as especially the type of Brahmá, or the creative power. Those who worshipped the meridian sun as Íśwara, the destructive and regenerative faculty; and those who reverenced the setting sun, as the prototype of Vishńu, or the attribute of preservation.

The fourth class comprehended the advocates of the *Trimúrti*, who addressed their devotions to the sun in all the preceding states, as the comprehensive type of these three divine attributes.

The object of the fifth form is not quite clearly stated, but it appears to have been the adoration of the sun as a positive and material body, and the marks on his surface, as his hair, beard, &c. The members of this class so far correspond with the *Sauras* of the present day, as to refrain from food until they had seen the sun.

The sixth class of *Sauras*, in opposition to the preceding, deemed it unnecessary to address their devotions to the visible and material sun: they provided a mental luminary, on which they meditated, and to which their adoration was offered: they stamped circular orbs en their foreheads, arms, and breasts with hot irons; a practice uniformly condemned by Śankara, as contrary to the laws of the *Vedas*, and the respect due to Brahmanical flesh and blood.

Gańeśa, as well as Súrya, had formerly six classes of adorers; in the present day he cannot boast of any exclusive worship, although he shares a sort of homage with almost all the other divinities: his followers were the worshippers of Mahá Gańapati, of Haridra Gańapati, or Ḍhúńḍí Ráj, who is still a popular form of Gańeśa, of Uchchhisht́ha G., of Navanı́ta G., of Swarńa G., and of Santána G. The left hand sub-division of the Uchchhisht́ha Gańapatí sect, also called *Hairamba*, abrogated all obligatory ritual and distinction of caste.

The adorers of the female personifications of divine power, appear to have been fully as numerous as at present, and to have worshipped the same ocjects, or Bhavání, Mahá Lakshmí, and Saraswatí: even as personifications of these divinities, however, the worship of Sítá and Rádhá, either singly, or in conjunction with Ráma and Krishńa, never makes its appearence. The worshippers of *Śakti* were then, as now, divided into two classes, a right and left hand order, and three sub-divisions of the latter are enumerated, who are still well known—the *Púrńábhishiktas*, *Akŕitárthas*, *Kŕitákŕityasamas*.

There can be little doubt, that the course of time and the presence of foreign rulers, have very much ameliorated the character of much of the Hindu worship: if the licentious practices of the Śáktas are still as prevalent as ever, which may well be questioned, they are, at least, carefully concealed from observation, and if they are not exploded, there are other observances of a more ferocious description, which seem to have disappeared. The worship of Bhairava still prevails amongst the *Śáktas* and the *Jogís;* but in upper India, at least, the naked mendicant, smeared with funeral ashes, armed with a trident or a sword, carrying a hollow skull in his hand, and half intoxicated with the spirits which he has quaffed from that disgusting wine-cup, prepared, in short, to perpetrate any act of violence and crime, the *Kápálika* of former days, is now rarely, if ever, encountered. In the work of Ánanda Giri, we have two of these sectaries introduced, one a Brahman by birth, is the genuine *Kápálika:* he drinks wine, eats flesh, and abandons all rites and observances in the spirit of his faith, his eminence in which has armed him with supernatural powers, and rendered Bhairava himself the reluctant, but helpless minister of his will. The other *Kápálika* is an impostor, the son of a harlot, by a gatherer of *Tádí*, or Palm juice, and who has adopted the character as an excuse for throwing off all social and moral restraint. The *Kápálikas* are often alluded to in controversial works, that appear to be the compositions of a period at least preceding the tenth century[1].

---

[1] See the Prabodha Chandrodaya, translated by Dr. Taylor [especially Act. III, Sc. 8 and ff.].

The next classes of sectaries, confuted by ŚANKARA, were various infidel sects, some of whom avowedly, and perhaps all covertly, are still in being: the list is also interesting, as discriminating opinions which, in the ignorance subsequent to their disappearance from Hindustan, have very commonly been, and, indeed, still are frequently confounded. These are the *Chárvákas,* or *Śúnya Vádís,* the *Saugatas,* the *Kshapańakas,* the *Jainas,* and the *Bauddhas.*

The *Chárvakas* were so named from one of their teachers, the MUNI CHÁRVÁKA. From VŔIHASPATI—some of whose dogmas have been quoted from the work of MÁDHAVA, they are termed also *Várhaspatyas.* The appellation *Śúnya Vádí* implies the asserter of the unreality and emptiness of the universe, and another designation, *Lokáyata,* expresses their adoption of the tenet, that this being is the *Be-all* of existence: they were, in short, the advocates of materialism and atheism, and have existed from a very remote period, and still exist, as we shall hereafter see.

The *Saugatas* are identified even by MÁDHAVA with *Bauddhas,* but there seems to have been some, although probably not any very essential difference: the chief tenet of this class, according to ÁNANDA GIRI, was their adopting the doctrine taught by SUGATA MUNI, that tenderness towards animated nature comprehends all moral and devotional duty, a tenet which is, in a great measure, common to both the *Bauddha* and *Jaina* schisms: it is to be feared, that the personal description of the *Saugata,* as a man of a fat body and small head, although possibly intended to characterise the genus, will not direct us to the discovery of its origin or history. The *Kshapańaka* again has always been described by *Hindu* writers as a *Bauddha*, or sometimes even a *Jaina* naked mendicant: in the work before us he appears as the professor of a sort of astrological religion, in which[1] time is the principal divinity, and he is described as carrying, in either hand, the implements of his science, or a *Gola Yantra*, and *Túrya Yantra*, the former of which is an armillary sphere, and the latter a kind of quadrant, apparently for ascertaining time[2]; from the geographical controversy that occurs between him and Śankara, it appears that he entertains the doctrine regarding the descent of earth in space, which is attributed by the old astronomers to the *Bauddhas*, and controverted by the author of the *Súrya Siddhánta*[3], and subsequently by Bháskara: the former is quoted by Śankara, according to our author. These doctrines, the commentators on Bháskara's work, and

---

[1] Time is the Supreme Deity. Íśwara cannot urge on the present. He who knows time knows Brahma. Space and time are not distinct from God.

किञ्च कालः परमदेवता। प्रत्यचञ्च लयितुमीश्वरो न समर्थः।
कालविद्ब्रह्मविदिति दिक्कालौ नेश्वरादतिरिच्येते॥

[2] तूर्य्ययन्त्रं मण्डलचतुर्भागमित्यर्थः।

The *Túrya Yantra* is the fourth part of an orb.

तत्र यन्त्रोपरि कीलद्वयमखिलं कृत्वा।
तन्मध्ये दृष्ट्वा च विज्ञानेन कालज्ञानं जायते॥

Fixing above it two pins, and looking between them, the time is ascertained by science.

[3] [at least implicitly in the śloka XII: 32.] A. R. XII: 229.

even he, himself, commenting on his own text, say, belong to the *Jainas*, not to the *Bauddhas;* but, possibly, the correction is itself an error, it does not appear that the *Kshapańaka* of ÁNANDA GIRI argues the existence of a double set of planetary bodies, which is, undoubtedly, a *Jaina* doctrine[1], and the descent of the earth in space may have been common to all these sects.

The *Jainas* that existed in the time of ÁNANDA GIRI appear as *Digambaras* only; he does not notice their division into *Digambaras* and *Swetámbaras*, as they at present are found, and existed indeed prior to the age of MÁDHAVA. The *Bauddhas* are introduced personally, although it may be questioned whether they were very numerous in India in so comparatively modern a period: according to ÁNANDA GIRI, a persecution of this sect, and of the *Jainas*, took place in one part of the peninsula, the state of *Rudrapur*, during ŚANKARA's life time, but he, as well as MÁDHAVA[2], excludes ŚANKARA from being at all concerned in it. He ascribes its occurrence to the same source, the instigation of a *Bhaťťa*, from the north, or, in fact, of KUMÁRILA BHAŤŤA, a *Bengáli*, or *Maithíli Brahman*.

A long series of sectaries then ensues, of a more orthodox description, and who only err in claiming primeval and pre-eminent honors for the objects of their adoration—none of these are to be found; and, although, of a certain extent, the places of some of

---

[1] A. R. IX: 321.

[2] Preface to Wilson's Sanscrit and English Dictionary.

them may be supplied by the local deities of the villagers, and by the admission of others to a participation in the worship paid to the presiding deities of each sect, yet there can be little doubt, that a large portion of the Hindu Pantheon formerly enjoyed honours, which have for some centuries past been withheld. In this predicament are INDRA, KUVERA, YAMA, VARUŃA, GÁRUḊA, ŚESHA, and SOMA, all of whom, in the golden age of Hindu idolatry, had, no doubt, temples and adorers: the light and attractive service of the god of love, indeed, appears to have been formerly very popular, as his temples and groves make a distinguished figure in the[1] tales, poems, and dramas of antiquity: it is a feature that singularly characterises the present state of the Hindu religion, that if in some instances it is less ferocious, in others it has ceased to address itself to the amiable propensities of the human character, or the spontaneous and comparatively innocent feelings of youthful natures. The buffoonery of the *Holi*, and barbarity of the *Charak Pújá*, but ill express the sympathies which man, in all countries, feels with the vernal season, and which formerly gave rise to the festive *Vasantotsava* of the Hindus, and the licentious homage paid to *Śakti* and BHAIRAVA, has little in common with the worship, that might be supposed acceptable to KÁMA and his lovely bride, and which it would appear they formerly enjoyed.

---

[1] In the *Vrihat Kathá*, *Daśa Kumára*, *Málati Mádhava*, *Mrichchhakati*, &c.

Besides the adorers of the secondary divinities, we have a variety of sects who direct their devotions to beings of a still lower rank, and of whom none, at present, exist as distinct bodies, although individuals may be found, either detached or comprehended in other classes, who, more or less, reverence similar objects. Thus, the worship of *Ákáś*[1], or *Ether*, as the supreme deity, is still occasionally met with: all classes pay daily homage to the *Pitŕis* or Manes, and a few of the *Tántrikas* worship the *Siddhas*, or Genii, in the hope of acquiring super-human powers: the same class furnishes occasional votaries of the *Vasus*, *Yakshas*, and *Gandharvas*, and even of the *Vetálas* and *Bhútas*, or goblins and ghosts, and the latter also receive still, from the fears of the villagers, propitiatory adoration. It does not appear, that in any form, the worship of the moon and stars, of the elements, and divisions of the universe, is still practised, although that of the *Tírthas*, or holy places and rivers, is as popular as ever.

We have thus completed the enumeration of the sects as described by the author of the *Śankara Vijaya*, and have had an opportunity of observing, that, although the outlines of the system remain the same, the details have undergone very important alterations, since the time at which this work was composed: the

---

[1] I have encountered but one Professor, however, of this faith, a miserable mendicant, who taught the worship of Ether, under the strange name of *Baghela*.

rise of most of the existing modifications, we can trace satisfactorily enough, as will hereafter appear, and it is not improbable, that the disappearance of many of those, which no longer take a part in the idolatry of the Hindus, may be attributed to the exertions of Śankara and his disciples: his object, as appears from the work we have hitherto followed, was by no means the suppression of acts of outward devotion, nor of the preferential worship of any acknowledged and pre-eminent deity: his leading tenet is the recognition of *Brahma Para Brahma*[1], as the sole cause and supreme ruler of the universe, and as distinct from Śiva, Vishńu, Brahmá, or any individual member of the pantheon: with this admission, and in regard to the weakness of those human faculties, which cannot elevate themselves to the conception of the inscrutable first cause, the observance of such rites, and the worship of such deities, as are either prescribed by the *Vedas*, or the works not incompatible with their authority, were left undisturbed by this teacher[2]; they even received, to a certain extent, his particular sanction, and the following divisions of the Hindu faith were, by his express per-

---

[1] As in these texts of the Vedas सदेव सौम्येदमग्र आसीत् । and आत्मा वा इदमेक एवाग्र आसीत् । [quoted by Śank. in his Brahmasútrabháshya, Calc., 1854, p. 54. See also Bŕihad Árańy. Upan. I, 4, 1. p. 125.]

[2] आगमेतिहासपुराणोक्ताचारस्तु वेदानुकूलवृत्त्या ग्राह्यः । अग्राह्य एव तत्प्रतिकूले ।

Ordinances founded on the *Tantras,* the *Puráńas,* or historical record, are admissible if accordant with the *Vedas*; they must be rejected if repugnant.

mission, taught by some of his disciples, and are, consequently, regarded by the learned Brahmans in general, as the only orthodox and allowable forms in the present day[1]. The *Śaiva* faith was instituted by PARAMATA KÁLÁNALA, who is described as teaching at Benares, and assuming the insignia that characterise the *Dańdís* of modern times. The *Vaishńava* worship was taught at *Kánchi*, or *Conjeveram*, by LAKSHMAŃA ÁCHÁRYA and HASTÁMALAKA; and the latter seems to have introduced a modified adoration of VISHŃU, in the character of KŔISHŃA. The *Saura* sect was continued under the auspices of DIVÁKARA, *Brahmachárí*, and the *Śákta*, under those of the *Sannyásí*, TRIPURA-KUMÁRA: the *Gáńapatya* were allowed to remain under the presidence of GIRIJAPUTRA, and from such persons as had not adopted either of the preceding systems, BATUKANÁTH, the professor of the *Kápálika*, or *Bhairava* worship, was permitted to attract followers: all these teachers were converts and disciples of ŚANKARA,

---

[1] कलावस्मिन्युगे नानापापध्वस्तज्ञानाङ्कुरेषु मर्त्येषु शुद्धाद्वैतविद्यायामनधिकारिषु तेषां वृत्तिः पुनरपि यथेप्सिता भवतीति विचार्य्य लोकरक्षार्थं वर्णाश्रमपरिपालनार्थं च परमतत्त्वकल्पनां जीवेशभेदास्पदां च रचयितुमुपक्रम्य निजशिष्यमाह ।

In the present impure age, the bud of wisdom being blighted by iniquity, men are inadequate to the apprehension of pure unity; they will be apt, therefore, again to follow the dictates of their own fancies, and it is necessary for the preservation of the world, and the maintenance of civil and religious distinctions, to acknowledge those modifications of the divine spirit which are the work of the SUPREME. These reflexions having occurred to ŚANKARA, he addressed his disciple, &c.

and returned to his superintending guidance, when they had effected the objects of their missions.

The notice that occurs in the *Sarva Darśana* of any of the sects which have yet been mentioned, has been already incidentally adverted to: this work is less of a popular form than the preceding, and controverts the speculative rather than the practical doctrines of other schools: besides the atheistical *Bauddha* and *Jaina* sects, the work is occupied chiefly with the refutation of the followers of *Jaimini*, *Gautama*, and *Patanjali*, and we have no classes of worshippers introduced but those of the *Vaishńavas* who follow Rámánuja, and *Madhwácharya*, of the *Śaivas*, the *Páśupatas*, the followers of Abhinava Gupta, who taught the *Mantra* worship of *Śiva*; and the alchemical school, or worshippers of Śiva's type in quicksilver, and the *Rasendra Linga*: most of these seem to have sprung into being in the interval between the 10th and 13th centuries, and have now either disappeared, or are rapidly on the decline: those which actually exist, we shall recur to in the view we are now prepared to take of the actual condition of the Hindu faith.

SECTION III.

PRESENT DIVISIONS OF THE HINDUS, AND OF THE VAISHŃAVAS IN PARTICULAR.

The classification adopted by the works, I especially follow, if not unexceptionable, is allowable and convenient, and may, therefore, regulate the following details: it divides all the Hindus into three great classes, or *Vaishńavas*, *Śaivas*, and *Śáktas*, and refers to a fourth or miscellaneous class, all not comprised in the three others.

The worshippers of Vishńu, Śiva, and Śakti, who are the objects of the following description, are not to be confounded with the orthodox adorers of those divinities: few Brahmans of learning, if they have any religion at all, will acknowledge themselves to belong to any of the popular divisions of the Hindu faith, although, as a matter of simple preference, they more especially worship some individual deity, as their chosen, or *Ishťa Devatá*: they refer also to the *Vedas*, the books of law, the Puráńas, and Tantras, as the only ritual they recognise, and regard all practices not derived from those sources as irregular and profane: on the other hand, many of the sects seem to have originated, in a great measure, out of opposition to the Brahmanical order: teachers and disciples are chosen from any class, and the distinction of caste is, in a great measure, sunk in the new one, of similarity of schism: the ascetics and mendicants, also in many instances, affect to treat the Brahmans with particular contempt, and this is generally repaid with interest by the Brahmans. A portion, though not a large one, of the populace is still attached to the *Smárta* Brahmans, as their spiritual guides, and are so far distinct from any of the sects we shall have to specify, whilst most of the followers, even of the sects, pay the ordinary deference to the Brahmanical order, and especially evince towards the Brahmans of their own fellowship, of whom there is generally abundance, the devotedness and submission which the original Hindu Code so perpetually inculcates.

Excluding, therefore, those who may be regarded as the regular worshippers of regular gods, we have the following enumeration of the several species of each class:

VAISHŃAVAS.

1 Rámánujas, or Śrí Sampradáyís, or Śrí Vaishńavas.
2 Rámánandís, or Rámávats.
3 Kabír Panthís.
4 Khákís.
5 Malúk Dásís.
6 Dádú Panthís.
7 Ráya Dásís.
8 Senáís.
9 Vallabháchárís, or Rudra Sampradáyís.
10 Mírá Báís.
11 Madhwáchárís, or Brahma Sampradáyís.
12 Nímávats, or Sanakádi Sampradáyís.
13 The Vaishńavas of Bengal.

14 Rádhá Vallabhís.
15 The Sakhí Bhávas.
16 Charań Dásís.
17 Hariśchandís.
18 Sadhná Panthís.
19 Mádhavís.
20 Sannyásís, Vairágís and Nágas.

Śaivas.

1 Dańďís and Daśnámís.
2 Jogís.
3 Jangamas.
4 Paramahansas.
5 Úrdhabáhús, Ákáś Mukhís, and Nakhís.
6 Gúdaras.
7 Rúkharas, Súkharas and Úkharas.
8 Kańá Lingís.
9 Sannyásís, &c.

Śáktas.

1 Dakshińís.
2 Vámís.
3 Káncheliyas.
4 Karárís.

Miscellaneous Sects.

1 Gáńapatyas.
2 Saurapatas.
3 Nának Sháhís of seven classes.
  1 Udásís.
  2 Ganjbakhshís.
  3 Rámráyís.
  4 Suthrá Sháhís.

5 Govind Sinhís.
6 Nirmalas.
7 Nágas.
4 Jainas of two principal orders.
1 Digambaras.
2 Śwetámbaras.
5 Bábá Lálís.
6 Práń Náthís.
7 Sádhs.
8 Śatnámís.
9 Śiva Náráyańís.
10 Śúnyavádís.

These will be regarded as varieties enough, it may be presumed, especially when it is considered, that most of them comprise a number of sub-divisions, and that besides these acknowleged classifications, many individual mendicants are to be found all over India, who can scarcely be included within the limits of any of them, exercising a sort of independence both in thought and act, and attached very loosely, if at all, to any of the popular schismatical sects[1].

---

[1] Some of the popular works adopt a different classification, and allude to 90 *Páshańdas*, or heresies, which are thus arranged:—

Amongst the Brahmans,	24
Sannyásís,	12
Vairágis,	12
Sauras,	18
Jangamas,	18
Jogís,	12

VAISHŃAVAS.

ŚRÍ SAMPRADÁYÍS, or RÁMÁNUJAS.

Amongst other divisions of lecs importance, the *Vaishńavas* are usually distinguished into four principal *Sampradáyas*, or *sects*[1]; of these, the most an-

---

[1] Thus the *Bhakta Málá*: चौबीस प्रथम हरि वपु धर्‍यौ त्यौं चतुर व्युह कलियुग प्रगट। श्रीरामानुज उद्दार सुधानिधि अवनि कल्पतरु। विष्णुस्वामी वोहितसिंधु संसार पारकरु। मध्वाचारज मेघभक्ति शरत सर भरिया। निम्बादित्य आदित्य कुहर अज्ञान जुहरिया। जन्मकर्म्म भागौत धर्म्मसम्प्रदायथापी अघट। चौबीस प्रथम हरिइत्यादि। "Hari, in preceding ages, assumed twenty-four principal shapes, but four were manifest in the *Kali Jug*: the magnanimous *Rámánuja*, a treasure of Ambrosia and terrestrial tree of plenty: the ocean of kindness and transporter across the sea of the universe, *Vishńu Swámí*: *Madhu Áchárj*, a rich cloud in the autumnal season of piety: and *Nimbáditya*, a sun that illumined the cave of ignorance; by them acts of piety and obligation were divided, and each sect was severally established." There are also Sanskrit texts authorising the different institution, and characteristic term of each *Sampradáya*, one of these is from the *Padma Puráńa*:

सम्प्रदायविहीना ये मन्त्रास्ते निष्फला मताः।
अतः कलौ भविष्यन्ति चत्वारः सम्प्रदायिनः॥
श्रीमाध्वीरुद्रसनका वैष्णवाः क्षितिपावनाः।
चत्वारस्ते कलौ देवि सम्प्रदायप्रवर्त्तकाः॥

"Those *Mantras*, which belong to no system, are of no virtue; and, therefore, in the *Kali* age, there shall be followers of four sects. *Śri*, *Mádhwí*, *Rudra* and *Sanaka*, shall be *the Vaishńavas*, purifying the world, and these four, *Dévi*, (*Śiva* speaks,) shall be the institutors of the *Sampradáyas* in the *Kali* period." We may here observe in passing, that if this text is genuine, the *Padma Puráńa* must be very modern: another similar text is the following:

cient and respectable is the *Śrí Sampradáya*, founded by the *Vaishńava* reformer *Rámánuja Ácárya*, about the middle of the twelfth century[1].

The history of RÁMÁNUJA, and his first followers, is well known in the south of India, of which he was a native, and is recorded in various legendary tracts and traditional narratives.

According to the *Bhárgava Upapuráńa*, RÁMÁNUJA is said to have been an incarnation of the serpent *Śesha*, whilst his chief companions and disciples were the embodied *Discus*, *Mace*, *Lotus*, and other insignia of *Vishńu*. In a *Kanara* account of his life, called the *Divya Charitra*, he is said to have been the son of

---

रामानुजं श्रीःस्वीचक्रे मध्वाचार्यं चतुर्मुखः ।
श्रीविष्णुस्वामिनं रुद्रो निम्बादित्यं चतुस्सनः ॥

"LAKSHMI selected *Rámánuja*; BRAHMA *Madhwáchárya*; *Rudra* gave the preference to *Vishńu Swámí*, and the four *Sanakas* to *Nimbáditya*." The cause of the election is not very evident, as the creeds taught by those teachers, have little connexion with the deity who lends the appellation to the sects.

[1] The *Smŕiti Kála Taranga* places the date of RÁMÁNUJA's appearance in *Śaka*—1049 or A. D. 1127. A note by Colonel Mackenzie on an inscription, given in the Asiatic Researches 9, 270, places the birth of RÁMÁNUJA in A. D. 1008: various accounts, collected by Dr. Buchanan, make it 1010 and 1025 (Buchanan's Mysore 2, 80) and 1019 (ibid. 3, 413). Inscriptions make him alive in 1128, (ibid.) which would give him a life of more than a century: according to COL. WILKS, indeed (History of Mysore 1, 41, note and appendix), he was alive in 1133. The weight of authority seems to be in favour of the more recent date, and we may conclude that he was born about the end of the eleventh century, and that the first half of the twelfth century was the period at which his fame, as a teacher, was established.

Śrí Keśava Áchárya and *Bhúmi Deví*; and, as before, an incarnation of *Śesha*. He was born at *Perumbur*, and studied at *Kánchi*, or *Conjeveram*, where also he taught his system of the *Vaishńava* faith. He afterwards resided at *Śrí Ranga*, worshipping *Vishńu* as *Śrí Ranga Nátha*, and there composed his principal works, he then visited various parts of India, disputing with the professors of different creeds, overcoming them of course, and reclaiming various shrines, then in possession of the *Śaivas*, for the worshippers of *Vishńu*, particularly the celebrated temple of *Tripeti.*

On his return to *Śrí Ranga*, the disputes between the *Vaishńava* and *Śaiva* religions, became exceedingly violent, and the *Chola* monarch, who according to some accounts, was at that time Kerikála Chola, subsequently named Kŕimi Końd́a Chola, being a devout worshipper of *Śiva*, commanded all the *Brahmans* in his dominions to sign an acknowledgement of the supremacy of that divinity, bribing some of the most refractory, and terrifying others into acquiescence. Rámánuja, however, was impracticable, and the king sent armed men to seize him. With the assistance of his disciples, he effected his escape, and ascending the Gháts, found refuge with the *Jain* sovereign of Mysore, Vitala Deva, *Vellála Ráya.* In consequence of rendering medical service to the daughter of this prince, or in the terms of the legend, expelling an evil spirit, a *Brahma Rákshasa*, by whom she was possessed, he obtained the monarch's grateful regard, and finally converted him to the *Vaishńava* faith. The *Rájá* assumed the title of *Vishńu Vardhana*. Rámánuja remained several years in Mysore, at a temple founded by the *Rája* on *Yádava Giri*, now known as *Mail Cotay*, for the reception of an image called *Chavala Ráya*, a form of *Rańachhoŕ*, or *Kŕishńa*, which the local traditions very ridiculously pretend he obtained from the *Mohammedan* sovereign of Delhi. Rámánuja resided here twelve years, but on the death of his persecutor, the *Chola* king, he returned to *Śrí Ranga*, on the *Káverí*, and there spent the remainder of his life in devout exercises and religious seclusion.

The establishments of the Rámánujíyas are numerous in the Dekhan still, and the same country comprehends the site of the *Gaddí*, the pillow or seat of the primitive teacher; his spiritual throne, in fact, to which his disciples are successively elevated[1]. This circumstance gives a superiority to the *Ácháryas* of the *Dakshińa*, or south, over those of the *Uttara*, or north, into which they are at present divided.

---

[1] According to information obtained by Dr. Buchanan, Rámánuja founded 700 *Maths*, of which four only remain; one of the principal of these is at *Mail Cotay*, or *Dakshińa Badarikáśrama*, the *Badari* station of the south. Rámánuja also established 74 hereditary *Guruships* amongst his followers, the representatives of which still remain and dispute the supremacy with the *Sannyási* members of the order; these last, however, are generally considered of the highest rank (Buchan. Mysore 2, 75). In another place (1, 144), he says that 89 *Guruships* were established, 5 in the *Sannyási* class, and 84 in the secular order: the *Madams* of the five former are *Ahobilam, Toiádri, Raméśwara, Śrí Rangam*, and *Kánji*.

The worship of the followers of RÁMÁNUJA, is addressed to VISHŃU and to LAKSHMÍ, and their respective incarnations, either singly or conjointly; and the *Śrí Vaishńavas*, by which general name the sect is known, consist of corresponding subdivisions, as NÁRÁYAŃA, or LAKSHMÍ, or LAKSHMÍ NÁRÁYAŃA, or RÁMA or SÍTÁ, or SÍTÁ RÁMA, or KRISHŃA, or RUKMIŃÍ, or any other modifications of *Vishńu*, or his consort, is the preferential object of the veneration of the votary[1]. The *Śrí Vaishńava* worship in the north of India, is not very popular, and the sect is rather of a speculative than practical nature, although it does not require, in its teachers, secession from the

[1] Mr. Colebrooke, A. R. 7, [Essays &c. London: 1858. p. 124.] says the *Rámánujas* are of three classes, those who worship RÁMA alone, SÍTÁ alone, and SÍTÁ and RÁMA conjointly. One of my authorities, *Mathurá Náth*, says, they worship *Mahá Lakshmí*, and other information agrees with his; from the texts quoted in the *Sarva Darśana Sangraha*, [Calcutta: 1858. pp. 54. 55.] VISHŃU as VÁSUDEVA, is the deity to be worshipped, but no doubt all the varieties exist: without, however, affecting the identity of the sect, the real object of whose devotion is VISHŃU, as the cause and creator of the world, and any of his, or his *Śakti*'s more especial manifestations, are consequently entitled to reverence. The term *Śrí Vaishńavas*, most commonly applied to them, denotes an original preference of the female deity or *Mahá Lakshmí*: the worship of RÁMA is more properly that of the *Rámánandis*, and they may be the persons intended by Mr. Colebrooke's informants, as those of the *Rámánujíyas* who worship RÁMA only (A. R. 7, 281). It may also be observed, that the *Rámánujíyas* unite with KŔISHŃA, *Rukmini*, not *Rádhá*, the latter being his mistress only, not his wife, and being never named in the *Bhágavat*, except in one ambiguous passage.

world: the teachers are usually of the Brahmanical order, but the disciples may be of any caste[1].

Besides the temples appropriated to VISHŃU and his consort, and their several forms, including those of KŔISHŃA and RÁMA, and those which are celebrated as objects of pilgrimage, as *Lakshmí-Balaji*, *Rámnáth*, and *Ranganáth*, in the south; *Badarínáth*, in the *Himálaya*, *Jagannáth*, in *Orissa*, and *Dwáraká*, on the Malabar Coast, images of metal or stone are usually set up in the houses of the private members of this sect, which are daily worshipped, and the temples and dwellings are all decorated with the *Sálagrám* stone and *Tulasí* plant.

The most striking peculiarities in the practices of this sect, are the individual preparation, and scrupulous privacy of their meals: they must not eat in cotton garments, but having bathed, must put on woollen or silk: the teachers allow their select pupils to assist them, but, in general, all the *Rámánujas* cook for themselves, and should the meal during this process, or whilst they are eating, attract even the looks of a stranger, the operation is instantly stopped, and the viands buried in the ground: a similar delicacy, in this respect, prevails amongst some other classes of Hindus, especially of the *Rájaput* families, but it is not carried to so preposterous an extent[2].

---

[1] The *Mantra*, and mark, are never bestowed on any person of impure birth.—Buchan. Mysore 1, 146.

[2] It is said, however, that there are two divisions of the sect,

The chief ceremony of initiation in all Hindu sects, is the communication by the teacher to the disciple of the *Mantra*, which generally consists of the name of some deity, or a short address to him; it is communicated in a whisper, and never lightly made known by the adept to profane ears. The *Mantra* of the RÁMÁNUJA sect is said to be the six syllable *Mantra*—or *Om Rámáya namah́*; or Om, salutation to RÁMA[1].

Another distinction amongst sects, but merely of a civil character, is the term or terms with which the religious members salute each other when they meet, or in which they are addressed by the lay members. This amongst the *Rámánujas* is the phrase, *Dáso 'smi*, or *Dáso 'ham*; I am your slave; accompanied with the *Prańám*, or slight inclination of the head, and the application of the joined hands to the forehead. To the *Ácháryas*, or supreme teachers of this sect, the rest perform the *Ashťánga Dańďawat* or prostration of the body, with the application of eight parts—the forehead, breast, hands, knees, and insteps of the feet, to the ground.

---

one called *Ávarańi*, from *Ávarańa*, screening, or surrounding, and the other *Anávarańi*, from the members not observing such punctilious privacy.

[1] In giving the *Mantras*, as they have been communicated to me, it may be necessary to suggest a doubt of their accuracy; a Hindu evades what he dislikes to answer, and will not scruple a falsehood to stop enquiry; men above prejudice, in other respects, find it so difficult to get over that of communicating the *Mantra*, that when they profess to impart it, even their sincerity can scarcely be admitted without a doubt.

The Hindu sects are usually discriminated by various fantastical streaks on their faces, breasts, and arms: for this purpose, all the *Vaishńavas* employ especially a white earth called *Gopíchandana*, which, to be of the purest description, should be brought from *Dwáraká*, being said to be the soil of a pool at that place, in which the Gopís drowned themselves when they heard of *Kŕishńa*'s death. The common *Gopíchandana*, however, is nothing but a *Magnesian* or *Calcareous Clay*.

The marks of the *Rámánujas* are two perpendicular white lines, drawn from the root of the hair to the commencement of each eye-brow, and a transverse streak connecting them across the root of the nose: in the centre is a perpendicular streak of red, made with red Sanders, or *Rolí*, a preparation of Turmeric and Lime; they have also patches of *Gopíchandana*, with a central red streak on the breast, and each upper arm: the marks are supposed to represent the *Śankh*, *Chakra*, *Gadá*, and *Padma*[1], or Shell, Discus, Club, and Lotus, which Vishńu bears in his four hands, whilst the central streak is Śrí, or Lakshmí[2]. Some

---

[1] The *Vaishńava* is thus described in the *Bhakta Málá*, the text is probably that of the *Bhágavat*—

ये कण्ठलग्नतुलसीनलिनाक्षमालाः ये बाहुमूलपरिचिह्नितशङ्खचक्राः ।
ये वा ललाटपटले लसदूर्ध्वपुण्ड्रास्ते वैष्णवा भुवनमाशु पवित्रयन्ति ॥

"They who bear the *Tulasí* round the neck, the rosary of Lotus seeds, have the shell and discus impressed upon their upper arm, and the upright streak along the centre of the forehead, they are *Vaishńavas*, and sanctify the world."

[2] The efficacy of these marks is very great: we are told in the *Kásí Khańd*, that Yama directs his ministers to avoid such as

have these objects carved on wooden stamps, with which they impress the emblems on their bodies, and others carry their devotion so far as to have the parts cicatrized with heated metallic models of the objects they propose to represent, but this is not regarded as a creditable practice[1]: besides these marks, they wear a neclace of the wood of the *Tulasí*, and carry a rosary of the seeds of the same plant, or of the Lotus.

The principal authorities of this sect are the comments of the founder on the *Sútras* of Vyása, and other Vaidika works: they are written in Sanskrit,

---

bear them, and the same work observes, that no sin can exist in the individuals who make use of them, be they of whatever caste.

ब्राह्मणः क्षत्त्रियो वैश्यः शूद्रो वा यदि वेतरः ।
विष्णुभक्तिसमायुक्तो ज्ञेयः सर्वोत्तमश्च सः ॥
शङ्खचक्राङ्किततनुः शिरसा मञ्जरीधरः ।
गोपीचन्दनलिप्ताङ्गो दृष्टश्चेत्तदघं कुतः ॥

[1] The *Vrihan Náradíya Puráńa* sentences every Brahman adopting the practice to endless degradation, and even to the infernal regions.

तथाहि संतप्तशङ्खादिलिङ्गचिह्नतनुर्नरः ।
स सर्वपतकभोगी चाण्डालो जन्मकोटिभिः ॥
तं द्विजं तप्तशङ्खादिलिङ्गाङ्किततनुं हरः ।
संभाव्य रौरवं याति यावदिन्द्राश्चतुर्दश ॥

The reason also occurs—

ब्राह्मणस्य तनुर्ज्ञेया सर्वदेवानामाश्रिता ।
सा चेत्संतापिता राजन्किमु वत्स्यामहे वयम् ॥

"The body of a Brahman is the abode of all the Gods, if that is consumed, where shall we abide?" It appears, however, that stamping the mark with a hot iron, is commonly in use in the *Dekhan*. A similar practice seems to have been known to some of the early Christians, and baptizing with fire was stamping the cross on the forehead with a hot iron.

and are the *Śrí Bháshya*, the *Gítá Bháshya*, the *Vedártha Sangraha*, *Vedánta Pradípa*, and *Vedánta Sára*: besides these, the works of *Venkata Áchárya*, are of great repute amongst them, as the *Stotra Bháshya*, and *Śatadúshińí*, and others: the *Chańda Máruta Vaidika*, and *Trinśatadhyánam*, are also works of authority, as is the *Páncharátra* of Nárada: of the *Puráńas* they acknowledge only six as authorities, the *Vishńu*, *Náradiya*, *Gáruda*, *Padma*, *Váráha* and the *Bhágavat*: the other twelve are regarded as *Támasa*, or originating in the principles of darkness and passion, as we have already observed. Besides these, the *Rámánujas* have a variety of popular works in the dialects of the South, one of which, the *Guru Para*, containing an account of the life of Rámánuja, was procured by Dr. Buchanan, in the course of his statistical researches in *Mysore*.

The chief religious tenet of the *Rámánujas*, is the assertion that *Vishńu* is Brahmá; that he was before all worlds, and was the cause and the creator of all. Although they maintain that *Vishńu* and the universe are one, yet, in opposition to the *Vedánta* doctrines, they deny that the deity is void of form or quality, and regard him as endowed with all good qualities, and with a two-fold form: the supreme spirit, *Paramátmá*, or cause, and the gross one, the effect, the universe or matter. The doctrine is hence called the *Viśishthádwaita*, or doctrine of unity with attributes. In these assertions they are followed by most of the *Vaishńava* sects. Creation originated in the wish of

VISHŃU, who was alone, without a second, to multiply himself: he said, I will become many; and he was individually embodied as visible and etherial light. After that, as a ball of clay may be moulded into various forms, so the grosser substance of the deity became manifest in the elements, and their combinations: the forms into which the divine matter is thus divided, are pervaded by a portion of the same vitality which belongs to the great cause of all, but which is distinct from his spiritual or eterial essence; here, therefore, the *Rámánujas* again oppose the *Vedántikas*, who identify* the *Paramátmá* and *Jívátmá*, or etherial and vital spirit: this vitality, though endlessly diffusible, is imperishable and eternal, and the matter of the universe, as being the same in substance with the Supreme Being, is alike without beginning or end: PURUSHOTTAMA, or NÁRÁYAŃA, after having created man and animals, through the instrumentality of those subordinate agents whom he willed into existence for that purpose, still retained the supreme authority of the universe: so that the *Rámánujas* assert three predicates of the universe, comprehending the deity: it consists of *Chit*, or spirit, *Achit*, or matter, and *Íśwara*, or God, or the enjoyer, the thing enjoyed, and the ruler and controller of both. Besides his primary and secondary form as the creator, and creation, the deity has assumed, at different times, particular forms and appearances, for the benefit

* [See, however, Colebr. M. E., London, 1858, p. 169.]

of his creatures: he is, or has been visibly present amongst men, in five modifications: in his ARCHÁ, objects of worship, as images, &c.; in the *Vibhavas*, or *Avatáras*, as the fish, the boar, &c.; in certain forms called *Vyúhas*, of which four are enumerated, VÁSUDEVA, or KŔISHŃA, BALARÁMA, PRADYUMNA, and ANIRUDDHA; fourthly, in the *Súkshma* form, which, when perfect, comprises six qualities: *Virajas*, absence of human passion; *Vimŕityu*, immortality; *Viśoka*, exemption from care or pain; *Vijighatsá*, absence of natural wants; *Satyakáma*, and *Satyasankalpa*, the love and practice of truth; and sixthly, as the *Antarátmá*, or *Antaryámí*, the human soul, or individualised spirit: these are to be worshipped seriatim, as the ministrant ascends in the scale of perfection, and adoration therefore is five-fold; *Abhigamanam*, cleaning and purifying the temples, images, &c. *Upádánam*, providing flowers and perfumes for religious rites; *Ijyá*, the presentation of such offerings, blood offerings being uniformly prohibited, it may be observed, by all the *Vaishńavas*; *Swádhyáya*, counting the rosary and repeating the names of the divinity, or any of his forms; and *Yoga*, the effort to unite with the deity*: the reward of these acts is elevation to the seat of VISHŃU, and enjoyment of like state with his own, interpreted to be perpetual residence in *Vaikuńtha*, or *Vishńu*'s heaven, in a condition of pure ecstasy and eternal rapture.

* [Sarva Darśana Sangraha, p. 54–56.]

The *Rámánujas* are not very numerous in the north of India, where they are better known as *Śrí Vaishńavas*; they are decidedly hostile to the *Śaiva* sect, and are not on very friendly terms with the modern votaries of Kŕishńa, although they recognise that deity as an incarnation of Vishńu[1].

Rámánandís, or Rámávats.

The followers of Rámánand are much better known than those of Rámánuja in upper Hindustan: they are usually considered as a branch of the Rámánuja sect, and address their devotions peculiarly to Rámachandra, and the divine manifestations connected with Vishńu in that incarnation, as Sítá, Lakshmańa, and Hanumán.

---

[1] Dubois, in his 8th Chapter, has some details of the *Vaishńava* mendicants, as met with in the Dekhan: his account, however, does not apply to the *Rámánuja*, or any other Vaishńava sect, as known in these provinces, although a few of the particulars may be true, if confined to the Vaishńava Vairágis — the *Dakhińi Vaishńavas* must be, therefore, a very different class from those that are met within any other part of India, or the *Abbé* must have mixed, as is not unusual with him, a small quantum of truth, with a very large portion of error: it is, indeed, impossible to think him correct, when he states, that "the sectaries of *Vishńu* eat publicly of all sorts of meat, except beef, and drink spirituous liquors without shame or restraint, and that they are reproached with being the chief promoters of that abominable sacrifice, the *Śakti Pújá*:" now, it is not true of any sect in Upper India, that the practices the *Abbé* mentions occur at all, except in the utmost privacy and secrecy, and if even in that way they do occur, it is certainly not amongst the *Vaishńava Vairágis*, but with very different sects, as we shall hereafter see.

Rámánand is sometimes considered to have been the immediate disciple of Rámánuja, but this appears to be an error: a more particular account makes him the fifth in descent from that teacher, as follows—the pupil and successor of Rámánuja was Devánand; of Devánand, Harinand; of Harinand, Rághavánand, and of this last, Rámánand, an enumeration which, if correct, would place Rámánand about the end of the 13th century[1]: there is great reason, however, to doubt his being entitled to so remote a date, and consequently to question the accuracy of his descent from Rámánuja: we shall have occacion to infer, hereafter, from the accounts given of the dates of other teachers, that Rámánand was not earlier than the end of the 14th, or beginning of the 15th century.

According to common tradition, the schism of Rámánand originated in resentment of an affront offered him by his fellow disciples, and sanctioned by his teacher. It is said, that he had spent some time in travelling through various parts of India, after which he returned to the *Math*, or residence of his superior: his brethren objected to him, that in the course of his peregrinations, it was impossible he could have observed that privacy in his meals, which is a vital observance of the *Rámánuja* sect, and as Rághavánand admitted the validity of the objection, Rámánand was

---

[1] The enumeration in the *Bhakta Málá* is different: it there occurs 1. Rámánuja, 2. Deváchárj, 3. Rághavánand, 4. Rámánand; making him the fourth.

condemned to feed in a place apart from the rest of the disciples: he was highly incensed at the order, and retired from the society altogether, establishing a schism of his own.

The residence of RÁMÁNAND was at Benares, at the *Pancha Gangá Ghát*, where a *Math*, or monastery of his followers, is said to have existed, but to have been destroyed by some of the Musalman princes: at present there is merely a stone plat-form, in the vicinity, bearing the supposed impression of his feet, but there are many *Maths* of his followers, of celebrity at *Benares*, whose *Pancháyat*, or council, is the chief authority amongst the *Rámávats* in Upper India: we shall have frequent occasion to mention these *Maths*, or convents, and a short account of them may, therefore, here be acceptable.

Most of the religious sects of which we have to give an account, comprise various classes of individuals, resolvable, however, especially into two, whom (for want of more appropriate terms) we must call, perhaps, *Clerical* and *Lay*: the bulk of the votaries are generally, but not always of the latter order, whilst the rest, or the *Clerical* class, are sometimes monastic, and sometimes secular: most of the sects, especially the *Vaishńavas*, leave this distinction a matter of choice: the *Vallabhácháris*, indeed, give the preference to married teachers, and all their *Gosáins* are men of business and family: the preference, however, is usually assigned to teachers of an ascetic or cœnobitic life, whose pious meditations are not distracted by the affections of kindred, or the cares of the world: the doctrine that introduced similar unsocial institutions into the Christian church, in the fourth century, being still most triumphantly prevalent in the east, the land of its nativity; the establishments of which we are treating, and the still existing practices of solitary mortification, originating in the "specious appearance and pompous sound of that maxim of the ancient philosophy, that in order to the attainment of true felicity and communion with God, it was necessary that the soul should be separated from the body even here below, and that the body was to be macerated and mortified for that purpose." (*Mosheim.* i. 378.)

Of the cœnobitic members of the different communities, most pursue an erratic and mendicant life: all of them, indeed, at some period have led such a life, and have travelled over various parts of India singly or in bodies, subsisting by alms, by merchandise, and sometimes, perhaps, by less unexceptionable means, like the *Sarabaites* of the east, or the mendicant friars of the Latin Church: they have, however, their fixed rallying points, and are sure of finding, in various parts of their progress, establishments of their own, or some friendly fraternity where they are for a reasonably moderate period lodged and fed. When old or infirm, they sit down in some previously existing *Math*, or establish one of their own.

The *Maths*, *Asthals*, or *Akhádás*, the residences of the monastic communities of the Hindus, are scattered over the whole country: they vary in structure and extent, according to the property of which the proprietors are possessed; but they generally comprehend a set of huts or chambers for the *Mahant*[1], or Superior, and his permanent pupils; a temple, sacred to the deity whom they worship, or the *Samádhi*, or shrine of the founder of the sect, or some eminent teacher; and a *Dharma Śálá*, one or more sheds, or buildings for the accommodation of the mendicants or travellers, who are constantly visiting the *Math*: ingress and egress is free to all; and, indeed, a restraint upon personal liberty seems never to have entered into the conception of any of the religious legislators of the Hindus.

---

[1] The following description of the residence of MANDANA MIŚRA, from the *Śankara Vijaya* of ÁNANDA GIRI, is very applicable to a modern *Math*.

"At the distance of four Yojanas, west from Hastinapur, was a square plot of ground, extending a cos on each side; in the centre of it stood a large mansion, constructed of the timber of the Tal, and exactly facing it another a hundred cubits in length; upon the top of this last were many cages full of parrots, and within it resided five hundred pupils, occupied in the study of various Śástras: the first was the dwelling of the Teacher, like Brahmá with four heads, like the Serpent King, with a thousand faces, and Rudra, with a five-fold head, amongst his disciples like the waves of the ocean, and enabling them to overcome the universe in unparalleled profundity and extent of knowledge: he was attended by numerous slaves of both sexes: attached to his dwelling were wells and reservoirs, and gardens and orchards, and his person was pampered with the choicest viands procured daily by his disciples. In his court-yard were two Temples, on a circular mound, for the worship of the *Viśvadevas* and the *Sálagrám*, in the form of *Lakshmí Náráyańa*."

The *Math* is under the entire controul of a *Mahant*, or Superior, with a certain number of resident *Chelás*, or disciples; their number varies from three or four to thirty or forty, but in both cases there are always a number of vagrant or out-members: the resident *Chelás* are usually the elders of the body, with a few of the younger as their attendants and scholars; and it is from the senior and more proficient of these ascetics, that the *Mahant* is usually elected.

In some instances, however, where the *Mahant* has a family, the situation descends in the line of his posterity: where an election is to be effected, it is conducted with much solemnity, and presents a curious picture of a regularly organised system of church policy, amongst these apparently unimportant and straggling communities.

The *Maths* of various districts look up to some one of their own order as chief, and they all refer to that connected with their founder, as the common head: under the presidence, therefore, of the *Mahant* of that establishment, wherever practicable, and in his absence, of some other of acknowledged pre-eminence, the *Mahants* of the different *Maths* assemble, upon the decease of one of their brethren, to elect a successor. For this purpose they regularly examine the *Chelás*, or disciples of the deceased, the ablest of whom is raised to the vacant situation: should none of them be qualified, they choose a *Mahant* from the pupils of some other teacher, but this is rarely necessary, and unless necessary, is never had recourse to. The new *Mahant* is then regularly installed, and is formally invested with the cap, the rosary, the frontal mark, or *Ṫíká*, or any other monastic insignia, by the president of the assembly. Under the native Government, whether Mohammedan or Hindu—the election of the superior of one of these establishments was considered as a matter of sufficient moment to demand the attention of the Governor of the province, who, accordingly, in person, or by his deputy, presided at the election: at present, no interference is exercised by the ruling authorities, and rarely by any lay character, although occasionally, a *Rájá*, or a *Zemíndár*, to whose liberality the *Math* is indebted, or in whose lands it is situated, assumes the right of assisting and presiding at the election.

The *Mahants* of the sects, in which the election takes places, are generally assisted by those of the sects connected with them: each is attended by a train of disciples, and individuals of various mendicant tribes repair to the meeting; so that an assemblage of many hundreds, and sometimes of thousands, occurs: as far as the resources of the *Math*, where they are assembled, extend, they are maintained at its expence; when those fail, they must shift for themselves; the election is usually a business of ten or twelve days, and during the period of its continuance, various points of polity or doctrine are discussed in the assembly.

Most of the *Maths* have some endowments of land, but with the exception of a few established in large cities, and especially at Benares, the individual amount of these endowments is, in general, of little value. There are few *Maths* in any district that possess five hundred Bíghás of land, or about one hundred and seventy acres, and the most usual quantity is about thirty or forty Bíghás only: this is sometimes let out for a fixed rent; at other times it is cultivated by the *Math* on its own account; the highest rental met with, in any of the returns procured, is six hundred and thirty rupees per annum. Although, however, the individual portions are trifling, the great number of these petty establishments renders the aggregate amount considerable, and as the endowed lands have been granted *Máfí*, or free of land tax, they form, altogether, a serious deduction from the revenue of each district.

Besides the lands they may hold, the *Maths* have other sources of support: the attachment of lay votaries frequently contributes very liberally to their wants: the community is also sometimes concerned, though, in general, covertly, in traffic, and besides those means of supply, the individual members of most of them sally forth daily to collect alms from the vicinity, the aggregate of which, generally in the shape of rice or other grains, furnishes forth the common table: it only remains to observe, that the tenants of these *Maths*, particularly the *Vaishńavas*, are most commonly of a quiet inoffensive character, and the *Mahants* especially are men of talents and respectability, although they possess, occasionally, a little of that self-importance, which the conceit of superior sanctity is apt to inspire: there are, it is true, exceptions to this innocuous character, and robberies, and murders have been traced to these religious establishments.

The especial object of the worship of RÁMÁNANDA's followers is VISHŃU, as RÁMACHANDRA: they, of course, reverence all the other incarnations of VISHŃU, but they maintain the superiority of RÁMA, in the present or *Kali Yug*; hence they are known collectively as *Rámávats*, although the same variety prevails amonst them, as amongst the *Rámánujas*, as to the exclusive or collective worship of the male and female members of this incarnation, or of *Ráma* and *Sítá*, singly, or jointly, or *Sítá Ráma*[1]: individuals of them also pay particular veneration to some of the other forms of VISHŃU, and they hold in like estimation, as the *Rámánujas*, and every *Vaishńava* sect, the *Sálagrám* stone and *Tulasí* plant; their forms of worship correspond with those of the Hindus generally, but some of the mendicant members of the sect, who are very numerous, and are usually known as *Vairágís*, or *Viraktas*, consider all form of adoration superfluous, beyond the incessant invocation of the name of KŔISHŃA and RÁMA.

The practices of this sect are of less precise nature than those of the RÁMÁNUJAS, it being the avowed object of the founder to release his diciples from those

---

[1] Amongst the temples of this sect at Benares, are two dedicated to *Rádhá Kŕishńa*, although attached to *Maths* belonging to the *Rámávat* order, and not at all connected with the followers of VALLABHA, or of CHAITANYA and NITYÁNAND.

fetters which he had found so inconvenient: in allusion to this, indeed, he gave, it is said, the appellation *Avadhúta*, or *Liberated*, to his scholars, and they admit no particular observances with respect to eating or bathing[1], but follow their own inclination, or comply with the common practice in these respects. The initiatory *Mantra* is said to be *Śrí Ráma*—the salutation is *Jaya Śrí Ráma*, *Jaya Rám*, or *Sítá Rám*: their marks are the same as those of the preceding, except that the red perpendicular streak on the forehead is varied, in shape and extent, at the pleasure of the individual, and is generally narrower than that of the RÁMÁNUJAS.

Various sects are considered to be but branches of the *Rámánandí Vaishńavas*, and their founders are asserted to have been amongst his disciples: of these disciples, twelve are particularised as the most eminent, some of whom have given origin to religious distinctions of great celebrity, and, although their doctrines are often very different from those of RÁMÁNAND, yet the popular tradition is so far corroborated, that they maintain an amicable intercourse with the followers of RÁMÁNAND, and with each other.

The twelve chief disciples of RÁMÁNAND are named, as follows—ÁŚÁNAND, KABÍR, the weaver, RAIDÁS, the *Chamár*, or currier, PÍPÁ, the *Rájaput*, SURSU-

---

[1] The *Vairágis* of this sect, and some others, eat and drink together, without regard to tribe or caste, and are thence called *Kulaíúí*, or *Varńaíúí*.

RÁNAND, SUKHÁNAND, BHAVÁNAND, DHANNA the *Ját*, SENA, the barber—MAHÁNAND, PARAMÁNAND, and ŚRÍÁNAND[1], a list which shews, that the school of RÁMÁNAND admitted disciples of every caste: it is, in fact, asserted in the *Bhakta Málá*, that the distinction of caste is inadmissible according to the tenets of the *Rámánandís*: there is no difference, they say, between the BHAGAVÁN and the *Bhakt*, or the deity and his worshipper; but BHAGAVÁN appeared in inferior forms, as a *Fish*, a *Boar*, a *Tortoise*, &c., so therefore the *Bhakt* may be born as a *Chamár*, a *Kolí*, a *Chhípí*, or any other degraded caste.

The various character of the reputed disciples of RÁMÁNAND, and a consideration of the tenets of those sects which they have founded, lead to a conclusion, that this individual, if he did not invent, gave fresh force to a very important encroachment upon the orthodox system: he, in fact, abrogated the distinction of caste amongst the religious orders, and taught, that the holy character who quitted the ties of nature and society, shook off, at the same time, all personal distinction—this seems to be the proper import of the term *Avadhúta*, which RÁMÁNAND is said to have affixed to his followers, and they were liberated from

---

[1] The *Bhakta Málá* has a rather different list: 1. RAGHUNÁTH, 2. ANANTÁNAND, 3. KABÍR, 4. SUKHÁSUR, 5. JÍVA, 6. PADMÁVAT, 7. PÍPÁ, 8. BHAVÁNAND, 9. RAIDÁS, 10. DHANNA, 11. SENA, 12. SURSURA. His successors, again, were somewhat different, or 1. RAGHUNÁTH, 2. ANANTÁNÁND, JOGÁNAND, RÁMDÁS, ŚRÍ RANJA, and NARAHARI.

more important restraints than those of regimen and ablution: the popular character of the works of this school corroborates this view of RÁMÁNANDA's innovation; ŚANKARA and RÁMÁNUJA writing to and for the Brahmanical order alone, composed chiefly, if not solely, Sanskrit commentaries on the text of the *Vedas*, or Sanskrit expositions of their peculiar doctrines, and the teachers of these opinions, whether monastic or secular, are indispensably of the Brahmanical caste—it does not appear that any works exist which are attributed to RÁMÁNAND himself, but those of his followers are written in the provincial dialects, and addressed to the capacity, as well as placed within the reach, of every class of readers, and every one of those may become a *Vairágí*, and rise, in time, to be a *Guru* or *Mahant*.

We shall have occasion to speak again particularly of such of the above mentioned disciples of RÁMÁNAND, as instituted separate sects, but there are several who did not aspire to that distinction, and whose celebrity is, nevertheless, still very widely spread throughout Hindustan: there are also several personages belonging to the sects of particular note, and we may, therefore, here pause, to extract a few of the anecdotes which the *Bhakta Málá* relates of those individuals, and which, if they do not afford much satisfactory information regarding their objects, will at least furnish some notion of the character of this popular work.

PÍPÁ, the *Rájaput*, is called the Rájá of *Gángaraun*: he was originally a worshipper of DEVÍ, but abandoned her service for that of VISHŃU, and repaired to Benares to put himself under the tuition of RÁMÁNAND. Having disturbed the sage at an inconvenient season, RÁMÁNAND angrily wished that he might fall into the well of his court-yard, on which PÍPÁ, in the fervour of his obedience, attempted to cast himself into it to accomplish the desire of the saint. This act was with difficulty prevented by the by-standers, and the attempt so pleased RÁMÁNAND that he immediately admitted the *Rájá* amongst his disciples.

PÍPÁ, after some time, abandoned his earthly possessions, and accompanied by only one of his wives, named SÍTÁ, as ardent a devotee as himself, adopting a life of mendicity, accompanied RÁMÁNAND and his disciples to *Dwáraká.* Here he plunged into the sea to visit the submarine shrine of KŔISHŃA, and was affectionately received by that deity: after spending some days with him, PÍPÁ returned, when the fame of the occurrence spread, and attracted great crowds to see him. Finding them incompatible with his devotions, PÍPÁ left *Dwáraká* privately: on the road some Patťháns carried off his wife, but RÁMA himself rescued her, and slew the ravishers. The life of this vagrant *Rájá* is narrated at considerable length in the *Bhakta Málá*, and is made up of the most absurd and silly legends. On one occasion the *Rájá* encounters a furious lion in a forest; he hangs a rosary round his neck, whispers the Mantra of *Ráma*, and makes him tranquil in a moment; he then lectures the lion on the impropriety of devouring men and kine, and sends him away penitent, and with a pious purpose to do so no more.

Of Sursuránand we have a silly enough story of some cakes that were given to him by a *Mlechchha* being changed when in his mouth into a *Tulasí* leaf. Of Dhanna, it is related that a Brahman, by way of a frolic, gave him a piece of stone, and desired him to offer to it first, whatever he was about to eat. Dhanna obeyed, looking upon the stone as the representative of Vishńu, who, being pleased with his devotion, appeared, and constantly tended the cattle of the simple *Ját*: at last he recommended his becoming the disciple of Rámánand, for which purpose he went to Benares, and having received the Mantra, returned to his farm. Raghunáth, or in the text Áśánand, succeeded Rámánand in the *Gaddí*, or the Pillow of the *Mahant*. Narahari or Haryánand was also a pupil of Rámánand, whom it is difficult to identify with any one in the list above given: we have a characteristic legend of him.

Being one day in want of fuel to dress his meat, he directed one of his pupils to proceed to a neighbouring temple of Devi, and bring away from it any portion of the timber he could conveniently remove: this was done, to the great alarm, but utter helplessness of the goddess, who could not dispute the authority of a mortal of Haryánand's sanctity. A neighbour who had observed this transaction laboured under a like want of wood: at the instigation of his wife, he repaired also to the temple, and attempted to remove one of the beams, when the goddess, indignant at his presumption, hurled him down and broke his neck: the widow hearing of her husband's fate, immediately hastened to the temple, and liberally abused the vindictive deity. DEVÍ took advantage of the business to make a bargain for her temple, and restored the man to life, on condition that he would ever afterwards buy fuel for HARYÁNAND.

The legends of such other disciples of RÁMÁNAND as occur in the *Bhakta Málá* will be given in their proper places, and it will be sufficient here to confine our further extracts from that authority to NÁBHÁJI, the author, SÚR DÁS, and TULASÍ DÁS, to whose poetical talents the late version of it is largely indebted, and JAYADEVA, whose songs have been translated by Sir William Jones.

NÁBHÁJI, the author of the *Bhakta Málá*, was by birth a *Ďom*, a caste whose employ is making baskets and various sorts of wicker work. The early commentators say he was of the *Hanumán Vanś*, or Monkey tribe, because, observes the modern interpreter, *Bánar*, a monkey, signifies in the *Marwar* language a *Ďom*, and it is not proper to mention the caste of a *Vaishńava* by name: he was born blind, and when but five years old, was exposed by his parents, during a time of scarcity, to perish in the woods: in this situation he was found by AGRADÁS and KÍL, two *Vaishńava* teachers: they had compassion upon his helplessness, and KÍL sprinkled his eyes with the water of his *Kamańdalu*, or water pot, and the child saw: they carried

NÁBHÁJI to their *Math*, where he was brought up, and received the initiatory Mantra from AGRADÁS: when arrived at maturity, he wrote the *Bhakta Málá* by desire of his *Guru*. The age of NÁBHÁJI must be about two centuries, or two and a half, as he is made cotemporary with MÁN SINH, the Rájá of *Jaynagar*, and with AKBAR. He should date much earlier, if one account of his spiritual descent which makes him the fourth from RÁMÁNAND[1] be admitted, but in the *Bhakta Málá*, KŔISHŃA DÁS, the second in that account, does not descend in a direct line from RÁMÁNAND, but derives his qualifications as teacher from the immediate instructions of VISHŃU himself: there is no necessity, therefore, to connect NÁBHÁJI with RÁMÁNAND. The same authority places him also something later, as it states that TULASÍ DÁS, who was contemporary with SHÁH JEHÁN, visited NÁBHÁJI at *Bŕindávan*. It is probable, therefore, that this writer flourished at the end of AKBAR's reign, and in the commencement of that of his successor.

The notices we have of SÚR DÁS are very brief: he was blind, a great poet, and a devout worshipper of VISHŃU, in whose honour all his poems are written: they are songs and hymns of various lengths, but usually short, and the greater number are *Padas*, or simply stanzas of four lines, the first line forming a subject, which is repeated as the last and the burthen

---

[1] 1. RÁMÁNAND, 2. ÁŚÁNAND, 3. KŔISHŃA DÁS, 4. KIL and AGRADÁS, 5. NÁBHÁJI. See the next division of this section.

of the song, *Padas* being very generally sung, both at public entertainments, and the devotional exercises of the *Vaishńava* ascetics. SÚR DÁS is said to have composed 125,000 of these *Padas*: he is almost entitled to be considered as the founder of a sect, as blind beggars carrying about musical instruments, to which they chaunt stanzas in honour of VISHŃU, are generally termed *Súr Dásis*. The tomb of SÚR DÁS, a simple mound of earth, is considered to be situated in a tope near *Śivpur*, a village about two miles to the north of Benares. There is also an account of a saint of the same name in the *Bhakta Málá*, who is possibly a different person from the blind bard. This was a Brahman, *Amín*, or collector of the Pergunnah of *Sańdíla*, in the reign of AKBAR, and who with more zeal than honesty made over his collections to the shrine of MADANA MOHANA, a form of KŔISHŃA, at *Bŕindávan*, and sent to the treasury chests filled with stones[1]: the minister TOḌAR MALL, however, although a Hindu, was not disposed to confirm this transfer, and he had the defaulter arrested and thrown into prison. SÚR DÁS then applied to AKBAR, and the good

---

[1] He accompanied them also with the following rhyme,

तेरह लाख संडीले उपजे सब सन्तन मिलि गटके।
सूरदास मदनमोहन आधी रात हि सटके॥

which may be thus rendered:

The Saints have shared Sańdíla's taxes,
Of which the total thirteen lacks is,
A fee for midnight service owen,
By me *Súr Dás* to *Madan Mohen*.

[Price's Hindee and Hindust. Selections. Calc., 1827. I, p. 100.]

natured monarch, who probably thought his collector more fool than knave, set him at liberty. He retired to *Bŕindávan* and there continued to lead a religious and ascetic life.

The account of TULASÍ DÁS in the *Bhakta Málá* represents him as having been incited to the peculiar adoration of RÁMA by the remonstrances of his wife, to whom he was passionately attached: he adopted a vagrant life, visited Benares, and afterwards went to *Chitrakúta*, where he had a personal interview with *Hanumán*, from whom he received his poetical inspiration, and the power of working miracles: his fame reached *Dehli*, where SHÁH JEHÁN was emperor: the monarch sent for him to produce the person of RÁMA, which TULASÍ DÁS refusing to do, the king threw him into confinement; the people of the vicinity, however, speedily petitioned for his liberation, as they were alarmed for their own security: myriads of monkies having collected about the prison, and begun to demolish it, and the adjacent buildings. SHÁH JEHÁN set the poet at liberty, and desired him to solicit some favour as a reparation for the indignity he had suffered: TULASÍ DÁS, accordingly, requested him to quit ancient *Dehli*, which was the abode of RÁMA, and in compliance with this request the emperor left it, and founded the new city, thence named *Sháh Jehánábád*. After this, TULASÍ DÁS went to *Bŕindávan*, where he had an interview with NÁBHÁJI: he settled there, and strenuously advocated the worship of *Sítá Ráma*, in preference to that of *Rádhá Kŕishńa*.

Besides these legendary tales of this celebrated writer, whose works exercise more influence upon the great body of Hindu population than the whole voluminous series of Sanskrit composition, we have other notices of him collected from his own works, or preserved by tradition, that differ in some respects from the above. From these it appears, that TULASÍ DÁS was a Brahman of the *Sarvárya* branch, and a native of *Hájípur*, near *Chitrakúta*; when arrived at maturity, he settled at *Benares*, and held the office of *Díwán* to the *Rájá* of that city: his spiritual preceptor was JAGANNÁTH DÁS, a pupil, as well as NÁBHÁJI, of AGRADÁS: he followed this teacher to *Govardhan*, near *Bŕindávan*, but afterwards returned to Benares, and there commenced his Hindi version of the *Rámáyańa*, in the year of Samvat 1631, when he was thirty-one years of age. Besides this work, which is highly popular, TULASÍ DÁS is the author of a *Sat Sai**, or collection of one hundred stanzas on various subjects: of the *Rám Guńávali*, a series of verses in praise of RÁMA, of a *Gítávali*, and *Vinaya Patriká*, poetical compositions of a devotional or moral tendency, and of a great variety of *Hymns*—as *Rágas*, *Kavits*, and *Padas*, in honour of his tutelary deity and his consort, or RÁMA and SÍTÁ. TÚLASÍ DÁS continued to reside at Benares, where he built a temple to *Sítá*

* [The word *Sat Sai* = सप्तशती rather implies a collection of seven-hundred stanzas or ślokas, such as e. g. the Deví-máhátmya. See Śabdakalpadruma s. v.]

Ráma, and founded a *Math* adjoining, both which are still in existence: he died in the year of the *Samvat* era, 1680, or A. D. 1624, in the reign of JEHÁNGÍR[1], and the legendary story of his intercourse with SHÁH JEHÁN, is consequently an anachronism.

JAYADEVA was an inhabitant of a village called *Kinduvilva*, where he led an ascetic life, and was distinguished for his poetical powers, and the fervour of his devotion to VISHṄU. He at first adopted a life of continence, but was subsequently induced to marry. A Brahman had dedicated his daughter to JAGANNÁTH, but on his way to the shrine of that deity was addressed by him, and desired to give the maiden to JAYADEVA who was one with himself. The saint, who it should appear had no other shelter than the shade of a tree, was very unwilling to burthen himself with a bride, but her father disregarded his refusal, and leaving his daughter with him departed. JAYADEVA then addressed the damsel, and asked her what she proposed to do, to which she replied: "whilst I was in my father's house, I was obedient to his will; he has now presented me to you, and I am subject to your pleasure; if you reject me, what remains for me but to die?" The saint finding there was no help, turned householder, and removed the image he had worshipped in the air into his dwelling, by desire, it

[1] According to this memorial verse:

संवत सोलह सय असी गंगाके तीर।
सावण शुक्ला सत्तमी तुलसी तज्यौ शरीर॥

is said, of the object of his adoration. In his new condition he composed the *Gítá Govinda*, in which KRISHŃA himself assisted, for on one occasion, JAYADEVA being puzzled how to describe the charms of RÁDHÁ, laid down the paper for a happier moment, and went to bathe. KRISHŃA, assuming his person, entered his house, and wrote the requisite description, much to the poet's astonishment on his return home.

Of the *Gítá Govinda* it is said, that the *Rájá of Níláchala* (Orissa) composed a poem similarly named, but when the two works were placed before JAGANNÁTH, he took the work of JAYADEVA to his bosom, and threw that of the *Rájá* out of his temple. It is also said, that the *Gítá Govinda* was sung in the court of VIKRAMA, thus assigning to it an antiquity which there is no reason to suspect it can justly claim.

JAYADEVA being desirous of performing a particular rite for his idol, resumed his erratic habits, and succeeded in collecting a considerable sum of money for this purpose: on the road he was attacked by *Ťhags*, or thieves, who robbed him, and cut off his hands and feet. In this state he was found by a *Rájá* who took him home, and had his wounds healed. Shortly afterwards the thieves, disguised as religious mendicants, came to the court of the Rájá. JAYADEVA recognized them, and overwhelmed them with benefits. On their departure, two of the Rájá's people were sent to attend them to the confines of the *Ráj*, who on their way asked them how they had merited the saint's particular regard. To this they replied, that they had been his fellows in the service of a Rájá, who had ordered them to put him to death: they however only mutilated him, and his gratitude for their sparing his life was the reason he had treated them so kindly. They had no sooner uttered these words, than the earth opened and swallowed them. The servants of the Rájá returned, and reported the occurrence, when a fresh miracle took place—the hands and feet of JAYADEVA sprouted forth again. The *Rájá* being filled with astonishment, requested the saint to explain these events, which he did by narrating what had befallen him.

After remaining some time with the *Rájá* where he restored to life his own wife PADMÁVATÍ, who had voluntarily put an end to herself, he returned to *Kinduvilva*. Here the Ganges, which was then eighteen cos distant, and to which he went daily to bathe, requested him not to undergo so much fatigue, as she would rather come to him. The proposal was accepted by the saint, and according to our guide, the river now runs close to the village.

The ascetic and mendicant followers of RÁMÁNAND, known indiscriminately as *Rámánandis* or *Rámávats*, are by far the most numerous class of sectaries in Gangetic India: in Bengal they are comparatively few: beyond this province, as far as to *Allahábád*[1], although

[1] Some of the principal Maths at Benares are the following: RÁMJIT, *Mahant*, a temple of RÁMA. MÁYÁ RÁM, *Mahant*, a temple of RÁMA. RÁMÁNUJA, *Khâki*, *Mahant*, a temple of SÍTÁ RÁM. PURUSHOTTAMA DÁS, *Khâki*, *Mahant*, a temple of RÁMA.

perhaps the most numerous, they yield in influence and wealth to the *Śaiva* branches, especially to the *Atíts*: hence, however, they predominate, and either by themselves, or their kindred divisions, almost engross the whole of the country along the *Ganges* and *Jamna*: in the district of *Agra*, they alone constitute seven-tenths of the ascetic population. The *Rámánandís* have very numerous votaries, but they are chiefly from the poorer and inferior classes, with the exception of the *Rájaputs* and military *Brahmans*, amongst whom the poetical works of Súr Dás and Tulasí Dás maintain the pre-eminence of *Ráma* and his *Bhakts*.

KABÍR PANTHÍS.

Amongst the twelve disciples of Rámánand the most celebrated of all, and one who seems to have produced, directly or indirectly, a greater effect on the state of popular belief than any other, was Kabír: with an unprecedented boldness he assailed the whole system of idolatrous worship, and ridiculed the learning of the *Pańdits*, and doctrines of the Śástras, in a

---

Pitámbara Dás, *Mahant*, Sitá Rám; this is the *Mandir* of *Tulasí Dás*. Govind Dás, *Mahant*, Rádhá Kŕishńa. Rámacharań, ditto, ditto.

At a late meeting (1820) to elect a *Mahant* of one of the Vaishńava *Maths*, in the vicinity of Benares, about 5000 Mendicants of the various branches of the sect attended; of these at least 3000 were *Rámávats*, the rest were *Śrí Vaishńavas*, *Kabír Panthís*, and others.

style peculiarly well suited to the genius of his countrymen to whom he addressed himself, whilst he also directed his compositions to the Musalman, as well as to the Hindu faith, and with equal severity attacked the *Mullá* and *Korán*. The effect of his lessons, as confined to his own immediate followers, will be shewn to have been considerable, but their indirect effect has been still greater; several of the popular sects being little more than ramifications from his stock, whilst *Nának Sháh*, the only Hindu reformer who has established a national faith, appears to have been chiefly indebted for his religious notions to his predecessor KABÍR[1]. This sect therefore claims particular attention.

---

[1] MALCOLM says, that NÁNAK constantly referred to the writings of the celebrated Mohammedan CABIR, (A. R. XI, 267.) and the *Kabir Panthís* assert, that he has incorporated several thousand passages from *Kabir*'s writings. As to *Kabir*'s being a Mohammedan, I shall allude to the improbability, I may say impossibility, of this in the text; nor is COL. MALCOLM more accurate when he calls him a celebrated *Ssúfi*, for his doctrines have nothing in common apparently with that sect; indeed I think it not at all improbable that no such person as KABÍR ever existed, and that his name is a mere cover to the innovations of some freethinker amongst the Hindus: perhaps some one of those considered as his principal disciples: his names are very suspicious, and *Jnáni*, the sage, or *Kabir*, the greatest, are generic rather than individual denominations: at any rate, even if the individual were distinct, we must suppose that the name which occurs in his writings is nothing more than the *Takhallus*, or assumed name, under which both *Musalman* and *Hindu* poets have been accustomed to send their compositions into the world. To return, however, to the obligations which the popular reli-

The origin of the founder of this sect is variously narrated, although in the main points the traditions are agreed: the story told in the *Bhakta Málá* is, that he was the son of the virgin widow of a Brahman, whose father was a follower of RÁMÁNAND: at his daughter's repeated request, he took her to see RÁMÁNAND, and that teacher, without adverting to her situation, saluted her with the benediction he thought acceptable to all women, and wished her the conception of a son: his words could not be re-called, and the young widow, in order to conceal the disgrace thus inflicted on her, contrived to be privately delivered, and exposed the child: it was found by a weaver and his wife, and brought up as their own.

The followers of KABÍR do not admit more than the conclusion of this legend: according to them, the child, who was no other than the incarnate deity, was found floating on a Lotus in *Lahartaláb*, a lake, or pond near Benares, by the wife of a weaver, named NIMÁ*, who, with her husband NÚRÍ, was attending a wedding procession: she took the child up, and shewed it to her husband, who being addressed by the child, and

---

gions owe to the real or supposed KABÍR, I find him avowedly or unavowedly cited by *Bábá Lál*, and in the writings of the *Sádhs*, the *Satnámís*, the *Śrí Nárdínís* and *Śúnyávádís*, and I am told that the *Dádú Panthís*, and *Daryá Dásís* are equally indebted to him.

* [According to the text of the Bhakta Málá, as printed in Price's „Hindee and Hindustanee Selections", Calcutta: 1827. Vol. I, p. 84. *Kabír* was found by a weaver of the name of *Alí* (a Muhammedan?), — अली जुलाहा ने पाया.]

desired to take him to *Kási*, fled with terror, thinking they had got hold of some incarnate demon: after having run to the distance of about a mile, he was surprised to find the child before him, by whom his fear was tranquillised, and he was persuaded to return to his wife, and bring up, without anxiety or alarm, the infant they had so marvellously discovered.

All traditions concur in making Kabír the disciple of Rámánand, although various stories are narrated of the method by which he obtained that distinction, and overcame the objections started to him as a man of low caste, or, according to very general belief, of the Mohammedan persuasion: he succeeded at last by surprise, having put himself in the way of that teacher on the steps of the *ghát* down which he went at day-break to bathe, so as to be struck with his foot, on which Rámánand exclaimed, *Rám, Rám*, words that Kabír assumed, and Rámánand acknowledged to be the initiatory Mantra, which forms the bond of union between a *Guru* and his disciple.

The story of Kabír's being a disciple of Rámánand, however told, and, although perhaps not literally true in any fashion, may be so far correct, that Kabír was roused by the innovations of that sectary to adopt and extend the schism, and seems to place at contiguous periods the eras at which they flourished: according to the *Kabír Panthís*, their founder was present in the world three hundred years, or from 1149 to 1449[1],

---

[1] सम्वत् बारहसवे औ पांच मों ज्ञानी कियौ विचार । काशी

but of these dates we cannot admit the accuracy of more than one at most, and as the latter is the more recent, it is the more probable: agreeable to this is the connexion of KABÍR's writings with the faith of NÁNAK SHÁH, who began to teach about 1490, and it also confirms a particular account, current amongst his followers, of his openly vindicating his doctrines before SEKANDER SHÁH[1], in whose time FERISHTA has

---

मांहि प्रगट भयौ शब्द कहौ टकसार ॥ सम्वत् पंद्रहसये औ पांच मौं मगर कियौ गवन। अगहन् सुदी येकादसी मिले पवन सों पवन॥
"In the Samvat 1205 JNÁNÍ meditated, was manifest at *Káśí*, and declared the text called *Ṫaksár*: in the Samvat 1505 he journeyed to *Magar*, and on the 11th of the light fortnight of *Aghan*, air mixed with air."

[1] There is a *Ramaini* to that effect, and the following story is told, with the usual marvellous embellishments, in the *Bhakta Málá*; in that work it is said, his mother complained to SEKANDER *Pádsháh* of her son's having deserted the true faith, on which the king sent for him; he appeared with the *Ṫiká* and *Málá*, and when told to make the customary *Salám*, he replied, "I know none but *Rám*, what use is there in prostrating myself to a monarch?" Enraged at his behaviour, the king ordered him to be chained hand and foot, and thrown into the river. The water bore him to shore. He then commanded him to be cast into fire, but the flames played harmless round him. He then directed him to be trodden to death by an elephant, but as soon as the animal saw the sage, he turned tail and ran away. The king mounted his own elephant, resolved to execute his commands in person, but when he approached, KABÍR transformed himself into a lion. The Monarch then convinced of his divine character alighted, and falling at his feet, offered him any lands and villages he might choose: these offers he declined, saying, "RÁM is my wealth: of what avail are worldly possessions, but

noticed, that some religious disputes, possibly connected with the history of KABÍR, or that of some of his disciples, did occur.

These circumstances, connected with the acknowledged date of his death, render it exceedingly probable that *Kabír* flourished about the beginning of the 15th century—and as it is also not unlikely that his innovations were connected with the previous exertions of RÁMÁNAND, consequently that teacher must have lived about the end of the 14th.

According to one account, KABÍR was originally named *Jnáni,* the knowing or wise. The Musalmans, it is said, claim him as one of their persuasion, but

---

to set father, and son, and brother, at deadly variance?" He returned to his abode, and remained unmolested. [Price, Hindee and Hindust. Sel. I, 86.]

COLONEL MALCOLM in the note before cited, places him in the reign of SHÍR SHÁH; this is, however, at variance with his own statements; NÁNAK was in the height of his career in 1527, (A. R. XI, 206.) then imparting to BABER tenets which he had partly borrowed from the writings of KABÍR, and which must consequently have been some time *previously* promulgated: but SHÍR SHÁH did not commence his reign till 1542, and it was therefore impossible for KABÍR to have lived in his reign, and at the same time to have instigated by his own innovations the more successful ones of NÁNAK. KABÍR's being contemporary with SEKANDER, is also mentioned in PRIYA DÁSA's expansion of the *Bhakta Málá*: it is likewise stated in the *Kholassat al tawárikh,* and is finally established by ABULFAZL, who says that KABÍR, the Unitarian, lived in the reign of *Sultán* SECANDER LODÍ (*Ay*: *Ac*: 2, 38.). [G. de Tassy, histoire de la littérature Hindoui et Hindoustani. Paris: 1839 & 47. Vol. I, p. 275. II, 6.]

his conversancy with the *Hindu Śástras*, and evidently limited knowledge of the Mohammedan authorities in matters of religion, render such a supposition perfectly unwarrantable: at any rate tradition represents it to have occasioned a contest between them and the Hindus respecting the disposal of his corpse, the latter insisting on burning, the Musalmans on burying it; in the midst of the dispute, KABÍR himself appeared amongst them, and desiring them to look under the cloth supposed to cover his mortal remains, immediately vanished: on obeying his instructions, they found nothing under the cloth, but a heap of flowers: one half of these BANÁR *Rájá* or BÍRSINHA *Rájá*, then Rájá of Benares, removed to that City, where they were burnt, and where he appropriated the spot now called the *Kabír Chaura* to the reception of their ashes, whilst BIJILÍ KHÁN *Paṭṭhán*, the head of the Mohammedan party, erected a tomb over the other portion at *Magar* near *Gorakhpur*, where KABÍR had died. This latter place was endowed by MANSÚR ALÍ KHÁN with several villages, and it divides with the *Chaura* the pilgrimage of the followers of this sect.

The *Kabír Panthís* in consequence of their Master having been the reputed disciple of RÁMÁNAND, and of their paying more respect to VISHṄU, than the other Members of the Hindu triad, are always included amongst the *Vaishṅava* sects, and maintain with most of them, the *Rámávats* especially, a friendly intercourse and political alliance: it is no part of their faith, however, to worship any Hindu deity, or to observe any of the rites or ceremonials of the Hindus, whether orthodox or schismatical; such of their members as are living in the world conform outwardly to all the usages of their tribe and caste, and some of them even pretend to worship the usual divinities, although this is considered as going rather farther than is justifiable. Those however who have abandoned the fetters of society, abstain from all the ordinary practices, and address their homage, chiefly in chanting Hymns, exclusively to the invisible KABÍR: they use no *Mantra* nor fixed form of salutation; they have no peculiar mode of dress, and some of them go nearly naked, without objecting however to clothe themselves in order to appear dressed, where clothing is considered decent or respectful—the *Mahants* wear a small scull cap: the frontal marks, if worn, are usually those of the *Vaishńava* sects, or they make a streak with Sandal, or *Gopichandan* along the ridge of the nose: a necklace and rosary of *Tulasi* are also worn by them, but all these outward signs are considered of no importance, and the inward man is the only essential point to be attended to[1].

---

[1] To avoid unnecessary contention, and its probable concomitant in other days, persecution, was the object probably of the following prudent maxim, one of the *Sákhis* of their founder:

सब से हिलिये सब से मिलिये सब का लिजिये नाऊं।
हां जी हां जी सब से किजिये वसे आपने गाऊं॥

"Associate and mix with all, and take the names of all; say to every one, yes Sir, yes Sir. Abide in your own abode."—They do not admit that taking the names of all implies the in-

The doctrines of KABÍR are taught in a great variety of works in different dialects of Hindi; they are the acknowledged compositions of his disciples and successors, but they are mostly in the form of dialogues, and profess to be of his utterance, either in his own words, with the phrase, *Kaháhi Kabír*, '*Kabír* verily says', or to the same substance, which is marked by the qualification, *Kahai Kabír*, '*Kabír* has said', or they are given in the language of his followers, when the expression *Dás Kabír*, the slave of *Kabír*, is made use of. The style of all their works is very peculiar, they are written in the usual forms of *Hindi* verse, the *Dohá*, *Chaupai* and *Samay*; and are very voluminous, as may be inferred from the following collection, preserved as the *Kháss Grantha*, or *The Book* at the *Chaura*.

1. *Sukh Nidhán.*
2. *Gorakhnáth ki Goshthi.*
3. *Kabír Pánji.*
4. *Balakh ki Ramaini.*
5. *Rámánand ki Goshthi.*
6. *Ánand Rám Ságara.*
7. *Śabdávali*, containing 1,000 *Śabdas*, or short doctrinal expositions.

---

vocation of the illusory deities of the Hindu Pantheon, but means that they should reply as they are addressed, whether the phrase be *Bandagi, Dańdáwat*, or *Rám Rám*: the proper salutation of an inferior to a superior amongst them, if any be particularly proper, is *Bandagi Sáhib*, Service, Sir: to which the latter replies, *Guru Ki Dayá*, the mercy of the Lord be upon you.

8. *Mangala*, 100 short poems, amongst which is the account of KABÍR's discovery as given above.

9. *Vaśant*, 100 hymns in that *Rága*.

10. *Holi*, 200 of the songs called *Holi*.

11. *Rekhtas*, 100 odes.

12. *Jhúlanas*, 500 odes, in a different style.

13. *Kaháras*, 500 odes, in a different style.

14. *Hindolas*, 12 ditto ditto. The subject of all these odes, or hymns, is always moral or religious.

15. *Bárah Máśa*, the 12 months in a religious view, agreeably to KABÍR's system.

16. *Chancharas* 22.

17. *Chautiśas* 2: the 34 letters of the *Nágarí* alphabet, with their religious signification.

18. *Alefnámah*, the Persian alphabet in the same manner.

19. *Ramainís*, short doctrinal or argumentative poems.

Sákhís 5,000, these may be considered as texts, consisting of one stanza each.

20. The *Bíjak*, in 654 Sections[1].

---

[1] There are two *Bíjaks*, however, only differing in the occasional omission of some passages and introduction of others; the longer of the two, they say, was communicated by KABIR himself to the *Rájá* of Benares. I rather suspect, however, that the varieties are only those common to most Hindu Manuscripts, and that many more than two varieties are to be found. A curious Italian work on the *Kabir Panthis*, entitled, but not accurately, *Mulapanci*, intending no doubt *Múlapanthí*, or Radical disciple, not as rendered, *Della Radice*, is published in the third volume of the *Mines of the East*: it was found amongst the papers

There are also a variety of stanzas, called *Ágams*, *Váńís*, &c. composing a very formidable course of study to those who wish to go deep into the doctrine of this school, and one in which the greatest proficients amongst the *Kabír Panthís* are but imperfectly versed. A few *Sákhís*, *Śabdas* and *Rekhtas*, with the greater portion of the *Bíjak*, constituting their acquirements: these, however, they commit to memory, and quote in argument with singular readiness and happiness of application; the *Goshṫhís*, or disputations of KABÍR with those opposed to him, as GORAKHNÁTH, RÁMÁNAND, and even in spite of chronology with *Mohammed* himself, are not read till more advanced, whilst the *Sukh Nidhán*, which is the key to the whole, and which has the singularity of being quite clear and intelligible, is only imparted to those pupils whose studies are considered to approach perfection.

The author or compiler of the *Bíjak* or *Víjak*, was

---

of the Propaganda, and is communicated by Monsignore MÜNTER, Bishop of Zealand, in Denmark; an eminent Scholar, the author of a valuable work on the Sahidic Version of the N. T. &c. It is to be presumed, that it is intended to be a translation of some KABÍRÍ work, but how correctly it deserves this character, may be questioned; much of the phraseology of the sect is indeed closely followed, but the minute and ridiculous details of its cosmogony are, with very few exceptions, exceedingly different from those notions entertained by the followers of *Kabir*, as explained in the *Bíjaks*, or *Sukh Nidhán*. The extract published in the *Mines*, appears to be a portion, the second book, of some work thus described: "Il libro primario dei Cabiristi (Specie di riforma della gentilità,) si chiama *Satnam Kabir*: questo libro e fra le carte di Propaganda."

Bhagodás[1], one of KABÍR's immediate disciples: it is the great authority amongst the *Kabir Panthis* in general; it is written in very harmonious verse, and with great ingenuity of illustration: its style, however, is more dogmatical than argumentative, and it rather inveighs against other systems than explains its own: in the latter respect it is, indeed, so inexplicit and obscure, that it is perhaps impossible to derive from it any satisfactory conclusion as to the real doctrines of KABÍR. The followers of the *Sect* admit this obscurity, and much difference of opinion prevails amongst them in the interpretation of many passages: some of the teachers have a short work professedly written as a key to the most difficult parts, but this is in the hands of a chosen few: it is of no great value, however, as it is little less puzzling than the original, of a few passages of which the following translations will best exemplify the description thus given:

RAMAINÍ THE 1ST.—God, light, sound, and one woman; from these have sprung HARI, BRAHMÁ, and TRIPURÁRI. Innumerable are the emblems of ŚIVA and BHAVÁNÍ, which they have established, but they know not their own beginning nor end: a dwelling has been prepared for them: HARI, BRAHMÁ, and ŚIVA, are the three headmen, and each has his own village: they have formed the *Khaṅdas* and the egg of *Brahmá*, and have invented the six *Darśanas*—and ninety-six *Páshaṅdas*: no one has ever read the *Vedas* in the womb, nor has any infant been born a member of *Islám*. 'The woman', relieved from the burthen of the embryo, adorned her person with every grace. I and you

[1] Of the shorter work: it is undoubtedly the one most generally current.

are of one blood, and one life animates us both; from one mother is the world born: what knowledge is this that makes us separate? no one knows the varieties of this descent, and how shall one tongue declare them? nay should the mouth have a million of tongues, it would be incompetent to the task. *Kabir* has said, I have cried aloud from friendship to mankind; from not knowing the name of Ráma, the world has been swallowed up in death.

In this *Ramaini*, the first passage contains an allusion to the notions of the sect regarding the history of creation. God is called Antar, *Inner*, that which was in all, and in which all was, meaning the first self-existent and all-comprehensive being. *Jyotish* is the luminous element, in which he manifested himself, and *Śabda*, the primitive *sound* or *word* that expressed his essence—the woman is *Máyá*, or the principle of error and delusion: the next passage relates to the impotence of the secondary gods, and the unnatural character of religious distinctions: "the *woman*" is Máyá, the self-born daughter of the first deity, and at once the mother and wife of Brahmá, Vishńu, and Śiva. "*I and you, &c.*" is addressed by her to them, "*no one knows, &c.*" is an allusion to the blindness of all worldly wisdom, and the passage winds up with a word of advice, recommending the worship of Ráma, implying the true God, agreeably to the system of Kabír.

The style of the whole *Bíjak* is of this kind: straggling allusions to the deceits of *Májá*, to the errors of other sects, and the superiority of their own, being strung together with very little method: it will not, however, be necessary to analyse any more of the passages, and they will become clear by reference to the general view of the system, with which we shall be furnished from the *Sukh Nidhán*: it may be sufficient here to observe, that the doctrines of *Kabír* are said to be conveyed in four-fold language, or that of *Máyá*, *Átmá*, *Man* or intellect, and the *Vedas*.

Ramaini the 6th.—(*Máyá*'s account of the first being, and of herself.) What is his colour, form, and shape; what other person has beheld him; the *Omkára* did not witness his beginning, how then can I explain it; can you say from what root he sprang; he is neither the stars, nor sun, nor moon; he has neither father, nor mother: he is neither water, nor earth, nor fire, nor air: what name or description can I give of him: to him is neither day nor night, nor family nor caste; he resides on the summit of space; a spark of his substance was once manifest, of which emanation I was the bride; the bride of that being who needs no other.

Śabda the 56th.—To Alí and Ráma we owe our existence, and should, therefore, shew similar tenderness to all that live: of what avail is it to shave your head, prostrate yourself on the ground, or immerse your body in the stream; whilst you shed blood you call yourself pure, and boast of virtues that you never display: of what benefit is cleaning your mouth, counting your beads, performing ablution, and bowing yourself in temples, when, whilst you mutter your prayers, or journey to *Mecca* and *Medína*, deceitfulness is in your heart. The Hindu fasts every eleventh day, the Musalman during the *Ramazán*. Who formed the remaining months and days that you should venerate but one. If the Creator dwell in Tabernacles, whose residence is the universe? who has beheld *Ráma* seated amongst images, or found him at the shrine to which the Pilgrim has directed his steps? The city of Hara is to the east, that of Alí to the west; but explore your own heart, for there are both *Ráma* and *Karím*. Who talks of the lies of the *Veds* and *Tebs*; those who understand not their essence. Behold but one in all things, it is the second that leads you astray. Every man and woman that has ever been born is of the same nature with yourself. *He*, whose is the world, and whose are the children of *Alí* and *Rám*, He is my *Guru*, He is my *Pír*.

The following *Śabda* is peculiarly illustrative of the mystical and unintelligible style of parts of the *Bíjak*; the explanation of the terms is taken from the key above referred to, but the interpreter is, perhaps, the most unintelligible of the two.

Śabda the 69th.—Who is the (1) magistrate of this city, (2) the meat (3) is exposed, and the (4) Vulture sits guarding it, the (5) Rat is converted into a (6) boat, and the (7) Cat is in charge of the helm; the (8) Frog is asleep, and the (9) Snake stands sentinel; the (10) Ox bears; the (11) Cow is barren; and the (12) Heifer is milked thrice a day; the (13) Rhinoceros is attacked by the (14) Jackal; very few know the (15) station of *Kabír*. (16)

Key. 1. *Man* the pride of intellect. 2. The body. 3. The *Vedas*, or scriptural writings of any sect. which teach the true nature of God. 4. The *Paṅḋit*, or worldly expounder of divine truths. 5. *Man* or intellect. 6. A mere vehicle for the diffusion of 7. *Máyá*, illusion and falsehood. 8. The *Siddha* or saint. 9. *Parameśvara*, the supreme being. 10. *Vishṅu*. 11. *Máyá* or *Deví*. 12. *Parameśvara*, the supreme. 13. A holy man. 14. Intellectual or doctrinal pride. 15. The divine nature. 16. God identified with man and nature.

The *Sákhis* of *Kabír* deserve, perhaps, a more copious exemplification: they are very gradually current even amongst those not his followers, they contain much curious matter, and they have often been referred to without their character being duly understood; there are some thousands of them, of which the *Bíjak* comprehends between three and four hundred:

one hundred will be sufficient, as a specimen of the whole: they are taken with one or two exceptions, from the *Bíjak* of the *Kabír Chaura*, in the order in which they occur.

Sákhis.

1. When man springs from the womb, he is void of every care: pass but the sixth day, and he feels the pains of separation.

2. My word is of the word; hear it, go not astray; if man wishes to know the truth, let him investigate the word.

3. My word is from the first; the word has been deposited in life; a basket has been provided for the flowers; the horse has eaten up the *Ghí.*

4. My word is from the first; meditate on it every moment; you will flourish in the end like the *Joár* plant, which shews externally but beards and leaves.

5. Without hearing the word, it is utter darkness; say, whither shall any one go; without finding the gate-way of the word, man will ever be astray.

6. There are many words, but take the pith of them; he who takes not the essence, saith Kabír, will live a profitless life.

7. For the sake of the word, some have died, and some have resigned dominion: he who has investigated the word, has done his work.

8. Lay in your provender, and provide your carriage, for if your food fail, and your feet be weary, your life is in the hands of another.

9. Lay in provender sufficient for the road, whilst time yet serves: evening comes on; the day is flown, and nothing will be provided.

10. Now is the time to prepare, henceforth the path is difficult: the travellers all hasten to purchase where there is neither trade nor market.

11. He who knows what life is will take the essence of his own; such as it is now, he will not possess it a second time.

12. If you know how mankind pass their lives, you will live

according to your knowledge; fetch water for your own drinking, nor demand it from others and drink.

13. Why go about to offer water? there is abundance in every house: when man is really thirsty, he needs no solicitation, but will drink by force.

14. The goose (the world or life) sells pearls; a gold vessel is full of them; but with him who knows not their value, what can be done?

15. The goose abandons the lake, the body is withered and dry: *Kabír* has called aloud, here is a path, there is a resting place!

16. The goose abandons the lake, and lodges in a water jar. *Kabír* calls aloud, repair to your village, nor demolish your habitation.

17. The goose and the paddy-bird are of one colour, and frolic in the same pool: the goose extracts the milk from the water, and the paddy-bird drinks the mire.

18. Why comes the feeble doe to the green pool; numerous foes lie in wait for her; how should she escape?

19. The three worlds form a cage; vice and virtue spread a net; life is the prey; and time the fowler.

20. The half of a *Sákhi* is sufficiently arduous, if duly investigated; of what avail are the books of the *Paṅdit*, or incessant study?

21. Having combined the five elements, I found one offspring; now I ask the *Paṅdit*, whether life or the word be the greater.

22. Of the five elements, the body was formed: when the body was formed what was done? subservient to action, it is called life, but by action life is destroyed.

23. The offspring of the five elements is called *Man*; if one element be withdrawn, the whole compound is destroyed.

24. With the five elements is the abode of a great mystery; when the body is decomposed, has any one found it? the word of the teacher is the guide.

25. Colour proceeds from colour, yet behold all are but one: of what colour then is life? think well of this.

26. Life is wakefulness: the word is like *Borax*, white: who has seen the yellow drop, saith *Kabír*, that has turned the water of that colour?

27. There is a mirror in the heart; but the face is not visible in it: then only will the face be reflected there, when doubleness of heart shall disappear.

28. The dwelling of *Kabír* is on the peak of a mountain, and a narrow path leads to it, an ant cannot put its foot upon it, but the pious man may drive up an ox.

29. The blind man talks of a district, which he has not seen; they are possessed of a salt pit, and offer camphor for sale.

30. The road that SANAKA and his brethren, that BRAHMÁ, VISHŃU, and MAHEŚA have travelled, is still traversed by mankind: what advice can I bestow?

31. The plough ascends the hill; the horse stops in the village: the bee seeks for honey, where there are no flowers: declare the name of the plant.

32. Sandal! restrain thy fragrance: on thy account, the wood is cut down; the living slay the living, and regard only the dead.

33. The sandal (the soul) is guarded by serpents (passion); what can it effect? every hair is impregnated with venom; where shall Ambrosia enter?

34. The seizer (death) lets not go his hold; though his tongue and beak be scorched: where it deems a dainty, the *Chakor* devours the burning coals.

35. The *Chakor* (hill partridge) in its passion for the moon, digests the burning coal, KABÍR declares it does not burn him, such is the fervour of his affection.

36. The village is on the top of a mountain, and so is the abode of the stout man. Choose, *Kabír*, one for your protector, who can really give you an asylum.

37. The crowd has taken the road travelled by the *Pańdit*: *Kabír* has ascended the steep defile, where lies the abode of RÁM.

38. What, ho! *Kabír*, descend, together with your car and provender; your provender will fail, your feet will grow weary, and your life will be in the hands of another.

39. From the contest of swinging and being swung no one

has escaped. GORAKH (the founder of the *Jogis*) was stopped at the city of time; who shall be called exempt?

40. GORAKH, enamoured as he was of RÁMA, is dead; his body was not burnt: (the Jogís bury the dead,) the flesh has decayed, and is turned to clay, and such rank as the *Kauravas* enjoy does he obtain (bodily annihilation).

41. The young camel flying from the wood has fallen into the stream; how shall the animal proclaim its misfortune, who shall learn it?

42. After a search of many days an empty shrine is raised: the camel's calf has strayed into a pit, and repents its heedlessness, when assistance is far off.

43. KABÍR (mankind) hat not escaped error, he is seized in various forms: without knowledge of its lord the heart will be but ashes.

44. Although not subject to fine, a heavy fine has been imposed upon the world: it has proved unprofitable: avarice has disposed of it; the juice of the cane yields both clayed and candied sugar.

45. In the confines of the *Malaya* Mountain (where Sandal grows) the *Palás* (Butea) tree acquires fragrance; were the *Bamboo* to grow there for ages, it would never gain perfume.

46. In the Woods of the *Malaya* Mountain grow trees of every kind, they may be called Sandal, but they yield not the Sandal of *Malaya*.

47. Walking, walking still, the feet are weary; the city is yet far off, a tent is erected by the road side; say, who is to blame?

48. The end of the journey is sunset, but night comes on mid-way: it is from the embrace of many lovers that the wanton is barren.

49. *Man* (the pride of intellect) enquires, when may I be allowed to go? the heart asks, when shall I go? the village (truth) that I have been these six months in quest of (investigating the six Darśanas, or systems), is not half a mile remote.

50. He has left his dwelling as an Ascetic, and goes to the thickets to practice penance: tired of the *Pán*-box, he beats the betel-vender, and eats split pease.

51. When a man (intending, however, here a *Jogí*) becomes acquainted with the name of RÁM, his body becomes a mere skeleton; his eyes taste no repose; his limbs retain no flesh.

52. He who sows RÁM, never puts forth the buds of wrath: he attaches no value to the valueless; he knows neither pleasure nor pain.

53. The cut mango will not blossom, the slit ear cannot be reunited; whose loss is it, if they apply not the philosopher's stone, that GORAKH had?

54. They have not regarded good advice, but have determined for themselves. *Kabír* says and cries aloud, the world has passed away like a dream.

55. When fire (evil) burns amidst the ocean (the world), no one sees the smoke: he is conscious of the fire who lighted it, and he who perishes in the flame.

56. The incendiary orders the fire to be kindled, and he who lights it singes his wings: he expiates his own act: the thatch escapes, but the house is burned.

57. When fire (truth) burns in the ocean (the mind), as it burns, it clears away the rubbish (worldly care). *Pańďits* from the east and from the west have died in the discussion.

58. When fire blazes in the ocean, the thatch of the house falls to pieces. Mankind weep as they resign their breath, and the inestimable jewel is lost.

59. That a drop falls into the ocean, all can perceive; but that the drop and the ocean are but one, few can comprehend.

60. The poison still remains in the soil, although the latter has been a hundred times sprinkled with ambrosia—man quits not the evil practices to which he has been long addicted.

61. The bellows is applied to the damp wood, which calls aloud with pain: if again it is caught in the blacksmith's forge, it will be burned the second time.

62. The soul that pines in absence, vainly flies to medicaments for relief; sigh follows sigh; it faints repeatedly and recovers, to exist, restless and distressed.

63. The separated (spirit) is like the moist fuel which smokes and blazes by fits: then only will it be exempted from pain, when all is utterly consumed.

64. An invitation has been issued in metre, and no one has understood the stanza; fortunate is the scholar who comprehends the word.

65. Take the true word of *Kabír* to your heart; the mind has received, but not understood it, although it has been divulged throughout the four ages.

66. If you are a true dealer, open the market of veracity; keep clean your inward man, and repel oppression to a distance.

67. The house is of wood, fire is all around it; the *Paṅḋit* with his learning is burnt: the prudent man makes his escape.

68. Drops fall from heaven on the verdure of *Śrávaṅ*: all the world are *Vaishṅavas*, no one listens to the teacher.

69. The bather dives nor comes up again; I think within myself, should sleep surprise him in the stream of fascination, what will befall him?

70. The *Sákhi* (text) is uttered, but not obeyed; the road is pointed out, but not followed: the stream of fascination sweeps him away; he finds no place to put his feet.

71. Many there are that talk, but few that take care to be found: let him pass on without regard, who practices not what he professes.

72. One by one, let each be considered, and adhered to, so shall error be stopped: he who is double-faced like a drum, shall be slapped (like a drum) on both cheeks.

73. He who has no check upon his tongue, has no truth in his heart; keep him not company: he will kill you on the high way.

74. Life has been destroyed by the repeated falsehoods of the tongue; it has strayed on the path of pride, and been whirled in the swing of time.

75. Put a check upon the tongue; speak not much; associate with the wise; investigate the words of the teacher.

76. The body is wounded by a spear, the head is broken off, and left in the flesh; it cannot be extracted without the loadstone: a thousand other stones are of no avail.

77. At first the ascent is difficult, but afterwards the way is easy; the beauty is behind the curtain, far from the pregnant woman.

78. Worldly existence is the season for reflecting what is the *Yoga*: the season is passing away; think ye, who have understanding.

79. Doubt has overcome the world, and no one has triumphed over doubt: he will refute doubt, who has investigated the word.

80. The eyes see dimly from incessant babbling, KABÍR cries aloud, and says, understand the word that is spoken.

81. Life is the philosopher's stone, the world is of iron: *Pársí (Máyá)* comes from *Páras* (God), the mintage is of the former.

82. Affection is the garment in which man dresses for the dance: consign yourself hand and foot to him, whose body and soul are truth.

83. In the concavity of the mirror the image is formed: the dog seeing his likeness barks at it till he dies.

84. But as a man viewing his reflexion in a mirror, knows that it and the original are but one, so should he know that *this* element, is but *that* element, and that thus the world proceeds.

85. KABÍR cries aloud to his fellows: ascend the sandal ridge; whether there be a road prepared or not; what matters it to me?

86. Truth, provided there be truth in the heart, is the best of all; there can be no happiness without truth, let man do as he will.

87. Let truth be your rate of interest, and fix it in your heart; a real diamond should be purchased, the mock gem is waste of capital.

88. Truth is the best of all, if it be known for truth—when truth combines with truth, then a real union is effected.

89. No act of devotion can equal truth; no crime is so heinous as falsehood; in the heart where truth abides, there is my abode.

90. The net of error catches the heron; the simpleton falls into the snare: KABÍR declares, that *he* will escape the toils, who has discrimination in his heart.

91. Like the harlot companion of the minstrel is life *(Jiv)*, associated with intellect *(man)*, at his command, she dances various steps, and is never separated from him.

92. This pride of intellect is manifold; now a swindler, now

a thief; now a liar, now a murderer; men, sages, gods, have run after it in vain; its mansion has a hundred gates.

93. The snake of separation has attached itself to the body, and darted its fangs into the heart: into the body of the *Sádh* it finds no admission: prepare yourself for what may happen.

94. How is it possible to reach the city when the guide cannot point out the road? when the boat is crazy, how shall the passengers get clear of the *Ghát*?

95. When the master is blind, what is to become of the scholar? when the blind leads the blind, both will fall into the well.

96. Yet the master is helpless when the scholar is unapt: it is blowing through a *bambu*, to teach wisdom to the dull.

97. The instruction of the foolish is waste of knowledge; a *maund* of soap cannot wash charcoal white.

98. The tree bears not fruit for itself, nor for itself does the stream collect its waters: for the benefit of others alone does the sage assume a bodily shape.

99. I have wept for mankind, but no one has wept with me; *he* will join in my tears, who comprehends the word.

100. All have exclaimed, master, master, but to me this doubt arises: how can they sit down with the master, whom they do not know?

The preceding will serve as exemplifications of the compositions of this school: they are necessarily unsatisfactory, as amongst some hundreds of similar passages the business of selection, when confined to the few admissible in this place, is unavoidably perplexing and incomplete: they are, however, sufficient for the present purpose, as the perusal of the entire work from which they have been selected would not convey any more positive notions of the doctrines of *Kabír*: these we shall now proceed to state according to the authority of the *Sukh Nidhán*.

The *Sukh Nidhán* is supposed to be addressed by

Kabír himself to *Dharmadás*, his chief pupil, and a follower of *Rámánand's* doctrines; it is said to be the work of ŚRUTGOPÁL, the first of KABÍR'S disciples.

From this authority it appears, that, although the *Kabír Panthís* have withdrawn, in such a very essential point as worship, from the Hindu communion, they still preserve abundant vestiges of their primitive source; and that their notions are in substance the same as those of the Pauráńic sects, especially of the Vaishńava division. They admit of but one God, the creator of the world, and in opposition to the *Vedánta* notions of the absence of every quality and form, they assert that he has a body formed of the five elements of matter, and that he has mind endowed with the three *Guńas*, or qualities of being; of course of ineffable purity and irresistible power: he is free from the defects of human natures, and can assume what particular shape he will: in all other respects he does not differ from man, and the *pure* man, the Sádh of the *Kabír* sect, is his living resemblance, and after death is his associate and equal; he is eternal, without end or beginning, as in fact is the elementary matter of which he consists, and of which all things are made residing in him before they took their present form, as the parts of the tree abide in the seed, or flesh, blood and bone may be considered to be present in the seminal fluid: from the latter circumstance, and the identity of their essential nature, proceeds the doctrine, that God and man are not only the same, but that they are both in the same manner every thing that lives and moves and has its being. Other sects have adopted these phrases literally, but the followers of *Kabír* do not mean by them to deny the individuality of being, and only intend these texts as assertions of all nature originally participating in common elementary principles.

The *Paramapurusha* was alone for seventy-two ages, for after the *Pauráńiks* the *Kabír Panthís* maintain successive and endless creations: he then felt a desire to renew the world, which desire became manifest in a female form[1], being the *Máyá*, from whom all the mistaken notions current amongst mankind originate: with this female the *Ádi Bhavání Prakŕiti* or *Śakti*, the *Parama Purusha*, or first male, cohabits, and begets the Hindu triad, *Brahmá*, *Vishńu* and *Śiva*: he then disappears, and the lady makes advances to her own sons: to their questions of her origin and character, she tells them, she was the bride of the first great invisible being, without shape and void, and whom she describes agreeably to the *Vedánta* notions; that she is now at liberty, and being of the same nature as themselves, is a fit associate for them: the deities hesitate, and *Vishńu* especially, putting some rather puzzling queries to *Máyá*, secured the respect of the *Kabír Panthís*, and excited the wrath

[1] These notions are common to the whole Hindu system—diversified according to the favorite object of worship, but essentially the same in all sects; we shall have occasion to discuss them more fully under the division *Śáktas*, or worshippers of Śakti.

of the goddess: she appears as *Mahá Máyá*, or *Durgá*, and frightens her sons into a forgetfulness of their real character, assent to her doctrines, and compliance with her desires: the result of this is the birth of *Saraswati*, *Lakshmi* and *Umá*, whom she weds to the three deities, and then establishing herself at *Jwálamukhi*, leaves the three wedded pairs to frame the universe, and give currency to the different errors of practice and belief which they have learnt from her.

It is to the falsehood of *Máyá* and her criminal conduct that the *Kabír Panthís* perpetually allude in their works, and in consequence of the deities pinning their faith upon her sleeve, that they refuse them any sort of reverential homage: the essence of all religion is to know *Kabír* in his real form, a knowledge which those deities and their worshippers, as well as the followers of Mohammed, are all equally strange to, although the object of their religion, and of all religions, is the same.

Life is the same in all beings, and when free from the vices and defects of humanity, assumes any material form it pleases: as long as it is ignorant of its source and parent, however, it is doomed to transmigration through various forms, and amongst others we have a new class of them, for it animates the planetary bodies, undergoing a fresh transfer, it is supposed, whenever a star or meteor falls: as to heaven and hell, they are the inventions of *Máyá*, and are therefore both imaginary, except that the *Swarga* of the Hindus, and *Bihisht* of the Musalmans, imply worldly luxury and sensual enjoyment, whilst the *Narak* and *Jehannam* are those cares and pains which make a hell upon earth.

The moral code of the *Kabír Panthís* is short, but if observed faithfully is of a rather favourable tendency. Life is the gift of God, and must not therefore be violated by his creatures; *Humanity* is, consequently, a cardinal virtue, and the shedding of blood, whether of man or animal, a heinous crime. *Truth* is the other great principle of their code, as all the ills of the world, and ignorance of God, are attributable to original falsehood. *Retirement* from the world is desirable, because the passions and desires, the hopes and fears which the social state engenders, are all hostile to tranquillity and purity of spirit, and prevent that undisturbed meditation on man and God which is necessary to their comprehension. The last great point is the usual sum and substance of every sect amongst the Hindus[1], implicit devotion in word, act, and thought to the *Guru*, or spiritual guide: in this, however, the characteristic spirit of the *Kabír Panthís* appears, and the pupil is enjoined to scrutinize his teacher's doctrines and acts, to be first satisfied that he is the sage he pretends to be, before he resigns

[1] The *Bhágavat* declares the Deity and *Guru* to be the same:

आचार्यं मां विजानीयान्नावमन्येत कर्हिचित् ।
न मर्त्त्यबुद्ध्यासूयेत सर्वदेवमयो गुरुः ॥

NÁBHÁJI declares the Deity, *Guru*, worshipper, and worship, to be four names and one substance:

भक्तिभक्तभगवंतगुरु चतुर्नाम वपु एक ॥

himself to his control. This sect, indeed, is remarkably liberal in this respect, and the most frequently recurring texts of *Kabír* are those which enforce an attentive examination of the doctrine, that he offers to his disciples. The chief of each community has absolute authority over his dependents: the only punishments he can award, however, are moral, not physical—irregular conduct is visited by reproof and admonition: if the offender does not reform, the *Guru* refuses to receive his salutation; if still incurable, the only further infliction is expulsion from the fraternity.

The doctrine of outward conformity, and the absence of visible objects of worship have prevented this sect from spreading very generally throughout India: it is, however, very widely diffused, and, as I have observed, has given rise to many others, that have borrowed its phraseology, and caught a considerable portion of its spirit: the sect itself is split into a variety of subdivisions, and there are no fewer than twelve branches of it traced up to the founder, between which a difference of opinion as well as descent prevails: the founders of these twelve branches, and the position of their descendants, are the following:—

1. Śrutgopál Dás, the author of the *Sukh Nidhán*: his successors preside over the *Chaura* at *Benares*, the *Samádh* at *Magar*, an establishment at *Jagannáth*, and one at *Dwáraká*.

2. *Bhago Dás*, the author of the *Bíjak*: his successors reside at *Dhanauti*.

3. *Náráyań Dás*, and

4. *Churámań Dás*; these two were the sons of Dharma Dás, a merchant of the *Kasaundhya* tribe, of the *Śrí Vaishńava* sect, and one of *Kabír*'s first and most important converts; his residence was at *Bandho* near *Jabbalpur*, where the *Maths* of his posterity long remained: the *Mahants* were family men, thence termed *Vanś Gurus*: the line of Náráyań Dás is extinct, and the present successor of *Churámań*, being the son of a concubine, is not acknowledged as a *Mahant* by all the other branches.

5. *Jaggo Dás*; the Gaddí or Pillow at Cuttack.

6. *Jívan Dás*, the founder of the *Satnámí* sect, to whom we shall again have occasion to advert.

7. *Kamál.*—Bombay: the followers of this teacher practice the *Yoga*. *Kamál* himself is said to have been the son of *Kabír*, but the only authority for this is a popular and proverbial phrase[1].

8. *Ták Sálí.*—Baroda.

9. *Jnání.*—Majjhní near Sahásram.

10. *Sáheb Dás.*—Cuttack: his followers have also some distinct notions, and form a sect called *Múla Panthís*.

11. *Nityánand.*

12. *Kamál Nád*: these two settled somewhere in the Dekhan, but my informant could not tell me exactly where. There are also some popular, and per-

---

[1] डूबा वंश कबीर का जो उपजा पुत कमाल ॥ "The Race of *Kabír* became extinct when his son Kamál was born," Kamál adopting, on principle, a life of celibacy, or being a person of worldly appetites.—*Roebuck*'s Proverbs, II, 1, 656.

haps local, distinctions of the sect, as *Hansa Kabíris, Dána Kabíris,* and *Mangrela Kabíris,* but in what respect, except appellation, they differ from the rest has not been ascertained.

Of these establishments the *Kabír Chaura,* at Benares, is pre-eminent in dignity, and it is constantly visited by wandering members of the sect, as well as by those of other kindred heresies: its Mahant receives and feeds these visitors whilst they stay, although the establishment has little to depend upon, except the occasional donations of its lay friends and followers. Balvant Sinh, and his successor, Chеit Sinh, were great patrons of it, and the latter granted to the *Chaura* a fixed monthly allowance. Cheit Sinh also attempted to form some estimate of the numbers of the sect, and if we may credit the result, they must be very considerable indeed, as at a grand meeting, or *Melá,* which he instituted near Benares, no fewer than 35,000 *Kabír Panthís* of the Monastic and Mendicant class are said to have been collected. There is no doubt that the *Kabír Panthís,* both clerical and lay, are very numerous in all the provinces of upper and central India, except, perhaps, in Bengal itself: the quaker-like spirit of the sect, their abhorrence of all violence, their regard for truth, and the inobtrusiveness of their opinions, render them very inoffensive members of the state: their mendicants also never solicit alms, and in this capacity even they are less obnoxious than the many religious vagrants, whom the rank soil of Hindu superstition and the enervating operation of an Indian climate so plentifully engender.

KHÁKÍS.

This division of the *Vaishńavas* is generally derived, though not immediately, from RÁMÁNAND, and is undoubtedly connected in its polity, and practice, with his peculiar followers. The reputed founder is KÍL, the disciple of KŔISHŃADÁS, whom some accounts make the disciple of ÁŚÁNAND, the disciple of RÁMÁNAND, but the history of the *Khákí* sect is not well known, and it seems to be of modern origin, as no notice of it occurs in the *Bhakta Málá*, or in any other work that has been consulted: the sectaries, though believed to be rather numerous, appear to be either confined to a few particular districts, or to lead wholly an erratic life, in which latter character they are confounded with the class of *Vairágís*: as no written accounts have been procured, and the opportunities of obtaining oral information have been rare and imperfect, a very brief notice of this sect is all that can here be offered.

The *Khákís*, as the name implies, are distinguished from the other *Vaishńavas*, by the application of clay and ashes to their dress or persons: those who reside in fixed establishments generally dress like other *Vaishńavas*, but those who lead a wandering life go either naked or nearly so, smearing their bodies with the pale grey mixture of ashes and earth, and making, in this state, an appearance very incompatible with the mild and decent character of the *Vaishńava* sects: the *Khákís* also frequently wear the *Jaṫá*, or braided hair, after the fashion of the votaries of *Śiva*, and, in fact, it appears that this sect affords one of the many instances of the imitative spirit common amongst the Hindu polytheists, and has adopted, from the *Śaivas*, some of their characteristic practices, blending them with the preferential adoration of VISHŃU, as *Raghunáth* or *Ráma*: the *Khákís* also worship SÍTÁ, and pay particular veneration to HANUMÁN.

Many *Khákís* are established about Furúkhábád, but their principal seat on this side of India is at *Hanumán Gaṙh*, near *Ayodhyá*, in Oude: the *Samádh* or spiritual throne of the founder, is said to be at *Jaypur*: the term *Samádh* applied to it, however, would seem to indicate their adopting a like practice with the *Jogís*, that of burying their dead, as the word is more generally used to express a tomb or mausoleum[1].

---

[1] The little information given in the text, was obtained from the Superior of a small, but neat establishment on the bank of the river, above *Viśránta Ghát*, at Furúkhábád. The *Ghát* and *Maṫh* had been recently erected by a merchant of Lucknow: the tenants, three or four in number, were a deputation from *Ayodhyá*, in Oude, and were but little acquainted with their own peculiarities, although not reluctant to communicate what they knew; other *Khákís* encountered here were *Nágas* and *Brahmachárís*, with whom no satisfactory communication was attainable; there were other establishments, but time did not permit their being visited.

MALÚK DÁSÍS.

The *Malúk Dásís* form another subdivision of the *Rámánandí Vaishńavas*, of comparatively uncertain origin and limited importance: they are generally traced from *Rámánand* in this manner: 1. *Rámánand*, 2. *Áśánand*, 3. *Kŕishńa Dás*, 4. *Kíl*, 5. *Malúk Dás*; making the last, consequently, contemporary with the author of the *Bhakta Málá*, and placing him in the reign of Akbar, or about 250 years ago.

We had occasion, in the notice taken of Nábhájí, to shew that the spiritual genealogy now enumerated could scarcely be correct, for as Rámánand must have flourished prior to the year 1400, we have but three generations between him and the date even of Akbar's succession 1555, or a century and a half: it was then mentioned, however, that according to the *Bhakta Málá*, Kŕishńa Dás was not the pupil of Áśánand, and consequently the date of succession was not necessarily uninterrupted: we might therefore place Malúk Dás, where there is reason to place Nábhájí, about the end of Akbar's reign, as far as this genealogy is to be depended upon, but there is reason to question even its accuracy, and to bring down Malúk Dás to a comparatively recent period: the uniform belief of his followers is indeed sufficient testimony on this head, and they are invariably agreed in making him contemporary with Aurengzeb.

The modifications of the *Vaishńava* doctrines introduced by Malúk Dás, appear to have been little more than the name of the teacher, and a shorter streak of red upon the forehead: in one respect indeed there is an important distinction between these and the *Rámánandí* ascetics, and the teachers of the *Malúk Dásís* appear to be of the secular order, *Gríhasthas*, or house-holders, whilst the others are all cœnobites: the doctrines, however, are essentially the same: Vishńu, as Ráma, is the object of their practical adoration, and their principles partake of the spirit of quietism, which pervades these sects: their chief authority is the *Bhagavad Gítá*, and they read some small Sanskrit tracts, containing the praise of *Ráma*: they have also some Hindi *Sákhís*, and *Vishńu Padas* attributed to their founder, as also a work in the same language, entitled the *Daśratan*: the followers of this sect are said to be numerous in particular districts, especially amongst the trading and servile classes, to the former of which the founder belonged[1].

The principal establishment of the *Malúk Dásís* is at *Kara Manikpur*, the birth-place of the founder, and still occupied by his descendants[2]; the present *Mahant*

---

[1] A verse attributed to Malúk Dás is so generally current, as to have become proverbial, it is unnecessary to point out its resemblance to Christian texts:

अजगर करै न चाकरी पंक्षी करै न काम।
दास मलूका यों कहै सब का दाता राम॥

"The snake performs no service, the bird discharges no duty. Malúk Dás declares, Rám is the giver of all." [*Roebuck's* Proverbs, II, 1, 36.]

[2] There is some variety in the accounts here, Mathurá Náth says, the *Tomb* is at *Kara*; *Purán Dás* asserts, that it is at

is the eighth in descent from him: the series is thus enumerated:

1. MALÚK DÁS. 2. RÁMSANÁHI. 3. KṘISHṄASNÁHI. 4. ṪHÁKUR DÁS. 5. GOPÁL DÁS. 6. KUNJ BEHÁRI. 7. RÁMSÁHÚ. 8. SEOPRASÁD DÁS. 9. GANGÁ PRASÁD DÁS, the present *Mahant*.

The *Math* at *Kara* is situated near the river, and comprises the dwellings of the *Mahant*, and at the time it was visited, of fifteen resident *Chelás*, or disciples, accommodations for numerous religious mendicants who come hither in pilgrimage, and a temple dedicated to *Rámachandra*: the *Gaddi*, or pillow of the sect, is here, and the actual pillow originally used by MALÚK DÁS is said to be still preserved. Besides this establishment, there are six other *Maths* belonging to this sect, at *Alláhábád*, *Benares*, *Bṙindávan*, *Ayodhyá*, *Lucknow*, which is modern, having been founded by *Gomati Dás*, under the patronage of *Asef ad Daula*, and *Jagannáth*, which last is of great repute as rendered sacred by the death of MALÚK DÁS.

Jagannáth, and the birth-place at *Kara*—he has been at both: the establishment at *Jagannáth* is of great repute; it is near to a *Math* of KABIR PANTHÍS, and all ascetics who go to this place of pilgrimage consider it essential to receive the *Malúk Dás ká Tukrá*, from the one, and *Kabír ká Tarañi*, from the other, or a piece of bread and spoonful of sour rice water. This and most of the other particulars were procured for me from the present *Mahant* by a young officer, Lieut. WILTON, stationed for a short time at *Kara*.

DÁDÚ PANTHÍS.

This class is one of the indirect ramifications of the *Rámánandí* stock, and is always included amongst the *Vaishńava* schisms: its founder is said to have been a pupil of one of the *Kabír Panthí* teachers, and to be the fifth in descent from RÁMÁNAND, according to the following genealogy:—

1. *Kabír.*	4. *Vimal.*
2. *Kamál.*	5. *Buddhan.*
3. *Jamál.*	6. *Dádú.*

The worship is addressed to *Ráma*, but it is restricted to the *Japa*, or repetition of his name, and the *Ráma* intended is the deity, as negatively described in the *Vedánta* theology: temples and images are prohibited.

Dádú was a cotton cleaner by profession: he was born at *Ahmedábád*, but in his twelfth year removed to *Sambhur*, in Ajmír: he thence travelled to *Kalyánpur*, and next removed to *Naraina*, in his thirty-seventh year, a place four cos from *Sambhur*, and twenty from *Jaypur*. When here, he was admonished, by a voice from heaven, to addict himself to a religious life, and he accordingly retired to *Baheraňa* mountain, five cos from *Naraina*, where, after some time, he disappeared, and no traces of him could be found. His followers believe he was absorbed into the deity. If the list of his religious descent be accurate, he flourished about the year 1600, at the end of *Akbar*'s reign, or in the beginning of that of *Jehángír*. The followers of *Dádú* wear no peculiar frontal mark nor *Málá*, but carry a rosary, and are further distinguished by a peculiar sort of cap, a round white cap, according to some, but according to others, one with four corners, and a flap hanging down behind; which it is essential that each man should manufacture for himself.

The *Dádú Panthís* are of three classes: the *Viraktas*, who are religious characters, who go bare-headed, and have but one garment and one water-pot. The *Nágas*, who carry arms, which they are willing to exercise for hire, and, amongst the Hindu princes, they have been considered as good soldiers. The third class is that of the *Vistar Dhárís*, who follow the occupations of ordinary life. A further sub-division exists in this sect, and the chief branches again form fifty-two divisions, or *Thambas*, the peculiarities of which have not been ascertained. The *Dádú Panthís* burn their dead at dawn, but their religious members not unfrequently enjoin, that their bodies, after death, shall be thrown into some field, or some wilderness, to be devoured by the beasts and birds of prey, as they say that in a funeral pile insect life is apt to be destroyed.

The *Dádú Panthís* are said to be very numerous in *Márwár* and *Ajmír*: of the *Nága* class alone the Rájá of *Jaypur* is reported to entertain as soldiers more than ten thousand: the chief place of worship is at *Naraina*, where the bed of *Dádú*, and the collection of the texts of the sect are preserved and worshipped: a small building on the hill marks the place of his disappearance—a *Melá*, or fair, is held annually, from the day of new moon to that of full moon in Phalgun (Febr.-March) at *Naraina*. The tenets of the sect are contained in several *Bháshá* works, in which it is said a vast number of passages from the *Kabír* writings are inserted, and the general character of which is certainly of a similar nature[1]. The *Dádú Panthís* maintain a friendly intercourse with the followers of *Kabír*, and are frequent visitors at the *Chaura*.

[To supply the deficiency alluded to in the note, we reprint from the 6th volume of the Journal of the Asiatic Society of Bengal pp. 484-87, and 750-56, the translation, by Captain *G. R. Siddons*, of two chapters from one of the granths or manuals of the Dádúpanthís. The translator gives (p. 750) the following particulars respecting his visit to one of their Maths:

"When not interested in the subject, I chanced to visit one of the Dádúpanthí institutions at a village near Sambhur, and was particularly struck by the contented and severe countenances of the sectaries. There were a Principal and several Professors, which gave the place the appearance of a College. The former occupied a room at the top of the building, and seemed quite absorbed in meditation.—The sect is maintained by the admission to it of proselytes, and marriage is, I believe, forbidden; as also the growing any hair about the face, which gives to the priests the appearance of old women."

---

[1] I had prepared a list of the contents of one of their manuals, and a translation of a few passages, but the Manuscript has been mislaid. The work was lent me for a short time by one of the sect, who would on no account part with it. The above notice was taken partly from a statement in Hindi, procured at *Naraina* by Lieut. Col. Smith, and partly from verbal information obtained at Benares. *Dádú* is not mentioned in the *Bhakta Málá*, but there is some account of him in the *Dabistán*. [Engl. translation, II, p. 233.]

The Chapter on Faith,—विश्वास का अङ्ग.

1. Whatever RÁM willeth, that, without the least difficulty, shall be; why, therefore, do ye kill yourselves with grief, when grief can avail you nothing?

2. Whatsoever hath been made, God made. Whatsoever is to be made, God will make. Whatsoever is, God maketh,—then why do any of ye afflict yourselves?

3. DÁDÚ sayeth, Thou, oh God! art the author of all things which have been made, and from thee will originate all things which are to be made. Thou art the maker, and the cause of all things made. There is none other but thee.

4. He is my God, who maketh all things perfect. Meditate upon him in whose hands are life and death.

5. He is my God, who created heaven, earth, hell, and the intermediate space; who is the beginning and end of all creation; and who provideth for all.

6. I believe that God made man, and that he maketh every thing. He is my friend.

7. Let faith in God characterize all your thoughts, words, and actions. He who serveth God, places confidence in nothing else.

8. If the remembrance of God be in your hearts, ye will be able to accomplish things which are impracticable. But those who seek the paths of God are few!

9. He who understandeth how to render his calling sinless, shall be happy in that calling, provided he be with GOD.

10. If he that perfecteth mankind occupy a place in your hearts, you will experience his happiness inwardly. RÁM is in every thing; RÁM is eternal.

11. Oh foolish one! God is not far from you. He is near you. You are ignorant, but he knoweth every thing, and is careful in bestowing.

12. Consideration and power belong to God, who is omniscient. Strive to preserve God, and give heed to nothing else.

13. Care can avail nothing; it devoureth life: for those things shall happen which God shall direct.

14. He who causeth the production of all living things, giveth

to their mouths milk, whilst yet in the stomach. They are placed amidst the fires of the belly: nevertheless they remain unscorched.

15. Oh, forget not, my brother, that God's power is always with you. There is a formidable pass within you, and crowds of evil passions flock to it: therefore comprehend God.

16. Commend the qualities which God possesseth. He gave you eyes, speech, head, feet, mouth, ears, and hands. He is the lord of life and of the world.

17. Ye forget God, who was indefatigable in forming every thing, and who keepeth every thing in order; ye destroy his doctrines. Remember God, for he endued your body with life: remember that beloved one, who placed you in the womb, reared and nourished you.

18. Preserve God in your hearts, and put faith into your minds, so that by God's power your expectations may be realized.

19. He taketh food and employment, and distributeth them. God is near; he is always with me.

20. In order that he may diffuse happiness, God becometh subservient to all; and although the knowledge of this is in the hearts of the foolish, yet will they not praise his name.

21. Although the people every where stretch out their hands to God; although his power is so extensive, yet is he sometimes subservient to all.

22. Oh God, thou art as it were exceeding riches; thy regulations are without compare, thou art the chief of every world, yet remainest invisible.

23. DÁDÚ sayeth, I will become the sacrifice of the Godhead; of him who supporteth every thing; of him who is able, in one moment, to rear every description of animal, from a worm even to an elephant.

24. Take such food and raiment as it may please God to provide you with. You require naught besides.

25. Those men who are contented, eat of the morsel which is from God. Oh disciple! why do you wish for other food, which resembles carrion?

26. He that partaketh of but one grain of the love of God, shall be released from the sinfulness of all his doubts and actions.

Who need cook, or who need grind? Wherever ye cast your eyes, ye may see provisions.

27. Meditate on the nature of your bodies, which resemble earthen vessels; and put every thing away from them, which is not allied to God.

28. DÁDÚ sayeth, I take for my spiritual food, the water and the leaf of RÁM. For the world I care not, but God's love is unfathomable.

29. Whatever is the will of God, will assuredly happen; therefore do not destroy yourselves by anxiety, but listen.

30. What hope can those have elsewhere, even if they wandered over the whole earth, who abandon God? oh foolish one! righteous men who have meditated on this subject, advise you to abandon all things but God, since all other things are affliction.

31. It will be impossible for you to profit any thing, if you are not with God, even if you were to wander from country to country; therefore, oh ignorant, abandon all other things, for they are affliction, and listen to the voice of the holy.

32. Accept with patience the offering of truth, believing it to be true; fix your heart on God, and be humble as though you were dead.

33. He who meditateth on the wisdom which is concealed, eateth his morsel and is without desires. The holy praise his name, who hath no illusion.

34. Have no desires, but accept what circumstances may bring before you; because whatever God pleaseth to direct, can never be wrong.

35. Have no desires, but eat in faith and with meditation whatever chances to fall in your way. Go not about, tearing from the tree, which is invisible.

36. Have no desires, but take the food which chances to fall in your way, believing it to be correct, because it cometh from God; as much as if it were a mouthful of atmosphere.

37. All things are exceeding sweet to those who love God; they would never style them bitter, even if filled with poison; on the contrary, they would accept them, as if they were ambrosia.

38. Adversity is good, if on account of God; but it is useless to pain the body. Without God, the comforts of wealth are unprofitable.

39. He that believeth not in the one God, hath an unsettled mind; he will be in sorrow, though in the possession of riches: but God is without price.

40. The mind which hath not faith, is fickle and unsettled, because, not being fixed by any certainty, it changeth from one thing to another.

41. Whatever is to be, will be: therefore long not for grief nor for joy, because by seeking the one, you may find the other. Forget not to praise God.

42. Whatever is to be, will be: therefore neither wish for heaven nor be apprehensive on account of hell. Whatever was ordained, is.

43. Whatever is to be, will be; and that which God hath ordained can neither be augmented nor decreased. Let your minds understand this.

44. Whatever is to be, will be; and nothing else can happen. Accept that which is proper for you to receive, but nothing else.

45. Whatever God ordereth, shall happen, so why do ye vex yourselves? Consider God as supreme over all; he is the sight for you to behold.

46. DÁDÚ sayeth, Do unto me, oh God! as thou thinkest best—I am obedient to thee. My disciples! behold no other God; go nowhere but to him.

47. I am satisfied of this, that your happiness will be in proportion to your devotion. The heart of DÁDÚ worshippeth God night and day.

48. Condemn nothing which the creator hath made. Those are his holy servants who are satisfied with them.

49. We are not creators—the Creator is a distinct being; he can make whatever he desireth, but we can make nothing.

50. KABIRA left *Benares* and went to *Mughor* in search of God. RÁM met him without concealment, and his object was accomplished.

51. DÁDÚ sayeth, My earnings are God. He is my food and

my supporter; by his spiritual sustenance, have all my members been nourished.

52. The five elements of my existence are contented with one food: my mind is intoxicated; hunger leaveth him who worshippeth no other but God.

53. God is my clothing and my dwelling. He is my ruler, my body, and my soul.

54. God ever fostereth his creatures; even as a mother serves her offspring, and keepeth it from harm.

55. Oh God, thou who art the truth, grant me contentment, love, devotion, and faith. Thy servant DÁDÚ prayeth for true patience, and that he may be devoted to thee.

The Chapter on Meditation,—विचार का अङ्ग.

Reverence to thee, who art devoid of illusion, adoration of God, obedience to all saints, salutation to those who are pious. To God the first, and the last.

He that knoweth not delusion is my God.

1. DÁDÚ hath said, in water there exists air, and in air water; yet are these elements distinct. Meditate, therefore, on the mysterious affinity between God and the soul.

2. Even as ye see your countenance reflected in a mirror, or your shadow in the still water, so behold RÁM in your minds, because he is with all.

3. If ye look into a mirror, ye see yourselves as ye are, but he in whose mind there is no mirror cannot distinguish evil from good.

4. As the *til* plant contains oil, and the flower sweet odour, as butter is in milk, so is God in every thing.

5. He that formed the mind, made it as it were a temple for himself to dwell in; for God liveth in the mind, and none other but God.

6. Oh! my friend, recognize that being with whom thou art so intimately connected; think not that God is distant, but believe that like thy own shadow, He is ever near thee.

7. The stalk of the lotus cometh from out of water, and yet the lotus separates itself from the water! For why? Because it loves the moon better.

8. So let your meditations tend to one object, and believe that he who by nature is void of delusion, though not actually the mind, is in the mind of all.

9. To one that truly meditateth, there are millions, who, outwardly only, observe the forms of religion. The world indeed is filled with the latter, but of the former there are very few.

10. The heart which possesseth contentment wanteth for nothing, but that which hath it not, knoweth not what happiness meaneth.

11. If ye would be happy, cast off delusion. Delusion is an evil which ye know to be great, but have not fortitude to abandon.

12. Receive that which is perfect into your hearts, to the exclusion of all besides; abandon all things for the love of God, for this DÁDÚ declares is the true devotion.

13. Cast off pride, and become acquainted with that which is devoid of sin. Attach yourselves to RÁM, who is sinless, and suffer the thread of your meditations to be upon him.

14. All have it in their power to take away their own lives, but they cannot release their souls from punishment; for God alone is able to pardon the soul, though few deserve his mercy.

15. Listen to the admonitions of God, and you will care not for hunger nor for thirst; neither for heat, nor cold; ye will be absolved from the imperfections of the flesh.

16. Draw your mind forth, from within, and dedicate it to God; because if ye subdue the imperfections of your flesh, ye will think only of God.

17. If ye call upon God, ye will be able to subdue your imperfections and the evil inclinations of your mind will depart from you; but they will return to you again when ye cease to call upon him.

18. DÁDÚ loved RÁM incessantly; he partook of his spiritual essence and constantly examined the mirror which was within him.

19. He subdued the imperfections of the flesh, and overcame all evil inclinations; he crushed every improper desire, wherefore the light of RÁM will shine upon him.

20. He that giveth his body to the world, and rendereth up his soul to its Creator, shall be equally insensible to the sharpness of death, and the misery which is caused by pain.

21. Sit with humility at the foot of God, and rid yourselves of the impurities of your bodies. Be fearless and let no mortal qualities pervade you.

22. From the impurities of the body there is much to fear, because all sins enter into it; therefore let your dwelling be with the fearless and conduct yourselves towards the light of God.

23. For there neither sword nor poison have power to destroy, and sin cannot enter. Ye will live even as God liveth, and the fire of death will be guarded, as it were with water.

24. He that meditateth will naturally be happy, because he is wise and suffereth not the passions to spread over his mind. He loveth but one God.

25. The greatest wisdom is to prevent your minds from being influenced by bad passions, and, in meditating upon the one God. Afford help also to the poor stranger.

26. If ye are humble ye will be unknown, because it is vanity which impelleth us to boast of our own merits, and which causeth us to exult, in being spoken of by others. Meditate on the words of the holy, that the fever of your body may depart from you.

27. For when ye comprehend the words of the holy, ye will be disentangled from all impurities, and be absorbed in God. If ye flatter yourselves, you will never comprehend.

28. When ye have learned the wisdom of the invisible one from the mouth of his priests, ye will be disentangled from all impurities; turn ye round therefore, and examine yourselves well in the mirror which crowneth the lotus.

29. Meditate on that particular wisdom, which alone is able to increase in you the love and worship of God. Purify your minds, retaining only that which is excellent.

30. Meditate on him by whom all things were made. Pandits and Qázís are fools: of what avail are the heaps of books which they have compiled?

31. What does it avail to compile a heap of books? Let your minds freely meditate on the spirit of God, that they may be enlightened regarding the mystery of his divinity. Wear not away your lives, by studying the Vedas.

32. There is fire in water and water in fire, but the ignorant

know it not. He is wise that meditateth on God, the beginning and end of all things.

33. Pleasure cannot exist without pain, and pain is always accompanied with pleasure. Meditate on God, the beginning and end, and remember that hereafter there will be two rewards.

34. In sweet there is bitter, and in bitter there is sweet, although the ignorant know it not. DÁDÚ hath meditated on the qualities of God, the eternal.

35. Oh man! ponder well ere thou proceedest to act. Do nothing until thou hast thoroughly sifted thy intentions.

36. Reflect with deliberation on the nature of thy inclinations before thou allowest thyself to be guided by them; acquaint thyself thoroughly with the purity of thy wishes, so that thou mayest become absorbed in God.

37. He that reflecteth first, and afterwards proceedeth to act, is a great man, but he that first acteth, and then considereth is a fool whose countenance is as black as the face of the former is resplendent.

38. He that is guided by deliberation, will never experience sorrow or anxiety: on the contrary he will always be happy.

39. Oh ye who wander in the paths of delusion, turn your minds towards God, who is the beginning and end of all things; endeavour to gain him, nor hesitate to restore your soul, when required, to that abode from whence it emanated.]

RAI DÁSÍS.

RAI DÁS was another of RÁMÁNAND's disciples, who founded a sect, confined, however, it is said, to those of his own caste, the *Chamárs*, or workers in hides and in leather, and amongst the very lowest of the Hindu mixed tribes: this circumstance renders it difficult, if not impossible, to ascertain whether the sect still exists: the founder must once have enjoyed some celebrity, as some of his works are included in the *Ádi*

Granth of the Sikhs; he is there named Ravi Dása, which is the Sanskrit form of his name: some of his compositions also form part of the collection of hymns and prayers used by that sect at Benares: there appears to be but little known of him of any authentic character, and we must be contented with the authority of the *Bhakta Málá*, where he makes a rather important figure: the legend is as follows:—

One of Rámánand's pupils was a *Brahmachári*, whose daily duty it was to provide the offering presented to the deity: on one of these occasions, the offering consisted of grain, which the pupil had received as alms from a shop-keeper, who supplied chiefly the butchers with articles of food, and his donation was, consequently, impure: when Rámánand, in the course of his devotions, attempted to fix his mind upon the divinity, he found the task impracticable, and suspecting that some defect in the offering occasioned such an erratic imagination, he enquired whence it had been obtained: on being informed, he exclaimed, *Há Chamár*, and the *Brahmachári* soon afterwards dying was born again as Rai Dás, the son of a worker in hides and leather.

The infant Rai Dás retained the impression left upon his mind by his old master's anger, and refused to take any nourishment: the parents, in great affliction, applied to Rámánand, who, by order of the deity, visited the child, and recognising the person at once whispered into his ear the initiating *Mantra*: the effect was instantaneous: the child immediately accepted the breast, and throve, and grew up a pious votary of Ráma.

For some time the profits of his trade maintained Rai Dás, and left him something to divide amongst the devout; but a season of scarcity supervening reduced him to great distress, when *Bhagaván*, in the semblance of a *Vaishńava*, brought him a piece of the Philosopher's stone, and shewing him its virtue made him a present of it. Rai Dás paid little regard to the donation, replying to the effect of the following *Pada*, as since versified by *Súr Dás*.

Pada. "A great treasure is the name of Hari to his people: it multiplieth day by day, nor doth expenditure diminish it: it abideth securely in the mansion, and neither by night nor by day can any thief steal it. The Lord is the wealth of *Súr Dás*, what need hath he of a stone?"

The miraculous stone was thrown aside, and when, thirteen months afterwards, *Vishńu* again visited his votary, he found no use had been made of it: as this expedient had failed, the deity scattered gold coin in places where Rai Dás could not avoid finding it: the discovery of this treasure filled the poor Currier with alarm, to pacify which *Kŕishńa* appeared to him in a dream, and desired him to apply the money either to his own use or that of the deity, and thus authorised, Rai Dás erected a temple, of which he constituted himself the high priest, and acquired great celebrity in his new character.

The reputation of Rai Dás was further extended by its attracting a persecution, purposely excited by

Vishńu to do honour to his worshipper, the deity well knowing that the enmity of the malignant is the most effective instrument for setting open to the world the retired glory of the pious: he therefore inspired the Brahmans to complain thus to the king.

Śloka (Sanskrit stanza). "Where things profane are reverenced, where sacred things are profanely administered, there three calamities will be felt, famine, death, and fear*."

A *Chamár,* oh king, ministers to the *Sálagrám,* and poisons the town with his *Prasád*[1]; men and women, every one will become an outcast; banish him to preserve the honour of your people.

The king accordingly sent for the culprit, and ordered him to resign the sacred stone. Rai Dás expressed his readiness to do so, and only requested the *Rájá*'s presence at his delivery of it to the *Brahmans,* as, he said, if after being given to them it should return to him, they would accuse him of stealing it. The *Rájá* assenting, the *Sálagrám* was brought, and placed on a cushion in the assembly. The Brahmans were desired to remove it, but attempted to take it away in vain: they repeated hymns and charms, and

* [अपूज्या यत्र पूज्यन्ते पूज्यपूजाव्यतिक्रमः ।
तत्र त्रीणि प्रवर्त्तन्ते दुर्भिक्षं मरणं भयं ॥
See Panchatantra III, 202.]

[1] The *Prasád* is any article of food that has been consecrated by previous presentation to an idol, after which it is distributed amongst the worshippers on the spot, or sent to persons of consequence at their own houses.

read the *Vedas*, but the stone was immoveable. RAI DÁS then addressed it with this *Pada*:—

Pada. "Lord of Lords, thou art my refuge, the root of Supreme happiness art thou, to whom there is none equal: behold me at thy feet: in various wombs have I abided, and from the fear of death have I not been delivered. I have been plunged in the deceits of sense, of passion, and illusion; but now let my trust in thy name dispel apprehension of the future, and teach me to place no reliance on what the world deems virtue. Accept, oh God, the devotions of thy slave RAI DÁS, and be thou glorified as the Purifier of the sinful."

The saint had scarcely finished, when the *Sálagrám* and cushion flew into his arms, and the king, satisfied of his holy pretensions, commanded the Brahmans to desist from their opposition. Amongst the disciples of RAI DÁS was JHÁLÍ, the *Ráni* of Chitore: her adopting a *Chamár*, as her spiritual preceptor, excited a general commotion amongst the Brahmans of her state, and, alarmed for her personal safety, she wrote to RAI DÁS to request his counsel and aid. He repaired to her, and desired her to invite the Brahmans to a solemn feast: they accepted the invitation, and sat down to the meal provided for them, when between every two Brahmans there appeared a RAI DÁS. This miraculous multiplication of himself had the desired effect, and from being his enemies and revilers they became his disciples.

Such are the legends of the *Bhakta Málá*, and whatever we may think of their veracity, their tenor, representing an individual of the most abject class, an absolute outcast in Hindu estimation, as a teacher and a saint, is not without interest and instruction.

SENÁ PANTHÍS.

SENÁ, the barber, was the third of *Rámánand's* disciples, who established a separate schism; the name of which, and of its founder, is possibly all that now remains of it. SENÁ and his descendants were, for sometime, however, the family-*Gurus* of the Rájás of *Bandhogaŕh*, and thence enjoyed considerable authority and reputation: the origin of this connexion is the subject of a ludicrous legend in the *Bhakta Málá*.

SENÁ, the barber of the Rájá of *Bandhogaŕh*, was a devout worshipper of VISHŃU, and a constant frequenter of the meetings of the pious: on one of these occasions, he suffered the time to pass unheeded, when he ought to have been officiating in his tonsorial capacity, and VISHŃU, who noticed the circumstance, and knew the cause, was alarmed for his votary's personal integrity. The god, therefore, charitably assumed the figure of SENÁ, and equipping himself suitably, waited on the Rájá, and performed the functions of the barber, much to the Rájá's satisfaction, and without detection, although the prince perceived an unusual fragrance about his barber's person, the ambrosial odour that indicated present deity, which he supposed to impregnate the oil used in lubricating his royal limbs. The pretended barber had scarcely departed, when the real one appeared, and stammered out his excuses: his astonishment and the Rájá's were alike, but the discernment of the latter was more acute, for he immediately comprehended the whole business, fell at his barber's feet, and elected for his spiritual guide an individual so pre-eminently distinguished by the favour and protection of the deity.

RUDRA SAMPRADÁYÍS, or VALLABHÁCHÁRÍS.

The sects of *Vaishńavas* we have hitherto noticed are chiefly confined to professed ascetics, and to a few families originally from the south and west of India, or, as in the case of the *Rámávats* and *Kabír Panthís*, to such amongst the mass of society, as are of a bold and curious spirit; but the opulent and luxurious amongst the men, and by far the greater portion of the women, attach themselves to the worship of Kŕishńa and his mistress Rádhá, either singly, or conjointly, as in the case of Vishńu and Lakshmí, amongst the *Rámánujas*, and Sítá and Rám, amongst the *Rámávats*. There is, however, another form, which is perhaps more popular still, although much interwoven with the others. This is the Bála Gopála, the infant Kŕishńa, the worship of whom is very widely diffused amongst all ranks of Indian society, and which originated with the founder of the *Rudra Sampradáyi* sect, Vallabha Áchárya; it is perhaps better known, however, from the title of its teachers, as the religion of the *Gokulastha Gosáins*.

The original teacher of the philosophical tenets of this sect is said to have been Vishńu Swámí, a commentator on the texts of the *Vedas*, who, however, admitted disciples from the Brahmanical cast only, and considered the state of the *Sannyási*, or ascetic, as essential to the communication of his doctrines. He was succeeded by JNÁNA DEVA, who was followed by NÁMA DEVA and TRILOCHANA, and they, although whether immediately or not does not appear, by VALLABHA SWÁMÍ, the son of LAKSHMAŃA BHAŤŤ, a *Tailinga* Brahman: this *Sannyási* taught early in the sixteenth century: he resided originally at *Gokul*, a village on the left bank of the Jamna, about three cos to the east of Mathurá: after remaining here sometime, he travelled through India as a pilgrim, and amongst other places he visited, according to the *Bhakta Málá*, the court of KŔISHŃA DEVA, king of *Vijayanagar*, apparently the same as KŔISHŃA RÁYALU, who reigned about the year 1520, where he overcame the *Smárta* Brahmans in a controversy, and was elected by the *Vaishńavas* as their chief, with the title of *Áchárj*: hence he travelled to *Ujayin*, and took up his abode under a *Pípal* tree, on the banks of the *Siprá*, said to be still in existence, and designated as his *Baiťhak*, or station. Besides this, we find traces of him in other places. There is a *Baiťhak* of his amongst the *Gháts* of *Muttrá*, and about two miles from the fort of *Chanár* is a place called his well, *Áchárj kúán*, comprising a temple and *Math*, in the court yard of which is the *well* in question; the saint is said to have resided here sometime. After this peregrination VALLABHA returned to *Bŕindávan*, where, as a reward for his fatigues and his faith, he was honoured by a visit from Kŕishńa in person, who enjoined him to introduce the worship of *Bálagopál*, or *Gopál Lál*, and founded the faith which at present exists in so flourishing a condition. Vallabha is supposed to have closed his career in a miracle: he had finally settled at *Jethan Beŕ*, at Benares, near which a *Math* still subsists, but at length, having accomplished his mission, he is said to have entered the *Ganges* at *Hanumán Ghát*, when, stooping into the water, he disappeared: a brilliant flame arose from the spot, and, in the presence of a host of spectators, he ascended to heaven, and was lost in the firmament.

The worship of Kŕishńa as one with Vishńu and the universe dates evidently from the *Mahábhárat*[1], and his more juvenile forms are brought pre-eminently to notice in the account of his infancy, contained in the *Bhágavat*[2], but neither of these works discriminates him from Vishńu, nor do they recommend his infantine or adolescent state to particular veneration. At the same time some hints may have been derived from them for the institution of this division of the

---

[1] The well known passage in the *Bhagavad Gítá* [XI, 26–30.], in which Arjuna sees the universe in the mouth of Kŕishńa, establishes this identity.

[2] Particularly in the tenth book, which is appropriated to the life of Kŕishńa. The same subject occupies a considerable portion of the *Hari Vanś* section of the *Mahábhárat*, of the *Pátála* section of the *Padma Puráńa*, the fifth section of the *Vishńu Puráńa*, and the whole of the *Ádi Upapuráńa*.

Hindu faith[1]. In claiming, however, supremacy for Kṛishṇa, the *Brahma Vaivartta Puráṅa* is most decided, and this work places Kṛishṇa in a heaven, and society exclusively his own, and derives from him all the objects of existence*.

According to this authority, the residence of Kṛishṇa is denominated *Goloka*; it is far above the three

---

[1] Thus in the *Vana Parva* of the *Mahábhárat* [v. 12895 ff.], Márkaṅḋeya Muni, at the time of a minor destruction of the world, sees, "amidst the waters, an Indian Fig tree of vast size, on a principal branch of which was a bed ornamented with divine coverings, on which lay a child with a countenance like the moon." The saint, though acquainted with the past, present, and future, cannot recognise the child, who therefore appears of the hue, and with the symbols of Kṛishṇa, and desires the sage to rest within his substance from his weary wanderings over the submerged world.

In the *Bhágavat* [X, 3, 9. 10.] it is stated, that when first born, Vasudeva beheld the child of the hue of a cloud, with four arms, dressed in a yellow garb, and bearing the weapons, the jewels and the diadem of Vishṅu:

तमद्भुतं बालकमम्बुजेक्षणं चतुर्भुजं शंखगदाद्युदायुधं श्रीवत्सलक्ष्मं गलशोभिकौस्तुभं पीताम्बरं सान्द्रपयोदसौभगं । महार्हवैदूर्यकिरीटकुण्डलत्विषापरिष्वक्तसहस्रकुन्तलं उद्दामकाञ्च्यङ्गदकङ्कणादिभिर्विरोचमानं वसुदेव ऐक्षत ॥

and the same work describes Yaśodá, his adoptive mother, as seeing the universe in the mouth of the child [X, 7, 36. 37. (30. 31. Calcutta edition):

पीतप्रायस्य जननी सुतस्य रुचिरस्मितम् ।
मुखं लालयती राजन् जृम्भतो ददृशे इदम् ॥
खं रोदसी ज्योतिरनीकमाशाः सूर्येन्दुवह्निश्वसनाम्बुधींश्च ।
द्वीपान्नगांस्तद्दुहितॄर्वनानि भूतानि यानि स्थिरजङ्गमानि ॥]

* [Journal of the As. Soc. of Bengal, Vol. I, p. 217–37.]

worlds, and has, at five hundred millions of Yojanas below it, the separate *Lokas* of VISHŃU and ŚIVA, *Vaikuńtha*, and *Kailás*. This region is indestructible, whilst all else is subject to annihilation, and in the centre of it abides KŔISHŃA, of the colour of a dark cloud, in the bloom of youth, clad in yellow raiment, splendidly adorned with celestial gems, and holding a flute. He is exempt from *Máyá*, or delusion, and all qualities, eternal, alone, and the *Paramátmá*, or supreme soul of the world.

KŔISHŃA being alone in the *Goloka*, and meditating on the waste of creation, gave origin to a being of a female form endowed with the three *Guńas*, and thence the primary agent in creation. This was *Prakŕiti*, or *Máyá*, and the system so far corresponds with that of the other Vaishńavas, and of the Puráńas generally speaking. They having adopted, in fact, the *Sánkhya* system, interweaving with it their peculiar sectarial notions.

Crude matter, and the five elements, are also made to issue from KŔISHŃA, and then all the divine beings. NÁRÁYAŃA, or VISHŃU, proceeds from his right side, MAHÁDEVA from his left, BRAHMÁ from his hand, DHARMA from his breath, SARASWATÍ from his mouth, LAKSHMÍ from his mind, DURGÁ from his understanding, RÁDHÁ from his left side. Three hundred millions of *Gopís*, or female companions of RÁDHÁ, exude from the pores of her skin, and a like number of *Gopas*, or companions of KŔISHŃA, from the pores of his skin: the very cows and their calves, properly the tenants of *Goloka*, but destined to inhabit the Groves of *Brindávan*, are produced from the same exalted source.

In this description of creation, however, the deity is still spoken of as a young man, and the *Puráńa* therefore affords only indirect authority in the marvels it narrates of his infancy for the worship of the child. Considering, however, that in this, or in any other capacity, the acts of the divinity are his *Lílá*, or sport, there is no essential difference between those who worship him either as a boy or as a man, and any of his forms may be adored by this class of *Vaishńavas*, and all his principal shrines are to them equally objects of pilgrimage. As the elements and chief agents of creation are thus said to proceed from the person of KŔISHŃA, it may be inferred that the followers of this creed adopt the principles of the *Vedánta* philosophy, and consider the material world as one in substance, although in an illusory manner, with the supreme. Life is also identified with spirit, according to the authority of a popular work[1]. None of the

---

[1] According to the *Várttá*, VALLABHA advocated this doctrine with some reluctance, by the especial injunction of the juvenile *Kŕishńa*:

तब श्री आचार्य्य जी ने कहा। जो तुम जीव को स्वभाव जानती हो दोषवंत है। तो तुम सो सम्बन्ध कैसे होय। तब श्री आचार्य्य जी सो श्री ठाकुर जी कहे। जो तुम जीव को ब्रह्म सम्बन्ध करो हों तिन को अङ्गीकार करोंगो॥

"Then *Áchárj Jí* said, you know the nature of Life, it is full of defects, how can it be combined with you? to which *Śrí Thákur Jí* (KŔISHŃA) replied: Do you unite *Brahma* and *Life* in

philosophical writings of the chief teachers of this system have been met with.

Amongst other articles of the new creed, VALLABHA introduced one, which is rather singular for a Hindu religious innovator or reformer: he taught that privation formed no part of sanctity, and that it was the duty of the teachers and his disciples to worship their deity, not in nudity and hunger, but in costly apparel and choice food, not in solitude and mortification, but in the pleasures of society, and the enjoyment of the world. The *Gosáins*, or teachers, are almost always family men, as was the founder VALLABHA; for after he had shaken off the restrictions of the monastic order to which he originally belonged, he married, by the particular order, it is said, of his new god. The *Gosáins* are always clothed with the best raiment, and fed with the daintiest viands by their followers, over whom they have unlimited influence: part of the connexion between the *Guru* and teacher being the three-fold *Samarpań*, or consignment of *Tan*, *Man*, and *Dhan*, body, mind, and wealth, to the spiritual guide. The followers of the order are especially numerous amongst the mercantile community, and the *Gosáins* themselves are often largely engaged, also, in maintaining a connexion amongst the commercial establishments of remote parts of the country, as they are constantly travelling over India, under pretence

---

what way you will, I shall concur, and thence all its defects will be removed."

of pilgrimage, to the sacred shrines of the sect, and notoriously reconcile, upon these occasions, the profits of trade with the benefits of devotion: as religious travellers, however, this union of objects renders them more respectable than the vagrants of any other sect.

The practices of the sect are of a similar character with those of other regular worshippers: their temples and houses have images of Gopál, of Kríshńa and Rádhá, and other divine forms connected with this incarnation, of metal chiefly, and not unfrequently of gold: the image of Kríshńa represents a chubby boy, of the dark hue of which Vishńu is always represented: it is richly decorated and sedulously attended; receiving eight times a day the homage of the votaries. These occasions take place at fixed periods and for certain purposes; and at all other seasons, and for any other object, except at stated and periodical festivals, the temples are closed and the deity invisible. The eight daily ceremonials are the following:—

1. *Mangala;* the morning levee: the image being washed and dressed is taken from the couch, where it is supposed to have slept during the night, and placed upon a seat about half an hour after sun-rise: slight refreshments are then presented to it, with betel and *Pán*: lamps are generally kept burning during this ceremony.

2. *Śríngára;* the image having been anointed and perfumed with oil, camphor, and sandal, and splendidly attired, now holds his public court: this takes

place about an hour and a half after the preceding, or when four *Gharis* of the day have elapsed.

3. *Gwála;* the image is now visited, preparatory to his going out to attend the cattle along with the cow-herd; this ceremony is held about forty-eight minutes after the last, or when six *Gharis* have passed.

4. *Rája Bhóga:* held at mid-day, when KRISHṄA is supposed to come in from the pastures, and dine: all sorts of delicacies are placed before the image, and both those and other articles of food dressed by the ministers of the temple are distributed to the numerous votaries present, and not unfrequently sent to the dwellings of worshippers of some rank and consequence.

5. *Utthápan;* the calling up: the summoning of the god from his siesta: this takes place at six *Gharis*, or between two and three hours before sun-set.

6. *Bhóga;* the afternoon meal, about half an hour after the preceding.

7. *Sandhyá:* about sun-set, the evening toilet of the image, when the ornaments of the day are taken off, and fresh unguent and perfume applied.

8. *Śayan;* retiring to repose: the image, about eight or nine in the evening, is placed upon a bed, refreshments and water in proper vases, together with the betel box and its appartenances, are left near it, when the votaries retire, and the temple is shut till the ensuing morning.

Upon all these occasions the ceremony is much the

same, consisting in little more than the presentation of flowers, perfumes, and food by the priests and votaries, and the repetition, chiefly by the former, of Sanskrit stanzas in praise of Kŕishńa, interspersed with a variety of prostrations and obeisances. There is no established ritual, indeed, in the Hindu religion for general use, nor any prescribed form of public adoration.

Besides the diurnal ceremonials described, there are several annual festivals of great repute observed throughout India: of these, in Bengal and Orissa, the *Rath Játra,* or procession of Jagannáth in his car, is the most celebrated, but it is rarely held in upper India, and then only by natives of Bengal established in the provinces: the most popular festival at Benares, and generally to the westward, is the *Janmáshtami,* the nativity of Kŕishńa, on the eighth day of *Bhádra* (August[1]). Another is the *Rás Yátra*, or annual

---

[1] Great difference of practice prevails on occasion of this observance. Kŕishńa was born on the eighth lunar day of the waning moon of *Bhádra*, at midnight, upon the moon's entrance into *Rohini,* in commemoration of which a fast is to be held on the day preceding his birth, terminating, as usual, in a feast; but the day of his birth is variously determinable, according to the adoption of the civil, the lunar, or lunar-sydereal computations, and it rarely happens that the eighth lunation comprises the same combination of hours and planetary positions, as occurred at Kŕishńa's birth. Under these circumstances, the followers of the *Smŕiti,* with the *Śaivas* and *Śáktas,* commence their fast with the commencement of the lunation, whenever that takes place; the *Rámánujas* and *Mádhwas* observe such part of the eighth day of the moon's age as includes sun rise, and forms the

commemoration of the dance of the frolicsome deity with the sixteen Gopís. This last is a very popular

eighth day of the calendar, or civil day, whilst some of the *Rámánujas*, and the *Nimáwats* regulate the duration of their fast by the moon's passage through the asterism *Rohini*. The consequence is, that the *Smártas* often fast on the 7th, one set of *Vaishnávas* on the 8th, and another on the 9th, whilst those who affect great sanctity sometimes go thirty hours without food; an extract from last year's calendar will very well exemplify these distinctions.

3rd Bhádra, 17th August 1825, Tuesday, Saptamí, 10 Dańdas 17 Palas. The Janmásht́amí Vrata and a Fast.

4th Bhádra, 18th August, Wednesday, Asht́amí, 9 Dańdas 18 Palas. Fast according to the Vaishńavas of Braj.

5th Bhádra, 19th August, Thursday, Navamí, 7 Dańdas 4 Palas. Rohiní Nakshatra, till 10 Dańdas 52 Palas, at which hour *Páraňa*, the end of the fast.

Now the 3d day of the *Solar Bhádra* was the 7th of the *Lunar* Month, but it comprised little more than ten *Dańdas* or four hours of that lunation: as it included sun-rise, however, it was the 7th of the calendar, or *civil* day. The eighth *Tithi*, or lunation, therefore, began about that time, or four hours after sun-rise, and the *Smártas, Śaivas,* and *Śáktas* observed the fast on that day; they began with sun-rise, however, as there is a specific rule for the *Sankalpa*, or pledge, to perform the usual rite at dawn. This *Asht́amí* comprised midnight, and was the more sacred on that account.

The 4th of *Bhádra* was the *Asht́ami,* or eighth of the *Vaishńavas*, although the lunation only extended to 9 *Dańdas*, or less than four hours after sun-rise, but they are particularly enjoined to avoid the *Saptamí*, or the *Asht́amí* conjoined with it, and therefore they could not commence their fast earlier, although they lost thereby the midnight of the eighth lunation, which they were, consequently, compelled to extend into the night of the ninth. They fasted till the next morning, unless they chose to eat after midnight, which, on this occasion, is allowable.

festival, and not an uninteresting one: vast crowds, clad in their best attire, collecting in some open place in the vicinity of the town, and celebrating the event with music, singing, and dramatic representations of Kŕishńa's sports: all the public singers and dancers lend their services on this occasion, and trust for a remuneration to the gratuities of the spectators: at Benares the *Rás Yátra* is celebrated at the village of *Śivapur,* and the chief dancers and musicians, ranging themselves under the banners of the most celebrated of the profession, go out in formal procession: tents, huts, and booths are erected, swings and round-abouts form a favourite amusement of the crowd, and sweetmeats and fruits are displayed in tempting profusion: the whole has the character of a crowded fair in Europe, and presents, in an immense concourse of people, an endless variety of rich costume, and an infinite diversity of picturesque accompaniment, a most lively and splendid scene. The same festival is held from the tenth day of the light half of *Kúár* (Septr.-Octr.) to the day of the full moon at *Bŕindávan,*

The 5th of *Bhádra* was the *Navami,* or ninth of the calendar, but it included a portion of the moon's passage through *Rohiní,* and the strict *Vaishńavas* of the different sects should not have performed the *Párańa,* the close of the fast, earlier, or before 10 Dańdas and 52 Palas after sun-rise, or about nine o'clock. Those *Vaishńavas,* however, who wholly regulate their observance by the Asterism, and referring also to the necessity of commencing it with sun-rise, would only have begun their fast on the calendar *Navami,* and have held the *Párańa* on Friday the 10th, the third day after the proper birth-day of their deity.

where a stone plat-form, or stage, has been built for the exhibition of the mimic dance in a square near the river side. Besides their public demonstrations of respect, pictures and images of Gopála are kept in the houses of the members of the sect, who, before they sit down to any of their meals, take care to offer a portion to the idol. Those of the disciples who have performed the triple *Samarpańa* eat only from the hands of each other; and the wife or child that has not exhibited the same mark of devotion to the *Guru* can neither cook for such a disciple nor eat in his society.

The mark on the forehead consists of two red perpendicular lines meeting in a semicircle at the root of the nose, and having a round spot of red between them. The *Bhaktas* have the same marks as the *Śrí Vaishńavas* on the breasts and arms, and some also make the central spot on the forehead with a black earth, called *Śyámabandí*, or any black metallic substance: the necklace and rosary are made of the stalk of the *Tulasí*. The salutations amongst them are *Śrí-kŕishńa* and *Jaya Gopál*.

The great authority of the sect is the *Bhágavat*, as explained in the *Subodhiní*, or Commentary of Vallabhácharya: he is the author also of a *Bháshya* on part of Vyása's *Sútras*, and of other Sanskrit works, as the *Siddhánta Rahasya*, *Bhágavata Lílá Rahasya*, and *Ekánta Rahasya*; these, however, are only for the learned, and are now very rare. Amongst the votaries in general, various works upon the history of

Kŕishńa are current, but the most popular are the *Vishńu Padas*, stanzas in *Bháshá*, in praise of Vishńu, attributed to Vallabha himself; the *Braj Vilás*, a *Bhákhá* poem of some length, descriptive of Kŕishńa's life, during his residence at *Bŕindávan*, by Braj Vásí Dás; the *Ashta Chháp*, an account of Vallabha's eight chief disciples, and the *Várttá*, or *Bárttá*, a collection in *Hindústání* of marvellous and insipid anecdotes of Vallabha and his primitive followers, amounting to the number of eighty-four, and including persons of both sexes, and every class of Hindus. The *Bhakta Málá* also contains a variety of legends regarding the different teachers of this sect, but it is less a text-book with this sect than any other class of *Vaishńavas*, as the *Várttá* occupies its place amongst the worshippers of *Gopál*. The following are specimens of this work, and by no means the most unfavourable:—

Dámodar Dás, of *Kanoj*, was a disciple of Śrí Áchárya (Vallabháchárya). Like the rest of the members of this sect, he had an image of Kŕishńa in his house. One day it was exceedingly hot, and when night came, *Śrí Ṫhákur ji* (the image) woke the maid servant, and desired her to open the doors of his chamber, as it was very warm. She obeyed, and taking a *pankha*, fanned him—Early in the morning, Dámodar Dás observed the doors of the chamber open, and enquired how this had happened: the girl mentioned the circumstance, but her master was much vexed that she had done this, and that *Śrí Ṫhákur ji* hat not called him to do it. *Śrí Ṫhákur ji* knowing his thoughts said: I told her to open the doors, why are you displeased with her? you shut me up here in a close room, and go to sleep yourself on an open and cool terrace. Then Dámodar Dás made a vow, and said: I will not taste consecrated food until I have built a new temple, but his wife advised him, and urged: this is not a business of five or six days, why go without the consecrated food so long? Then he said: I will not partake of the consecrated sweetmeats, I will only eat the fruits. And so he did, and the temple was completed, and *Śri Ṫhákur ji* was enshrined in it, and DÁMODAR DÁS distributed food to the *Vaishńavas,* and they partook thereof.

Śri Ṫhákur ji had a faithful worshipper in a Mahratta lady, whom, with the frolicsomeness of boyhood, he delighted to teaze. One day, a woman selling vegetables having passed without the *Bái* noticing her, *Śri Ṫhákur ji* said to her: will you not buy any vegetables for me to-day? she replied: whenever any one selling them comes this way, I will buy some; to which he answered: one has just now passed. The *Bái* replied: no matter, if one has gone by, another will presently be here. But this did not satisfy the little deity, who leaping from his pedestal ran after the woman, brought her back, and, after haggling for the price with her himself, made his protectress purchase what he selected.

As RÁŃÁVYÁS and JAGANNÁTH, two of VALLABHÁCHÁRYA's disciples, were bathing, a woman of the *Rájput* caste came down to the river to burn herself with her husband; on which JAGANNÁTH said to his companion: what is the fashion of a woman becoming a *Sati?* RÁŃÁVYÁS shook his head, and said: the fruitless union of beauty with a dead body. The *Rájputáni* observing RÁŃÁVYÁS shake his head, her purpose at that moment was changed, and she did not become a *Sati,* on which her kindred were much pleased. Some time afterwards, meeting with the two disciples, the *Rájputáni* told them of the effect of their former interview, and begged to know what had passed between them. RÁŃÁVYÁS being satisfied that the compassion of *Śri Áchárj* was extended to her, repeated what he had said to JAGANNÁTH, and his regret that her charms should not be devoted to the service of *Śri Ṫhákur ji,* rather than be thrown away upon a dead body. The *Rájputáni* enquired how the service of *Ṫhákur ji* was to be performed, on which RÁŃÁVYÁS, after making her bathe, communicated to her the initiating prayer, and she thenceforth performed the menial service of the deity, washing his garments, bringing him water, and discharging other similar duties in the dwelling of RÁṄÁVYÁS with entire and fervent devotion, on which account she obtained the esteem of *Śrí Áchráj*, and the favour of the deity.

RÁM DÁS was married in his youth, but adopting ascetic principles, he refused to take his wife home: at last his father-in-law left his daughter in her husband's dwelling, but RÁM DÁS would have nothing to say to her, and set off on a pilgrimage to *Dwáraká*: his wife followed him, but he threw stones at her, and she was compelled to remain at a distance from him. At noon he halted and bathed the god, and prepared his food, and presented it, and then took the *Prasád* and put it in a vessel, and fed upon what remained, but it was to no purpose, and he was still hungry. Thus passed two or three days, when RAṄACHHOṘ appeared to him in a dream, and asked him why he thus ill-treated his wife. He said, he was *Virakta* (a cœnobite), and what did he want with a wife. Then RAṄACHHOṘ asked him, why he had married, and assured him that such an unsocial spirit was not agreeable to *Śrí Áchárya*, and desired him to take his wife unto him; for RAṄACHHOṘ could not bear the distress of the poor woman, as he has a gentle heart, and his nature has been imparted to the *Achárya* and his disciples. When morning came, RÁM DÁS called to his wife, and suffered her to accompany him, by which she was made happy. When the time for preparing their food arrived, RÁM DÁS prepared it himself, and after presenting the portion to the image, gave a part of it to his wife. After a few days RAṄACHHOṘ again appeared, and asked him, why he did not allow his wife to cook, to which RÁM DÁS replied, that she had not received the initiating name from *Śrí Áchárya*, and was, therefore, unfit to prepare his food. RAṄACHHOṘ, therefore, directed him to communicate the *Nám* (*the* name) to his wife, and after returning to the *Áchárya*, get him to repeat it. Accordingly RÁM DÁS iniated his wife, and this being confirmed by the *Áchárya*, she also became his disciple, and, with her husband, assiduously worshipped *Śrí Ṫhákur ji*.

VALLABHA was succeeded by his son VITALA NÁTH, known amongst the sect by the appellation of *Śrí Gosáin Jí*, VALLABHA's designation being *Śrí Áchárj Jí*. VITALA NÁTH, again, had seven sons, GIRDHARÍ RÁE, GOVIND RÁE, BÁLA KŔISHŃA, GOKUL NÁTH, RAGHUNÁTH, YADUNÁTH, and GHANAŚYÁMA; these were all teachers, and their followers, although in all essential points the same, form as many different communities. Those of GOKULNÁTH, indeed, are peculiarly separate from the rest, looking upon their own *Gosáins* as the only legitimate teachers of the faith, and withholding all sort of reverence from the persons and *Maths* of the successors of his brethren: an exclusive preference that does not prevail amongst the other divisions of the faith, who do homage to all the descendants of all VITALA NÁTH's sons.

The worshippers of this sect are very numerous and opulent, the merchants and bankers, especially those from Guzarat and Málwa, belonging to it: their temples and establishments are numerous all over India, but particularly at Mathurá and Bŕindávan, the latter of which alone is said to contain many hundreds, amongst which are three of great opulence. In Benares are two temples of great repute and wealth, one sacred to *Lál jí*, and the other to *Purushottama jí*[1]. *Jagannáth* and *Dwáraká* are also particularly venerated by

[1] Many of the bankers of this city, it is said, pay to one or other of the temples a tax of one-fourth of an *áná*, on every bill of exchange, and the cloth merchants, half an *áná* on all sales.

this sect, but the most celebrated of all the *Gosáin* establishments is at *Śrí Náth Dwár*, in Ajmír. The image at this shrine is said to have transported itself thither from *Mathurá*, when *Aurengzeb* ordered the temple it was there placed in to be destroyed.— The present shrine is modern, but richly endowed, and the high priest, a descendant of GOKUL NÁTH, a man of great wealth and importance[1]. It is a matter of obligation with the members of this sect to visit *Śrí Náth Dwár* at least once in their lives; they receive there a certificate to that effect, issued by the head *Gosáin*, and, in return, contribute according to their means to the enriching of the establishment: it is not an uncurious feature in the notions of this sect, that the veneration paid to their *Gosáins* is paid solely to their descent, and unconnected with any idea of their sanctity or learning; they are not unfrequently destitute of all pretensions to individual respectability, but they not the less enjoy the homage of their followers; the present chief, at *Śrínáth Dwár*, is said not to understand the certificate he signs.

MÍRÁ BÁÍS.

These may be considered as forming a subdivision of the preceding, rather than a distinct sect, although, in the adoption of a new leader, and the worship of KŔISHŃA under a peculiar form, they differ essentially

---

[1] Every temple is said to have three places of offering: the image, the pillow of the founder, and a box for *Śrí Náth Dwár*.

from the followers of VALLABHA: at the same time it is chiefly amongst those sectarians, that MÍRÁ BÁÍ and her deity, RAŃACHHOŔ, are held in high veneration, and, except in the west of India, it does not appear that she has many immediate and exclusive adherents.

MÍRÁ BÁÍ is the heroine of a prolix legend in the *Bhakta Málá*, which is a proof at least of her popularity: as the author of sacred poems addressed to the deity, as *Vishńu*, she also enjoys a classical celebrity, and some of her odes are to be found in the collections which constitute the ritual of the deistical sects, especially those of *Nának* and *Kabír*: according to the authority cited, she flourished in the time of *Akbar*, who was induced by her reputation to pay her a visit, accompanied by the famous musician *Tán Sen*, and it is said, that they both acknowledged the justice of her claim to celebrity.

MÍRÁ was the daughter of a petty Rájá, the sovereign of a place called *Mertá*; she was married to the *Ráńá* of *Udayapur*, but soon after being taken home by him quarrelled with her mother-in-law, a worshipper of *Deví*, respecting compliance with the family adoration of that goddess, and was, in consequence of her persevering refusal to desert the worship of KŔISHŃA, expelled the *Ráńá*'s bed and palace: she appears to have been treated, however, with consideration, and to have been allowed an independent establishment, owing, probably, rather to the respect paid to her abilities, than a notion of her personal sanctity, although the latter was attested, if we may believe our guide, by her drinking unhesitatingly a draught of poison presented to her by her husband, and without its having the power to do her harm. In her uncontrolled station she adopted the worship of RAṄACHHOṘ, a form of the youthful KṘISHṄA; she became the patroness of the vagrant *Vaishṅavas*, and visited in pilgrimage *Bṙindávan* and *Dwáraká*: whilst at the latter, some persecution of the *Vaishṅavas* at *Udayapur* appears to have been instituted, and Brahmans were sent to bring her home from *Dwáraká*: previously to departing, she visited the temple of her tutelary deity, to take leave of him, when, on the completion of her adorations, the image opened, and MÍRÁ leaping into the fissure, it closed, and she finally disappeared. In memory of this miracle it is said, that the image of MÍRÁ BÁÍ is worshipped at *Udayapur* in conjunction with that of RAṄACHHOṘ. The *Padas* that induced this marvel, and which are current as the compositions of MÍRÁ BÁÍ*, are the two following:

Pada 1.— Oh, sovereign RAṄACHHOṘ, give me to make *Dwáraká* my abode: with thy shell, discus, mace, and lotus, dispel the fear of YAMA: eternal rest is visiting thy sacred shrines; supreme delight is the clash of thy shell and cymbals: I have abandoned my love, my possessions, my principality, my husband. MÍRÁ, thy servant, comes to thee for refuge, oh, take her wholly to thee.

Pada 2.—If thou knowest me free from stain, so accept me:

---

* [Price's Hindee and Hindustanee Selections, I, p. 99. 100.]

save thee, there is none other that will show me compassion: do thou, then, have mercy upon me: let not weariness, hunger, anxiety, and restlessness consume this frame with momentary decay. Lord of MÍRÁ, GIRDHARA her beloved, accept her, and never let her be separated from thee.

BRAHMA SAMPRADÁYÍS, or MADHWÁCHÁRÍS.

This division of the *Vaishńavas* is altogether unknown in Gangetic Hindustan. A few individuals belonging to it, who are natives of southern India, may be occasionally encountered, but they are not sufficiently numerous to form a distinct community, nor have they any temple or teachers of their own. It is in the peninsula, that the sect is most extensively to be found*, and it is not comprised, therefore, in the scope of this sketch: as, however, it is acknowledged to be one of the four great *Sampradáyas*, or religious systems, such brief notices of it as have been collected will not be wholly out of place.

The institution of this sect is posterior to that of the *Śrí Vaishńavas*, or *Rámánujas*: the founder was MADHWÁCHÁRYA[1], a Brahman, the son of MADHIGE BHAŤŤA, who was born in the Śaka year 1121 (A. D. 1199) in *Tuluva*: according to the legendary belief of

* [Dr. Graul's Reise nach Ostindien. Leipzig: 1855. Vol. IV, p. 139.]

[1] In the *Sarvadarśana Sangraha* he is cited by the name *Púrńa Prajna* — a work is also quoted as written by him under the name of *Madhya Mandira*. Reference is also made to him by the title, most frequently found in the works ascribed to him, of *Ánanda Tírtha* [Sarvad. Sangr. p. 73.].

his followers, he was an incarnation of *Váyu*, or the god of air, who took upon him the human form by desire of Náráyańa, and who had been previously incarnate as *Hanumán* and *Bhíma*, in preceding ages. He was educated in the convent established at *Ananteśvar*, and in his ninth year was initiated into the order of Anachorets by Achyuta Pracha, a descendant of Sanaka, son of Brahmá. At that early age also he composed his *Bháshya*, or commentary on the *Gítá*, which he carried to *Badarikáśrama*, in the Himalaya, to present to Vedavyása, by whom he was received with great respect, and presented with three *Sálagráms*, which he brought back and established as objects of worship in the Maths of *Udipi*, *Madhyatala*, and *Subrahmańya*—he also erected and consecrated at *Udipi* the image of Kŕishńa, that was originally made by Arjuna, of which he became miraculously possessed.

A vessel from *Dwáraká*, trading along the Malabar coast, had taken on board, either accidentally or as ballast, a quantity of *Gopíchandana*, or the sacred clay, from that city, in which the image was immersed: the vessel was wrecked off the Coast of *Tuluva*, but Madhwa receiving divine intimation of the existence of the image had it sought for, and recovered from the place where it had sunk[1], and established it as

[1] This story is rather differently told by the late Colonel Mackenzie in his account of the Marda Gooroos, published in the Asiatic Annual Register for 1804.

the principal object of his devotion at *Udipi*, which has since continued to be the head quarters of the sect. He resided here for some time himself, and composed, it is said, thirty-seven works[1]. After some time he went upon a controversial tour, in which he triumphed over various teachers, and amongst others, it is said, over *Śankara Áchárya*—he finally, in his 79th year, departed to *Badarikáśrama*, and there continues to reside with Vyása, the compiler of the Vedas and Puráńas.

Before his relinquishing charge of the shrine he had established, Madhwácharya had very considerably extended his followers, so that he was enabled to establish eight different temples, in addition to the principal temple, or that of *Kŕishńa*, at *Udipi*: in these were placed images of different forms of *Vishńu*[2], and the superintendance of them was entrusted to the brother of the founder, and eight *Sannyásis*, who were Brahmans, from the banks of the *Godávarí*. These establishments still exist, and, agreeably to the code of the founder, each *Sannyási*, in turn, officiates as superior of the chief station at *Udipi* for two years,

---

[1] The principal of these are—the Gítá Bháshya, Sútra Bháshya, Rig-bháshya, Daśopanishad Bháshya—Anuvákánunaya Vivarńa, Anuvedánta Rasa Prakarańa, Bhárata Tátparya Nirńaya, Bhágavata-tátparya, Gitátátparya, Kŕishńámŕita Mahárńava, Tantra Sára. [See Burnouf, Bhágav. Pur., I, LIX.]

[2] 1. Ráma with Sítá.—2. Sítá and Lakshmań.—3. Káliya Mardana, with two arms.—4. Káliya Mardana, with four arms.—5. Suvitala.—6. Sukara.—7. Nŕisinha.—8. Vaśanta Vitala.

or two years and a half. The whole expense of the establishment devolves upon the superior for the time being, and, as it is the object of each to outvie his predecessor, the charges[1] are much heavier than the receipts of the institution, and, in order to provide for them, the *Sannyásis* employ the intervals of their temporary charge in travelling about the country, and levying contribution on their lay votaries, the amount of which is frequently very large, and is appropriated for the greater part to defray the costs of the occasional pontificate.

The eight *Maths* are all in *Tuluva*, below the Gháts[2], but, at the same time, Madhwácharya authorised the foundation of others above the Gháts under Padmanábha Tírtha, to whom he gave images of Ráma, and the *Vyása Sálagrám*, with instructions to disseminate his doctrines, and collect money for the use of the shrine at *Udipi*: there are four establishments under the descendants of this teacher above the Gháts, and the superiors visit *Udipi* from time to time, but never officiate there as pontiffs.

The superiors, or *Gurus*, of the *Mádhwa* sect, are Brahmans and *Sannyásis*, or profess cœnobitic observances: the disciples, who are domesticated in the several *Maths*, profess also perpetual celibacy. The

---

[1] Buchanan states them at 13,000 Rupees at least, and often exceeding 20,000.

[2] They are at Kánúr, Pejáwar, Admár, Phalamár, Kríshńapur, Sirúr, Sode, and Putti.

lay votaries of these teachers are members of every class of society, except the lowest, and each *Guru* has a number of families hereditarily attached to him, whose spiritual guidance he may sell or mortgage to a Brahman of any sect.

The ascetic professors of MADHWÁCHÁRYA's school adopt the external appearance of *Dańd́is,* laying aside the Brahmanical cord, carrying a staff and a water-pot, going bare-headed, and wearing a single wrapper stained of an orange colour with an ochry clay: they are usually adopted into the order from their boyhood, and acknowledge no social affinities nor interests. The marks common to them, and the lay votaries of the order, are the impress of the symbols of *Vishńu* upon their shoulders and breasts, stamped with a hot iron, and the frontal mark, which consists of two perpendicular lines made with *Gopichandana,* and joined at the root of the nose like that of the *Śrí Vaishńavas*; but instead of a red line down the centre, the *Madhwáchárís* make a straight black line with the charcoal from incense offered to *Náráyańa,* terminating in a round mark made with turmeric.

The essential dogma of this sect, like that of the *Vaishńavas* in general, is the identification of *Vishńu* with the Supreme Spirit, as the pre-existent cause of the universe[1], from whose substance the world was

---

[1] In proof of these doctrines they cite the following texts from the ŚRUTI, or VEDAS:

एको नारायण आसीन्न ब्रह्मा न च शङ्करः ।

"*Náráyańa* alone was; not *Brahmá* nor *Śankara.*"

made[1]. This primeval *Vishńu* they also affirm to be endowed with real attributes[2], most excellent, although indefinable and independent. As there is one independent, however, there is also one dependent, and this doctrine is the characteristic dogma of the sect, distinguishing its professors from the followers of RÁMÁNUJA as well as ŚANKARA, or those who maintain the qualified or absolute unity of the deity. The creed of the *Mádhwas* is *Dwaita*, or duality[3]. It is not, however, that they discriminate between the principles of good and evil, or even the difference between spirit and matter, which is the duality known to other sects of the Hindus. Their distinction is of a more subtle character, and separates the *Jívátmá* from the *Paramátmá*, or the principle of life from the Supreme Being. Life, they say, is one and eternal, dependent upon the Supreme, and indissolubly connected with, but not the same with him[4]. An important conse-

---

आनन्द एक एवाग्र आसीन्नारायणः प्रभुः ।
"Happy and alone before all was *Náráyańa* the Lord."

[1] "The whole world was manifest from the body of VISHŃU," विष्णोर्देहाज्जगत्सर्वमाविरासीत् ।

[2] "VISHŃU is independent, exempt from defects, and endowed with all good qualities."—*Tattwa Vivek.*: स्वतन्त्रो भगवान्विष्णुर्निर्दोषोऽशेषसद्गुणः ।

[3] "Independent and dependent is declared to be the two-fold condition of being."—*Tattwa Vivek.*: स्वतन्त्रमस्वतन्त्रं च द्विविधं तत्त्वमिष्यते । [Sarvadarśana Sangraha, p. 61.]

[4] "As the bird and the string, as juices and trees, as rivers and oceans, as fresh water and salt, as the thief and his booty, as man and objects of sense, so are God and Life distinct, and

quence of this doctrine is the denial of *Moksha*, in its more generally received sense, or that of absorption into the universal spirit, and loss of independent existence after death. The *Yoga* of the *Śaivas*, and *Sáyujyam* of the *Vaishńavas*, they hold to be impracticable[1].

The Supreme Being resides in *Vaikuńtha*, invested with ineffable splendour, and with garb, ornaments, and perfumes of celestial origin, being the husband also of *Lakshmí*, or *glory*, *Bhúmi*, the earth, and *Nílá*, understood to mean *Deví*, or *Durgá*, or personified matter. In his primary form no known qualities can be predicated of him, but when he pleases to associate with *Máyá*, which is properly his desire, or wish, the three attributes of purity, passion, or ignorance, or the *Sattwa*, *Rajas*, and *Tamas Guńas*, are manifested, as *Vishńu*, *Brahmá*, and *Śiva*, for the

---

both are ever indefinable."—*Mahopanishad*: यथा पक्षी च सूत्रं च नानावृक्षरसा यथा यथा नद्यः समुद्राश्च शुद्धोदलवणे यथा। चोरापहार्य्यौ च यथा यथा पुंविषयावपि तथा जीवेश्वरौ भिन्नौ सर्व्वदैव विलक्षणौ ॥ [ib. p. 69.]

[1] In confirmation of which they adduce texts from the *Purá-ńas* and *Vedas*:

"From the difference between Omniscience and partial knowledge, Omnipotence and inferior power, supremacy and subservience, the union of God and Life cannot take place."—*Garuda Puráńa*: सर्वज्ञाल्पज्ञाभेदात्सर्वशक्त्यल्पशक्तिनः। स्वातन्त्र्यपारतन्त्र्याभ्यां सम्भोगो नेशजीवयोः ॥ गां पुरं ॥ "Spirit is Supreme, and above qualities; Life is feeble and subordinate."—*Bhállaveya Upanishad*: आत्मा हि परमस्वतन्त्रो ऽधिगुणो जीवो ऽल्पशक्तिरस्वतन्त्रः। भां ॥

creation, protection, and destruction of the world. These deities, again, perform their respective functions through their union with the same delusive principle to which they owed their individual manifestation. This account is clearly allegorical, although the want of some tangible objects of worship has converted the shadows into realities, and the allegory, when adapted to the apprehensions of ordinary intellects, has been converted into the legend known to the followers of *Kabír*, of the Supreme begetting the Hindu TRIAD by MÁYÁ, and her subsequent union with her sons[1]. Other

---

[1] Colonel MACKENZIE, in his account of the sect, gives this legend in a different and rather unusual form, and one that indicates some relation to the *Śaiva* sects. It is not, however, admitted as orthodox by those members of the sect whom I have encountered, nor do any traces of it appear in the works consulted.

"The Lord of the Creation, by whose supremacy the world is illuminated, and who is infinitely powerful, creating and destroying many worlds in a moment, that Almighty Spirit, in his mind, contemplating the creation of a world for his pleasure, from his wishes sprung a goddess, named Itcha Sacktee; at her request, he directed her to create this world. Then the Sacktee, by the authority of God, immediately created three divine persons, generally called by Hindus the Moortee-trium, by their several names of Brahma, Vishnû and Siva, committing to them, separately, their respective charges in the expected world; Surstee, Sthutee, and Sayom, or the power of creating, nourishing, and destroying. When she had made these three lords, she requested of one after the other, that they might be her consort; but Brahma and Vishnû, disapproving of her request, she consumed them with the fire of her third eye, and proposed the same thing to Siva; then Sadaseevû, considering in his mind that

legends are current amongst the MÁDHWAS, founded on this view of the creation, in which BRAHMÁ and ŚIVA and other divinities are described as springing from his mind, his forehead, his sides, and other parts of his body. They also receive the legends of the *Vaishńava Puráńas*, of the birth of BRAHMÁ from the *Lotus*, of the navel of VISHŃU, and of RUDRA from the tears shed by BRAHMÁ on being unable to comprehend the mystery of creation.

The modes in which devotion to VISHŃU is to be expressed are declared to be three, *Ankana*, *Námakarańa*, and *Bhajana*, or marking the body with his symbols[1], giving his names to children, and other ob-

---

her demands were not agreeable to the divine law, replied that he could not be her consort, unless she granted her third eye to him. The goddess was pleased with his prudence, and adorned him with her third eye. So soon as Siva was possessed of that, he immediately destroyed her by a glance of the flaming eye, and revived Brahma and Vishnû, and of her ashes made three goddesses, Saraswatee, Latchmi, and Paravatee, and united one of them to each of the Trimoortee."

(*Account of the Marda Gooroos.—Asiatic Annual Register*, 1804.)

This legend is probably peculiar to the place where it was obtained, but the ideas and the notions adverted to in the text appear to have been misunderstood by Dr. BUCHANAN, who observes, that the MARDAS believe in the generation of the gods, in a literal sense, thinking VISHŃU to be the Father of BRAHMÁ, and BRAHMÁ the Father of ŚIVA.—Mysore, Vol. I, 14.

[1] Especially with a hot iron, which practice they defend by a text from the VEDAS. Whose body is not cauterised, does not obtain liberation. अतप्ततनुर्न तदा मोचमश्नुते ॥ [Sarvad. S. p. 64.] To which, however, *Sankaráchárya* objects, that *Tapta* does not

jects of interest, and the practice of virtue in word, act, and thought. Truth, good council, mild speaking, and study belong to the first; liberality, kindness, and protection, to the second, and clemency, freedom from envy, and faith, to the last. These ten duties form the moral code of the *Mádhwas**.

The usual rites of worship[1], as practiced by the *Vaishńavas* of this sect, are observed, and the same festivals. In the *Pújá,* however, there is one peculiarity which merits notice as indicative of a friendly leaning towards the *Śaiva* sects: the images of Śiva, Durgá, and Gańeśa are placed on the same shrine with the form of Vishńu, and partake in the adoration offered to his idol. Rites are conducive to final happiness only, as they indicate a desire to secure the favor of Vishńu. The knowledge of his supremacy is essential to the zeal with which his approbation may be sought, but they consider it unnecessary to attempt an identification with him by abstract meditation, as

---

mean cauterised, but purified with *Tapas,* or ascetic mortification.—

* [Sarvad. S. p. 65.]

[1] The daily ceremonies at *Udipi* are of nine descriptions: 1. *Malavisarjana,* cleaning the temple, 2. *Upasthána,* awaking Krishńa, 3. *Panchámrita,* bathing him with milk, &c., 4. *Udvarttana,* cleaning the image, 5. *Tírtha Pújá,* bathing it with holy water, 6. *Alankára,* putting on his ornaments, 7. *Ávritta,* addressing prayers and hymns to him, 8. *Mahápújá,* presenting fruits, perfumes, &c., with music and singing, 9. *Rátri Pújá,* nocturnal worship, waving lamps before the image, with prayers, offerings, and music.

that is unattainable[1].—Those who have acquired the regard of VISHŃU are thereby exempted from future birth, and enjoy felicity in *Vaikuńtha* under four conditions, as *Sárúpya*, similarity of form, *Sálokya*, visible presence, *Sánnidhya*, proximity, and *Sárshthi*, equal power*.

Besides the writings of the founder, the following works are considered as forming the *Śástra*, or scriptural authority, of this sect. The four Vedas, the *Mahábhárat*, the *Páncharátra*, and the genuine or original *Rámáyańa*.

It seems not improbable, that the founder of the *Mádhwa* sect was originally a *Śaiva* priest, and, although he became a convert to the *Vaishńava* faith, he encouraged an attempt to form a kind of compromise or alliance between the *Śaivas* and *Vaishńaivas*. MADHWA was first iniated into the faith of ŚIVA at *Ananteśwar*, the shrine of a *Linga*, and one of his names, ÁNANDA TÍRTHA, indicates his belonging to the class of *Daśnámí Gosáins*, who were instituted by ŚANKARÁCHÁRYA; one of his first acts was to establish a *Sálagrám*, a type of VISHŃU, at the shrine of SUBRAHMAŃYA, the warrior son of ŚIVA, and, as observed above, the images of ŚIVA are allowed to par-

---

[1] "Emancipation is not obtained without the favour of VISHŃU. His favour is obtained from knowledge of his excellence, and not from a knowledge of his identity."—*Śruti*: मोचस्तु विष्णुप्रसादान्तरेण न लभ्यते प्रसादश्च गुणोत्कर्षज्ञानादेव नाभेदज्ञानात्। [Sarvad. S. p. 68.]

* [See also Mahánáráyańa Upan. 15. ap. Weber, Ind. Stud. II, 94.]

take, in the *Mádhwa* temples, of the worship offered to Vishńu. The votaries of the *Mádhwa Gurus*, and of the *Śankaráchárí Gosáins*, offer the *Namaskár*, or reverential obeisance, to their teachers mutually, and the *Śríngeri* Mahant visits *Udipi*, to perform his adorations at the shrine of Kŕishńa. It is evident, therefore, that there is an affinity between these orders, which does not exist between the *Śaivas* and *Vaishńavas* generally, who are regarded by the *Mádhwas*, even without excepting the *Rámánujas*, as *Páshańd́ís*, or *heretics*, whether they profess the adoration of Vishńu or of Śiva.

SANAKÁDI SAMPRADÁYÍS, or NÍMÁVATS.

This division of the *Vaishńava* faith is one of the four primary ones, and appears to be of considerable antiquity: it is one also of some popularity and extent, although it seems to possess but few characteristic peculiarities beyond the name of the founder, and the sectarial mark.

Nimbáditya is said to have been a *Vaishńava* ascetic, originally named *Bháskara Áchárya*, and to have been, in fact, an incarnation of the *sun* for the suppression of the heretical doctrines then prevalent: he lived near *Bŕindávan*, where he was visited by a *Dańd́í*, or, according to other accounts, by a *Jaina* ascetic, or *Jati*, whom he engaged in controversial discussion till sunset: he then offered his visitant some refreshment, which the practice of either mendicant renders unlawful after dark, and which the guest was, therefore, compelled to decline: to remove the difficulty, the host stopped the further descent of the sun, and ordered him to take up his abode in a neighbouring *Nimb* tree, till the meat was cooked and eaten: the sun obeyed, and the saint was ever after named *Nimbárka*, or *Nimbáditya*, or the *Nimb* tree sun.

The *Nímávats* are distinguished by a circular black mark in the centre of the ordinary double streak of white earth, or *Gopíchandan*: they use the necklace and rosary of the stem of the *Tulasí*: the objects of their worship are Kṛishṅa and Rádhá conjointly: their chief authority is the *Bhágavat*, and there is said to be a *Bháshya* on the *Vedas* by Nimbárka: the sect, however, is not possessed of any books peculiar to the members, which want they attribute to the destruction of their works at *Mathurá* in the time of Aurengzeb.

The *Nímávats* are scattered throughout the whole of Upper India. They are met with of the two classes, cœnobitical and secular, or *Viraktas* and *Gṛihastas*, distinctions introduced by the two pupils of Nimbákra, Keśava Bhaṫṫ, and Hari Vyás: the latter is considered as the founder of the family which occupies the pillow of Nimbárka at a place called *Dhruva Kshetra*, upon the Jamna, close to *Mathurá*: the *Mahant*, however, claims to be a lineal descendant from Nimbárka himself, and asserts the existence of the present establishment for a past period of 1400 years: the antiquity is probably exaggerated: the *Nímávats* are very numerous about *Mathurá*, and they are also the most numerous of the *Vaishńava* sects in Bengal, with the exception of those who may be considered the indigenous offspring of that province.

VAISHŃAVAS OF BENGAL.

The far greater number of the worshippers of VISHŃU, or more properly of KŔISHŃA, in Bengal, forming, it has been estimated, one-fifth of the population of the province[1], derive their peculiarities from some *Vaishńava* Brahmans of *Nadíya* and *Śántipur*, who flourished about the end of the fifteenth century. The two leading men in the innovation then instituted were ADWAITÁNAND and NITYÁNAND, who, being men of domestic and settled habits, seem to have made use of a third, who had early embraced the ascetic order, and whose simplicity and enthusiasm fitted him for their purpose, and to have set up CHAITANYA as the founder and object of a new form of *Vaishńava* worship.

The history of CHAITANYA has been repeatedly written, but the work most esteemed by his followers is the *Chaitanya Charitra* of BŔINDÁVAN DÁS, which was compiled from preceding works by MURÁRI GUPTA and DÁMODARA, who were the immediate disciples of CHAITANYA, and who wrote an account, the first of his life as a *Gŕihastha*, or the *Ádi Lílá*, and the second of his proceedings as a pilgrim and ascetic, or

[1] WARD on the Hindus, 2, 175. In another place he says five-sixteenths, p. 448.

the *Madhya* and *Anta Lílá*. An abridgment of the composition of Bŕindávan Dás, under the title of *Chaitanya Charitámŕita*, was made by Kŕishńa Dás about 1590: although described by the author as an abridgment, it is a most voluminous work, comprising, besides anecdotes of Chaitanya and his principal disciples, the expositions of the doctrines of the sect: it is written in Bengali, but it is interspersed most thickly with the Sanskrit texts on which the faith is founded, and which are taken from the *Brahma Sanhitá*, the *Vishńu Puráńa*, the *Bhagavad Gítá*, and, above all, the *Śrí Bhágavat*, the work that appears about this period to have given a new aspect to the Hindu faith throughout the whole of Hindustan. The accounts we have to offer of Chaitanya and his schism are taken from the *Chaitanya Charitámŕita*.

Chaitanya was the son of a Brahman settled at *Nadíya*, but originally from *Śríhatta*, or *Silhet*. His father was named Jagannáth Miśra, and his mother Sachí: he was conceived in the end of Magha 1484, but not born till *Phalgun* 1485, being thirteen months in the womb—his birth was accompanied by the usual portentous indications of a super-human event, and, amongst other circumstances, an eclipse of the moon was terminated by his entrance into the world. Chaitanya was, in fact, an incarnation of Kŕishńa, or *Bhagaván*, who appeared for the purpose of instructing mankind in the true mode of worshipping him in this age: with the like view he was, at the same time, incarnate in the two greater teachers of the sect as principal *Anśas*, or portions of himself, animating the form of Adwaitánand, whilst Nityánand was a personal manifestation of the same divinity, as he had appeared formerly in the shape of Balaráma: the female incarnation was not assumed on this occasion, being, in fact, comprised in the male, for Rádhá, as the *Púrńa-Śakti*, or comprehensive energy, and Kŕishńa, as the *Púrńa-Śaktimán*, or possessor of that energy, were both united in the nature of the *Nadíya* saint.

The father of Chaitanya died in his son's childhood, and his elder brother, Viśvarúpa, had previously assumed the character of an ascetic: to take care of his mother, therefore, Chaitanya refrained from following his inclinations, and continued in the order of the *Gŕihastha*, or householder, till the age of twenty-four, during which time he is said to have married the daughter of Vallabháchárya. At twenty-four[1], he shook off the obligations of society, and becoming a *Vairágí*, spent the next six years in a course of peregrinations between *Mathurá* and *Jagannáth*, teaching his doctrines, acquiring followers, and extending the worship of Kŕishńa. At the end of this period, having nominated Adwaitáchárya and Nityánand to preside over the *Vaishńavas* of Bengal, and Rúpa and Sanátana over those of *Mathurá*, Chaitanya settled at *Níláchal*, or *Cuttack*, where he remained twelve

[1] Not forty, as stated by Mr. Ward (2, 173): his whole life little exceeded that age, as he disappeared at forty-two.

years, engaging deeply in the worship of *Jagannáth*, to whose festival he seems at least to have communicated great energy and repute[1]. The rest of his time was spent in tuition and controversy, and in receiving the visits of his disciples, who came annually, particularly the Bengalis, under ADWAITA and NITYÁNAND to *Nílúchal* in the performance of acts of self denial, and in intent meditation on KRISHŃA: by these latter means he seems to have fallen ultimately into a state of imbecility approaching to insanity, which engendered perpetually beatific visions of KRISHŃA, RÁDHÁ, and the Gopis: in one of these, fancying the sea to be the *Jamna*, and that he saw the celestial cohort sporting in its blue waters, he walked into it, and fainting with ecstasy, would have been drowned, if his emaciated state had not rendered him buoyant on the waves: he was brought to shore in a fisherman's net, and recovered by his two resident disciples, SVARÚPA and RÁMÁNAND: the story is rendered not improbable by the uncertain close of CHAITANYA's career: he disappeared; how, is not known: of course

[1] It may be observed, that in the frequent descriptions of the celebration of the *Rath Yátra*, which occur in the work of KRISHŃA DÁS, no instance is given of self-sacrifice amongst the numerous votaries collected, neither is there any passage that could be interpreted as commendatory of the practice: it is, in fact, very contrary to the spirit of *Vaishńava* devotion, and is probably a modern graft from *Śaiva* or *Śákta* superstition. ABULFAZL does not notice the practice, although he mentions that those who assist in drawing the car think thereby to obtain remission of their sins.

his disciples suppose he returned to *Vaikuṅtha*, but we may be allowed to conjecture the means he took to travel thither, by the tale of his marine excursion, as it is gravely narrated by KŔISHŃA DÁS: his disappearance dates about A. D. 1527.

Of ADWAITÁNAND and NITYÁNAND no marvels, beyond their divine pervasion, are recorded: the former, indeed, is said to have predicted the appearance of KŔISHŃA as CHAITANYA; a prophecy that probably wrought its own completion: he sent his wife to assist at the birth of the saint, and was one of his first disciples. ADWAITÁNAND resided at *Śántipur*, and seems to have been a man of some property and respectability: he is regarded as one of the three *Prabhus*, or *masters* of the sect, and his descendants, who are men of property, residing at *Śántipur*, are the chief *Gosáins*, or spiritual superiors, conjointly with those of NITYÁNAND, of the followers of this faith. NITYÁNAND was an inhabitant of *Nadiya*, a *Rádhiya* Brahman, and a householder: he was appointed especially by CHAITANYA, the superior of his followers in Bengal, nothwithstanding his secular character, and his being addicted to mundane enjoyments[1]: his descendants

---

[1] Thus, according to KŔISHŃA DÁS, when RAGHUNÁTH DÁS visits him, he finds him at a feast with his followers, eating a variety of dainties; amongst others a dish called *Pulina*, and when he good humouredly notices it, NITYÁNAND replies:—

गोपजाति आमि बङ्गगोपसङ्गे आमि सुखपाइ ए पुलीन भोजन रङ्गे॥

"I am of the *Gopa* cast (i. e. fig.: a companion of KŔISHŃA, the

are still in existence, and are divided into two branches: those of the male line reside at *Kharda*, near Barrackpore; and those of the female at *Bálagor*, near *Sukhságar*: there are other families, however, of nearly equal influence in various parts of Bengal, descended from the other *Gosáins*, the *Kavirájas* and original *Mahants*.

Besides the three *Prabhus*, or CHAITANYA, ADWAITA, and NITYÁNAND, the *Vaishńavas* of this order acknowledge six *Gosáins* as their original and chief teachers, and the founders, in some instances, of the families of the *Gosáins* now existing, to whom, as well as to the *Gokulastha Gosáins*, hereditary veneration is due. The six *Gauďiya*, or Bengal, *Gosáins*, appear to have all sattled at *Brindávan* and *Mathurá*, where many of their descendants are still established, and in possession of several temples: this locality, the agreement of dates, and the many points of resemblance between the institutions of VALLABHA and CHAITANYA render it extremely probable that their origin was connected, and that a spirit of rivalry and opposition gave rise to one or other of them.

The six *Gosáins* of the Bengal *Vaishńavas* are RÚPA,

---

cow-herd), and am amidst many *Gopas*, and such as we are, consider *Pulína* a delicacy."

A verse is also ascribed to him, said to have become proverbial:

मत्स्येर् झोल् कामिनीर् कोल्। आनन्दे तोरासबे हरिहरि बोल्॥
"Let all enjoy fish, broth, and woman's charms—be happy, and call upon HARI."

Sanátan, Jíva, Raghunáth Bhaṭṭ, Raghunáth Dás, and Gopál Bhaṭṭ. Rúpa and Sanátan[1] were brothers in the employ of the Mohammedan governor of Bengal, and were hence regarded as little better than *Mlechhas*, or outcasts, themselves: the sanctity of Chaitanya's life and doctrine induced them to become his followers, and as it was a part of his system to admit all castes, even Musalmans, amongst his disciples, they were immediately enlisted in a cause, of which they became the first ornaments and supports: they were men of learning, and were very indefatigable writers, as we shall hereafter see, and the foundation of two temples at *Bŕindávan*, the most respectable reliques of the Hindu faith existing in upper Hindustan, is ascribed to their influence and celebrity[2]. Jíva was the nephew

[1] From the indistinct manner in which they are conjointly described in the *Bhakta Málá* it might be thought that *Rúpa Sanátana* was but a single individual, but, in one passage, the work indicates their being two brothers, conformably to the *Charitámŕita*, and the tradition in general currency. [Price's Hindee and Hindust. Selections I, p. 132.]

[2] The temples of *Govind Deva* and *Madanmohan*, both in ruins; a Sanskrit inscription in the former, however, attributing it to Mán Sinh Deva, a descendant of Pŕithu Ráo, is dated Samvat 1647, or A. D. 1591. Besides the authority of Kŕishńa Dás for these two brothers being cotemporary with Chaitanya, who died in 1527, I have a copy of the *Vidagdha Mádhava*, of which Rúpa is the author, dated 1525; it is not therefore likely, that Sanátan actually founded the temple of *Govind Deva*, although he may have been instrumental to its being undertaken. The interior of this temple is far superior to any of the religious structures to be met with along the *Ganges* and *Jamna*, and may almost be

of the preceding, the son of their younger brother: he was likewise an author, and the founder of a temple at *Bŕindávan*, dedicated to *Rádhá Dámodara*. Raghunáth Bhaṫṫ and Raghunáth Dás were both Brahmans of Bengal, but they established themselves in the vicinity of *Mathurá* and *Bŕindávan*. Gopál Bhaṫṫ founded a temple and establishment at *Bŕindávan*, which are still maintained by his descendants; the presiding deity is Rádhá Ramaṅa.

Next to the six *Gosáins*, several learned disciples and faithful companions of Chaitanya are regarded with nearly equal veneration: these are Śrínivás, Gadádhar *Paṅḋit*, Śrí Svarúpa, Rámánand, and others, including Hari Dás: the last, indeed, has obtained almost equal honour with his master, being worshipped as a divinity in some places in Bengal. It is recorded of him, that he resided in a thicket for many years, and during the whole time he repeated the name of Kŕishṅa three hundred thousand times daily. In addition to these chiefs, the sect enumerates eight *Kavi Rájas*, or eminent and orthodox bards, amongst whom is Kŕishṅa Dás, the author of the *Chaitanya Charitámŕita*, and they also specify sixty-four *Mahantas*, or heads of religious establishments.

The object of the worship of the Chaitanyas is

---

considered handsome: the exterior of that of *Madanmohan* is remarkable for its being built something after the plan of the pyramidical temples of *Tanjore*; or rather its exterior corresponds with that of the temples at *Bhuvaneśvara* in *Cuttack*. As. Res. Vol. XV, plate.

Kŕishńa: according to them he is *Paramátmá*, or supreme spirit, prior to all worlds, and both the cause and substance of creation: in his capacity of creator, preserver, and destroyer he is Brahmá, Vishńu, and Śiva, and in the endless divisions of his substance or energy he is all that ever was or will be: besides these manifestations of himself, he has, for various purposes, assumed specific shapes, as *Avatárs*, or descents; *Anśas*, or portions; *Anśánsás*, portion of portions, and so on ad infinitum: his principal appearance and, in fact, his actual sensible manifestation was as Kŕishńa, and in this capacity he again was present in Chaitanya, who is therefore worshipped as the deity, as are the other forms of the same god, particularly as Gopál, the cow-herd, or Gopínáth, the lord of the milk-maids of *Bŕindávan*; his feats, in which juvenile characters are regarded, are his *Lílá*, or sport.

It is not worth while to enter upon the prolix series of subtle and unmeaning obscurities in which this class of Kŕishńa's worshippers envelop their sectarial notions: the chief features of the faith are the identification of *Vishńu* with *Brahma*, in common with all the *Vaishńava* sects, and the assertion of his possessing, in that character, sensible and real attributes, in opposition to the *Vedánta* belief of the negative properties of God: these postulates being granted, and the subsequent identity of Kŕishńa and Chaitanya believed, the whole religious and moral code of the sect is comprised in one word, *Bhakti*, a term that signifies a union of implicit faith with incessant devotion, and which, as illustrated by the anecdote of Hari Dás above given, is the momentary repetition of the name of Kŕishńa, under a firm belief, that such a practice is sufficient for salvation.

The doctrine of the efficacy of *Bhakti* seems to have been an important innovation upon the primitive system of the Hindu religion. The object of the *Vedas*, as exhibiting the *Vedánta*, seems to have been the inculcation of fixed religious duties, as a general acknowledgment of the supremacy of the deities, or any deity, and, beyond that, the necessity of overcoming material impurities by acts of self-denial and profound meditation, and so fitting the spiritual part for its return to its original sources; in a word, it was essentially the same system that was diffused throughout the old pagan world. But the fervent adoration of any one deity superseded all this necessity, and broke down practice and speculation, moral duties, and political distinctions. Kŕishńa himself declares in the *Bhágavat*, that to his worshipper that worship presents whatever he wishes—paradise, liberation, Godhead, and is infinitely more efficacious than any or all observances, than abstraction, than knowledge of the divine nature, than the subjugation of the passions, than the practice of the *Yoga*, than charity, than virtue, or than any thing that is deemed most meritorious[1]. Another singular and important consequence

[1] यत्कर्मभिर्यत्तपसा ज्ञानवैराग्यतश्च यत् । योगेन दानधर्मेण

results from these premises, for as all men are alike capable of feeling the sentiments of faith and devotion, it follows, that all castes become by such sentiments equally pure. This conclusion indeed is always admitted, and often stoutly maintained in theory, although it may be doubted whether it has ever been acted upon, except by CHAITANYA himself and his immediate disciples, at a period when it was their policy to multiply proselytes[1]. It is so far observed,

---

श्रेयोभिरितरैरपि । सर्वं मद्भक्तियोगेन मद्भक्तो लभते ऽञ्जसा । स्वर्गापवर्गं मद्धाम कथञ्चिद्यदि वाञ्छति ॥ *Bhágavat*, 11th Section [20, 33. 34. See also BURNOUF, Bhág. Pur., Vol. I, p. c.].

[1] CHAITANYA admitted amongst his followers five *Paíháns*—who purposed to attack and plunder him, but were stopped by his sanctity, and converted by his arguments: one of these, who was a *Pír,* he new-named RÁM DÁS, another, their leader, was a young prince *(a Rájakumár)* whom he named *Bijjili Khán.* CHAITANYA communicated the *Upadeśa,* or initiating *Mantra,* to them, and they all became famous *Vaishńavas*; पाठान वैष्णवनिहैल तांर ख्याति ॥ CHAITANYA uniformly maintains the pre-eminence of the faith over caste: the mercy of God, he says, regards neither tribe nor family: ईश्वरेर कृपा जाति कुल नाहि माने॥ KRISHŃA did not disdain to eat in the house of *Vidura,* a *Śúdra*: विदुरेर घरे कृष्ण करिल भोजन ॥ and he cites *Sanskrit* texts for his authority—as शुचिसद्भक्तिदीप्ताग्नि: दग्धदुर्जातिकल्मषः । श्वपाको ऽपि बुधैः श्लाघ्यो न वेदज्ञो ऽपि नास्तिकः ॥ "The *Cháńdála,* whose impurity is consumed by the chastening fire of holy faith, is to be reverenced by the wise, and not the unbelieving expounder of the *Vedas.*" Again: न मे भक्तश्चतुर्वेदी मद्भक्तः श्वपचः प्रियः । तस्मै देयं ततो ग्राह्यं स च पूज्यो यथा ह्यहम् ॥ "The teacher of the four *Vedas* is not my disciple; the faithful *Cháńdála* enjoys my friendship; to him be given, and from him be received: let him be reverenced, even as I am reverenced." These pas-

however, that persons of all castes and occupations are admitted into the sect, and all are at liberty to sink their civil differences in the general condition of mendicant and ascetic devotees, in which character they receive food from any hands, and of course eat and live with each other without regard to former distinctions. As followers of one faith all individuals are, in like manner, equally entitled to the *Prasád*, or food which has been previously presented to the deity, and it is probably the distribution of this, annually, at *Jagannáth*, that has given rise to the idea, that at this place all castes of Hindus eat together: any reservation, however, on this head is foreign to the tenets of this sect, as well as of the *Ramánandí Vaishńavas*[1], and in both community of schism is a close connecting link, which should, in deed as well as word, abrogate every other distinction.

The *Bhakti* of the followers of this division of the Hindu faith is supposed to comprehend five *Rasas* or *Ratis*, tastes or passions: in its simplest form it is mere *Śánti*, or quietism, such as was practiced by the *Yogendras*, or by sages, as SANAKA and his brethren, and other saints: in a more active state it is servitude, or *Dásya*, which every votary takes upon himself; a higher condition is that of *Sákhya*, a personal regard or friendship for the deity, as felt by BHÍMA,

---

sages are from the *Chaitanya Charitámŕita*, where many others of similar purport may be found.

[1] See remark on the *Rámánandí Vaishńavas*; page 56.

Arjuna, and others, honoured with his acquaintance. *Vátsalya*, which is a higher station, is a tender affection for the divinity, of the same nature as the love of parents for their children, and the highest degree of *Bhakti* is the *Mádhurya*, or such passionate attachment as that which pervaded the feelings of the *Gopís* towards their beloved Kŕishńa.

The modes of expressing the feelings thus entertained by his votaries towards Kŕishńa do not differ essentially from those prevalent amongst the followers of the *Gokulastha Gosáins*: the secular worshippers, however, pay a less regular homage in the temples of Kŕishńa, and in most parts of Bengal his public adoration occurs but twice a day, or between nine and twelve in the morning, and six and ten at night: occasionally, however, it does take place in a similar manner, or eight times a day. The chief ritual of the Bengal *Vaishńavas* of the class is a very simple one, and the *Náma Kírtana*, or constant repetition of any of the names of Kŕishńa, or his collateral modifications, is declared to be the peculiar duty of the present age, and the only sacrifice the wise are required to offer; it is of itself quite sufficient to ensure future felicity: however, other duties, or *Sádhanas*, are enjoined, to the number of sixty-four, including many absurd, many harmless, and many moral observances; as fasting every eleventh day, singing and dancing in honour of Kŕishńa, and suppressing anger, avarice, and lust. Of all obligations, however, the *Guru Pádáśraya*, or servile veneration of the spiritual teacher, is the most important and compulsory: the members of this sect not only are required to deliver up themselves and every thing valuable to the disposal of the *Guru*, they are not only to entertain full belief of the usual *Vaishńava* tenet, which identifies the votary, the teacher, and the god, but they are to look upon the *Guru* as one with the present deity, as possessed of more authority even than the deity, and as one whose favour is more to be courted, and whose anger is more to be deprecated, than even that of KŔISHŃA himself[1]. We have already had occasion to observe that this veneration is hereditary, and is paid to the successor of a deceased *Gosáin*, although, in the estimation perhaps of his own worshippers, he is in his individual capacity more deserving of reprobation than of reverence. This blind and extravagant adoration of the *Guru* is, perhaps, the most irrational of all Hindu irrationalities, and it is but justice to the foun-

---

[1] On this subject the following text occurs in the *Upásana Chandrámŕita*: यो मन्त्रः स गुरुः साक्षाद्यो गुरुः स हरिः स्वयम् ॥ "The *Mantra* is manifest in the *Guru*, and the *Guru* is HARI himself." प्रथमं तु गुरुः पूज्यस्ततश्चैव ममार्चनम् । "First the *Guru* is to be worshipped, then I am to be worshipped." गुरुरेव सदाराध्यः श्रेष्ठो मन्त्रादभेदतः । गुरौ तुष्टे हरिस्तुष्टः नान्यथा कल्पकोटिभिः ॥ "The *Guru* is always to be worshipped: he is most excellent from being one with the *Mantra*. HARI is pleased when the *Guru* is pleased: millions of acts of homage else will fail of being accepted." Again: हरौ रुष्टे गुरुस्त्राता गुरौ रुष्टे न कश्चनः । "When HARI is in anger, the *Guru* is our protector, when the *Guru* is in anger, we have none." These are from the *Bhajanámŕita.*

ders of the system to acquit them of being immediately the authors of this folly. The earliest works inculcate, no doubt, extreme reverence for the teacher, but not divine worship; they direct the disciple to look upon his *Guru* as his second father, not as his God: there is great reason to suppose, that the prevailing practice is not of very remote date, and that it originates chiefly with the *Śrí Bhágavat*: it is also falling into some disrepute, and as we shall presently see, a whole division of even CHAITANYA's followers have discarded this part of the system.

Liberation from future terrestrial existence is the object of every form of Hindu worship. The prevailing notion of the means of such emancipation is the re-union of the spiritual man with that primitive spirit, which communicates its individual portions to all nature, and which receives them, when duly purified, again into its essence. On this head, however, the followers of CHAITANYA, in common with most of the *Vaishńava* sects, do not seem to have adopted the *Vedánta* notions; and, although some admit the *Sáyujya*, or identification with the deity, as one division of *Mukti*, others are disposed to exclude it, and none acknowledge its pre-eminence. Their *Moksha* is of two kinds: one, perpetual residence in *Svarga*, or Paradise, with possession of the divine attributes of supreme power, &c. and the other, elevation to *Vaikuńtha*—the heaven of VISHŃU, which is free from the influence of *Máyá*, and above the regions of the *Avatárs*, and where they enjoy one or all of the relations to

Kṛishṅa, which have been enumerated when speaking of the followers of Rámánuja and Madhwáchárya.

The doctrines of the followers of Chaitanya are conveyed in a great number of works, both in Sanskrit and Bengali. The sage himself, and the two other *Mahápràbhus*, Nityánand and Adwaita, do not appear to have left any written compositions, but the deficiency was amply compensated by Rúpa and Sanátan, both of whom were voluminous and able writers. To Rúpa are ascribed the following works; the *Vidagdha Mádhava*, a drama; the *Lalitá Mádhava*, *Ujjvala Nílamańi*, *Dána Kéli Kaumudí*, poems in celebration of Kṛishṅa and Rádhá; *Bahustavávali*, hymns; *Ashṭádaśa Lílá Khańḍ*; *Padmávali*, *Govinda Virudávali*, and its *Lakshańa*, or exposition; *Mathurá Máhátmya*, panegyrical account of *Mathurá*, *Náṭaka Lakshańa*, *Laghu Bhágavat*, an abridgment of the *Śrí Bhágavat*, and the *Vraja Vilása Varńanam*, an account of Kṛishńa's sports in *Bṛindávan*. Sanátan was the author of the *Hari Bhakti Vilás*, a work on the nature of the deity and devotion, the *Rasámṛita Sindhu*, a work of high authority on the same subjects, the *Bhágavatámṛita*, which contains the observances of the sect, and the *Siddhánta Sára*, a commentary on the 10th Chapter of the *Śrí Bhágavat*. Of the other six *Gosáins*, Jíva wrote the *Bhágavat Sandarbha*, the *Bhakti Siddhánta*, *Gopála Champú*, and *Upadeśámṛita*, and Raghunáth Dás, the *Manaśśikshá* and *Guńaleśa Sukhaḍa*. These are all in Sanskrit. In Bengali, the *Rágamaya Kóńa*, a work on subduing the passions, is ascribed to RÚPA, and *Rasamaya Kaliká*, on devotedness to KŔISHŃA, to SANÁTAN. Other Sanskrit works are enumerated amongst the authorities of this sect, as the *Chaitanya Chandrodaya*, a drama*, *Stava Málá*, *Stavámŕita Laharí*, by VIŚVANÁTH CHAKRAVARTÍ; *Bhajanámŕita*, *Śrí Smarańa Darpańa*, by RÁMCHANDRA *Kavirája*; the *Gopípremámŕita*, a comment on the *Kŕishńa Karńámŕita*, by KŔISHŃA DÁS *Kavirája*; and the *Kŕishńa Kírtana*, by GOVIND DÁS and VIDYÁPATI.—The biographical accounts of CHAITANYA have been already specified in our notice of the *Chaitanya Charitámŕita*, and besides those, there enumerated, we have the *Chaitanya Mangala*, a history of the saint, by LOCHANA, and the *Gauragańoddeśa dípiká*, an account of his chief disciples. The principal works of common reference, and written in *Bengali*, though thickly interspersed with *Sanskrit* texts, are the *Upásanáchandrámŕita*, a ritual, by LÁL DÁS, the *Premabhakti Chandriká*, by ṪHÁKUR *Gosáin*, the *Páshańda Dalana*, a refutation of other sects, by RÁDHÁMÁDHAVA, and the *Vaishńava Varddhana*, by DAIVAKÍ NANDANA. There are no doubt many other works circulating amongst this sect, which is therefore possessed of a voluminous body of literature of its own[1].

---

* [by KAVIKARŃAPURA.]

[1] The particulars of the above are taken chiefly from the CHAITANYA CHARITÁMŔITA, others from the *Upásaná Chandrámŕita*, and a few from the list given by Mr. WARD: "Account of the Hindus", Vol. 2, 448.

The *Vaishńavas* of this sect are distinguished by two white perpendicular streaks of sandal, or *Gopichandana*, down the forehead, uniting at the root of the nose, and continuing to near the tip; by the name of *Rádhá Kŕishńa* stamped on the temples, breast and arms; a close necklace of *Tulasí* stalk of three strings, and a rosary of one hundred and eight or sometimes even of a thousand beads made of the stem of the *Tulasí*; the necklace is sometimes made of very minute beads, and this, in upper India, is regarded as the characteristic of the *Chaitanya* sect, but in Bengal it is only worn by persons of the lowest class. The *Chaitanya* sectaries consist of every tribe and order, and are governed by the descendants of their *Gosáins*. They include some *Udáśínas*, or *Vairágís*, men who retire from the world, and live unconnected with society in a state of celibacy and mendicancy: the religious teachers are, however, married men, and their dwellings, with a temple attached, are tenanted by their family and dependents. Such cœnobitical establishments as are common amongst the *Rámánandís* and other ascetics are not known to the great body of the *Chaitanya Vaishńavas*.

Besides the divisions of this sect arising from the various forms under which the tutelary deity is worshipped, and thence denominated *Rádháramańís*, *Rádhípális*, *Viháríjí* and *Govindjí*, and *Yugala Bhaktas*, and which distinctions are little more than nominal, whilst also they are almost restricted to the Bengal *Vaishńavas* about *Mathurá* and *Bŕindávan*, there are in Bengal three classes of this sect, that may be regarded as seceders from the principal body; these are denominated *Spashtha Dáyakas*, *Kartá Bhájas* and *Sáhujas*.

The *Spashtha Dáyakas* are distinguished from perhaps every other Hindu sect in India by two singularities—denial of the divine character, and despotic authority of the *Guru*, and the, at least professedly, platonic association of male and female cœnobites in one conventual abode[1].

The secular followers of this sect are, as usual, of every tribe, and of the *Gríhastha*, or householder order: the teachers, both male and female, are *Udásína*, or mendicants and ascetics, and lead a life of celibacy: the sectarial marks are a shorter *Tilaka* than that used by the other *Chaitanyas*, and a single string of *Tulasí* beads worn close round the neck: the men often wear only the *Kaupína*, and a piece of cloth round the waist, like an apron, whilst the women shave their heads, with the exception of a single slender tress: those amongst them who are most rigid in their conduct, accept no invitations nor food from any but persons of their own sect.

The association of men and women is, according to their own assertions, restricted to a residence within the same inclosure, and leads to no other than such intercourse as becomes brethren and sisters, or than

[1] Like the brethren and sisters of the free spirit, who were numerous in Europe in the 13th century. See MOSHEIM 3, 379.

the community of belief and interest, and joint celebration of the praise of KṚISHṄA and CHAITANYA, with song and dance: the women act as the spiritual instructors of the females of respectable families, to whom they have unrestricted access, and by whom they are visited in their own dwellings: the institution is so far political, and the consequence is said to be actually that to which it obviously tends, the growing diffusion of the doctrines of this sect in Calcutta, where it is especially established.

The *Kartá Bhájas*, or worshippers of the Creator, are a sect of very modern origin, having been founded no longer than thirty years ago by RÁMA ŚARAṄ PÁLA, a *Gwála*, an inhabitant of *Ghospara*, a village near *Sukh Ságar*, in Bengal[1]. The chief peculiarity of this sect is the doctrine of the absolute divinity of the *Guru*, at least as being the present *Kṛishṅa*, or deity incarnate, and whom they therefore, relinquishing every other form of worship, venerate as their *Ishṫa Devatá*, or elected god: this exclusive veneration is,

---

[1] See Mr. WARD's account of this sect, Vol. 2, 175; in a note he has given a translation of the *Mantra*: "Oh! sinless Lord — Oh! great Lord, at thy pleasure I go and return, not a moment am I without thee, I am even with thee, save, Oh! great Lord:" the following is the original: कर्ता आउले महाप्रभु आमि तोमार सुखे चलि फिरि तिलार्द्ध तोमा छाडा नहि आमि तोमार सङ्गे आछि दोहाइ महाप्रभु ॥ This is called the *Solah áná Mantra*, the *Neophyte* paying that sum, or sixteen annas, for it: it is perhaps one singularity in the sect, that this *Mantra* is in *Bengali*, a common spoken language — in all other cases it is couched in Sanskrit, the language of the gods.

however, comprehended within wide limits: we have seen that it prevails amongst the followers of *Chaitanya* generally, and it need scarcely have been adopted as a schismatical distinction: the real difference, however, is the person, not the character of the *Guru*, and the innovation is nothing, in fact, but an artful encroachment upon the authority of the old hereditary teachers or *Gosáins*, and an attempt to invest a new family with spiritual power: the attempt has been so far successful, that it gave affluence and celebrity to the founder, to which, as well as his father's sanctity, the son, Rámdulál Pál has succeeded. It is said to have numerous disciples, the greater proportion of whom are women. The distinctions of caste are not acknowledged amongst the followers of this sect, at least when engaged in any of their religious celebrations, and they eat together in private, once or twice a year: the initiating *Mantra* is supposed to be highly efficacious in removing disease and barrenness, and hence many infirm persons and childless women are induced to join the sect.

The remaining division of the Bengal *Vaishńavas* allow nothing of themselves to be known: their professions and practices are kept secret, but it is believed that they follow the worship of *Śakti*, or the female energy, agreeably to the left handed ritual, the nature of which we shall hereafter have occasion to describe.

The chief temples of the Bengal *Vaishńavas*, besides those which at *Dwáraká* and *Bŕindávan*, and particularly at *Jagannáth*, are objects of universal reverence, are three, one at *Nadíya* dedicated to CHAITANYA, one at *Ambiká* to NITYÁNAND and the same, and one at *Agradwípa* dedicated to GOPÍNÁTH: at the latter a celebrated *Melá*, or annual fair, is held in the month of March, at which from 50 to 100,000 persons are generally collected.

RÁDHÁ VALLABHÍS.

Although the general worship of the female personifications of the Hindu deities forms a class by itself, yet when individualised as the associates of the divinities, whose energies they are, their adoration becomes so linked with that of the male power, that it is not easy, even to their votaries, to draw a precise line between them: they, in fact, form a part of the system, and *Lakshmí* and *Sítá* are the preferential objects of devotion to many of the followers of RÁMÁNUJA and RÁMÁNAND, without separating them from the communion of the sect.

In like manner RÁDHÁ, the favourite mistress of KŔISHŃA, is the object of adoration to all the sects who worship that deity, and not unfrequently obtains a degree of preference that almost throws the character from whom she derives her importance into the shade: such seems to be the case with the sect now noticed, who worship KŔISHŃA as *Rádhá Vallabha*, the lord or lover of RÁDHÁ.

The adoration of RÁDHÁ is a most undoubted innovation in the Hindu creed, and one of very recent origin. The only RÁDHÁ that is named in the *Mahá-*

*bhárat** is a very different personage, being the wife of DURYODHANA's charioteer, and the nurse of KARŃA. Even the *Bhágavat* makes no particular mention of her amongst the *Gopís* of *Bŕindávan*, and we must look to the *Brahma Vaivartta Puráńa*, as the chief authority of a classical character, on which the pretensions of RÁDHÁ are founded; a circumstance which is of itself sufficient to indicate the comparatively modern date of the *Puráńa*.

According to this work**, the primeval being having divided himself into two parts, the right side became KŔISHŃA, and the left RÁDHÁ, and from their union, the vital airs and mundane egg were generated. RÁDHÁ being, in fact, the *Ichchhá Śakti*, the will or wish of the deity, the manifestation of which was the universe.

RÁDHÁ continued to reside with KŔISHŃA in *Goloka*, where she gave origin to the *Gopís*, or her female companions, and received the homage of all the divinities. The *Gopas*, or male attendants of KŔISHŃA, as we have formerly remarked, were in like manner produced from his person. The grossness of Hindu personification ascribes to the KŔISHŃA of the heavenly *Goloka* the defects of the terrestial cowherd, and the RÁDHÁ of that region is not more exempt from the causes or effects of jealousy than the nymph of *Bŕindávan*. Being on one occasion offended with KŔISHŃA for his infidelity, she denied him access to her palace,

* [V, 4759. 60.] ** [II, 45. 46.]

on which she was severely censured by SUDÁMÁ, a *Gopa*, and confidential adviser of KŔISHŃA. She therefore cursed him, and doomed him to be born on earth as an *Asura*, and he accordingly appeared as ŚANKHACHÚDA. He retaliated by a similar imprecation, in consequence of which RÁDHÁ was also obliged to quit her high station, and was born at *Bŕindávan* on earth, as the daughter of a *Vaiśya*, named VŔISHABHÁNU, by his wife KALÁVATÍ. KŔISHŃA having, at the same time, become incarnate, was married to her at *Bŕindávan*, when he was fourteen, and she was twelve years of age: as a further result of the imprecation, she was separated from him after he attained maturity, until the close of his earthly career; when she preceded him to the celestial *Goloka*, and was there reunited with him. The following is a further illustration of the notions of RÁDHÁ entertained by this sect. It is the address of GAŃEŚA to her, in the *Brahma Vaivartta Puráńa* *, after she had set the example of presenting offerings to him.

"Mother of the universe, the worship thou hast offered affords a lesson to all mankind. Thou art of one form with *Brahma*, and abidest on the bosom of KŔISHŃA. Thou art the presiding goddess of his life, and more dear than life to him, on the lotus of whose feet meditate the gods *Brahmá*, *Śiva*, *Śesha*, and the rest, and *Sanaka* and other mighty munis, and the chiefs of the sages, and holy men, and all the faithful. RÁDHÁ is the created left half, and MÁDHAVA the right, and the great *Lakshmí*, the mother of the world, was made from thy left side. Thou art the

* [IV, 123.]

great goddess, the parent of all wealth, and of the *Vedas*, and of the world. The primeval *Prakṛiti*, and the universal *Prakṛiti*, and all the creations of the will, are but forms of thee. Thou art all cause and all effect. That wise *Yogí*, who first pronounces thy name, and next that of KṚISHṆA, goes to his region; but he that reverses this order, incurs the sin of Brahminicide [1]. Thou art the mother of the world. The *Paramátmá* HARI is the father. The *Guru* is more venerable than the father, and the mother more venerable than the *Guru*. Although he worship any other god, or even KṚISHṆA, the cause of all, yet the fool in this holy land who reviles RÁDHIKÁ shall suffer sorrow and pain in this life, and be condemned to hell, as long as the sun and moon endure. The spiritual preceptor teaches wisdom, and wisdom is from mystical rites and secret prayers; but they alone are the prayers of wisdom, that inculcate faith in KṚISHṆA and in you. He who preserves the *Mantras* of the gods through successive births, obtains faith in DURGÁ, which is of difficult acquisition. By preserving the *Mantra* of DURGÁ he obtains SAMBHU, who is eternal happiness and wisdom. By preserving the *Mantra* of SAMBHU, the cause of the world, he obtains your lotus feet, that most difficult of attainments. Having found an asylum at your feet, the pious man never relinquishes them for an instant, nor is separated from them by fate. Having with firm faith received, in the holy land of *Bharata*, your *Mantra* (initiating prayer) from a *Vaishṇava*, and adding your praises *(Stava)* or charm *(Kavacha)*, which cleaves the root of works, he delivers himself (from future births) with thousands of his kindred. He who having properly worshipped his *Guru* with clothes, ornaments, and sandal, and assumed thy *Kavacha* (a charm or prayer, carried about the person in a small gold or silver casket) is equal to VISHṆU himself."

In what respect the *Rádhá Vallabhís* differ from those followers of the Bengali *Gosáins*, who teach the

---

[1] Accordingly the formula used by the *Rádhá Vallabhí* sect, and the like, is always RÁDHÁ KṚISHṆA, never KṚISHṆA RÁDHÁ.

worship of this goddess in conjunction with Kṛishṅa, does not appear, and perhaps there is little other difference than that of their acknowledging separate teachers. Instead of adhering to any of the hereditary *Gosáins*, the members of this sect consider a teacher named Hari Vanś as their founder. This person settled at *Bṛindávan*, and established a *Math* there, which in 1822 comprised between 40 and 50 resident ascetics. He also erected a temple there that still exists, and indicates, by an inscription over the door, that it was dedicated to *Śrí Rádhá Vallabha* by Hari Vanś, in *Samvat* 1641, or A. D. 1585. A manual, entitled *Rádhá Sudhá Nidhi*, which is merely a series of Sanskrit verses in praise of Rádhá, is also ascribed to the same individual. A more ample exposition of the notions of the sect, and of their traditions and observances, as well as a collection of their songs or hymns, is the *Sevá Sakhí Vání*, a work in *Bhákhá*, in upwards of forty sections. There are other works in the vernacular dialects, and especially in that of *Braj*, or the country about *Mathurá* and *Bṛindávan*, which regulate or inspire the devotion of the worshippers of *Rádhá Vallabha*.

SAKHÍ BHÁVAS.

This sect is another ramification of those which adopt Kṛishṅa and Rádhá for the objects of their worship, and may be regarded as more particularly springing from the last named stock, the *Rádhá Vallabhis*. As Rádhá is their preferential and exclusive divinity, their devotion to this personification of the *Śakti* of KŔISHŃA is ridiculously and disgustingly expressed. In order to convey the idea of being as it were her followers and friends, a character obviously incompatible with the difference of sex, they assume the female garb, and adopt not only the dress and ornaments, but the manners and occupations of women: the preposterous nature of this assumption is too apparent, even to *Hindu* superstition, to be regarded with any sort of respect by the community, and, accordingly, the *Sakhí Bhávas* are of little repute, and very few in number: they occasionally lead a mendicant life, but are rarely met with: it is said that the only place where they are to be found, in any number, is *Jaypur*: there are a few at Benares, and a few in Bengal.

CHARAŃ DÁSÍS.

Another *Vaishńava* sect conforming with the last in the worship of *Rádhá* and *Kŕishńa* was instituted by CHARAŃ DÁS, a merchant of the *Dhúsar* tribe, who resided at *Dehli* in the reign of the second ALEMGÍR. Their doctrines of universal emanation are much the same as those of the *Vedánta* school, although they correspond with the *Vaishńava* sects in maintaining the great source of all things, or *Brahma*, to be KŔISHŃA: reverence of the *Guru*, and assertion of the pre-eminence of faith above every other distinction, are also common to them with other *Vaishńava* sects, from whom, probably, they only differ in requiring no particular qualification of caste, order, nor even of sex, for their teachers: they affirm, indeed, that originally they differed from other sects of *Vaishńavas* in worshipping no sensible representations of the deity, and in excluding even the *Tulasi* plant and *Sálagrám* stone from their devotions: they have, however, they admit, recently adopted them, in order to maintain a friendly intercourse with the followers of RÁMÁNAND: another peculiarity in their system is the importance they attach to morality, and they do not acknowledge faith to be independent of works: actions, they maintain, invariably meet with retribution or reward: their moral code, which they seem to have borrowed from the *Mádhwas*, if not from a purer source, consists of ten prohibitions. They are not to lie, not to revile, not to speak harshly, not to discourse idly, not to steal, not to commit adultery, not to offer violence to any created thing, not to imagine evil, not to cherish hatred, and not to indulge in conceit or pride. The other obligations enjoined are, to discharge the duties of the profession or caste to which a person belongs, to associate with pious men, to put implicit faith in the spiritual preceptor, and to adore HARI as the original and indefinable cause of all, and who, through the operation of MÁYÁ, created the universe, and has appeared in it occasionally in a mortal form, and particularly as KŔISHŃA at *Brindávan*.

The followers of CHARAN DÁS are both clerical and secular; the latter are chiefly of the mercantile order;

the former lead a mendicant and ascetic life, and are distinguished by wearing yellow garments and a single streak of sandal, or *Gopichandana*, down the forehead; the necklace and rosary are of *Tulasi* beads: they wear also a small pointed cap, round the lower part of which they wrap a yellow turban. Their appearance in general is decent, and their deportment decorous; in fact, although they profess mendicity, they are well supported by the opulence of their disciples; it is possible, indeed, that this sect, considering its origin, and the class by which it is professed, arose out of an attempt to shake off the authority of the *Gokulastha Gosáins*.

The authorities of the sect are the *Śri Bhágavat* and *Gítá*, of which they have *Bháshá* translations: that of the former is ascribed, at least in parts, to CHARAŃ DÁS himself: he has also left original works, as the *Sandeha Ságar* and *Dharma Jiháj*, in a dialogue between him and his teacher, SUKH DEVA, the same, according to the *Charań Dásis*, as the pupil of VYÁS, and narrator of the *Puráńas*. The first disciple of CHARAŃ DÁS was his own sister, SAHAJI BÁÍ, and she succeeded to her brother's authority, as well as learning, having written the *Sahaj Prakáś* and *Solah Nirńaya*: they have both left many *Śabdas* and *Kavits*: other works, in *Bháshá*, have been composed by various teachers of the sect.

The chief seat of the *Charań Dásis* is at *Dehli*, where is the *Samádh*, or monument of the founder: this establishment consists of about twenty resident members: there are also five or six similar *Maths* at *Dehli*, and others in the upper part of the *Doab*, and their numbers are said to be rapidly increasing.

HARIŚCHANDÍS, SADHNÁ PANTHÍS and MÁDHAVÍS.

These sects may be regarded as little more than nominal. The two first have originated, apparently, in the determination of some of the classes considered as outcaste, to adopt new religious as well as civil distinctions for themselves, as they were excluded from every one actually existing. The *Hariśchandís* are *Ḋoms*, or sweepers, in the western provinces: their name bears an allusion to the *Pauráṅik* prince *Hariśchandra*[1], who, becoming the purchased slave of a man of this impure order, instructed his master, it is said, in the tenets of the sect. What they were, however, is not known, and it may be doubted whether any exist.

SADHNÁ, again, was a butcher, but it is related of him, that he only sold, never slaughtered meat, but purchased it ready slain. An ascetic rewarded his humanity with the present of a stone, a *Sálagrám* which he devoutly worshipped, and, in consequence, VISHṄU was highly pleased with him, and conferred upon him all his desires. Whilst on a pilgrimage, the wife of a Brahman fell in love with him, but he replied to her advances, by stating, that a throat must be cut before he would comply, which she misinter-

---

[1] See the Story of *Hariśchandra* in WARD, Vol. I, p. 16. Note,

preting, cut off her husband's head: finding SADHNÁ regarded her on this account with increased aversion, she accused him of the crime, and as he disdained to vindicate his innocence, his hands were cut off as a punishment, but they were restored to him by JAGANNÁTH. The woman burnt herself on her husband's funeral pile, which SADHNÁ observing exclaimed: "No one knows the ways of women, she kills her husband, and becomes a *Sati*," which phrase has passed into a proverb. What peculiarity of doctrine he introduced amongst the *Vaishńavas* of his tribe, is no where particularised.

MÁDHO is said to have been an ascetic, who founded an order of mendicants called *Mádhavis*: they are said to travel about always with a *Saroda* or *Balian*, stringed instruments of the guitar kind, and to accompany their solicitations with song and music: they are rarely, if ever, to be met with, and their peculiarity of doctrine is not known. The founder appears to be the same with the MÁDHOJI of the *Bhakta Málá*, who was an inhabitant of *GáLágaŕh*, but there are several celebrated ascetics of the same name, especially a MÁDHO DÁS, a Brahman of *Kanoj*, who was a man of considerable learning, and spent some time in *Orissa* and *Brindávan*. He was probably a follower of CHAITANYA.

SANNYÁSÍS, VAIRÁGÍS, &c.

Much confusion prevails in speaking of the mendicant and monastic orders of the Hindus, by the indiscriminate use of the terms prefixed to this division of our subject, and from considering them as specific denominations. They are, on the contrary, generic terms, and equally applicable to any of the erratic beggars of the Hindus, be they of what religious order they may: they signify, in fact, nothing more than a man, who has abandoned the world, or has overcome his passions, and are therefore equally suitable to any of the religious vagrants we meet with in Hindustan: the term *Fakír* is of equally general application and import, although it is of Mohammedan origin, and in strictness more descriptive of the holy beggars of that faith.

Although, however, *Sannyásis* and *Vairágis*, and other similar denominations are used, and correctly used in a wide acceptation, yet we occasionally do find them limited in meaning, and designating distinct and inimical bodies of men. When this is the case, it may be generally concluded, that the *Sannyásis* imply the mendicant followers of Śiva, and the *Vairágis* those of Vishńu.

The distinction thus made requires, at its outset, a peculiar exception, for besides the indiscriminate application of the term *Sannyási* to the *Vaishńavas*, as well as other mendicants; there is a particular class of them to whom it really appertains, these are the *Tridańdis*, or *Tridańdi Sannyásis*.

The word *Dańda* originally imports a *staff*, and it figuratively signifies moral restraint; exercised in three ways especially, or in the control of speech, body, and mind; or word, deed, and thought: a joint reference to the literal and figurative sense of the term has given rise to a religious distinction termed *Dańđa Grahańam,* the taking up of the staff. or adopting the exercise of the moral restraints above-mentioned, and carrying, as emblematic of such a purpose, either one, or, as in the present instance, three small wands or staves. *Tridańđí* designates both these characteristics of the order.

The *Tridańđí Sannyásis* are such members of the *Rámánuja,* or *Śrí Vaishńava* sect, as have past through the two first states of the Brahmanical order, and entered that of the *Sannyásí,* or the ascetic life: their practices are, in some other respects, peculiar: they never touch metals nor fire, and subsist upon food obtained as alms from the family Brahmans of the *Śrí Vaishńava* faith alone: they are of a less erratic disposition than most other mendicants, and are rarely met with in upper India: they are found in considerable numbers, and of high character, in the south: in their general practices, their religious worship, and philosophical tenets, they conform to the institutes and doctrines of RÁMÁNUJA.

VAIRÁGÍS.

The term *Vairágí* implies a person devoid of passion[1], and is therefore correctly applicable to every religious mendicant, who affects to have estranged

---

[1] From *Vi* privative prefix, and *Rága* passion.

himself from the interests and emotions of mankind. *Virakta*, the dispassionate, and *Avadhúta*, the liberated, have a similar import, and are therefore equally susceptible of a general application: they are, indeed, so used in many cases, but it is more usual to attach a more precise sense to the terms, and to designate by them the mendicant *Vaishńavas* of the *Rámánandí* class, or its ramifications, as the disciples of KABÍR, DÁDÚ, and others.

The ascetic order of the *Rámánandi Vaishńavas* is considered to have been instituted especially by the twelfth disciple of RÁMÁNAND, ŚRÍ ÁNAND: they profess perpetual poverty and continence, and subsist upon alms: the greater number of them are erratic, and observe no form of worship, but they are also residents in the *Maths* of their respective orders[1], and the spiritual guides of the worldly votaries: it is almost impossible, however, to give any general cha-

[1] The *Rámánandi Vairágis*, although indigenous in upper India, have established themselves in the Dekhan, as mentioned by BUCHANAN (Mysore, II, 76). The account he gives there of the *Dakhińi Vairágis* is an excellent illustration of the confusion that prevails respecting the application of the term; as he has blended with the *Rámánandi* ascetics, who are accurately entitled to the designation, a variety of religious vagrants, to some of whom the name is rarely, and to others never applied: as *Paramahansas*, *Digambaras*, or *Nágas*, *Úrddhabáhus*, and even *Aghoris*; the latter are not named, but they, or similar *Śaiva* mendicants, are the only individuals "who extort compassion by burning themselves with torches, and cutting themselves with swords."

racter of these *Vairágis*, as, although united generally by the watch-word of VISHṆU, or his incarnations, there are endless varieties both of doctrine and practice amongst them: those who are collected in *Maths* are of more fixed principles than their vagrant brethren, amongst whom individuals are constantly appearing in some new form with regard to the deity they worship, or the practices they follow[1].

---

[1] Such are the *Sítá Pádrís*, *Ramati Ráms*, and others; also the new and scarcely yet known sects *Gulál Dásis*, and *Daryá Dásis*: mention is also made in the *Dabistán*, of a number of Hindu mendicants, who are no longer numerous, if ever to be encountered. It is not possible in general, however, to discriminate the classes to which they belong, as in the descriptions given by the writer, he usually confines himself to a few peculiarities of practice that afford no guide to the principles of the sect, and as in the case of the *Ḋheṙhs*, he confounds the distinction of caste, or occupation with that of religious belief. Many of the vagrant ascetics whom he notices belong also rather to the Mohammedan, than the Hindu religion, as in the followers of SHEIKH BEDÍA AD DIN MEDÁR [Dabist. II, 223 ff. G. de Tassy, la relig. musulmane dans l'Inde. Paris, 1831, p. 54-62.]—who, although they credit the divine mission of Mohammed, disregard the established forms of the Musalman faith, chew *Bhang*, and go naked, smearing their bodies with *Vibhúti*, or the ashes of burnt cow-dung, and twisting their hair into the *Jaṭá*, or braid worn by Hindu ascetics—except as professed worshippers of *Niranjan*, or the indescribable deity, and a belief in magic, these mendicants have little in common with the Hindu religion, or perhaps with any, although, with a facility of which innumerable instances occur in Hindustan, they have adopted many of the Hindu practices. The tomb of *Sheikh Medár* is still to be seen at *Makhanpur*, near *Firozábád*, in the *Doab*—where, at the time of the *Dabistán*, an annual meeting of his disciples was held. The tomb is an

NÁGAS.

All the sects include a division under this denomination. The *Nágas* are of the same description as the *Vairágís*, or *Sannyásís*, in all essential points, but in their excess of zeal they carry their secession from ordinary manners so far, as to leave off every kind of covering, and, as their name signifies, go naked; there are, however, other points in which they differ from the general character of Hindu mendicants, and they are unquestionably the most worthless and profligate members of their respective religions.

A striking proof of their propensities is their use of arms. They always travel with weapons, usually a matchlock and sword and shield, and that these implements are not carried in vain has been shewn on various occasions: the sanguinary conflicts of opposite sects of Hindu mendicants have been described in several publications with the customary indistinctness as to the parties concerned: these parties are the *Vaishńava* and *Śaiva Nágas* chiefly, assisted and probably instigated by the *Vairági* and *Sannyási* members of those two sects, and aided by abandoned characters from all the schisms connected respectively with the one or the other[1]: it would, however, be

---

extensive building, though in decay. The *Dabistán*, although it contains many curious, and some correct notices of the Hindu religion, affords too loose and inaccurate a description to be consulted with advantage.

[1] As. Res. VI, 317, and XII, 455; an occurence of a similar

doing an injustice to the mendicant orders of any sect, to suppose that they are universally or even generally implicated in these atrocious affrays.

ŚAIVAS.

The worship of Śiva in the districts along the Ganges presents itself under a very different aspect from that of Vishńu, and with some singular anomalies. It appears to be the most prevalent and popular of all the modes of adoration, to judge by the number of shrines dedicated to the only form under which Śiva is reverenced, that of the *Linga*; yet it will be generally observed, that these temples are scarcely ever the resort of numerous votaries, and that they are regarded with comparatively little veneration by the Hindus. *Benares*, indeed, furnishes exceptions, and the temple of *Viśveśvara*[1] is thronged

nature is recorded by the author of the Dabistán, who mentions, that in 1050 of the Hijra a severe conflict took place at Dwáraká between a set of Vaishńava ascetics termed *Muńḍis*, from shaving their heads, and the *Sannyásis*, in which a great number of the former were slain [Dabist. II, 197].

[1] "The Lord of all," an epithet of Śiva, represented as usual by a *Linga*. It is one of the twelve principal emblems of this description, and has been, for many centuries, the chief object of veneration at *Káśí* or *Benares*. The old temple was partially destroyed by the Mohammedans in the reign of Aurengzeb: the present was built by Ahalyá Bái, the Mahratta Princess, and, although small and without pretension to magnificence, is remarkable for the minute beauty of its architectural embellishments.

with a never-ceasing crowd of adorers. There is, however, little solemnity or veneration in the hurried manner in which they throw their flowers or fruits before the image[1]; and there are other temples, the dwellings of other divinities, that rival the abode of *Viśveśvara* in popular attraction.

The adoration of Śiva, indeed, has never assumed, in Upper India, a popular form. He appears in his shrines only in an unattractive and rude emblem, the mystic purpose of which is little understood, or regarded by the uninitiated and vulgar, and which offers nothing to interest the feelings or excite the imagination. No legends are recorded of this deity of a poetic and pleasing character: and above all, such legends

---

[1] A Hindu temple comprises an outer court, usually a quadrangle, sometimes surrounded by a piazza, and a central edifice constituting the shrine. This, which in Upper India is generally of small dimensions, is divided into two parts, the *Sabhá*, or vestibule, and the *Garbhagŕiha*, or adytum, in which the Image is placed. The course of worship is the circumambulating of the temple, keeping the right hand to it, as often as the devotee pleases: the worshipper then enters the vestibule, and if a bell is suspended there, as is commonly the case, strikes two or three times upon it. He then advances to the threshold of the shrine, presents his offering, which the officiating Brahman receives, mutters inaudibly a short prayer, accompanied with prostration, or simply with the act of lifting the hands to the forehead, and departs. There is nothing like a religious service, and the rapid manner in which the whole is performed, the quick succession of worshippers, the gloomy aspect of the shrine, and the scattering about of water, oil, and faded flowers, inspire any thing but feelings of reverence or devotion.

as are narrated in the Puráńas and Tantras, have not been presented to the Hindus in any accessible shape. The *Śaivas* have no works in any of the common dialects, like the *Rámáyańa*, the *Vártá*, or the *Bhaktamálá*. Indeed, as far as any enquiry has yet been instituted, no work whatever exists, in any vernacular dialect, in which the actions of Śiva, in any of his forms, are celebrated. It must be kept in mind, however, that these observations are intended to apply only to Gangetic Hindustan, for in the South of India, as we shall hereafter see, popular legends relating to local manifestations of Śiva are not uncommon.

Corresponding to the absence of multiplied forms of this divinity as objects of worship, and to the want of those works which attach importance to particular manifestations of the favourite god, the people can scarcely be said to be divided into different sects, any farther than as they may have certain religious mendicants for their spiritual guides. Actual divisions of the worshippers of Śiva are almost restricted to these religious personages, collected sometimes in opulent and numerous associations, but for the greater part detached, few, and indigent. There are no establishments amongst the *Śaivas* of Hindustan, like those of *Śrináth* or *Purí*; no individuals as wealthy as the *Gokulastha Gosáins*, nor even as influential as the descendants of Adwaita and Nityánand. There are no teachers of ancient repute except Śankara Áchárya, and his doctrines are too philosophical and speculative to have made him popular.

The worship of Śiva continues, in fact, to be what it appears to have been from a remote period, the religion of the *Bráhmaṅas*[1]. Śambhu is declared by Manu to be the presiding deity of the Brahmanical order, and the greater number of them, particularly those who practice the rites of the *Vedas*, or who profess the study of the *Śástras*, receive Śiva as their tutelary deity, wear his insignia, and worship the *Linga*, either in temples, in their houses, or on the side of a sacred stream, providing, in the latter case, extempore emblems kneaded out of the mud or clay of the river's bed. The example of the Brahmans and the practice of ages maintain the veneration universally offered to the type of Śiva; but it is not the prevailing, nor the popular condition of the Hindu faith, along the banks of the Ganges. We shall now proceed to specify the different classes into which the worshippers of Śiva, as distinct from the mass of Brahmans, may be distinguished.

DAṄDÍS and DAŚNÁMÍS.

It is customary to consider these two orders as forming but one division. The classification is not, in every instance, correct, but the practices of the two are, in many instances, blended, and both denominations are accurately applicable to the same individual. It will not be necessary, therefore, to deviate from the ordinary enumeration.

---

[1] See a preceding Note page 2. [The received text of Manu does not contain the śloka there quoted.]

The *Dańdis*, properly so called, and the *Tridańdis* of the *Vaishńavas*, are the only legitimate representatives of the fourth *Áśrama*, or mendicant life, into which the Hindu, according to the instructions of his inspired legislators, is to enter, after passing through the previous stages of student, householder and hermit[1]. It is not necessary, however, to have gone through the whole of the previous career, as the Brahman may pass from any one of the first orders to the last at once[2]: he is then to take up his staff and water-pot, to derive from begging such a portion of food as is sufficient for his mere sustenance, and to devote the remainder of his day to holy study and pious meditation[3].

---

[1] Thus MANU. 6, 33:

वनेषु तु विहृत्यैवं तृतीयं भागमायुषः ।
चतुर्थमायुषो भागं त्यक्त्वा सङ्गान्परिव्रजेत् ॥

"Having thus performed religious acts in a forest during the third portion of his life, let him become a *Sannyási* for the fourth portion of it, abandoning all sensual affection."

[2] So MANU, as expounded by KULLÚKA BHAŤŤA, 6, 38:

प्राजापत्यां निरूप्येष्टिं सर्ववेदसदक्षिणाम् ।
आत्मन्यग्नीन्समारोप्य ब्राह्मणः प्रव्रजेद्गृहात् ॥
ब्रह्मचर्यादेव प्रव्रजेद्गृहाद्वा वनाद्वा इति टीका ।

"Having performed the sacrifice of *Prajápati*, &c. a Brahman may proceed from his house, that is, from the second order, or he may proceed even from the first to the condition of a *Sannyási*." Indeed the intermediate stage of the *Vánaprastha* is amongst the prohibited acts in the *Kali* age.

[3] Agreeably to the high authority already quoted, 6, 41, 43:

आगारादभिनिष्क्रान्तः पवित्रोपचितो मुनिः ।
समुपोढेषु कामेषु निरपेक्षः परिव्रजेत् ॥

Adopting, as a general guide, the rules of original works, the *Dańdí* is distinguished by carrying a small *Dańd*, or wand, with several processes or projections from it, and a piece of cloth dyed with red ochre, in which the Brahmanical cord is supposed to be enshrined, attached to it: he shaves his hair and beard, wears only a cloth round his loins, and subsists upon food obtained ready-dressed from the houses of the Brahmans once a day only, which he deposits in the small clay pot that he carries always with him: he should live alone, and near to, but not within a city; but this rule is rarely observed, and in general the *Dańdís* are found in cities collected like other mendicants in *Maths*[1]. The *Dańdí* has no particular time

---

अनग्निरनिकेतः स्याद्ग्राममन्नार्थमाश्रयेत् ।
उपेक्षको ऽशंकुसुको मुनिर्भावसमाहितः ॥

"Departing from his house, taking with him pure implements, his water-pot, and staff, keeping silence, unallured by desire of objects near him, let him enter into the fourth order."

"Let him have no culinary fire, no domicile, let him when very hungry go to the town for food, let him patiently bear disease, let him study to know God, and fix his attention on God alone."

[1] These are all founded on the following texts of MANU:

क्लृप्तकेशनखश्मश्रुः पात्री दण्डी कुसुम्भवान् ।
विचरेन्नियतो नित्यं सर्वभूतान्यपीडयन् ॥
एककालं चरेद्भैक्षं न प्रसज्जेत विस्तरे ।
भैक्षे प्रसक्तो हि यतिर्विषयेष्वपि सज्जति ॥
विधूमे सन्नमुसले व्यङ्गारे भुक्तवज्जने ।
वृत्ते सरावसम्पाते भिक्षां नित्यं यतिश्चरेत् ॥
अलाभे न विषादी स्याल्लाभे चैव न हर्षयेत् ।
प्राणयात्रिकमात्रः स्यान्मात्रासङ्गाद्विनिर्गतः ॥

or mode of worship, but spends his time in meditation, or in practices corresponding with those of the *Yoga*, and in the study of the *Vedánta* works, especially according to the comments of Śankaráchárya. As that teacher was an incarnation of Śiva[1], the *Dańḍis* reverence that deity and his incarnations, in preference to the other members of the Triad, whence they are included amongst his votaries; and they so far admit the distinction as not unfrequently to bear the *Śaiva* mark upon the forehead, smearing it with the *Tripuń-ḍra*, a triple transverse line made with the *Vibhúti*, or ashes which should be taken from the fire of an *Agnihotra Bráhman*, or they may be the ashes of

---

"His hair, nails and beard being clipped, bearing with him a dish, a staff, and a water-pot, let him wander about continually without giving pain to any being." VI, 52.

"Only once a day let him demand food, let him not habituate himself to eat much at a time, for an anchorite habituated to eat much becomes inclined to sensual gratification." 55.

"At the time when the smoke of kitchen fires has ceased, when the pestle lies motionless, when the burning charcoal is extinguished, when people have eaten and when dishes are removed, that is, late in the day, let the *Sannyási* always beg food." 56.

"For missing it let him not be sorrowful, nor for gaining it let him be glad, let him care only for a sufficiency to support life, but let him not be anxious about his utensils." 57.

[1] This character is given to him in the *Śankara Vijaya* of Mádhava Áchárya; his followers in the *Dekhan* assert that Śiva's descent as Śankara was foretold in the *Skanda Puráńa*: a prophecy which, if found in that work, will assist to fix its date; but the passage has not been met with.

burnt cowdung from an oblation offered to the god[1]. They also adopt the initiating *Mantra* of all the *Śaiva* classes, either the five or six syllable Mantra, "*Nama Śiváya*," or, "*Om, Nama Śiváya.*" The genuine *Dańdí*, however, is not necessarily of the *Śaiva* or any other sect; and in their establishments it will be usually found that they profess to adore *Nirguńa* or *Niranjana*, the deity devoid of attribute or passion[2].

---

[1] The material, or *Vibhúti*, and the efficacy of the mark, the *Tripuńdra*, are thus described in the *Káśikhańda*:

आग्नेयमुच्यते भस्म दग्धगोमयसम्भवं ।
तदेव द्रव्यमित्युक्तं त्रिपुण्ड्रस्य महामुने ॥

"The ashes of fire made with burnt cowdung are the material fittest for the *Tripuńdra*."

त्रिपुण्ड्रं कुरुते यस्तु भस्मना विधिपूर्वकम् ।
महापातकसङ्घातैर्मुच्यते चोपपातकैः ॥
अमन्त्रेणापि यः कुर्याद्ज्ञात्वा महिमोन्नतिं ।
त्रिपुण्ड्रं भालफलके मुच्यते सर्वपातकैः ॥

"Whoever marks the *Tripuńdra* with ashes, agreeably to rule, is purified from sins of the first and second degree: who makes it on his forehead without the *Mantras*, being ignorant of its virtue, will be purified from every simple sin." The mode of making it is thus laid down:

भ्रुवोर्मध्ये समारभ्य यावदन्तो भवेद्भ्रुवोः ।
मध्यमानामिकाङ्गुल्योर्मध्ये तु प्रतिलोमतः ॥
अङ्गुष्ठेन कृता रेखा त्रिपुण्ड्राख्याभिधीयते ।

"Beginning between the eye-brows, and carrying it to their extremity, the mark made with the thumb reverted between the middle and third fingers is called the *Tripuńdra*." [Vŕihadbrahmottarakhańda 28, 41. 42. quoted in Catal. Codd. MSS. Sanscrit. Bibl. Bodl. I, p. 74.]

[2] The *Dańdis* of the North of India are the *Sannyásis*, or monastic portion of the *Smárta Bráhmańas* of the South, of

The *Dańďis*, who are rather practical than speculative, and who have little pretence to the appellation beyond the epithet and outward signs of the order, are those most correctly included amongst the *Śaiva* sects. Amongst these the worship of Śiva, as Bhairava, is the prevailing form, and in that case part of the ceremony of initiation consists in inflicting a small incision on the inner part of the knee, and drawing the blood of the novice as an acceptable offering to the god. The *Dańďis* of every description have also a peculiar mode of disposing of their dead, putting them into coffins and burying them; or, when practicable, committing them to some sacred stream. The reason of this is their being prohibited the use of fire on any account[1].

---

whom Buchanan gives the following account: "The most numerous class here, and which comprehends about one-half of all the Brahmans in the Lower Carnatic, is called the *Smárta* Sect, and its members are the followers of Śankara Áchárya. They are commonly said to be of the sect of Śiva, but they consider Brahmá, Vishńu and Íśvara to be the same as the creator, preserver, and destroyer of the universe. They are readily distinguished by three horizontal stripes on the forehead, made with the ashes of cowdung" (Buch. 1, 13). "The *Sannyásis* are the *Gurus* of this sect" (Ibid. 305); and the *Dańdis* have great influence and authority amongst *Śaiva* Brahmans of the North of India.

[1] In the South, the ascetic followers of both Śiva and Vishńu bury the dead (Dubois, 56); so do the *Vaishńava Vairágis* and *Sannyásis* in the North of India, and the *Śaiva Jogis*. The class of Hindu weavers called *Yogis*, have adopted a similar practice (Ward 1, 201); all the casts in the South, that wear the *Linga*, do the same (Buch. 1, 27).

Any Hindu of the three first classes may become *Sannyási* or *Dańdí*, or, in these degenerate days, a Hindu of any caste may adopt the life and emblems of this order. Such are sometimes met with, as also are Brahmans, who, without connecting themselves with any community, assume the character of this class of mendicants. These constitute the *Dańdis* simply so termed, and are regarded as distinct from the primitive members of the order, to whom the appellation of *Daśnámis* is also applied, and who admit none but Brahmans into their fraternity.

The *Daśnámi Dańdis*, who are regarded as the descendents of the original members of the fraternity, are said to refer their origin to Śankara Áchárya, an individual who appears to have performed a part of some importance in the religious history of Hindustan; and to whom an influence has been often attributed much exceeding that which he really exercised. His biography, like that of most of the Hindu saints, is involved in considerable obscurity; but a few facts may be gleaned from such accounts as we have of him, upon which reliance may be placed, and to which it may not be uninteresting here briefly to advert.

A number of works are current in the South of India relating to this teacher, under the titles of *Śankara Charitra*, *Śankara Kathá*, *Śankara Vijaya*, or *Śankara Digvijaya**, following much the same course of narration, and detailing little more than Śankara's

* [Mackenzie Collection, I, 98. 314.]

controversial victories over various sects; in most cases, no doubt, the fictions of the writers. Of the two principal works of the class one attributed to Ánandagiri, a pupil of *Śankara*, has already been noticed[1]. The other is the work of Mádhava Áchárya*, the minister of some of the earliest chiefs of *Vijayanagar*, and who dates, accordingly, in the fourteenth century. This is a composition of high literary and polemical pretension, but not equally high biographical value. Some particulars of Śankara's birth and early life are to be found in the *Kerala Utpatti***, or political and statistical description of *Malabar*, although the work is sometimes said to have been composed by Śankara himself.

With regard to the place of Śankara's birth, and the tribe of which he was a member, most accounts agree to make him a native of *Kerala*, or *Malabar*, of the tribe of *Nambúri* Brahmans, and in the mythological language of the sect an incarnation of Śiva. According to other traditions, he was born as *Chidambaram*, although he transferred his residence to *Malabar*, whilst the *Kerala Utpatti* recognises *Malabar* as his native place, and calls him the offspring of adultery, for which his mother Śrí Mahádeví was expelled her caste.

---

[1] Supra p. 14.

* [See Bhágav. Puráńa ed. Burnouf, I, p. LVII. Lassen, Ind. Alt. IV, p. 173, Note.]

** [Mackenzie Coll. II, 73 ff. F. H. H. Windischmann, Sancara. Bonn, 1833, pp. 39–48.]

In *Malabar* he is said to have divided the four original castes into seventy-two, or eighteen sub-divisions each, and to haxe assigned them their respective rites and duties. Notwithstandig this, he seems to have met with particular disrespect either on account of his opinions, origin, or his wandering life. On his return home, on one occasion, his mother died, and he had to perform the funeral rites, for which his relations refused to supply him with fire, and at which all the Brahmans declined to assist. Śankara then produced fire from his arm, and burnt the corpse in the court yard of the house, denouncing imprecations on the country to the effect, that the Brahmans there should not study the Vedas, that religious mendicants should never obtain alms, and that the dead should always be burned close to the houses in which they had resided—a custom which is said to have survived him.

All accounts concur in representing Śankara as leading an erratic life, and engaging in successful controversy with various sects, whether of the *Śaiva, Vaishńava,* or less orthodox persuasions. In the course of his peregrinations he established several *Maths*, or convents, under the presidence of his disciples, particularly one still flourishing at *Śŕingeri*, or *Śŕingagiri*, on the western Ghâts, near the sources of the *Tungabhadrá.* Towards the close of his life he repaired as far as to *Kashmír*, and seated himself, after triumphing over various opponents, on the throne of Sarasvatí. He next went to *Badarikáśrama*, and finally to *Kedárnáth*, in the *Himálaya*, where he died at the early age of thirty-two. The events of his last days are confirmed by local traditions, and the *Pítha*, or throne of SARASVATÍ, on which ŚANKARA sat, is still shown in *Kashmír*; whilst at the temple of ŚIVA, at *Badari*, a Malabar Brahman, of the *Nambúri* tribe, has always been the officiating priest[1].

The influence exercised by ŚANKARA in person, has been perpetuated by his writings, the most eminent of which are his *Bháshyas*, or Commentaries, on the *Sútras*, or Aphorisms, of VYÁSA. A Commentary on the *Bhagavad Gítá* is also ascribed to him, as is one on the *Nṛisinha Tapaníya Upanishad*; a cento of verses in praise of DURGÁ, the *Saundaryá Laharí*, is likewise said to be his composition, as sometimes is the *Amaru Śataka*, a collection of amatory Stanzas written in the name of AMARU, a Prince, whose dead body ŚANKARA is fabled to have animated, that by becoming familiarised with sensual enjoyments he might argue upon such topics with the wife of *Madana Miśra*, who was more than equal to him in discussions of this nature, and was the only disputant he was unable to subdue, until the period of his transmigration had expired, and he had thence become practiced in the gratification of the passions.

Although no doubt of ŚANKARA's existence or of the important part performed by him in the partial re-modelling of the Hindu system can be entertained,

---

[1] Asiat. Researches, Vol. XII, p. 536.

yet the exact period at which he flourished can by no means be determined. I have, in another place, expressed my belief that he may have existed about the eighth or ninth century[1]. Subsequent enquiry has failed to add any reasons to those assigned for such an inference; but it has offered nothing to weaken or invalidate the conclusion there proposed[2].

---

[1] Preface to the Sanscrit Dictionary [first edition], p. XVII.

[2] A *Hálakánara* Manuscript, in the possession of the late Col. MACKENZIE, entitled *Śankara Vijaya,* (Mackenzie Collection II, 34) gives the following list of the spiritual heads of the *Śringeri* establishment:

1. Govinda Páda.
2. Śankara Áchárya.
3. Sanandana Áchárya.
4. Surásura Áchárya.
5. Troṭaka Áchárya.
6. Hastámalaka Áchárya.
7. Jnánaghana Áchárya.
8. Jnánottama Áchárya.
9. Sinhagiriśvara Áchárya.
10. Íśvaratirtha Áchárya.
11. Nŕisinha Múrtti Áchárya.
12. Vitaraṅa Áchárya.
13. Vidyáśankara Áchárya.
14. Bhárati Krishńa Áchárya.
15. Vidyáraṅya Áchárya.
16. Chandra Śekhara Áchárya.
17. Nŕisinha Bhárati Áchárya.
18. Śankara Bhárati Áchárya.
19. Nŕisinha Bhárati Áchárya.
20. Purushottoma Bhárati Áchárya.
21. Rámachandra Bhárati Áchárya.
22. Nŕisinha Bhárati Áchárya.
23. Immádi Bhárati Áchárya.
24. Abhinava Nŕisinha Bhárati Áchárya.
25. SachchidánandaBháratiÁchárya.
26. Nŕisinha Bhárati Áchárya.
27. Immádi SachchidánandaBhárati Áchárya.
28. Abhinava Sachchidánanda Bhárati Áchárya.
29. Nŕisinha Bhárati Áchárya.

This gives 27 descents from ŚANKARA. As the *Mahant* is elected from the disciples either by the *Guru* when about to die, or by the *Swámalu,* the spiritual chiefs of other establishments of the same sect, he is raised probably to the station in the prime of manhood, and in the ease and dignity of his sanctity has a favourable prospect of a long life. Twenty-five years to a *Guru*

The spiritual descendants of Śankara, in the first degree, are variously named by different authorities, but usually agree in the number. He is said to have had four principal disciples, who, in the popular traditions, are called *Padmapáda*, *Hastámalaka*, *Sureśvara* or *Mandana*, and *Trotaka*. Of these, the first had two pupils, *Tírtha* and *Áśrama*; the second, *Vana* and *Araṅya*; the third had three, *Sarasvatí*, *Purí*, and *Bhárati*; and the fourth had also three, *Giri* or *Gir*, *Párvata*, and *Ságara*. These, which being all significant terms were no doubt adopted names, constitute collectively the appellation *Daśnámi*, or the *ten-named*, and when a Brahman enters into either class he attaches to his own denomination that of the class of which he becomes a member; as *Tírtha*, *Purí*, *Gir*, &c.[1]. The greater proportion of the ten

---

may therefore be but a fair average allowance, and the above list comprises at that rate an interval of 657 years: at what period it closes does not appear; but the *Hálakánara* language is obsolete, and the work is possibly not less than two or three centuries old. This series of *Gurus* is so far corroborative of the view elsewhere taken of Śankara's date; but as it has been extracted by a Paṅdit from a work which I could not consult myself, it is by no means certain that it is correct, and I do not wish to attach any undue importance to the authority.

[1] It is scarcely worth while perhaps to translate words of such common occurrence, but to prove what I have stated in the text, I subjoin their signification: *Tírtha*, a place of pilgrimage; *Áśrama*, an order, as that of student, householder, &c.; *Vana*, a wood; *Araṅya*, a wood; *Sarasvatí*, the goddess of speech and eloquence; *Purí*, a city; *Bhárati*, speech, or its goddess; *Giri*, a mountain; in common use it always occurs *Gír*, which implies

classes of mendicants, thus descended from ŚANKARA ÁCHÁRYA, have failed to retain their purity of character, and are only known by their epithets as members of the original order. There are but three, and part of a fourth mendicant class, or those called *Tírtha* or *Indra*, *Áśrama*, *Sarasvati*, and *Bhárati*, who are still regarded as really ŚANKARA's *Dańdis*. These are sufficiently numerous, especially in and about Benares. They comprehend a variety of characters; but amongst the most respectable of them, are to be found very able expounders of the *Vedánta* works. Other branches of Sanskrit literature owe important obligations to this religious sect[1]. The most sturdy beggars are also members of this order, although their contributions are levied particularly upon the Brahmanical class, as, whenever a feast is given to the Brahmans, the *Dańdis* of this description present themselves unbidden guests, and can only be got rid of by bestowing

---

speech; *Párvata*, a mountaineer; *Ságara*, an ocean; the names are always compounded with different terms. One of ŚANKARA's disciples we have seen called ÁNANDA GIRI. The famous MÁDHAVA, when he became a *Dańdi*, adopted the appellation of VIDYÁRAŃYA. PÚRANGIR has been elsewhere adverted to, and other like names occur in some of the following notes. *Bhárati* is the prevailing title of the latter *Śringagiri Gurus*.

[1] ŚANKARA and MÁDHAVA are well known by their numerous and excellent works. Tke chief Vedánta writers, in like manner, were *Dańdis*; and the author of the *Daśakumára*, RÁMÁŚRAMA, the Commentator on AMARA, and VIJNÁNEŚVARA, the Commentator on the texts of YÁJNAVALKYA, were of the same class of ascetics.

on them a due share of the cates provided for their more worldly-minded brethren. Many of them practice the *Yoga*, and profess to work miracles, although with less success than some members of the order in the days of the author of the *Dabistán* *, who specifies one *Dańďadhári* as able to suspend his breath for three hours, bring milk from his veins, cut bones with hair, and put eggs into a narrow-mouthed bottle without breaking them.

The remaining six and a half members of the *Daśnámí* class, although considered as having fallen from the purity of practice necessary to the *Dańďí*, are still, in general, religious characters, and are usually denominated *Atíts*[1]: the chief points of difference between them and the preceding are their abandonment of the staff; their use of clothes, money, and ornaments; their preparing their own food, and their admission of members from any order of Hindus. They are often collected in *Maths*, as well as the *Dańďís*, but they mix freely in the business of the world; they carry on trade, and often accumulate property, and they frequently officiate as priests at the shrines of the deities[2]: some of them even marry, but in that case they are distinguished by the term *Samyogí* from the other *Atíts*.

---

* [Vol. II, p. 148.]

[1] From अतीत *Atíta*, past away, liberated from worldly cares and feelings.

[2] The officiating priests at the celebrated shrine of ANNAPÚRŃA, in Benares, are *Atíts*.

The chief practices and designations of the *Dańḋis*, as generally characteristic of them, have been already adverted to, but a great variety prevails in the details[1]. Their philosophical tenets in the main are those of the *Vedánta* system, as taught by Śankara and his disciples; but they generally superadd the practice of the *Yoga*, as taught by the followers of Patanjali, and many of them have latterly adopted the doctrines of the *Tantras*. Besides Śankara, the different orders of *Dańḋis* hold in high veneration the Muni Dattátreya, the son of Atri and Anasúyá. By virtue of a boon bestowed upon Atri or, according to one legend, on his wife by the three deities Brahmá, Vishńu, and Śiva, that sage had three sons, Soma, Datta, and Durvásas, who were severally portions of the deities themselves[2]. Datta, or Dattátreya, was eminent for his practice of the *Yoga*, and hence is held in high estimation by the *Jogis*, of whom we are next to speak, whilst, as an incarnation of a portion of Vishńu, he is likewise venerated by the *Vaishńavas*.

YOGÍS or JOGÍS.

The *Dańḋis* are to the *Śaiva* sects what the followers of Rámánuja are to those of the *Vaishńava*

---

[1] A specimen of the independent but scarcely orthodox *Dańḋi* is presented in the well known personage *Purán Gir*, of whom Mr. Duncan published an account in the 5th volume of the Asiatic Researches.

[2] *Bhágavat*, Book IV, [1, 15. 33.] and *Márkańḋeya Puráńa*, Chapter XVI, [14 ff. XVII, 11. Vishńu Pur. p. 83.]

faith, and a like parallel may be drawn between the disciples of RÁMÁNAND and those of GORAKHNÁTH, or the *Kánphátá Jogis*, the first pair being properly restricted to the Brahmanical order, intended chiefly for men of learning; the two latter admitting members from every description of people, and possessing a more attractive popular character.

The term *Jogi* or *Yogi* is properly applicable to the followers of the *Yoga* or *Pátanjala* school of philosophy, which, amongst other tenets, maintained the practicability of acquiring, even in life, entire command over elementary matter by means of certain ascetic practices. The details of these it is unnecessary to particularize, and accounts of them and of the *Yoga* philosophy will be best derived from the translation of BHOJA DEVA's Comment on the *Pátanjala Sútras*, in WARD's Account of the Hindus, and Mr. COLEBROOKE's Essay on the *Sánkkya* and *Pátanjala* doctrines, in the 1st volume of the Transactions of the Royal Asiatic Society. It is sufficient here to observe, that the practices consist chiefly of long continued suppressions of respiration; of inhaling and exhaling the breath in a particular manner; of sitting in eighty-four different attitudes; of fixing the eyes on the top of the nose, and endeavouring, by the force of mental abstraction, to effect a union between the portion of vital spirit residing in the body and that which pervades all nature, and is identical with ŚIVA, considered as the supreme being and source and essence of all creation. When this mystic union is effected, the *Yogi* is liberated in his living body from the clog of material incumbrance, and acquires an entire command over all worldly substance. He can make himself lighter than the lightest substances, heavier than the heaviest; can become as vast or as minute as he pleases, can traverse all space, can animate any dead body by transferring his spirit into it from his own frame, can render himself invisible, can attain all objects, becomes equally acquainted with the past, present, and future, and is finally united with Śiva, and consequently exempted from being born again upon earth. These super-human faculties are acquired, in various degrees, according to the greater or less perfection with which the initiatory processes have been performed.

According to standard authorities the perfect fulfilment of the rites which the *Yogí* has to accomplish requires a protracted existence and repeated births, and it is declared to be unattainable in the present or *Kali* age[1]. The attempt is therefore prohibited, and the

---

[1] The *Káśíkhańda* thus enumerates the difficulty or impossibility of completing the *Yoga* in the present age:

चञ्चलेन्द्रियवृत्तित्वात्कलिकल्मषजृम्भणात् ।
अल्पायुष्यात्तथा नृणां क्वेह योगमहोदयः ॥

"From the unsteadiness of the senses, the prevalence of sin in the *Kali*, and the shortness of life, how can Exaltation by the *Yoga* be obtained?"

Again:

न सिध्यति कलौ योगो न सिध्यति कलौ तपः ।

"In the *Kali* age, the *Yoga* and severe penance are impracticable."

Yoga is prescribed in modern times. This inhibition is, however, disregarded, and the individuals who are the subjects of our enquiry endeavour to attain the super-human powers which the performance of the *Yoga* is supposed to confer. They especially practice the various gesticulations and postures of which it consists, and labour assiduously to suppress their breath and fix their thoughts until the effect does somewhat realise expectation, and the brain, in a state of over-wrought excitement, bodies forth a host of crude and wild conceptions, and gives to airy nothings a local habitation and a name[1]. A year's intense application is imagined enough to qualify the adept[2],

---

[1] Some who have commenced their career in this line, have carried the practice to several hours' duration, at which time they have described themselves as becoming perfectly exhausted, with strange objects passing before them, and sparks of fire flashing in their eyes. One individual quitted it from having at last a figure resembling himself always before him, and knowing this to be a deception, he wisely inferred the similar character of any other visionary creature of his contemplation and the absurdity of the practice. DUBOIS has some amusing anecdotes on this subject (page 357, &c.), they are fully authenticated by the similar accounts which many *Vairágís* in Upper India will readily furnish. The worthy ABBÉ may indeed be generally trusted when he confines himself to what he saw or knew: in much that he heard he was misled, and in almost every thing connected with the language and literature and the religion or philosophy, as taught by classical authority, he commits egregious blunders.

[2] ब्रह्मचारी मिताहारी योगी योगपरायणः।
अब्दादूर्द्धं भवेत्सिद्धो नात्र कार्या विचारणा॥

"Leading a life of chastity and abstemiousness, and diligent

whilst inferior faculties may be obtained by even a six month's practice.

There are few *Jogis*, however, who lay claim to perfection, and their pretensions are usually confined to a partial command over their physical and mental faculties. These are evinced in the performance of low mummeries or juggling tricks, which cheat the vulgar into a belief of their powers. A common mode of display is by waving a *Chaurí*, or bunch of peacock's feathers, over a sick or new-born infant, to cure it of any morbid affection or guard it against the evil eye. A trick of loftier pretence has of late attracted some notice in the person of a Brahman at Madras, who, by some ingenious contrivance, appeared to sit in the air, and who boasted of being able to remain for a considerable period under water. He and his followers ascribed the possession of these faculties to his successful practice of the obvervances of the *Yoga*[1].

---

in the practice of the *Yoga*, the *Yogí* becomes perfect after a year: of this there is do doubt." *Haṫha Pradípa*.

[1] "*Sitting in the Air.*—An exhibition at Madras has excited considerable curiosity. A Brahmin, old and slightly made, represented to be of high caste, contrives to poise himself in a most extraordinary manner in the air. He performs this feat at any gentleman's house, not for money, but as an act of courtesy. The following is a description from an eye-witness, given in a Calcutta paper:— "The only apparatus seen is a piece of plank, which, with four pegs, he forms into a kind of long stool; upon this, in a little brass saucer or socket, he places, in a perpendicular position, a hollow bamboo, over which he puts a kind

In referring to the origin of this system we must no doubt go back to some antiquity, although the want of chronological data renders it impossible to specify the era at which it was first promulgated. That it was familiarly known and practiced in the eighth century, we may learn from the plays of Bhavabhúti, particularly the *Málati* and *Mádhava*[1], and from several of the *Śaiva Puráńas*, in some of which, as the *Kúrma Puráńa*, we have a string of names which appear to be those of a succession of teachers[2].

---

of crutch, like that of a walking crutch, covering that with a piece of common hide: these materials he carries with him in a little bag, which is shown to those who come to see him exhibit. The servants of the houses hold a blanket before him, and when it is withdrawn, he is discovered poised in the air, about four feet from the ground, in a sitting attitude, the outer edge of one hand merely touching the crutch, the fingers of that hand deliberately counting beads; the other hand and arm held up in an erect posture. The blanket was then held up before him, and they heard a gurgling noise like that occasioned by wind escaping from a bladder or tube, and when the screen was withdrawn he was again standing on terra firma. The same man has the power of staying under water for several hours. He declines to explain how he does it, merely saying he has been long accustomed to do so." The length of time for which he can remain in his aerial station is considerable. The person who gave the above account says that he remained in the air for twelve minutes; but before the Governor of Madras he continued on his baseless seat for *forty minutes*."—*Asiatic Monthly Journal for March*, 1829.

[1] See especially the opening of the 5th Act, and Notes.

[2] Śiva, it is said, appeared in the beginning of the *Kali* age as Śveta for the purpose of benifiting the Brahmans. He re-

The cavern temples of the South of India, in the subjects of their sculptures and the decorations of Śiva

---

sided on the *Himálaya* mountains and taught the *Yoga*. He had four chief disciples, one also termed Śveta, and the others Śvetaśikha, Śvetáśva [V. L. Śvetásya], and Śvetalohita. They had twenty-eight disciples—*Sutára, Madana, Suhotra, Kankańa,* and twenty-four others. [In the 50th Chapter of the *Kúrma Puráńa*, as quoted in the *Śabdakalpadruma* s. v. Śvetal', the names of the 28 disciples are given as follows:

सुभावो दमनश्चाथ सुहोत्रः कङ्कणस्तथा ।
लोकाक्षिरथ योगीन्द्रो जैगीषव्यस्तु सप्तमे ॥
अष्टमे दधिवाहः स्यान्नवमे वृषभप्रभुः ।
भृगुस्तु दशमे प्रोक्तस्तस्मादुग्रः परः स्मृतः ॥
द्वादशे ऽत्रिः समाख्यातो बाली चाथ त्रयोदशे ।
चतुर्दशे गौतमस्तु वेदशीर्षा ततः परं ॥
गोकर्णश्चाभवत्तस्माद्गुहावासः शिखण्ड्यथ ।
जटामाल्यट्टहासश्च दारुको लाङ्गली क्रमात् ॥
श्वेतस्तथापरः शूली तिण्डी मुण्डी च वै क्रमात् ।
सहिष्णुः सोमशर्मा च नकुलीशो ऽन्तिमे प्रभुः ॥
वैवस्वते ऽन्तरे शम्भोरवतारास्त्रिशूलिनः ।
अष्टाविंशतिराख्याता ह्यन्ते कलियुगे प्रभोः ॥]

Of these, four, whose names are not mentioned, had ninety-seven disciples, masters of the *Yoga* and inferior portions of Śiva. Those Brahmans who recite the names of these teachers and offer to them libations acquire *Brahmavidyá*, or knowledge of spirit. That this long string of one hundred and twenty-five names is wholly fictitious, seems improbable, although the list is possibly not very accurate. The four primitive teachers may be imaginary; but it is a curious circumstance that the word *Śveta, white*, should be the leading member of each appellation, and that in the person of Śiva and his first disciple it should stand alone as Śveta, *the white*. Śiva, however, is always painted white, and the names may be contrived accordingly; but we are still at a loss to understand why the god himself should have a European complexion. [See also Weber, Ind. Stud., I, 420 ff. and Lassen, Ind. Alt., II, 1100.]

and his attendants, belong to the same sect[1]; whilst the philosophical tenets of *Patanjali* are as ancient perhaps as most of the other philosophical systems, and are prior to the *Puráńas* by which they are inculcated in a popular form. The practices of the *Yoga* are also frequently alluded to, and enforced in the *Mahábhárat*[2]. There is little reason to question therefore the existence and popularity of the *Yoga* in the early centuries of the Christian era, but whether it was known and cultivated earlier must be matter of vague conjecture alone. As represented in the *Śankaravijaya* (Section 41), the *Yogís* vindicate their doctrine by texts from the *Vedas*, but the applicability of the texts is there denied, and is certainly far from conclusive or satisfactory.

---

[1] In the temples of *Salsette, Elephanta,* and *Ellora* the principal figure is mostly Śiva, decorated with ear-rings, such as are still worn by the *Kánphátá Jogis;* the walls are covered with ascetics in the various *Ásanas*, or positions in which the *Yogí* is to sit; a favourite subject of sculpture at *Elephanta* and *Ellora* is the sacrifice of Daksha disconcerted, and the guests, though saints and gods, put to rout, bruised and mutilated by Vírabhadra and the *Gańas* of Śiva in revenge for that deity's not having been invited, a story told in most of the *Puráńas* which inculcate the *Yoga* tenets. The cells attached to some of the temples are also indicative of *Jogí* residence, and one of the caves of *Salsette* is named that of *Jogíśvara*, or Śiva, as lord of the *Jogís*. *Transactions of the Literary Society of Bombay.* Vols. 1 and 2.

[2] These allusions occur in the *Vana Parva* chiefly; whilst in the *Udyoga Parva* [c. 38-45. Vol. II, p. 144 ff.] the observances of the *Yoga* are detailed at considerable length, and strenuously enjoined.

The principal mode in which the *Yoga* takes a popular shape in Upper India is probably of comparatively recent origin. This is the sect of *Kánphátá Jogís*, who acknowledge as their founder a teacher named GORAKHNÁTH, traces of whom are found in a *Gorakhkshetra* at *Pesháwer*, mentioned by ABULFAZL, and in the district and town of *Gorakhpur*, where also exist a temple and religious establishment of his followers. They hold also in veneration a plain near *Dwáraká*, named *Gorakhkhetr*, and a cavern or subterraneous passage at *Haridwár*. The *Śaiva* temples of *Nepál*, those of *Śambunáth*, *Paśupatináth*, and others, belong to the same system, although local legends attached to them have combined in a curious manner the fictions of the *Bauddha* with those of the Brahmanical mythology[1].

From a *Goshthí*[2], or controversial dialogue, between KABÍR and GORAKHNÁTH it would seem that they were personally known to each other, but various texts in the *Bíjak* allude to him as if recently deceased. In either case these two teachers may have been cotemporaries, or nearly so, and the latter therefore flourished in the beginning of the 15th century. According to his followers he was an incarnation of ŚIVA; but in the controversial tract above named he calls

---

[1] See Asiatic Researches, Vol. XVI, page 471, and Note.

[2] This has been printed in the first volume of Hindee and Hindustani Selections, for the use of the Interpreters of the Bengal Army, compiled by Captain PRICE. The discussion, in the form of a dialogue, occurs page 140.

himself the son of MATSYENDRA NÁTH, and grandson of ÁDINÁTH[1]. MATSYENDRA NÁTH appears to have been the individual who introduced the *Yoga Śaivism* into *Nepál*: one of the works of the sect, the *Haṫha Pradípa*, makes MATSYENDRA prior to GORAKH by five spiritual descents[2], and this would place the former

---

[1] आदिनाथ के नाती मच्छेन्द्रनाथ के पूत।
मैं योगी गोरख् अवधूत॥

[2] The list of teachers is thus particularised [The names in parenthesis are the readings of the Berlin MS. ap. Weber. Catal. p. 195 ff.]:

1. *Ádináth.*
2. *Matsyendra.*
3. *Sambara [Śárada].*
4. *Ánanda.*
5. *Bhairava.*
6. *Chaurángi [Chaurangi].*
7. *Ména [Mína].*
8. *Goraksha.*
9. *Virúpáksha.*
10. *Vilesa [Vileśi].*
11. *Mantháṇa Bhairava.*
12. *Siddabuddha [Śuddhabuddha.]*
13. *Kanthada [Śrukandali].*
14. *Paurandaka [Puráṫanka].*
15. *Surananda.*
16. *Siddhapáda [Śuddhapáda].*
17. *Churpatí [Charpaṫi].*
18. *Káneri.*
19. *Pújyapáda [Púrvapáda].*
20. *Nityanátha [Dhvaninátha].*
21. *Niranjana.*
22. *Kapála [Kapáli].*
23. *Bindu [Bindunátha].*
24. *Kákachaṅḍíśvara.*
25. *Allama.*
26. *Prabhudeva.*
27. *Goráchili [Ghoḍácholi].*
28. *Dindima [Ṫiṅṫiṅi].*
29. *Bháluki.*
30. *Nágabodha.*
31. *Chaṅḍakápálika [Shaṅḍakápálika.]*

The author of the *Haṫha Pradípa*, ÁTMÁRÁMA, states that these and many more *Mahásiddhas*, or perfect *Yogís*, are in existence. His names are possibly those of the *Mahants* of a particular establishment: some of them are very unlike Hindu appellatives. If the date assigned to *Gorakhnáth* in the text be rightly conjectured, we cannot assign much more than fifteen years to each of his successors.

in the 14th century, supposing the *Kabír* work to be correct in the date it attributes to the latter.

If the date assigned by HAMILTON to the migration of the Hindu tribes from *Chitaur*, the beginning of the 14th century, be accurate[1], it is probable that this was the period at which the worship of ŚIVA, agreeably to the doctrines of MATSYENDRA, or GORAKH, was introduced there, and into the eastern provinces of Hindustan.

The temple of GORAKHNÁTH at *Gorakhpur*, according to the local tradition, was founded by ŚIVA in the second or *Treta* age. Of its revolutions subsequent to that period no account was preserved, until it was converted into a Mohammedan mosque by ALÁ-ADDÍN. The temple, after some interval, was re-built in a different situation by an association of the followers of GORAKHNÁTH, and this was possibly the period at which the sect assumed its present form. A similar fate, however, attended this edifice, and it was appropriated by AURANGZEB to the Mohammedan religion. A second interval elapsed before a shrine was again erected to GORAKHNÁTH, when it was re-built on the spot on which it now stands by BUDDHANÁTH according to instructions communicated to him by GORAKHNÁTH in person. The present temple is situated to the west of the City of *Gorakhpur*, and attached to it on the south are three temples consecrated to MAHÁDEVA, PAŚUPATINÁTH, and HANUMÁN. The inclosure also

---

[1] HAMILTON's *Nepal*, page 14.

comprehends the tombs of several eminent members of this communion and the dwellings of the Mahant and his resident disciples.

Gorakhnáth was a man of some acquirement, and has left specimens of his scholarship in two Sanskrit Compositions, the *Goraksha śataka* and *Goraksha kalpa*: third, the *Goraksha sahasra Náma* is, probably, of his writing. The celebrated Bhartŕihari, the brother of Vikramáditya, is said to have been one of his disciples, but chronology will not admit of such an approximation. According to the authorities of the sect Gorakh is but one of nine eminent teachers, or *Náths*. Of the perfect *Yogís*, or *Siddhas*, eighty-four are enumerated; but it is said, that there have been many more, of whom several are still upon the surface of the earth.

The *Jogís* of Gorakhnáth are usually called *Kánphátás* from having their ears bored and rings inserted in them at the time of their initiation. They may be of any cast; they live as ascetics, either singly or in *Maths*[1]. Śiva is the object of their worship—they

[1] Solitary and independent living, however, appears to be improper, if the authority of the *Hatha Pradipa* is to be depended upon:

सुराज्ये धार्मिके देशे सुभिक्षे निरुपद्रवे ।
एकान्ते मठिकामध्ये स्थातव्यं हठयोगिना ॥

"In a well-governed and well-regulated country, fertile and prosperous, the *Hatha Yogi* (he who upholds the world in eternal continuity) should reside in a solitary cell within the precincts of a *Math*." Other directions follow applicable to most establishments of a similiar nature. The cell should have a

officiate indeed as the priests of that deity in some places, especially at the celebrated *Lát*, or Staff, of BHAIRAVA at *Benares*. They mark the forehead with a transverse line of ashes, and smear the body with the same; they dress in various styles, but in travelling usually wear a cap of patch-work and garments dyed with red ochre. Some wear simply a *Dhotí*, or cloth round the loins.

The term *Jogí*, in popular acceptation, is of almost as general application as *Sannyásí* and *Vairágí*; and it is difficult to fix its import upon any individual class besides the *Kánphátá*: the vagrants so called following usually the dictates of their own caprice as to worship and belief, and often, it may be conceived, employing the character as a mere plea for a lazy livelihood. The *Jogís* are, indeed, particularly distinguished amongst the different mendicant characters by adding to their religious personification more of the mountebank than any others: most of the religious mendicants, it is true, deal in fortune-telling, interpretation of dreams, and palmistry; they are also often empirics, and profess to cure diseases with specific drugs, or with charms and spells: but besides these accomplishments, the *Jogí* is frequently musical, and plays and sings; he also initiates animals into his business, and often travels about with a small bullock, a goat, or a

small door, be neither too lofty, nor too low, be well smeared with cow-dung, and should be kept clean and free from reptiles: the *Math* should have a temple, a mound or altar, and a well adjoining, and be enclosed by a wall.

monkey, whom he has taught to obey his commands, and to exhibit amusing gesticulations. The dress of this class of *Jogis* is generally a cap and coat, or frock of many colours: they profess to worship Śiva, and often carry the *Linga*, like the *Jangamas*, in the cap; all classes and sects assume the character, and *Musalman Jogis* are not uncommon. One class of the *Hindu Jogis* is called *Sárangihár*, from their carrying a *Sárangi*, or small fiddle or lute, with which they accompany their songs: these are usually *Bháshá* stanzas on religious or mythological topics, amongst which stanzas ascribed to Bhatṙihari, and a *Pauráṅic* legend of the marriage of Śiva and Párvatí, are particularly celebrated. The *Sárangihárs* beg in the name of Bhairava: another sect of them, also followers of that deity, are termed *Ḋorihárs* from their trafficking in small pedlary, especially the sale of thread and silk, to the housewives of the villages; another class adopt the name of *Matsyendris*, or *Machchhendris*, from *Matsyendra*, whom they regard as their founder; and a fourth set are *Bhartṙiharis* from a traditional reference to him as the institutor of this particular order. The varieties of this class of mendicants, however, cannot be specified: they are all errants, fixed residences, or *Maths*, of any *Jogis* except the *Kánphátás* rarely occurring: an observation that will apply to perhaps all the *Śaiva* sects, of whom it yet remains to give an account.

JANGAMAS.

The worship of Śiva, under the type of the *Linga*, it has been observed, is almost the only form in which that deity is reverenced[1]. It is also perhaps the most

---

[1] Its prevalence throughout the whole tract of the *Ganges* as far as *Benares* is sufficiently conspicuous. In Bengal the temples are commonly erected in a range of six, eight, or twelve, on each side of a *Ghát* leading to the river. At *Kalna* is a circular group of one hundred and eight temples erected by the Raja of Bardwan. Each of the temples in Bengal consists of a single chamber, of a square form, surmounted by a pyramidal centre; the area of each is very small. the *Linga*, of black or white marble, occupies the centre; the offerings are presented at the threshold. *Benares*, however, is the peculiar seat of this form of worship: the principal deity Viśveśvara, as observed already, is a *Linga*, and most of the chief objects of the pilgrimage are similar blocks of stone. Particular divisions of the pilgrimage direct visiting forty-seven *Lingas*, all of pre-eminent sanctity; but there are hundreds of inferior note still worshipped, and thousands whose fame and fashion have passed away. If we may believe Śiva, indeed, he counted a hundred *Parárddhyas* in *Kásí*, of which, at the time he is supposed to tell this to Devi, he adds sixty crore, or six hundred millions, were covered by the waters of the Ganges. A *Parárddhya* is said, by the commentator on the *Kásí Khańda*, in which this dialogue occurs, to contain as many years of mortals as are equal to fifty of *Brahmá*'s years. Notwithstanding the acknowledged purport of this worship, it is but justice to state, that it is unattended in Upper India by any indecent or indelicate ceremonies, and it requires a rather lively imagination to trace any resemblance in its symbols to the objects they are supposed to present.. The absence of all indecency from public worship and religious establishments in the Gangetic Provinces was fully established by the Vindicator of the Hindus, the late General Stuart, and in every thing re-

ancient object of homage adopted in India subsequently to the ritual of the VEDAS, which was chiefly, if not wholly, addressed to the elements, and particularly to Fire. How far the worship of the *Linga* is authorised by the VEDAS, is doubtful, but it is the main purport of several of the *Puráńas*[1]. There can be not doubt of its universality at the period of the Mohammedan invasion of India. The idol destroyed by MAHMÚD of *Ghizní* was nothing more than a *Linga*, being, according to MIRKHOND, a block of stone four or five cubits long and of proportionate thickness[2].

---

lating to actual practice better authority cannot be desired. (Vindication, Part 1st, 99, and more particularly Part 2d, 135.)

[1] The *Skanda Puráńa*, which contains the *Kásí Khańda*, particularly inculcates the worship of ŚIVA in this form; so do the *Śiva, Brahmáńda,* and *Linga Puráńas.*

[2] The following is the passage from the *Rauzat us Ssafá* alluded to:

و آن خانه که سومنات در آنجا بود طول و عرض تمام داشت چنان که پنجاه و شش ستون و قایه سقف آن کرده بودند و سومنات صنمی بود از سنگ تراشیده طولش مقدار پنج گز و عرض آن ظاهر و دو گز در زیر زمین مخفي و یمین الدوله محمود بتخانه در آمده با گرز گران سنگ سومنات را درهم شکست و مقداری از آن سنگرا فرمود تا بار کرده بغزنین میبردند و در استانه مسجد جامع بینداختند

"The temple in which the Idol of *Somnáth* stood was of considerable extent, both in length and breadth, and the roof was supported by fifty-six pillars in rows. The Idol was of polished stone, its height was about five cubits, and its thickness in pro-

It was, in fact, one of the twelve great *Lingas* then set up in various parts of India, several of which,

---

portion: two cubits were below ground. MAHMÚD having entered the temple broke the stone *Somnáth* with a heavy mace: some of the fragments he ordered to be conveyed to *Ghizni*, and they were placed at the threshold of the great Mosque." Another authority, the *Tabakáti Akbari*, a history of Akbar's reign, with a preliminary Sketch of Indian History, has the following:

لشکر بجانب هندوستان بقصد سومنات کشیده و این سومنات
شهریست بزرگ بر ساحل دریا محیط معبد براهمنه است و بتان
در این بتخانه بسیار بودند و بت بزرگرا سومنات نامند در
تواریخ بنظر رسیده که در زمان ظهور حضرت ختمی پناه مصطفی
صلی الله علیه وسلم این بترا از خانه کعبه برآورده بودند نه
از این کتب سلف براهمنه معلوم میشود ذکر چنین است از
زمان کشن که چهار هزار سال میشد معبود براهمنه است و بقول
براهمنه کشن اینجا غیب نموده — انقصه چون سلطان به شهر
نهرواله پتن رسید شهررا خالی دید فرمود تا غلبه برداشتند و
راه سومنات پیش گرفته چون بسومنات رسیدند اهل آنجا قلعهرا
بر روی سلطان کشیدند و بعد از جنگ و تردد بسیار قلعه
مفتوح گشت لوازم بتاراج و غارت بعمل آمد و خلق کثیر بقتل
و اسیر شد بتخانها شکسته از بیخ برکندند و سنگ سومناترا
پارچه پارچه کرده پارهرا بغزنین برده بدر مسجد جامع گذاشتنه
و سالها سنگ اینجا بود

"In the year 415 *(Hijra)* MAHMÚD determined to lead an army against *Somnáth*, a city on the sea-shore, with a temple appertaining to the followers of BRAHMÁ; the temples contained many idols, the principal of which was named *Somnáth*. It is related in some histories that this idol was carried from the *Kaaba*, upon

besides *Someśvara*, or *Somanáth*, which was the name of the Śiva demolished by Mahmúd, were destroyed

---

the coming of the Prophet, and transported to India. The Brahmanical records, however, refer it to the time of Kŕishńa, or an antiquity of 4000 years. Kŕishńa himself is said to have disappeared at this place."

"When the Sultan arrived at *Neherwáleh* (the capital of Guzerat), he found the city deserted, and carrying off such provisions as could be procured he advanced to *Somnáth*: the inhabitants of this place shut their gates against him, but it was soon carried by the irresistible valour of his troops, and a terrible slaughter of its defenders ensued. The temple was levelled with the ground: the idol *Somnáth*, which was of stone, was broken to pieces, and in commemoration of the victory a fragment was sent to *Ghizní*, where it was laid at the threshold of the principal mosque, and was there many years." [See also Journ. As. Soc. Bengal, VII, p. 883 ff., XII. p. 73 ff. Journal of the Bombay Branch R. A. S., II, 11-21. Asiatic Journal for 1843, May and Novbr.]

These statements shew that the idol was nothing more than a block of stone of very moderate dimensions, like the common representation of the type of Śiva. Ferishta, however, has converted it into something very different, or a colossal figure of the deity himself, and following Colonel Dow's version of that compiler, the historian of British India gives the following highly coloured account of a transaction which never took place. "Filled with indignation at sight of the gigantic idol, Mahmúd aimed a blow at its *head* with his iron mace. The *nose* was struck off from its *face*. In vehement trepidation the *Brahmans* crowded round and offered millions to spare the god. The *Omráhs*, dazzled with the ransom, ventured to counsel acceptance. Mahmúd, crying out that he valued the title of breaker not seller of idols, gave orders to proceed with the work of destruction. At the next blow the *belly* of the *idol* burst open, and forth issued a vast treasure of diamonds, rubies and pearls, rewarding the holy perseverance of Mahmúd, and explaining the devout liberality of the *Brahmans*!" (Vol. I, 491.)

by the early Mohammedan conquerors[1]. Most, if not all of them, also are named in works, of which the

[1] The twelve *Lingas* are particularised in the *Kedára Kalpa*, of the *Nandi Upapuráńa* [See also *Śivapuráńa* c. 44–61 ap. Aufrecht, Cat. Codd. MSS. Sanskr. Bibl. Bodl., I, p. 64; ib. p. 81, and Weber, Catal. p. 347, No. 1242.], where Śiva is made to say: "I am omnipresent, but I am especially in twelve forms and places." These he enumerates, and they are as follow:

1. *Somanátha*, in *Saurashtra*, i. e. *Surat*, in its most extensive sense, including part of *Guzerat*, where, indeed, *Pattana Somnáth*, or the city of *Somnáth*, is still situated.

2. *Mallikárjuna*, or *Śri Śaila*, described by Colonel Mackenzie, the late Surveyor General. Asiatic Researches, Vol. 5th.

3. *Mahákála*, in *Ujjain*. This deity of stone was carried to *Dehli*, and broken there upon the capture of *Ujjain* by Altumsh. A. D. 1231,—Dow. According to the *Tabakáti Akbari* the shrine was then three hundred years old.

4. *Omkára* is said to have been in *Ujjain*, but it is probably the shrine of Mahádeo at *Omkára Mandatta [Mándhdttá]* on the *Narmadá*.

5. *Amareśvara* is also placed in *Ujjain*: an ancient temple of Mahádeo on a hill near *Ujjain* is noticed by Dr. Hunter, Asiatic Researches, Vol. 6th, but he does not give the name or form.

6. *Vaidyanáth*, at *Deogarh* in Bengal; the temple is still in being, and is a celebrated place of pilgrimage.

7. *Rámeśa*, at *Setubandha*, the island of *Ramisseram*, between Ceylon and the Continent; this *Lingam* is fabled to have been set up by Ráma. The temple is still in tolerable repair, and is one of the most magnificent in India. The gateway is one hundred feet high. It has been repeatedly described, and is delineated in Daniel's Superb Plates of Indian Antiquities, from which it has been copied into Langles' Monuments de L'Hindoostan.

8. *Bhimaśankara*, in *Ďákini*, which is in all probability the same with *Bhimeśvara*, a *Linga* worshipped at *Dracharam* in the *Rájamahendri* district, and there venerated as one of the principal twelve.

date cannot be much later than the eighth or ninth century, and it is therefore to be inferred with as much certainty as any thing short of positive testimony can afford, that the worship of Śiva, under this type, prevailed throughout India at least as early as the fifth or sixth century of the Christian era. Considered as one great branch of the universal public worship, its prevalence, no doubt, dates much earlier; but the particular modifications under which the several types received their local designations, and became entitled to special reverence, are not in every case of remote antiquity.

One of the forms in which the *Linga* worship appears is that of the *Lingáyats*, *Lingavants*, or *Jangamas*, the essential characteristic of which is wearing the emblem on some part of the dress or person. The type is of a small size, made of copper or silver, and is commonly worn suspended in a case round the neck, or sometimes tied in the turban. In common with the *Śaivas* generally the *Jangamas* smear their foreheads with *Vibhúti* or ashes, and wear necklaces, and carry rosaries, made of the *Rudráksha* seed. The

---

[9. *Viśveśvara*, at *Benares*.]

10. *Tryambaka*, on the banks of the *Gomatí*; whether the temple still exists I have no knowledge.

11. *Gautameśa* is another of the twelve, whose original site and present fate are uncertain.

12. *Kedáreśa*, or *Kedáranáth*, in the *Himálaya*, has been repeatedly visited by late travellers. The deity is represented by a shapeless mass of rock.

clerical members of the sect usually stain their garments with red ochre. They are not numerous in Upper India, and are rarely encountered except as mendicants leading about a bull, the living type of *Nandí*, the bull of Śiva, decorated with housings of various colours, and strings of Cowrí shells: the conductor carries a bell in his hand, and thus accompanied goes about from place to place, subsisting upon alms. In the South of India the *Lingáyats* are very numerous, and the officiating priests of the *Śaiva* shrines are commonly of this sect[1], when they bear the designations of *Áradhya* and *Pańďáram*[2]. The sect is also there known by the name of *Víra Śaiva*. The following account of the restorer, if not the founder of the faith, as well as a specimen of the legends by which it is maintained, are derived from the *Basava Puráńa*.

According to the followers of this faith, which prevails very extensively in the Dekhan, *Basva, Basava, Basvana*, or *Basvapa* or *Basavappa*, different modes of writing his name, only restored this religion, and did not invent it. This person, it is said, was the son of *Mádiga Ráya*, a Brahman, and *Madeví*, written also *Madala arasu* and *Mahámbá*, inhabitants of *Hingulesvar Parvati Agrahárám*, on the west of *Śrí Śaila*, and both devout worshippers of Śiva. In recompense of their piety *Nandí*, the bull of Śiva,

[1] They also officiate in this capacity at the temple of *Kedáranáth*, in *Benares*.

[2] This word seems to be properly *Páńduranga*, (पाण्डुरङ्ग:) pale complexioned, from their smearing themselves with ashes. It is so used in *Hemachandra*'s history of *Mahávíra*, when speaking of the *Śaiva Brahmans*.

was born on earth as their son, becoming incarnate by command of Śiva, on his learning from Nárada the decline of the *Śaiva* faith and prevalence of other less orthodox systems of religion. The child was denominated after the *Basva* or *Basava*, the bull of the deity. On his arriving at the age of investiture he refused to assume the thread ordinarily worn by Brahmans, or to acknowledge any *Guru* except Íśvara or Śiva. He then departed to the town of *Kalyán*, the capital of *Bijala* or *Vijala Rája*, and obtained in marriage *Gangámbá*, the daughter of the *Dańdanáyak*, or minister of police. From thence he repaired to *Sangameśvara*, where he received from *Sangameśvara Swámi* initiation in the tenets of the *Víra Śaiva* faith. He was invited back from this place to succeed his father-in-law upon his decease in the office he had held.

After his return to *Kalyán*, his sister, who was one of his first disciples, was delivered of a son, *Chenna Basava*, who is not unfrequently confounded with his uncle, and regarded, perhaps more correctly, as the founder of the sect.

After recording these events the work enumerates various marvellous actions performed by *Basava* and several of his disciples, such as converting grains of corn to pearls—discovering hidden treasures—feeding multitudes—healing the sick, and restoring the dead to life. The following are some of the anecdotes narrated in the *Puráńa*.

Basava having made himself remarkable for the profuse bounties he bestowed upon the *Jangamas*, helping himself from the Royal Treasury for that purpose, the other ministers reported his conduct to *Bijala*, who called upon him to account for the money in his charge. *Basava* smiled, and giving the keys of the Treasury to the king, requested him to examine it, which being done, the amount was found wholly undiminished. *Bijala* thereupon caused it to be proclaimed, that whoever calumniated *Basava* should have his tongue cut out.

A *Jangama*, who cohabited with a dancing girl, sent a slave for his allowance of rice to the house of *Basava*, where the messenger saw the wife of the latter, and on his return reported to the dancing girl the magnificence of her attire. The mistress of the *Jangama* was filled with a longing for a similiar dress, and the *Jangama* having no other means of gratifying her repaired to *Basava*, to beg of him his wife's garment. *Basava* immediately stripped *Gangámbá*, his wife, and other dresses springing from her body, he gave them all to the *Jangama*.

A person of the name of *Kanapa*, who regularly worshipped the image of Ekámreśvara, imagining the eyes of the deity were affected, plucked out his own, and placed them in the sockets of the figure. Śiva, pleased with his devotion, restored his worshipper his eyes.

A devout *Śaiva* named *Mahádevala Macháya*, who engaged to wash for all the *Jangamas*, having killed a child, the Rájá ordered *Basava* to have him secured and punished; but *Basava* declined undertaking the duty, as it would be unavailing to offer any harm to the worshippers of Śiva. *Bijala* persisting sent his servants to seize and tie him to the legs of an elephant, but *Macháya* caught the elephant by the trunk, and dashed him and his attendants to pieces. He then proceeded to attack the Rájá, who being alarmed applied to *Basava*, and by his advice humbled himself before the offended *Jangama*. *Basava* also deprecated his wrath, and *Macháya* being appeased forgave the king and restored the elephant and the guards to life.

A poor *Jangama* having solicited alms of *Kinnaráya*, one of *Basava*'s chief disciples, the latter touched the stones about them with his staff, and converting them into gold told the *Jangama* to help himself.

The work is also in many places addressed to the *Jainas* in the shape of a dialogue between some of the *Jangama* saints and the members of that faith, in which the former narrate to the latter instances of the superiority of the *Śaiva* religion, and the falsehood of the *Jain* faith, which appears to have been that of *Bijala Ráya*, and the great part of the population of *Kalyána*. In order to convert them *Ekánta Ramáya*, one of *Basava*'s disciples, cut off his head in their presence, and then marched five days in solemn procession through and round the city, and on the fifth day replaced his head upon his shoulders. The *Jain* Pagodas were thereupon, it is said, destroyed by the *Jangamas*.

It does not appear, however, that the king was made a convert, or that he approved of the principles and conduct of his minister. He seems, on the contrary, to have incurred his death by attempting to repress the extension of the *Vira Śaiva* belief. Different authorities, although they disagree as to the manner in which *Bijala* was destroyed, concur in stating the fact: the following account of the transaction is from the present work.

"In the city of *Kalyána* were two devout worshippers of Śiva, named *Allaya* and *Madhuvaya*. They fixed their faith firmly on the divinity they adored, and assiduously reverenced their spiritual preceptor, attending upon *Basava* whithersoever he went. The king, *Bijala,* well knew their merits, but closed his eyes to their superiority, and listening to the calumnious accusations of their enemies commanded the eyes of *Allaya* and *Madhuvaya* to be plucked out. The disciples of *Basava,* as well as himself, were highly indignant at the cruel treatment of these holy men, and leaving to *Jagaddeva* the task of putting *Bijala* to death, and denouncing imprecations upon the city, they departed from *Kalyána*. *Basava* fixed his residence at *Sangameśvara*.

Macháya, *Bommidevaya*, *Kinnara*, *Kannatha*, *Bommadeva*, *Kakaya*, *Masanaya*, *Kolakila Bommadeva*, *Kesirajaya*, *Mathirajaya*, and others, announced to the people that the fortunes of *Bijala* had passed away, as indicated by portentous signs; and accordingly the crows crowed in the night, jackals howled by day; the sun was eclipsed, storms of wind and rain came on, the earth shook, and darkness overspread the havens. The inhabitants of *Kalyána* were filled with terror.

When *Jagaddeva* repaired home, his mother met him, and told him that when any injury had been done to a disciple of the *Śaiva* faith his fellow should avenge him or die. When *Daksha* treated Śiva with contumely, Párvatí threw herself into the flames, and so, under the wrong offered to the saints, he should not sit down contented: thus saying, she gave him food at the door of his mansion. Thither also came *Mallaya* and *Bommaya*, two others of the saints, and they partook of *Jagaddeva*'s meal. Then smearing their bodies with holy ashes, they took up the spear, and sword, and shield, and marched together against *Bijala*. On their way a bull appeared, whom they knew to be a form of *Basava* come to their aid, and the bull went first even to the court of the king, goring any one that came in their way, and opening a clear path for them. Thus they reached the court, and put *Bijala* to death in the midst of all his courtiers, and then they danced, and proclaimed the cause why they had put the king to death. *Jagaddeva* on his way back recalling the words of his mother stabbed himself. Then arose dissension in the city, and the people fought amongst themselves, and horses with horses, and elephants with elephants, until, agreeably to the curse denounced upon it by *Basava* and his disciples, *Kalyána* was utterly destroyed.

Basava continued to reside at *Sangameśvara*, conversing with his disciples, and communing with the divine Essence, and he expostulated with Śiva, saying: 'By thy command have I, and thy attendant train, come upon earth, and thou hast promised to recall us to thy presence when our task was accomplished.' Then Śiva and Párvatí came forth from the *Sangameśvara Lingam*, and were visible to *Basava*, who fell on the ground before them. They raised him, and led him to the sanctuary, and all three disappeared in the presence of the disciples, and they praised their master, and flowers fell from the sky, and then the disciples spread themselves abroad, and made known the absorption of *Basava* into the emblem of Śiva."—Mackenzie Collect., Vol. 2nd. Hálakanara MSS. [pp. 3–12.]

The date of the events here recorded is not particularised, but from various authorities they may be placed with confidence in the early part of the eleventh century[1].

---

[1] Colonel Wilks gives the same date (Mysore, I, 506), but terms the founder *Dhen Bas Ishwar*, intending clearly *Chenna* (little) *Basava*, the nephew of *Basava*, or *Basaveśvara*. Buchanan has the name *Basvana* (Mysore, I, 240), but agrees nearly in the date, placing him about seven hundred years ago.

The MACKENZIE Collection, from which the above is taken, contains a number of works[1] of a similar description in the ancient *Kanara* dialect. There are also several works of the same nature in *Telugu*, as the *Basaveśvara Puráńa*, *Pańditárádhya Charitra*, and others. Although the language of these compositions may now have become obscure or obsolete, it is not invariably so, and at any rate was once familiar. This circumstance, and the marvellous character of the legends they relate, specimens of which have been given in the above account of the founder of the sect, adapted them to the comprehension and taste of the people at large, and no doubt therefore exercised a proportionate influence. Accordingly WILKS, BUCHANAN, and DUBOIS represent the *Lingavants* as very numerous in the *Dekhan*, especially in *Mysore*, or those countries constituting ancient *Kanara*, and they are also common in *Telingana*. In Upper India there are no popular works current, and the only authority is a learned *Bháshya*, or Comment, by NÍLKAŃTHA, on the *Sútras* of VYÁSA, a work not often met with, and, being in Sanskrit, unintelligible to the multitude[2].

---

[1] As the *Basvana Puráńa*, *Chenna Basava Puráńa*, *Prabhulinga Lílá*, *Saranu Lílámŕita*, *Viraktaru Kávyam*, and others, containing legends of a vast number of *Jangama* Saints and Teachers.— MACKENZIE Collection, Vol. 2, [pp. 12–32. See also *Madras Journal*, Vol. XI, p. 143 ff. and GRAUL, Reise nach Indien, Vol. V, p. 185 and 360.]

[2] Besides the *Jangama* priests of *Kedáranáth*, an opulent establishment of them exists at *Benares*: its wealth arises from

PARAMAHANSAS.

According to the introduction to the *Dwádaśa Mahávákya*, by a *Dańdi* author, Vaikuńt́ha Puri, the *Sannyási* is of four kinds, the *Kut́ichara*, *Bahúdaka*, *Hansa*, and *Paramahansa*: the difference between whom, however, is only the graduated intensity of their self-mortification and profound abstraction. The *Paramahansa*[1] is the most eminent of these grada-

---

a number of houses occupying a considerable space, called the *Jangam Bári*: the title to the property is said to be a grant to the *Jangamas*, regularly executed by Mán Sinh, and preserved on a copper plate: the story with which the vulgar are deluded is, that it was granted by one of the Emperors of Hindustan in consequence of a miracle performed by a *Jangama* devotee. In proof of the veracity of his doctrine he proposed to fly: the Emperor promised to give him as much ground as he could traverse in that manner: not quite satisfied of the impossibility of the feat, he had a check string tied to the ascetic's legs, and held by one of the attendants: the *Jangama* mounted, and when he reached the limits of the present *Jangama Bári*, the Emperor thinking that extent of ground sufficiently liberal had him constrained to fly back again.

[1] Moor, in his Hindu Pantheon (page 352), asserts, upon, as he says, authentic information, that the *Paramahansas* eat human flesh, and that individuals of this sect are not very unusually seen about *Benares*, floating down the river, and feeding upon a corpse: it is scarcely necessary to add that he is wholly wrong: the passage he cites from the Researches is quite correct, when it describes the *Paramahansa* as an ascetic of the orthodox sects, in the last stage of exaltation; and the practice he describes, although far from usual, is sometimes heard of as a filthy exhibition displayed for profit by individuals of a very different sect, those who occupy the ensuing portion of the present text—the *Aghoris*.

tions, and is the ascetic who is solely occupied with the investigation of Brahma, or spirit, and who is equally indifferent to pleasure or pain, insensible of heat or cold, and incapable of satiety or want*.

Agreeably to this definition, individuals are sometimes met with who pretend to have attained such a degree of perfection: in proof of it they go naked in all weathers, never speak, and never indicate any natural want: what is brought to them as alms or food, by any person, is received by the attendants, whom their supposed sanctity or a confederation of interest attaches to them, and by these attandants they are fed and served on all occasions, as if they were as helpless as infants. It may be supposed that, not unfrequently, there is much knavery in this helplessness, but there are many Hindus whose simple enthusiasm induces them honestly to practice such self-denial, and there is little risk in the attempt, as the credulity of their countrymen, or rather countrywomen, will in most places take care that their wants are amply supplied. These devotees are usually included amongst the *Śaiva* ascetics; but it may be doubted whether the classification is correct.

---

* [जातरूपधरो निर्द्वन्द्वो निरायहस्तत्त्वब्रह्ममार्गे सम्यक्सम्पन्नः शुद्धमानसः प्राणसंधारणार्थं यथोक्तकाले भैक्षमाचरन्लाभालाभौ समौ कृत्वा शून्यागारदेवगृहतृणकूटवल्मीकवृक्षमूलकुलालशालाग्निहोत्रनदीपुलिनगिरिकुहरकन्दरकोटरनिकरस्थण्डिलेष्वनिकेतवासी निष्प्रयत्नो निर्ममः शुक्लध्यानपरायणो ऽध्यात्मनिष्ठः शुभाशुभकर्मनिर्मूलनाय संन्यासेन देहत्यागं करोति यः स एव परमहंसो नाम ॥ *Jîvanmuktiviveka* (Weber, Catal. p. 195) quoted in the Śabdakalpadruma s. v. Paramahansah. See also Weber, Ind. Stud. II, 77. 78. 173-6.]

AGHORÍS.

The pretended insensibility of the *Paramahansa* being of a passive nature is at least inoffensive, and even where it is mere pretence the retired nature of the practice renders the deception little conspicuous or revolting. The same profession of worldly indifference characterises the *Aghorí*, or *Aghorapanthí*; but he seeks occasions for its display, and demands alms as a reward for its exhibition.

The original *Aghorí* worship seems to have been that of *Deví* in some of her terrific forms, and to have required even human victims for its performance[1]. In imitation of the formidable aspect under which the goddess was worshipped, the appearance of her votary was rendered as hideous as possible, and his wand and water-pot were a staff set with bones and the upper half of a skull: the practices were of a similar nature, and flesh and spirituous liquors constituted, at will, the diet of the adept.

The regular worship of this sect has long since been suppressed, and the only traces of it now left are pre-

[1] It may be credulity or calumny, but the *Bhils*, and other hill tribes, are constantly accused by Sanskrit writers of the eleventh and twelfth centuries as addicted to this sanguinary worship. The *Vríhat Kathá* is full of stories to this effect, the scene of which is chiefly in the *Vindhyá* range. Its covert existence in cities is inferable from the very dramatic situation in *Bhavabhúti's Drama, Málati* and *Mádhava*, where *Mádhava* rescues his mistress from the *Aghora Ghańta*, who is about to sacrifice *Málati* at the shrine of *Chámuńdá* [Act V, p. 83].

sented by a few disgusting wretches, who, whilst they profess to have adopted its tenets, make them a mere plea for extorting alms. In proof of their indifference to worldly objects, they eat and drink whatever is given to them, even ordure and carrion. They smear their bodies also with excrement, and carry it about with them in a wooden cup, or skull, either to swallow it, if by so doing they can get a few pice; or to throw it upon the persons, or into the houses of those who refuse to comply with their demands. They also for the same purpose inflict gashes on their limbs, that the crime of blood may rest upon the head of the recusants; and they have a variety of similar disgusting devices to extort money from the timid and credulous Hindu. They are fortunately not numerous, and are universally detested and feared.

ÚRDDHABÁHUS, ÁKÁŚ MUKHÍS, and NAKHÍS.

Personal privation and torture being of great efficacy in the creed of the Hindus, various individuals, some influenced by credulity, and some by knavery, have adopted modes of distorting their limbs, and forcing them out of their natural position, until they can no longer resume their ordinary direction.

The *Úrddhabáhus*[1] extend one or both arms above their heads, till they remain of themselves thus elevated. They also close the fist, and the nails being necessarily suffered to grow make their way between

---

[1] *Úrddha*, above, and *Báhu*, the arm.

the metacarpal bones, and completely perforate the hand. The *Úrddhabáhus* are solitary mendicants, as are all of this description, and never have any fixed abode: they subsist upon alms; many of them go naked, but some wear a wrapper stained with ochre; they usually assume the *Śaiva* marks, and twist their hair so as to project from the forehead, in imitation of the *Jatá* of Śiva.

The *Ákáśmukhis*[1] hold up their faces to the sky, till the muscles of the back of the neck become contracted, and retain it in that position: they wear the *Jatá*, and allow the beard and whiskers to grow, smearing the body with ashes: some wear coloured garments: they subsist upon alms.

The *Nakhis* are of a similar description with the two preceding, but their personal characteristic is of a less extravagant nature, being confined to the length of their finger nails, which they never cut: they also live by begging, and wear the *Śaiva* marks.

GÚDARAS.

The *Gúdaras* are so named from a pan of metal which they carry about with them, and in which they have a small fire, for the purpose of burning scented woods at the houses of the persons from whom they receive alms. These alms they do not solicit further than by repeating the word *Alakh*[2], expressive of the

---

[1] *Ákáś*, the sky, and *Mukha*, the face.

[2] *A*, the negative prefix, and *Lakshma*, a mark, a distinction.

indescribable nature of the deity. They have a peculiar garb, wearing a large round cap, and a long frock or coat stained with ochery clay. Some also wear ear-rings, like the *Kánphátá Jogís*, or a cylinder of wood passed through the lobe of the ear, which they term the *Khecharí Mudrá*, the seal or symbol of the deity, of him who moves in the heavens.

RÚKHARAS, SÚKHARAS, and ÚKHARAS.

The *Súkharas* are *Śaiva* mendicants, distinguished by carrying a stick three spans in length: they dress in a cap and sort of petticoat stained with ochery earth, smear their bodies with ashes, and wear ear-rings of the *Rudráksha* seed. They also wear over the left shoulder a narrow piece of cloth dyed with ochre, and twisted, in place of the *Zannár*.

The *Rúkharas* are of similar habits and appearance, but they do not carry the stick, nor wear the *Rudráksha* ear-rings, but in their place metallic ones: these two classes agree with the preceding in the watchword, exclaiming *Alakh*, as they pass along; the term is, however, used by other classes of mendicants.

The *Úkharas* are said to be members of either of the preceding classes, who drink spirituous liquors, and eat meat: they appear to be the refuse of the three preceding mendicant classes, who, in general, are said to be of mild and inoffensive manners.

KAŔÁ LINGÍS.

These are vagabonds of little credit; except sometimes amongst the most ignorant portions of the community, they are not often met with: they go naked, and to mark their triumph over sensual desires, affix an iron ring and chain on the male organ[1]: they are professedly worshippers of Śiva.

SANNYÁSÍS, BRAHMACHÁRÍS, and AVADHÚTAS.

Although the terms *Sannyásí* and *Vairágí* are, in a great measure, restricted amongst the *Vaishńavas* to peculiar classes, the same limit can scarcely be adopted with regard to the *Śaivas*. All the sects, except the *Samyogí Atíts*, are so far *Sannyásí*, or excluded from the world, as not to admit of married teachers, a circumstance far from uncommon, as we have seen amongst the more refined followers of Vishńu. Most of the *Śaiva* sects, indeed, are of a very inferior description to those of the *Vaishńavas*.

Besides the individuals who adopt the *Dańda Grahańa*, and are unconnected with the *Daśnámís*, there is a set of devotees who remain through life members of the condition of the *Brahmachárí*, or student[2]:

---

[1] These ascetics were the persons who attracted the notice of the earlier travellers, especially Bernier and Tavernier. They were more numerous then, probably, than they are at present, and this appears to be the case with most of the mendicants who practiced on the superstitious admiration of the vulgar.

[2] The *Dírghakála Brahmacharyam*. or protracted period of studentship, is however amongst the acts enumerated in various authorities of indisputable character, as those which are prohibited in the *Kali* age.

these are also regarded as *Sannyásís*, and where the term is used in a definite sense, these twelve kinds, the *Dańďis*, *Brahmachárís*, and ten *Daśnámí* orders are implied. In general, however, the term, as well as *Avadhúta*, or *Avdhauta*, and *Alakhnámí*, express all the *Śaiva* classes of mendicants, except perhaps the *Jogís*.

NÁGAS.

The *Śaiva Sannyásís* who go naked are distinguished by this term. They smear their bodies with ashes, allow their hair, beards, and whiskers to grow, and wear the projecting braid of hair, called the *Jaťá*; like the *Vairágí Nágas*, they carry arms, and wander about in troops, soliciting alms, or levying contributions. The *Śaiva Nágas* are chiefly the refuse of the *Dańďí* and *Atít* orders, or men who have no inclination for a life of study or business: when weary of the vagrant and violent habits of the *Nága*, they re-enter the better disposed classes, which they had first quitted. The *Śaiva Nágas* are very numerous in many parts of India, though less so in the Company's provinces than in any other: they were formerly in great numbers in *Búndelkhańď*[1], and HIMMET

[1] A party of them attacked Colonel GODDARD's troops in their march between *Ďoŕaval* and *Herapur*, the assailants were no more than four or five hundred, but about two thousand hovered about the rear of the army: they are called *Pańďárams* in the narrative, but were evidently *Śaiva Nágas*. PENNANT's Hindustan, 2, 192. The Vindicator of the Hindus, speaking of

BAHÁDUR was a pupil of one of their Mahants, RÁJENDRA GÍR, one of the lapsed *Daśnámí* ascetics. These *Nágas* are the particular opponents of the *Vairágí Nágas*, and were, no doubt, the leading actors in the bloody fray at *Haridwár*[1], which had excluded the *Vaishńavas* from the great fair there, from 1760, till the British acquired the country. The leader of the *Śaiva* party was called DHOKAL GÍR, and he, as well as the spiritual guide of HIMMET BAHÁDUR, was consequently of the *Daśnámi* order, which would thus seem to be addicted to violent and war-like habits. With respect to the sanguinary affray at *Haridwár*, in which we are told eighteen thousand *Vairágis* were left dead on the field, there is a different legend current of the origin of the conflict from that given in the Researches, but neither of them is satisfactory, nor indeed is any particular cause necessary, as the opposite objects of worship, and the pride of

---

them, observes, that they often engage in the rival contests of the Indian Chiefs, and, on a critical occasion some years ago, six thousand of them joined the forces of the Mahratta Chief SINDIAH, and enabled him, with an equal number of his own troops, to discomfit an army of thirty thousand men, headed by one of his rebellious subjects.

[1] As. Res. II, 455. It may be observed, that a very accurate account is given in the same place of the general appearance and habits of the *Śaiva Sannyásis* and *Jogis*, the *Vaishńava Vairágis*, and *Udásis* of *Nának Sháh*. The term *Gosáin*, as correlative to *Sannyási*, is agreeable to common usage, but, as has been elsewhere observed, is more strictly applicable to very different characters.

strength and numbers, and consequent struggle for pre-eminence are quite sufficient to account for the dispute[1].

ŚÁKTAS.

The worshippers of the ŚAKTI, the power or energy of the divine nature in action, are exceedingly numerous amongst all classes of Hindus[2]. This active energy is, agreeably to the spirit of the mythological system, personified, and the form with which it is invested, considered as the especial object of veneration, de-

[1] The irregular practices of these and other mendicants have attracted the lash of KABÍR in the following Ramaini:

RAMAINÍ 69.

ऐसा योगी न देखा भाई।
भूल फिरै लिये गफलाई, &c.

"I never beheld such a *Jogí*, oh brother! forgetting his doctrine he roves about in negligence. He follows professedly the faith of MAHÁDEVA, and calls himself an eminent teacher; the scene of his abstraction is the fair or market. MÁYÁ is the mistress of the false saint. When did DATTÁTREYA demolish a dwelling? when did ŚUKADEVA collect an armed host? when did NÁRADA mount a matchlock? when did VYÁSADEVA blow a trumpet? In making war, the creed is violated. Is he an *Atít*, who is armed with a quiver? Is he a *Virakta*, who is filled with covetousness? His garb is put to shame by his gold ornaments; he has assembled horses and mares, is possessed of villages, is called a man of wealth; a beautiful woman was not amongst the embellishments of *Sanaka* and his brethren; he who carries with him a vessel of ink, cannot avoid soiling his raiment."

[2] It has been computed, that of the Hindus of Bengal at least three-fourths are of this sect: of the remaining fourth three parts are *Vaishńavas*, and one *Śaivas*, &c.

pends upon the bias entertained by the individuals towards the adoration of VISHŃU or ŚIVA. In the former case the personified *Śakti* is termed LAKSHMÍ, or MAHÁ LAKSHMÍ, and in the latter, PÁRVATÍ, BHAVÁNÍ, or DURGÁ. Even SARASVATÍ enjoys some portion of homage, much more than her lord, BRAHMÁ, whilst a vast variety of inferior beings of malevolent character and formidable aspect receive the worship of the multitude. The bride of ŚIVA however, in one or other of her many and varied forms, is by far the most popular emblem in Bengal and along the Ganges.

The worship of the female principle, as distinct from the divinity, appears to have originated in the literal interpretation of the metaphorical language of the *Vedas*, in which the *will or purpose to create* the universe is represented as originating from the creator, and co-existent with him as his bride, and part of himself. Thus in the *Ŕig Veda* it is said "That divine spirit breathed without afflation, single with (*Svadhá*) her who is sustained within him; other than him nothing existed. First desire was formed in his mind, and that became the original productive seed"[1], and the *Sáma Veda*, speaking of the divine cause of creation, says, "He felt not delight, being alone. He wished another, and instantly became such. He caused his own self to fall in twain, and thus became husband

[1] As. Res. VIII, 393 [Colebrooke's Essays. London: 1858, p. 17. Müller's History of Anc. Sansk. Lit., p. 560 ff. Ŕig Veda X, 129].

and wife. He approached her, and thus were human beings produced"[1]. In these passages it is not unlikely that reference is made to the primitive tradition of the origin of mankind, but there is also a figurative representation of the first indication of *wish* or *will* in the Supreme Being. Being devoid of all qualities whatever, he was alone, until he permitted the wish to be multiplied, to be generated within himself. This wish being put into action, it is said, became united with its parent, and then created beings were produced. Thus this first manifestation of divine power is termed *Ichchhárúpa*, personified desire, and the creator is designated as *Svechchhámaya*[2], united with his own will, whilst in the *Vedánta* philosophy, and the popular sects, such as that of KABÍR, and others, in which all created things are held to be illusory, the *Śakti*, or active will of the deity, is always designated

---

[1] As. Res. VIII, 420 [Colebrooke's Essays, p. 37. Bṙihad Árańy. Up. I, 4, 3].

[2] Thus, in the *Brahma Vaivartta Puráńa*, which has a whole section dedicated to the manifestations of the female principle, or a *Prakṙiti Khańda*:

एवंरूपं विभ्रद्भगवानेक एव सः ।
दिग्भिश्च नभसा सार्द्धं शून्यं विश्वं ददर्श ह ॥
आलोच्य मनसा सर्वमेकमेवासहायवान् ।
स्वेच्छया स्रष्टुमारेभे सृष्टिं स्वेच्छामयः प्रभुः ॥

"The Lord was alone invested with the Supreme form, and beheld the whole world, with the sky and regions of space, a void. Having contemplated all things in his mind, he, without any assistant, began with the will to create all things,—He, the Lord, endowed with the wish for creation."

and spoken of as *Máyá* or *Mahámáyá*, original deceit or illusion[1].

Another set of notions of some antiquity which contributed to form the character of the *Śakti*, whether general or particular, were derived from the *Sánkhya* philosophy. In this system nature, *Prakŕiti*, or *Múla Prakŕiti*, is defined to be of eternal existence and independent origin, distinct from the supreme spirit, productive though no production, and the plastic origin of all things, including even the gods. Hence *Prakŕiti* has come to be regarded as the mother of gods and men, whilst as one with matter, the source of error, it is again identified with *Máyá*, or delusion, and as co-existent with the supreme as his *Śakti*, his personified energy, or his bride[2].

---

[1] So also in the authority last quoted:

सा च ब्रह्मस्वरूपा माया नित्या सनातनी ।

"She *(Prakŕiti)* one with *Brahma* is *Máyá*, eternal, everlasting;" and in the *Kálika Puráńa*

अभिन्ना प्रकृतिर्या सा जन्तून्सम्मोहति ।

Prakŕiti is termed "Inherent *Máyá*, because she beguiles all beings."

[2] In the *Gítá* [VII, 4] *Prakŕiti* is identified with all the elementary predicates of matter:

भूमिरापो ऽनलो वायुः खं मनो बुद्धिरेव च ।
अहंकार इतीयं मे भिन्ना प्रकृतिरष्टधा ॥

"This, my *Prakŕiti*, is inherently eight-fold, or earth, water, fire, air, ether, mind, intellect, individuality."

So also the *Kúrma Puráńa* (Chapter 12):

तस्य सर्वजगन्मूर्त्तिः शक्तिर्मायेति विश्रुता ।
तदेवं भ्रामयेदीशो मायावी पुरुषोत्तमः ॥

These mythological fancies have been principally disseminated by the *Puráńas*, in all which *Prakŕiti*, or *Máyá*, bears a prominent part. The aggregate of the whole is given in the *Brahma Vaivartta Puráńa*, one section of which, the *Prakŕiti Khańda*, is devoted to the subject, and in which the legends relating to the principal modifications of the female principle are narrated.

According to this authority, BRAHMA, or the supreme being, having determined to create the universe by his super-human power, became twofold, the right half becoming a male, the left half a female, which was *Prakŕiti*. She was of one nature with BRAHMA. She was illusion, eternal and without end: as is the soul, so is its active energy; as the faculty of burning is in fire[1]. In another passage it is said, that KŔISHŃA, who is in this work identified with the Supreme, being alone invested with the divine nature, beheld all one universal blank, and contemplating creation with his

---

सैषा मायात्मिका शक्तिः सर्वाकारा सनातनी ।
विश्वरूपं महेशस्य सर्वदा संप्रकाशयेत् ॥

"His Energy, being the universal form of all the world, is called *Máyá*, for so does the Lord the best of males and endowed will illusion cause it to revolve. That *Śakti*, of which the essence is illusion, is omniform and eternal, and constantly displays the universal shape of *Mahéśa*."

[1] योगेनात्मा सृष्टिविधौ द्विधारूपो बभूव सः ।
पुमांश्च दक्षिणार्द्धाङ्गो वामार्द्धा प्रकृतिः स्मृता ॥

"He, by the power of YOGA, became himself in the act of creation two-fold; the right half was the male, the left was called *Prakŕiti*." [1, 9. See Aufrecht, Catal. I, p. 23, a.]

mental vision, he began to create all things by his own will, being united with his will, which became manifest as Múla Prakŕiti[1]. The original Prakŕiti first assumed five forms[2]—Durgá the bride, *Śakti*, and *Máyá*, of Śiva, Lakshmí the bride, *Śakti* and *Máyá* of Vishńu, Saraswatí the same of Brahmá, or in the *Brahma Vaivartta Puráńa*, of Hari, whilst the next, Sávitrí is the bride of Brahmá. The fifth division of the original *Prakŕiti*, was Rádhá, the favourite of the youthful Kŕishńa, and unquestionably a modern intruder into the Hindu Pantheon.

Besides these more important manifestations of the female principle, the whole body of goddesses and nymphs of every order are said to have sprung from the same source, and indeed every creature, whether human or brutal, of the female sex, is referred to the same principle, whilst the origin of males is ascribed to the primitive *Purusha*, or male. In every creation of the universe it is said the Múla Prakŕiti assumes the different gradations of *Anśarúpińí*, *Kalárúpińí*, *Kalánśarúpińí*[3], or manifest herself in portions, parts,

---

1 स्वेच्छामयस्येच्छया च श्रीकृष्णस्य सिसृक्षया ।
सात्विर्बभूव सहसा मूलप्रकृतिरीश्वरी ॥

"From the wish which was the creative impulse of *Śrí Kŕishńa*, endowed with his will, she, *Múla Prakŕiti*, the Supreme, became manifest." [ibid. śl. 12.]

2 तदाज्ञया पञ्चविधा सृष्टिकर्मविभेदतः ।

"And she (the *Múla Prakŕiti*,) became in the act of creation five-fold by the will of the Supreme." [śl. 13.]

3 अंशरूपा कलारूपा कलांशांशस्य सम्भवा ।
प्रकृतेः प्रति विश्वेषु देव्याश्च दिव्ययोगिनः ॥

and portions of parts, and further subdivisions. The chief *Anśas* are, besides the five already enumerated, GANGÁ, TULASÍ, MANASÁ, SHASHṪHÍ, or DEVASENÁ, MANGALACHAŃḊIKÁ, and KÁLÍ*; the principal *Kalás* are SWÁHÁ, SWADHÁ, DAKSHIŃÁ, SWASTI, PUSHṪI, TUSHṪI, and others, most of which are allegorical personifications, as *Dhŕiti*, Fortitude, *Pratishṫhá*, Fame, and *Adharma*, Wickedness, the bride of *Mŕityu*, or Death. ADITI, the mother of the Gods, and DITI, the mother of the Demons, are also *Kalás* of PRAKŔITI. The list includes all the secondary goddesses. The *Kalánśas* and *Anśánśas*, or sub-divisions of the more important manifestations, are all womankind, who are distinguished as good, middling, or bad, according as they derive their being from the parts of their great original in which the *Satya*, *Rajas*, and *Tamo Guńa*, or property of goodness, passion, and vice predominates. At the same time as manifestations of the great cause of all they are entitled to respect, and even to veneration: whoever, says the *Brahma Vaivartta Puráńa*, offends or insults a female, incurs the wrath of PRAKŔITI, whilst he who propitiates a female, particularly the youthful daughter of a *Brahman*, with clothes, ornaments and perfumes, offers worship to PRAKŔITI herself. It is in the spirit of this last doctrine

---

"In every creation of the universe the *Deví*, through divine *Yoga*, assumes different forms, and becomes *Anśarúpá*, *Kalárúpá*, and *Kalánśarúpá*, or *Anśánśarúpá*."

* [and VASUNDHARÁ. See Aufrecht, l. l., p. 23, b.]

that one of the principal rites of the *Śáktas* is the actual worship of the daughter or wife of a *Brahman*, and leads with one branch of the sect at least to the introduction of gross impurities. But besides this derivation of PRAKṘITI, or ŚAKTI, from the Supreme, and the secondary origin of all female nature from her, those who adopt her as their especial divinity employ the language invariably addressed towards the preferential object of worship in every sect, and contemplate her as comprising all existence in her essence. Thus she is not only declared to be one with the male deity, of whose energy some one of her manifestations is the type, as DEVÍ with ŚIVA, and LAKSHMÍ with VISHṄU; but it is said, that she is equally in all things, and that all things are in her, and that besides her there is nothing[1].

Although the adoration of PRAKṘITI or ŚAKTI is, to a certain extent, authorised by the *Puráńas*, particu-

---

[1] Thus in the *Káśí Khańda*:

सर्वमन्त्रमयी त्वं ब्रह्माद्यास्त्वत्समुद्भवाः ।
चतुर्वर्गात्मकी त्वं वै चतुर्वर्गफलोदया ॥
त्वत्तः सर्वमिदं विश्वं त्वयि सर्वं जगन्निधे ।
यद्दृश्यं यददृश्यञ्च स्थूलसूक्ष्मस्वरूपतः ॥
यत्तत्त्वं शक्तिरूपेण किञ्चिन्न त्वदृते क्वचित् ।

"Thou art predicated in every prayer—*Brahmá* and the rest are all born from thee. Thou art one with the four objects of life, and from thee they come to fruit. From thee this whole universe proceeds, and in thee, asylum of the world, all is, whether visible or invisible, gross or subtle in its nature: what is, thou art in the *Śakti* form, and except thee nothing has ever been."

larly the *Brahma Vaivartta*, the *Skanda*, and the *Kálikâ*, yet the principal rites and formulæ are derived from an independent series of works known by the collective term of *Tantras*. These are infinitely numerous, and in some instances of great extent; they always assume the form of a dialogue between Śiva and his bride, in one of her many forms, but mostly as Umá and Párvatí, in which the goddess questions the god as to the mode of performing various ceremonies, and the prayers and incantations to be used in them. These he explains at length, and under solemn cautions that they involve a great mystery on no account whatever to be divulged to the profane.

The followers of the *Tantras* profess to consider them as a fifth *Veda*, and attribute to them equal antiquity and superior authority[1]. The observances they prescribe have, indeed, in Bengal almost superseded the original ritual. The question of their date is in-

---

[1] Thus, in the *Śiva Tantra*, Śiva is made to say:

मम पञ्चमुखेभ्यश्च पञ्चाम्नाया विनिर्गताः ।
पूर्वश्च पश्चिमश्चैव दक्षिणश्चोत्तरस्तथा ॥
ऊर्द्धाम्नायश्च पञ्चैते मोक्षमार्गाः प्रकीर्त्तिताः ।
आम्नाया बहवः सन्ति ऊर्द्धाम्नायेन नो समाः ॥

[See Aufrecht, Catal. I, p. 91.]

"The five Scriptures issued from my five mouths, and were the east, west, south, north, and upper. These five are known as the paths to final liberation. There are many Scriptures, but none are equal to the Upper Scripture." *Kullúka Bhaṭṭa*, commenting on the first verse of the second chapter of *Manu*, says: the *Śruti* is two-fold—*Vaidika* and *Tántrika*:

श्रुतिश्च द्विविधा वैदिकी तान्त्रिकी च ॥

volved in considerable obscurity. From the practices described in some of the *Puráńas*, particularly that of the *Díkshá* or rite of initiation, in the *Agni Púráńa*, from the specification of formulæ comprising the mystical monosyllables of the *Tántras* in that and other similar compilations, and from the citation of some of them by name in different *Pauráńic* works[1], we must conclude that some of the *Tantras* are prior to those authorities. But the date of the *Puráńas* themselves is far from determined, and whilst some parts of them may be of considerable antiquity, other portions of most, if not of all, are undoubtedly subsequent to the tenth century of the Christian era. It is not unlikely, however, that several of the *Tantras* are of earlier composition, especially as we find the system they inculcate included by ÁNANDAGIRI, in his life of ŚANKARÁCHÁRYA, amongst the heterodoxies which that Legislator succeeded in confuting. On the other hand there appears no indication of *Tántrika* notions in the

---

[1] As in the *Kúrma Puráńa* the *Kapála*, *Bhairava*, *Váma* and *Yámala*, and the *Páncharátra* in the *Varáha*: we have also a number mentioned in the *Śankara Vijaya*, of both *Ánandagiri* and *Mádhava*, as the *Śiva Gítá*, *Śiva Sanhitá*, *Rudra Yámala*, and *Śiva Rahasya*. It is also said in *Ánandagiri*'s work, that the *Bráhmańas* were cursed by *Gáyatri*, to become *Tántrikas* in the *Kali* age:

वेदोक्तकर्महीनाश्च तान्त्रिकाचारतत्पराः ।
यूयं कलौ भवन्त्वेवमिति तानाह सा रुषा ॥

"She being angry said to them: in the *Kali* age, after abandoning the *Veda* ritual, become followers of the *Tántrika* observances."

Mahábhárat, and the name of *Tantra,* in the sense of a religious text book, does not occur in the vocabulary of AMARA SINHA. It may therefore be inferred, that the system originated at some period in the early centuries of Christianity, being founded on the previous worship of the female principle, and the practices of the *Yoga* with the *Mantras*, or mystical formulæ of the *Vedas.* It is equally certain that the observances of the *Tantras* have been carried to more exceptionable extremes in comparatively modern times; and that many of the works themselves are of recent composition. They appear also to have been written chiefly in Bengal and the Eastern districts, many of them being unknown in the West and South of India, and the rites they teach having there failed to set aside the ceremonies of the *Vedas*, although they are not without an important influence upon the belief and the practices of the people.

The *Tantras* are too numerous to admit in this place of their specification, but the principal are the *Śyámá Rahasya*, *Rudra Yámala*, *Mantra Mahodadhi*, *Śáradá Tilaka*, and *Káliká Tantra,* whilst the *Kula-chúḋámańi*, *Kulárnava*, and similar works, are the chief authorities of one portion of the *Śáktas,* the sect being divided into two leading branches, the *Dakshińácháris* and *Vámácháris*, or followers of the right hand and left hand ritual.

DAKSHIŃAS, or BHÁKTAS.

When the worship of any goddess is performed in

a public manner, and agreeably to the *Vaidik* or *Pauráńic* ritual[1], it does not comprehend the impure practices which are attributed to a different division of the adorers of Śakti, and which are particularly prescribed to the followers of this system. In this form it is termed the *Dakshińa*, or right hand form of worship[2]. The only observance that can be supposed to form an exception to the general character of this mode is the *Bali*, an offering of blood, in which rite a number of helpless animals, usually kids, are annually decapitated. In some cases life is offered without shedding blood, when the more barbarous practice is adopted of pummelling with the fists the poor animal to death: at other times blood only is offered without injury to life. These practices, however, are not considered as orthodox, and approach rather to the ritual

---

[1] The peculiarities of this sect are described in the *Dakshińáchára Tantra Rája*, a modern summary of the system, by *Káśináth*: according to this authority:

दक्षिणाचारतन्त्रोक्तं कर्म तच्छुद्धं वैदिकम् ।

"The ritual declared in the *Tantras* of the *Dakshińáchâras* is pure and conformable to the *Vedas.*"

[2] वामागमो मदुक्तोऽयं सर्वशूद्रपरः प्रिये ।
ब्राह्मणो मदिरादानाद्ब्राह्मण्येन वियुज्यते ॥
न कर्त्तव्यं न कर्त्तव्यं न कर्त्तव्यं कदाचन ।
इदं तु साहसं देवि न कर्त्तव्यं कदाचन ॥

"The *Váma* ritual, although declared by me, was intended for *Śúdras* only. A *Brahman*, from receiving spirituous liquor, forfeits his Brahmanical character—let it not be done—let it not ever be done. Goddess, it is brutality, never let it be practiced."

of the *Vámáchárís*[1], the more pure *Bali* consisting of edible grain, with milk and sugar. Animal victims are also offered to Deví, in her terrific forms only, as Kálí or Durgá. The worship is almost confined to a few districts; and, perhaps, is carried to no great extent.

Although any of the goddesses may be objects of the *Śákta* worship, and the term *Śakti* comprehends them all, yet the homage of the *Śáktas* is almost restricted to the wife of Śiva, and to Śiva himself as identified with his consort[2]. The sect is in fact a ra-

---

1 द्विविधबलिराख्यातो राजसः सात्त्विको बुधैः।
राजसो मांसरक्ताद्यं पलत्रयसमन्वितः॥
मुद्गपायससंयुक्तो मधुरत्रयलोलितः।
ब्राह्मणो नियतः शुद्धः सात्त्विकं बलिमाहरेत्॥

"The *Bali* is of two kinds, *Rájasa* and *Sáttvika*; the first consists of meat, and includes the three kinds of flesh; the second of pulse and rice-milk, with the three sweet articles, (ghee, honey, and sugar,) let the *Brahman*, always pure, offer only the *Sáttvika Bali.*"

The *Brahmavaivartta* also observes: "The animal sacrifices, it is true, gratify Durgá; but they, at the same time, subject the sacrificer to the sin which attaches to the destroyer of animal life. It is declared by the *Vedas*, that he who slays an animal is hereafter slain by the slain."

2 शिवशक्तिमयं रूपं सम्पूज्यं साधकोत्तमैः॥
यस्तु सम्पूजयेच्छक्तिं शिवं नैव प्रपूजयेत्।
स एव पातकी रोगी मान्त्रिको दुर्गतिर्भवेत्॥

"The joint form of Śiva and Śakti is to be worshipped by the virtuous. Whoever adores Śakti, and offers not adoration to Śiva, that *Mántrika* is diseased: he is a sinner, and hell will be his portion." For it appears that some of the *Śáktas* elevate

mification from the common *Śaiva* stock, and is referred to ŚIVA himself as its institutor. In the *Tantras*, as has been noticed, he appears as its professor, expounding to PÁRVATÍ the mantras, tenets, and observances of the *Śákta* worship, whether of the right or left hand description.

The worship of DEVÍ, thus naturally resulting from the works on which the *Śákta* doctrines are founded, is one of considerable antiquity and popularity. Laying aside all uncertain and fabulous testimony, the adoration of *Vindhyá Vásini*, near *Mirzapur*[1], has existed for more than seven centuries, and that of *Jválámukhi at Nagarkot* very early attracted Mohammedan persecution[2]. These places still retain their reputation, and are the objects of pilgrimage to devout Hindus. On the eighth of the dark fortnight of *Chaitra* and

---

the ŚAKTI above the ŚAKTIMÁN, or deity: thus the *Vámis*, in the *Śankara Vijaya*, say:

शक्तिः शिवस्य बलकारिणी तया विना तस्य तृणचलनक्रियाया-
मसमर्थत्वात्। अतः शक्तिरेव शिवस्य कारणं।

"ŚAKTI gives strength to ŚIVA, without her he could not stir a straw. She is, therefore, the cause of ŚIVA."

नित्यपदार्थयोर्मध्ये शक्तेरधिकत्वं।

And again: "of the two objects which are eternal the greater is the ŚAKTI."

[1] It is freqnently mentioned in the *Vrihat Kathá*; the age of which work is ascertained to be about seven centuries. *Nagarkot* was taken by FIROZ the 3d, in 1360 (Dow 2, 55), at which time the goddess *Jválámukhi* was then worshipped there.

[2] For a full account of both the work of Mr. WARD may be advantageously consulted—II, 89 to 96, and 125 to 131.

Kártik in particular a numerous assemblage of pilgrims takes place at them.

The adoration of Kálí, or Durgá, is however particularly prevalent in Bengal, and is cultivated with practices scarcely known in most other provinces. Her great festival, the *Daśahará*, is in the West of India marked by no particular honors, whilst its celebration in Bengal occupies ten days of prodigal expenditure. This festival, the *Durgá Pújá*, is now well known to Europeans, as is the extensive and popular establishment near Calcutta, the temple of Kálí at *Kálí Ghát*. The rites observed in that place, and at the *Durgá Pújá*, however, almost place the *Bengali Śáktas* amongst the *Vámácháris*, notwithstanding the rank assigned them in the *Dakshiṅáchári Tantrarája*, which classes the *Gauras* with the *Keralas* and *Kashmirians*, as the three principal divisions of the purer worshippers of Śakti.

VÁMÍS, or VÁMÁCHÁRÍS.

The *Vámís* mean the left hand worshippers, or those who adopt a ritual contrary to that which is usual, and to what indeed they dare publicly avow[1]. They worship Deví, the *Śakti* of Śiva, but all the goddesses,

---

[1] The following verse is from the *Śyámá Rahasya*:

अन्तश्शाक्ता वहिश्शैवाः सभायां वैष्णवा मताः ।
नानारूपधराः कौला विचरन्ति महीतले ॥

"Inwardly *Śáktas*, outwardly *Śaivas*, or in society nominally *Vaishṅavas*, the *Kaulas* assuming various forms, traverse the earth."

as Lakshmí, Sarasvatí, the *Mátris*, the *Náyikás*, the *Yoginis*, and even the fiend-like *Ḋákinis* and *Śákinís*, are admitted to a share of homage. With them, as well as with the preceding sect, Śiva is also an object of veneration, especially in the form of Bhairava, with which modification of the deity it is the object of the worshipper to identify himself[1].

The worship of the *Vámácháris* is derived from a portion of the *Tantras*: it resolves itself into various subjects, apparently into different sects, of which that of the *Kaula*, or *Kulína*, is declared to be pre-eminent[2]. The object of the worship is, by the reverence of Deví or Śakti, who is one with Śiva, to obtain supernatural

---

1 भैरवो ऽहमिति ज्ञात्वा सर्वज्ञो ऽहं गुणान्वितः।
इति सञ्चिन्त्य योगीन्द्रः कुलपूजां समाचरेत्॥

"I am *Bhairava*, I am the omniscient, endowed with qualities. Having thus meditated, let the devotee proceed to the *Kula* worship."—*Śyámá Rahasya*.

2 सर्वेभ्यश्चोत्तमा वेदा वेदेभ्यो वैष्णवं परं।
वैष्णवादुत्तमं शैवं शैवाद्दक्षिणमुत्तमं॥
दक्षिणादुत्तमं वामं वामात्सिद्धान्तमुत्तमं।
सिद्धान्तादुत्तमं कौलं कौलात्परतरं न हि॥

"The *Vedas* are pre-eminent over all works, the *Vaishńava* sect excels the *Vedas*, the *Śaiva* sect is preferable to that of Vishńu, and the right hand Śákta to that of Śiva—the left hand is better than the right hand division, and the *Siddhánta* is better still—the *Kaula* is better than the *Sidhhánta*, and there is none better than it."—*Kulárńava*. The words *Kaula* and *Kulina* are both derivatives from *Kula*, family; and the latter is especially applied to imply of good or high family: these terms have been adopted to signify, that those who follow this doctrine are not only of one, but of an exalted race.

powers in this life, and to be identified after death with Śiva and Śakti.

According to the immediate object of the worshipper is the particular form of worship; but all the forms require the use of some or all of the five *Makáras*[1], *Mánsa, Matsya, Madya, Maithuna,* and *Mudrá,* flesh, fish, wine, women, and certain mystical gesticulations. Suitable *Mantras* are also indispensable, according to the end proposed, consisting of various unmeaning monosyllable combinations of letters of great imaginary efficacy[2].

---

[1] They are thus enumerated in the *Śyámá Rahasya*:

मद्यं मांसञ्च मत्स्यञ्च मुद्रा मैथुनमेव च ।
मकारपञ्चकञ्चैव महापातकनाशनम् ॥

"Wine, flesh, fish, *Mudrá,* and *Maithuna,* are the five-fold *Makára,* which takes away all sin." [See also Práńatoshańí, Calc. edition, p. 277, a.]

[2] Many specimens might be given, but one will be here sufficient. It is the combination H and S as हस, and is one of the very few to which any meaning is attempted to be given: it is called the *Prásáda Mantra,* and its virtues and import are thus described in the *Kulárńava* [chapter 3]:

श्रीप्रासादपरामन्त्रमूर्ध्वाम्नायप्रतिष्ठितम् ।
आवयोः परमाकारं यो वेत्ति सः शिवः स्वयम् ॥
शिवादिक्रिमिपर्यन्तं प्राणिनां प्राणवर्तनाम् ।
निश्वासोच्छ्वासरूपेण मन्त्रोऽयं वर्त्तते प्रिये ॥

"He who knows the excellent *Prásáda Mantra,* that was promulgated by the fifth *Veda,* (the *Tantras*) and which is the supreme form of us both, he is himself Śiva: this *Mantra* is present in all beings that breathe, from Śiva to a worm, and exists in states of expiration and inspiration." The letter H is the expirated, and S the inspirated letter, and as these two acts constitute life, the *Mantra* they express is the same with life: the

Where the object of the ceremony is to acquire an interview with and control over impure spirits, a dead body is necessary. The adept is also to be alone, at midnight, in a cemetery or place where bodies are burnt or buried, or criminals executed: seated on the corpse he is to perform the usual offerings, and if he does so without fear, the *Bhútas*, the *Yoginís*, and other male or female goblins become his slaves.

In this, and many of the observances practiced, solitude is enjoined; but all the principal ceremonies comprehend the worship of ŚAKTI, and require for that purpose the presence of a female as the living representative and the type of the goddess. This worship is mostly celebrated in a mixed society, the men of which represent *Bhairavas* or *Víras*, and the women *Bhairavís* and *Náyikás*. The ŚAKTI is personated by a naked female, to whom meat and wine are offered, and then distributed amongst the assistants, the recitation of various *Mantras* and texts, and the performance of the *Mudrá*, or gesticulations with the fingers, accompanying the different stages of the ceremony, and it is terminated with the most scandalous

---

animated world would not have been formed without it, and exists but as long as it exists, and it is an integral part of the universe, without being distinct from it, as the fragrance of flowers, and sweetness of sugar, oil of Sesamum seed, and ŚAKTI of ŚIVA. He who knows it needs no other knowledge —he who repeats it need practice no other act of adoration. The authority quoted contains a great deal more to the same purpose.

orgies amongst the votaries[1]. The ceremony is entitled the *Śrí Chakra*, or *Púrńábhisheka*, the Ring, or Full Initiation.

---

[1] It might have been sufficient to have given this general statement, or even to have referred to the similar but fuller account of Mr. Ward: his information was however merely oral, and may therefore be regarded as unsatisfactory; and as it seems to be necessary to show that the charge is not altogether unfounded, I shall subjoin the leading rites of the *Śakti Śodhana*, or *Śrí Chakra*, as they are prescribed in the *Deví Rahasya*, a section of the *Rudra Yámala*.

ŚAKTI ŚODHANA.

The object of the ceremony should be either:

नटी कपालिनी वेश्या रजकी नापिताङ्गना।
ब्राह्मणी शूद्रकन्या च तथा गोपालकन्यका॥
मालाकारस्य कन्याऽपि नवकन्याः प्रकीर्त्तिताः।
एतासु कांचिदानीय पूजयेच्[छक्ति]कौलिकः॥

[The *Práńatoshańí* in which (p. 300, b) the first 3 lines are quoted has instead of the fourth line the following:

विशेषवैदग्ध्ययुताः सर्व्वैव कुलाङ्गनाः॥
रूपयौवनसम्पन्ना शीलसौभाग्यशालिनी।
पूजनीया प्रयत्नेन ततः सिद्धिर्भवेद्ध्रुवम्॥]

"A dancing girl, a female devotee, a harlot, a washerwoman, or barber's wife, a female of the *Bráhmańical* or *Śúdra* tribe, a flower girl, or a milk maid." It is to be performed ad midnight, with a party of eight, nine, or eleven couple, as the *Bhairavas* and *Bhairavis*.

महानिशायामानीय नवकन्याश्च भैरवान्।
एकादश नवाष्टौ वा कौलिकः कौलिकेश्वरि।
शोधयेन्नवभिर्मन्त्रैः पूजयेत्कौलिकोत्तमः॥

Appropriate Mantras are to be used, according to the description of the person selected for the *Śakti*, who is then to be worshipped, according to prescribed form: she is placed disrobed, but richly ornamented, on the left of a circle *(Chakra)* described

The occurrence of these impurities is certainly countenanced by the texts, which the sects regard as

---

for the purpose, with various *Mantras* and gesticulations, and is to be rendered pure by the repetition of different formulas.

तदीयं मन्त्रमालिख्य तस्मिन्तामेव पूजयेत् ।
श्रीचक्रे स्थापयेद्वामे कन्यां भैरववल्लभाम् ॥
मुक्तकेशां वीतलज्जां सर्वाभरणभूषिताम् ।
आनन्दलीनहृदयां सौन्दर्यातिमनोहराम् ॥
शोधयेच्छुद्धिमन्त्रेण सुरानन्दामृताम्बुभिः ।

Being finally sprinkled over with wine, the act being sanctified by the peculiar *Mantra*,

मन्त्रेणानेन देवेशि कामिनीमभिषिञ्चयेत् ॥

The *Śakti* is now purified, but if not previously initiated, she is to be further made an adept by the communication of the radical *Mantra* whispered thrice in her ear, when the object of the ceremony is complete:

एवं शोधनमन्त्रास्ते संवर्णिताः पृथग्मया ।
योनौ जपेत्कुमारीणां कौलिकः करमालया ॥
सञ्जप्य दक्षकर्णे च मूलमन्त्रं त्रिरुच्चरेत् ।
अदीक्षिता ऽपि देवेशि दीक्षितैव भवेत्तदा ॥
दीक्षितां शोधितो वीरो भवेत्सर्वार्थसिद्धये ।

The finale is what might be anticipated, but accompanied throughout with *Mantras* and forms of meditation suggesting notions very foreign to the scene.

आनन्दतर्पितां कान्तां वीरः स्वानन्दविग्रहः ।
रतेन तर्पयेत्तत्र श्रीचक्रे वीरसंसदि ॥
पठन्प्रणवमुद्धृत्य मन्त्रराजं कुलेश्वरि ।
धर्माधर्महविर्दीप्ते स्वात्मा ऽग्नौ मनसा स्रुचा ॥
सुषुम्णा वर्त्मना नित्यमक्षवृत्तीर्जुहोम्यहम् ।
स्वाहान्तं मन्त्रमुच्चार्य जपमूलं स्मरन्परम् ॥
कुर्यान्निधुवनं मन्त्री मन्त्रसिद्धिमवाप्नुयात् ।
रतान्ते संजपेन्मूलं पठेन्मन्त्रमिदं पुनः ॥
तारद्वयान्तरगतं परमानन्दकारणम् ।
ओं प्रकाशाकाशहस्ताभ्यामवलम्ब्योन्मनी स्रुचा ॥

authorities, and by a very general belief of their occurrence. The members of the sect are enjoined secrecy, which, indeed, it might be supposed they would observe on their own account, and, consequently, will not acknowledge their participation in such scenes. They will not, indeed, confess that they are of the *Śákta* sect, although their reserve in this respect is said, latterly, to be much relaxed. It is contrary, however, to all knowledge of the human character, to admit the possibility of these transactions in their fullest extent; and, although the worship of the Śakti, according to the above outline, may be sometimes performed, yet there can be little doubt of its being practiced but seldom, and then in solitude and secrecy. In truth, few of the ceremonies, there is reason to believe, are ever observed; and, although the *Chakra* is said to be not uncommon, and by some of the zeallous *Śáktas* it is scarcely concealed, it is usually nothing more than a convivial party, consisting of the members of a single family, or at which men only are assembled, and the company are glad to eat flesh and drink spirits[1], under the pretence of a religious ob-

---

धर्माधर्मकलास्नेहपूर्णं वह्नौ जुहोम्यहम् ।
स्वाहान्ते वायुमन्त्रेण शुक्रमादाय पार्वति ॥
श्रीचक्रे तर्पयेद्देवि ततः सिद्धिमवाप्नुयात् ।
सम्पूज्य कान्तां संतर्प्य स्तुत्वा नत्वा परस्परम् ॥
संहारसन्धया मन्त्री शक्तिवीरान्विसर्जयेत् ।

[1] The zeal that is prescribed might suit some more civilized associations:

servance. In justice to the doctrines of the sect, it is to be observed that these practices, if instituted merely for sensual gratification, are held to be as illicit and reprehensible as in any other branch of the Hindu faith[1].

पीत्वा पीत्वा पुनः पीत्वा यावल्लुठति भूतले ।
उत्थाय च पुनः पीत्वा पुनर्जन्म न विद्यते ॥

Let him pledge the wine cup again and again,
Till he measures his length on the ground.
Let him rise and once more the goblet drain,
And with freedom for aye, from a life of pain,
Shall the glorious feat be crowned.

[1] The *Kulárńava* has the following and many similar passages; they occur constantly in other *Tantras*:

बहवः कौलिकं धर्मं मिथ्याज्ञानविडम्बकाः ।
स्वबुद्ध्या कलयन्तीत्थं पारम्पर्यविवर्जिताः ॥
मद्यपानेन मनुजा यदि सिद्धिं लभन्ति तत् ।
मद्यपानरताः सर्वे सिद्धिं यान्ति समीहिताम् ॥
मांसभक्षणमात्रेण यदि पुण्यगतिर्भवेत् ।
लोके मांसाशिनः सर्वे पुण्यवन्तो भवन्ति किम् ॥
स्त्रीसम्भोगेन देवेशि यदि मोक्षं व्रजन्ति तत् ।
सर्वेऽपि जन्तवो लोके मुक्ताः स्युः स्त्रीनिषेवनात् ।
कुलमार्गयुतो देवि न मया निन्दितः क्वचित् ।
आचाररहिता यत्र निन्दितास्ते न चेतरे ॥
कुलद्रव्याणि सेव्यन्ते येऽन्यदर्शनमाश्रिताः ।
तदङ्गरोमप्रमाणं पुनर्जन्म भविष्यति ॥

"Many false pretenders to knowledge, and who have not been duly initiated, pretend to practice the *Kaula* rites; but if perfection be obtained by drinking wine, independently of my commands, then every drunkard is a saint: if virtue consist in eating flesh, then every carnivorous animal in the world is virtuous: if eternal happiness be derived from sexual intercourse, then all beings will be entitled to it: a follower of the *Kula* doctrine is blameless in my sight, if he reproves those of other

The followers are considered as very numerous, especially amongst the Brahmanical tribe: all classes are however admissible, and are equal and alike at the ceremonies of the sect. In the world[1] they resume their characteristic distinctions, and wear the sectarial marks, and usually adopt the outward worship of any other division, whether orthodoxical or heretical. When they assume particular insignia, they are a semi-circular line or lines on the forehead, of red saunders or vermillion, or a red streak up the middle of the forehead, with a circular spot of red at the root of the nose. They use a rosary of *Rudráksha*

---

creeds who quit their established observances—those of other sects who use the articles of the *Kaula* worship, shall be condemned to repeated generations as numerous as the hairs of the body."—In fact, the texts of *Manu* are taken as authorities for the penance to be performed for the crimes of touching, smelling, looking at, or tasting the forbidden articles, except upon religious occasions, and when they are consecrated by the appropriate texts.

It is only to be added, that if the promulgators of these doctrines were sincere, which is far from impossible, they must have been filled with a strange phrenzy, and have been strangely ignorant of human nature.

1 प्रवृत्ते भैरवीतन्त्रे सर्वे वर्णा द्विजोत्तमाः।
निवृत्ते भैरवीतन्त्रे सर्वे वर्णाः पृथक्पृथक् ॥

"Whilst the *Bhairavi Tantra* is proceeding, all castes are *Brahmans*—when it is concluded, they are again distinct." *Śyámá Rahasya.* According to Ward, such of them as avow their creed, leading at the same time a mendicant life, are termed *Vyaktávadhútas,* or they who are openly free from restraints: those who conceal their creed and observe its practices in privacy are termed *Guptávadhútas,* the liberated in secret. II, 296.

seeds, or of coral beads, but of no greater length than may be concealed in the hand, or they keep it in a small purse, or a bag of red cloth. In worshipping they wear a piece of red silk round the loins, and decorate themselves with garlands of crimson flowers.

KÁNCHULÍYAS.

This is a sect of which the existence may be questioned, notwithstanding the assertion that it is not uncommon in the South of India. The worship is that of Śakti, and the practices are similar to those of the *Kaulas*, or *Vámácháris*. It is said to be distinguished by one peculiar rite, the object of which is to confound all the ties of female alliance, and to enforce not only a community of women amongst the votaries, but disregard even to natural restraints. On occasions of worship the female votaries are said to deposit their upper vests* in a box in charge of the *Guru*. At the close of the usual rites the male worshippers take each a vest from the box, and the female to whom the garment appertains, be she ever so nearly of kin to him, is the partner for the time of his licentious pleasures[1].

* [Called *Kanchuli* in Tamil; hence the name of the sect.]

[1] This sect appears in the *Śankara Vijaya*, as the *Uchchhishṭa Gaṅapati*, or *Hairamba* sect, who declare that all men and all women are of one caste, and that their intercourse is free from fault. पुरुषाणां सर्वजातिकानामेकजातिवद्दित्येको धर्मः स्त्रीणां सर्वजातिकानामेकजातिवद्दित्येको धर्मः। तासाञ्च तेषाञ्च संयोगे वियोगे च दोषाभावः।

KARÁRÍ.

The *Karárí* is the worshipper of DEVÍ, in her terrific forms, and is the representative of the *Aghora Ghańta* and *Kápálika*[1], who as lately only as seven or eight centuries ago, there is reason to suppose, sacrificed human victims to KÁLÍ, CHÁMUŃDÁ, CHHINNAMASTAKÁ, and other hideous personifications of the *Śakti* of ŚIVA. The attempt to offer human beings in the present day, is not only contrary to every known ritual, but it would be attended with too much peril to be practiced, and consequently it cannot be believed that this sect is in existence: the only votaries, if any there be, consisting of the miscreants who, more for

---

The same sort of story is told, but apparently with great injustice, of the Mohammedan *Vyavaháris* or *Bohras*, and of a less known Mohammedan sect, the *Chiraghkesh*: something of the same kind was imputed to the early Christians by their adversaries.

[1] The following description of the *Kápálika* is from the *Śankara Vijaya* of *Ánandagiri*:

चितिभस्मपूर्णकलेवरो नरकपालमालावृतगलः फालदेशरचितकज्जलरेखः सकलकेशरचितजटापारिर्व्याघ्रचर्मरचितकटिसूत्रकौपीनः कपालशोभितवामकरः सहनादघण्टाधृतदक्षिणकरः शम्भो भैरव अहो कालीश इति मुहुर्मुहुर्जपन् ।

"His body is smeared with ashes from a funeral pile, around his neck hangs a string of human skulls, his forehead is streaked with a black line, his hair is wove into the matted braid, his loins are clothed with a tiger's skin, a hollow skull is in his left hand (for a cup), and in his right he carries a bell, which he rings incessantly, exclaiming aloud, Ho, *Śambhu*, *Bhairava*— ho lord of *Káli*." [See also Prabodhachandr., ed. Brockhaus, Act III, p. 53, v. 10.]

pay than devotion, inflict upon themselves bodily tortures, and pierce their flesh with hooks or spits, run sharp pointed instruments through their tongues and cheeks, recline upon beds of spikes, or gash themselves with knives, all which practices are occasionally met with throughout India, and have become familiar to Europeans from the excess to which they are carried in Bengal at the *Charak Pújá*, a festival which, as a public religious observance, is unknown anywhere else, and which is not directed nor countenanced by any of the authorities of the Hindus, not even by the *Tantras*.

MISCELLANEOUS SECTS.

The sects that have been described are those of the regular system, and particularly of what may be called Brahmanical Hinduism, emanating, more or less directly, from the doctrines of the original creed. Besides these there are a number which it is not so easy to class, although they are mostly referable to a common source, and partake, in many respects, of the same notions, especially of those of a *Vaishńava* and *Vedánta* tendency. They exist in various degrees of popularity, and date from various periods, and in most instances owe their institution to enthusiastic or contemplative individuals, whose biography is yet preserved consistenly enough by tradition.

This is not the case, however, with the first two on the list—the *Saurapátas* and *Gáńapátas*: these are usually, indeed, ranked with the preceding divisions, and make with the *Vaishńavas*, *Śaivas*, and *Śáktas* the five orthodox divisions of the Hindus: they are of limited extent and total insignificance.

SAURAPÁTAS, or SAURAS.

The *Saurapátas* are those who worship Súryapati, the Sun-god, only; there are a few of them, but very few, and they scarcely differ from the rest of the Hindus in their general observances. The *Tilaka*, or frontal mark, is made in a particular manner, with red sandal, and the necklace should be of crystal: these are their chief peculiarities: besides which they eat one meal without salt on every Sunday, and each *Sankránti*, or the sun's entrance into a sign of the Zodiac: they cannot eat either until they have beheld the sun, so that it is fortunate that they inhabit his native regions.

GÁŃAPATYAS.

These are worshippers of Gańeśa, or Gańapati, and can scarcely be considered as a distinct sect: all the Hindus, in fact, worship this deity as the obviator of difficulties and impediments, and never commence any work, or set off on a journey, without invoking his protection. Some, however, pay him more particular devotion than the rest, and these are the only persons to whom the classification may be considered applicable. Gańeśa however, it is believed, is never exclusively venerated, and the worship, when it is paid, is addressed to some of his forms, particularly those of *Vaktratuńda* and *Ďhúńdhiráj*.

NÁNAK SHÁHÍS.

A sect of much greater importance is that which originated with Nának Sháh, and which, from bearing at first only a religious character, came, in time, to be a political and national distinction, through the influence of Mohammedan persecution and individual ambition. The enterprising policy of Govind Sinh and the bigotry of Aurangzeb converted the peaceful tenets of Nának into a military code, and his speculative disciples into the warlike nation of the *Śikhs*. It is not, however, in their political capacity that we are now to consider them, but as the professors of a peculiar form of faith, which branches into various sub-divisions, and is by no means restricted to the *Punjáb*. At the same time it is unnecessary to detail the tenets and practices of the *Śikhs*, as that has been already performed in a full and satisfactory manner.

The *Śikhs*, or *Nának Sháhis*, are classed under seven distinctions, all recognising *Nának* as their primitive instructor, and all professing to follow his doctrines, but separated from each other by variations of practice, or by a distinct and peculiar teacher. Of these the first is the sect of the *Udásis*.

UDÁSÍS.

These may be regarded as the genuine disciples of *Nának*, professing, as the name denotes, indifference to worldly vicissitudes. They are purely religious characters devoting themselves to prayer and meditation, and usually collected in *Sangats,* colleges or convents; they also travel about to places of pilgrimage, generally in parties of some strength. Individuals of them are to be met with in most of the chief cities of Hindustan, living under the patronage of some man of rank or property; but in all situations they profess poverty, although they never solicit alms; and although ascetics, they place no merit in wearing mean garments or dispensing altogether with clothes. On the contrary, they are, in general, well dressed, and, allowing the whiskers and beard to grow, are not unfrequently of a venerable and imposing appearance. Though usually practicing celibacy, it does not appear to be a necessary condition amongst the *Śikhs* to be found in the Gangetic provinces: they are usually the ministrant priests; but their office consists chiefly in reading and expounding the writings of Nának and Govind Sinh, as collected in the *Ádi Granth* and *Daś Pádsháh ká granth.* The perusal is enlivened by the chanting, occasionally, of Hindi *Padas* and *Rekhtas,* the compositions of Kabír, Mírá Báí, Súr Daś, and others. With that fondness for sensible objects of reverence which characterises the natives of India, the Book is also worshipped, and Rupees, flowers, and fruits are presented by the votaries, which become, of course, the property of the officiating *Udási.* In return, the *Udási* not uncommonly adopts the presentation of the *Prásáda,* and at the close of the ceremony sweetmeats are distributed amongst the congregation. In some of the establishments at *Benares* the service is held in the evening after sunset, and the singing and feasting continue through a great part of the night. Many of the *Udásís* are well read in *Sanskrit*, and are able expounders of the *Vedánta* philosophy, on which the tenets of NÁNAK are mainly founded.

The *Udási* sect was established by DHARMACHAND, the grandson of NÁNAK, through whom the line of the Sage was continued, and his descendants, known by the name of *Nának Putras*, are still found in the *Panjáb*, where they are treated by the *Śikhs* with especial veneration.

The doctrine taught by NÁNAK appears to have differed but little from that of KABÍR, and to have deviated but inconsiderably from the *Hindu* faith in general. The whole body of poetical and mythological fiction was retained, whilst the liberation of the spirit from the delusive deceits of *Máyá*, and its purification by acts of benevolence and self-denial, so as to make it identical even in life with its divine source, were the great objects of the devotee. Associated with these notions was great chariness of animal life, whilst with NÁNAK, as well as with KABÍR, universal tolerance was a dogma of vital importance, and both laboured to persuade *Hindus* and *Mohammedans* that the only essential parts of their respective creeds were common to both, and that they should discard the varieties of practical detail, or the corruptions of their teachers for the worship of one only Supreme, whether he was termed *Allah* or *Hari.* How far these doctrines are still professed by the *Nának Sháhis*, may be inferred from the translations in the eleventh volume of the Researches, to which the following may be added as part of the service solemnized at the *Śikh Sangat*, at *Benares.*

HYMN.

Thou art the Lord—to thee be praise.
All life is with thee.
Thou art my parents, I am thy child—
All happiness is derived from thy clemency.
No one knows thy end.
Highest Lord amongst the highest—
Of all that exists Thou art the regulator.
And all that is from thee obeys thy will.
Thy movements—thy pleasure—thou only knowest.
Nának, thy slave, is a free-will offering unto thee.

The Priest then says—

Meditate on the *Sáheb* of the Book, and exclaim *Wah Guru.*

The People accordingly repeat—

Wah Guru—Wah Guru ki fateh.

The Priest—

Meditating on *Rámachandra*, exclaim *Wah Guru.*

The People—

Wah Guru—Wah Guru ki fateh.

HYMN.

Love, and fix thy whole heart upon Him—
The world is bound to thee by prosperity—
No one is another's.
Whilst prosperity endures many will come,
And sit with thee and surround thee;

But in adversity they will fly,
And not one will be near thee.
The woman of the house who loves thee,
And is ever in thy bosom,
When the spirit quits the body,
Will fly with alarm from the dead.
Such is the way of the world
With all on which we place affection;
Do thou, *Nának*, at thy last hour,
Rely alone upon *Hari*.

Priest as before—

Meditating on the Sáheb of the Book, &c.

People as before—

Wah Guru, &c.

HYMN.

My holy teacher is he who teaches clemency—
The heart is awake within: who seeks may find.
Wonderful is that rosary, every bead of which is the breath.
Lying apart in its arbour, it knows what cometh to pass.
The Sage is he who is merciful; the merciless is a butcher.
Thou wieldest the knife and regardlessly exclaimest:
What is a goat, what is a cow, what are animals?
But the *Sáheb* declares that the blood of all is the same.
Saints, Prophets, and Seers have all passed in death.
Nának, destroy not life for the preservation of the body.
That desire of life which is in the heart do thou, brother, repress.
Nának, calling aloud, says: take refuge with *Hari*.

Priest as before—

Meditating on the *Sáheb*, &c.

People as before—

Wah Guru—Wah Guru ki fateh.*

---

* [For further specimens see *Journal of the As. Soc. of Bengal* XIX, 521–33, and XX, 314–20. 487–502: Translation of the Vichitra Nátak, by Capt. G. SIDDONS.]

GANJ BAKHSHÍS.

Of this division of the *Śikhs* no particulars, except the name, have been ascertained. This is said to have been derived from that of the founder. They are not numerous nor of any note.

RÁMRÁYÍS.

These derive their appellation from that of RÁMA RÁYA, the son or grandson of HARI RÁYA, and their distinction from the other *Śikhs* is more of a political than religious complexion. RÁMA RÁYA disputed the succession to the Pontificate with HARI KŔISHŃA, the son of HARI RÁYA, and was unsuccessful. His followers, however, maintain the superiority of his pretensions, and record many miracles wrought by him in proof of his sanctity. He flourished about A. D. 1660. The *Rámráyis* are not common in Hindustan.

SUTHRÁ SHÁHÍS.

These are more often met with than either of the two preceding, and the priests are recognisable by distinguishing marks. They make a perpendicular black streak down the forehead, and carry two small black sticks about half a yard in length, which they clash together when they solicit alms. They lead a vagabond life, begging and singing songs in the *Panjábí* and other dialects, mostly of a moral or mystic tendency. They are held in great disrepute, however, and are not unfrequently gamblers, drunkards, and thieves. They look up to TEGH BAHÁDUR, the father of GURU GOVIND, as their founder.

GOVIND SINHÍS.

These form the most important division of the *Śikh* community, being in fact the political association to which the name is applied, or to the *Śikh* nation generally[1]. Although professing to derive their national faith from *Nának*, and holding his memory in veneration, the faith they follow is widely different from the quietism of that reformer, and is wholly of a worldly and warlike spirit. GURU GOVIND devoted his followers to steel, and hence the worship of the sword, as well as its employment against both Mohammedans and Hindus. He also ordered his adherents to allow their hair and beards to grow, and to wear blue garments: he permitted them to eat all kinds of flesh, except that of kine, and he threw open his faith and cause to all castes, to whomsoever chose to abandon the institutes of *Hinduism*, or belief in the mission of Mohammed, for a fraternity of arms and life of predatory daring. It was then only that the *Śikhs* became

[1] Described by Sir JOHN MALCOLM, in the eleventh volume of the Asiatic Researches. The *Śikh* priest to whom he alludes (page 198) as one of his authorities, was afterwards well known to me, and was an individual every way worthy of confidence. His name was *Átmá Rám*, and although advanced in years, he was full of energy and intelligence, combining with them extreme simplicity and kindliness of disposition. The old man was a most favourable and interesting specimen of the *Panjábi* nation and disciples of *Nának*. He died a few years ago in Calcutta.

a people, and were separated from their *Indian* countrymen in political constitution, as well as religious tenets. At the same time the *Śikhs* are still, to a certain extent, *Hindus*: they worship the deities of the *Hindus*, and celebrate all their festivals: they derive their legends and literature from the same sources, and pay great veneration to the *Brahmans*. The impress of their origin is still, therefore, strongly retained, notwithstanding their rejection of caste, and their substituting the *Daś Pádsháh ká granth*[1], the compilation of GURU GOVIND, for the *Vedas*, and *Puráńas*.

NIRMALAS.

These differ but little from the *Udásis*, and are perhaps still closer adherents to the doctrines of the

---

[1] From the succession of Chiefs; GOVIND was tenth teacher in succession from *Nának*, and flourished at the close of the 17th and beginning of the 18th century.

The other standard authority of the Śikhs, the *Ádi Granth*, is a compilation chiefly of the works of *Nának*, and his immediate successors, made by *Arjunmal*, a *Śikh* teacher, in the end of the 16th century. As it is usually met with, however, it comprehends the writings of many other individuals, many of whom are *Vaishńavas*. At a *Śikh Sangat*, or Chapel, in Benares, the Book, a large folio, there denominated the *Śambhu Granth*, was said to contain the contributions of the following writers:—

Nának, Nám Deo, Kabír, Sheikh Feridaddín, Dhanna, Rámánand, Pípá, Sena, Jayadeva, Phandak, Sudámá, Prahlád, Dhuru, Raidás, Vibhíshańa, Mírá Bái, Karma Bái.

[Compare also G. de TASSY, hist. de la littérat. Hindoui et Hindoust., I, 385 ff. Journal R. As. Soc., IX, 43 ff. Dabistán, II, 246-98. Journal As. S. Bengal, XIV, 393.]

founder, as the name imports: they profess to be free from all worldly soil or stain and, consequently, lead a wholly religious life. They observe celibacy, and disregard their personal appearance, often going nearly naked. They are not, like the *Udásís*, assembled in colleges, nor do they hold any particular form of divine service, but confine their devotion to speculative meditation on the perusal of the writings of NÁNAK, KABÍR, and other unitarian teachers. They are always solitary, supported by their disciples or opulent individuals, and are often known as able expounders of the *Vedánta* philosophy, in which *Brahmans* do not disdain to become their scholars. They are not very numerous; but a few are almost always to be found at the principal seats of *Hindu* wealth and learning, and particularly at *Benares*[1].

NÁGAS.

The naked mendicants of the *Śikhs* are said to differ

---

[1] An interesting account of the religious service of the *Śikhs*, in their college at *Patna*, was published by Mr. WILKINS, in the first volume of the Asiatic Researches. I witnessed a similar ceremony at a *Śikh* establishment at Benares, and partook of the *Prásáda*, or sweetmeats, distributed to the assistants. Both Mr. WILKINS and Sir JOHN MALCOLM notice this eating in common, as if it were peculiar to the *Śikh* faith; but this, as elsewhere observed, is not the case. It prevails with most of the *Vaishńava* sects; but it should be remembered that it is always restricted to articles which have been previously consecrated by presentation to the object of worship, to the Idol, the sarcophagus, the sculptured foot-marks, or the book.

from those of the *Vaishńava* and *Śaiva* sects by abstaining from the use of arms, and following a retired and religious life. Except in going without clothes, they are not distinguishable from the *Nirmalas.*

JAINS.

A satisfactory account of the religion of the *Jains* would require a distinct dissertation, and cannot be comprised within the limits necessarily assigned to this general sketch of the *Hindu* sects. The subject is of considerable interest, as affecting a very large proportion of the population of India, and involving many important considerations connected with the history of the *Hindu* faith: an extended inquiry must, however, be left to some further opportunity; and in the meantime our attention will be confined to a few observations on the peculiar tenets and practices of the *Jain* religion, its past history, and actual condition.

Previously, however, to entering upon these subjects, it may be advisable to advert briefly to what has been already done towards their elucidation, and to the materials which exist in the original languages for a complete view. The latter are of the most extensive description, whilst the labours of European writers are by no means wanting to an accurate estimate of the leading doctrines of the *Jain* faith, or to an appreciation of the state in which it exists in various parts of *Hindustan.*

The first authentic notices of the *Jains* occur in the ninth volume of the Asiatic Researches, from the pens of the late Colonel MACKENZIE, Dr. BUCHANAN, and Mr. COLEBROOKE. The two first described the *Jains* from personal acquaintance, and from their accounts it appeared, that they existed, in considerable numbers and respectability, in Southern India, particularly in *Mysore*, and on the *Canara Coast*; that they laid claim to high antiquity, and enumerated a long series of religious teachers, and that they differed in many of their tenets and practices from the orthodox Hindus, by whom they were regarded with aversion and contempt. A further illustration of their doctrines, and a particular account of their deified teachers was derived by Mr. COLEBROOKE from some of their standard authorities, then first made known to Europeans.

Little more was published on the subject of the *Jains* until very lately, with exception of numerous but brief and scattered notices of the sect in the *Peninsula*, in BUCHANAN's Travels in Mysore. Some account of them also occurs in Colonel WILKS' Historical Sketch of the South of India, and in the work of the Abbé DUBOIS. Mr. WARD has an article dedicated to the *Jains*, in his account of the Hindus; and Mr. ERSKINE has briefly adverted to some of their peculiarities in his Observations on the Cave of *Elephanta*, and the remains of the *Bauddhas* in India, in the Proceedings of the *Bombay Literary Society*. It is, however, to the Transaction of the *Royal Asiatic Society* that we are indebted for the latest and most detailed accounts, and the papers of Mr. COLEBROOKE, Major DELAMAINE, Dr. HAMILTON, Colonel FRANKLIN and

Major TOD[1], furnish many interesting particulars relative to the doctrines and past or present condition of the *Jains*. Some valuable illustration of the latter subject is to be found in the Calcutta Quarterly Magazine[2]: some historical notices obtained from the inscriptions at *Abú* occur in the last volume of our Researches, whilst a novel and rather comprehensive view of *Jain* literature is contained in the Catalogue of Manuscripts collected by the late Colonel MACKENZIE[3].

From this latter authority we learn that the literature peculiar to *Jainas* comprises a number of works peculiar to the sect, the composition of their own writers, and on a variety of subjects[4]. They have a

---

[1] On the Philosophy of the Hindus, Part V, by Mr. COLEBROOKE, Vol. I [Essays, London, 1858, 243 ff. 280 ff.]. On the *Śrávaks*, or *Jains*, by Major DELAMAIN, Vol. I, 418. On Inscriptions in Jain Temples, in Behár, by Mr. COLEBROOKE, Dr. HAMILTON, and Colonel FRANKLIN, Vol. I, 520. On the *Śrávaks*, or *Jains*, by Dr. HAMILTON, Vol. I, 531. On the Religious Establishments in Mewar, by Major TOD, Vol. II, 270.

[2] Particularly in the Journal of a Native Traveller, from Calcutta and back again through Behár. The traveller was a learned *Jain*, in the service of Colonel MACKENZIE. There is also an interesting account of a visit to the temple of PARŚVANÁTH, at *Samet Śikhar*.

[3] Vol. I, page 144, &c.

[4] The List comprises 44 Works:

Puráńas, ...	7
Charitras and Legends, ...	10
Ritual, Prayers, &c..	18
Medicine, ...	1
Grammar, ...	2

series of works called *Puráńas,* as the *Adi* and *Uttara Puráńas, Chámuńda Ráya Puráńa,* and *Chaturvinśati Puráńa*[1]; but these are not to be confounded with the *Puráńas* of the *Hindus;* as, although they occasionally insert legends borrowed from the latter, their especial object is the legendary history of the *Tírthankaras,* or deified teachers, peculiar to the sect. The chief *Puráńas* are attributed to JINA SENA ÁCHÁRYA, whom some accounts make contemporary with VIKRAMÁDITYA; but the greater number, and most consistent of the traditions of the South, describe him as the spiritual preceptor of AMOGHAVARSHA, king of *Kánchí,* at the end of the ninth century of the Christian era. Analogous to the *Jain Puráńas* are works denominated *Charitras,* their subject being, in general, the marvellous history of some *Tírthankara,*

Arithmetic, ...	2
Miscellaneous, . . , ...	4

[1] HAMILTON says, the *Digambaras* have twenty-four *Puráńas,* twenty-three giving an account of each *Tírthankara,* and the twenty-fourth, of the whole; but this seems to be erroneous. The actions of the twenty-four *Tírthankaras* are described in a single *Puráńa,* but the section devoted to each is called after him severally as the *Puráńa* of each, as *Ŕishabha Deva Puráńa,* one section of the *Chámuńda Ráya Puráńa.* In the *Ádi* and *Uttara Puráńas,* forming in fact but one work, the *Ádi,* or first part, is appropriated to the first *Tírthankara,* whilst the *Uttara,* or last portion, contains the accounts of all the other deified Sages. There are several collections, comprehending what may be termed twenty-four *Puráńas;* but it does not appear that there are twenty-four distinct works so denominated.

or some holy personage, after whom they are denominated, as the *Jinadatta Ráya Charitra, Pújyapáda Charitra*, and others. They have a number of works explanatory of their philosophical notions and religious tenets of the sect, as well as rituals of practice, and a grammatical system founded on the rules of Śákaṫáyana is illustrated by glosses and commentaries. The *Jains* have also their own writers on astronomy and astrology, on medicine, on the mathematical sciences, and the form and disposition of the universe.

This general view of *Jain* literature is afforded by the Mackenzie Collection, but the list there given is very far from including the whole of *Jain* literature, or even a considerable proportion. The works there alluded to are, in fact, confined to Southern India, and are written in *Sanskrit*, or the dialects of the *Peninsula*; but every province of Hindustan can produce *Jain* compositions, either in Sanskrit or its vernacular idiom, whilst many of the books, and especially those which may be regarded as their scriptural authorities, are written in the *Prákrit* or *Mágadhí*, a dialect which, with the *Jains* as well as the *Bauddhas*, is considered to be the appropriate vehicle of their sacred literature.

The course of time, and the multiplication of writings, have probably rendered it almost impossible to reduce what may be considered as the sacred literature of the *Jains* to a regular system. They are said to have a number of works entitled *Siddhántas* and

Ágamas[1], which are to them what the *Vedas* are to the Brahmanical Hindus; and this appears to be the case, although the enumeration which is sometimes made of them is of a loose and popular character, and scarcely reconcileable with that to be derived from written authority[2].

---

[1] HAMILTON enumerates eight works as the *Ágamas* of the *Digambara* sect, the *Trailokya Sára*, the *Gomatisára*, *Panjiráj*, *Trailokya Dípiká*, *Kshepańasára*, *Tribhangisára*, and *Shaipávar*, attributed to the pupils of *Mahávíra*. He states also, that the *Śvetámbaras* have forty-five or, as some allege, eighty-four *Siddhántas*, amongst which he specifies the *Thánángi Sútra*, *Jnánanti Sútra*, *Sugorangi Sútra*, *Upásakadaśa*, *Mahápandanna*, *Nandi Sútra*, *Rayapsení*, *Jinábhigama*, *Jambudwípapaññatti*, *Súrapaññatti*, *Chandraságarapaññatti*, *Kalpa Sútra*, *Katantravibhrama Sútra*, *Śakti Sútra*, and *Sangrahańí Sútra*. Some of these are incorrectly named, and others inaccurately classed, as will be seen from what follows in the text.

[2] The following Works are either in my possession or in the library of the Sanskrit College of Calcutta. Compositions descriptive of the tenets or practices of the *Jain* religion: *Bhagavatyangam*. This is one of the eleven primary works, and is entitled also in *Prákrit Viváha Paññatti*, in *Sanskrit Viváha*, or *Vivádhá Prajnapti*, Instruction in the various sources of worldly pain, or in the paths of virtue. It consists of lessons given to GAUTAMA by MAHÁVÍRA, and is in *Prákrit*. It contains 36,000 stanzas. *Bhagavatyanga Vritti*, a *Sanskrit* Commentary on the preceding (defective.) *Thánánga Sútra*,—also one of the eleven *Angas*. *Kalpa Sútra*, the precepts of the *Jain* faith—these are originally 1250; but they are interspersed with legends of the *Tirthankaras*, and especially of MAHÁVÍRA, at the pleasure of the writer, and the several copies of the work therefore differ. *Prákrit*.

The author of the *Abhidhána Chintámańi*, a useful vocabulary, HEMACHANDRA, is well known as a zealous

---

Kalpa Sútra Bálabodha, a sort of abridgment of the preceding. *Prákrit.*
Kalpa Sútra Siddhánta, the essence of the *Kalpa Sútra. Prákrit.*
Daśavaikálika Sútra. Prákrit.
Ditto. *Tíká.*
Ráyapraśna Sútra Siddhánta. Tíká.
Gautamaprashńhá. Prákrit.
Sangrahińí Sútra. Prákrit.
Laghu Sangrahińí Sútra.
Nava Tattwa Sútra. Prákrit.
NavaTattwaPrakarańa. Prákrit.
Nava TattwaBálabodha. Prákrit.
Karma Grantha.
Jiva Vichára. Sanskrit.
Jíva Vinaya.
Smarańa Sútra. Prákrit.
Vŕiddhátichára. Prákrit.
Sindúraprakára Tíká. Sanskrit.
Ekavinśati Sthána. Bháshá.
Daśakshapańavratavidhi. Bháshá.
Upadeśa Málá. Prákrit.
Pratikramańa Vidhi. Prákrit.
Pratikramańa Sútra. Bháshá.
Chaturdaśa Gunasthána. Bháshá.
Chaturdaśa Gunanámáni.
Pakshi Sútra. Bháshá.
Shattrinśat Karmakathá. Bháshá.
Dharmabuddhi Chatushpádí. Bháshá.
Bálavibodha. Bháshá.
Upadhánavidhi. Prákrit.
Ashtáhnikamahotsava. Prákrit.
Ashtáhnikavyákhyána.
Mahámuni Svádhyáya.
Pragnasúkta Muktávalí.
Árádhana Prakára.
Párśvanátha Gítá.
Uttarádhyáyana Gítá.
Sádhusamáchárí.
Śrávakárádhana.
Jnánapújá.
Díkshámahotsava.
Bárah Vrata.
Saptavinśati Sádhu Lakshańa.
Rátribhojana Nishedha.
Sádhwapásana Vidhi.
Dwishashti Vákya.
Kshetrasamása Sútra.
Samyaktwádhyáyana.
Praśnottara Ratnamálá.
Navakáránta Bálabodha.
Asahyana Vidhi.
Santáraka Vidhi.
Átmánuśásana. Bháshá.
Panchástikáya, according to the *Digambara* faith.
Jinapratimá Sthápana Vidhi.
Jalakshálana Vidhi.
Sadopakára Muktávalí.
Moksha Márga.
Nítisangraha.
Vichúramanjarí.
Párśvanátha Daśabhávavisaha.
Śatavíśabháva.

and able propagator of the *Jain* doctrines in the twelfth century. He was no doubt well versed in the pecu-

---

Ánandaśrávaka Sandhi.
Rohińitapas.
Siddháchala Pújá.
Pújápaddhati. Bháshá.
Śilopadeśa Málá.
Snána Vidhi.
Navapattatapo Vidhi.
Amŕitáshtamitapas.
Dévapújá.
Varńabhávanasandhi. Bháshá.

Panegrics of the *Jain* teachers, &c., which are not unfrequently repeated in the temples:

Śánti Jina Stava. Bháshá.
Vŕihat Śánti Stava. Sanskrit.
Mahávira Stava. Bháshá.
Laghu Śánti Stava.
Ŕishabha Stava.
Párśvanátha Stava.
Párśvanátha Stuti. Prákrit.
Neminátha Stava.
Áśánta Stava. Prákrit.
Ajitaśánti Stava.
Bhaktamaya Stotra.
KalyáńaMandhraStotra. Sanskrit.
Chaturvinśati dańdakastava.
Sádhuvandana.
Śatrunjaya Stava.
Párśvanátha Namaskára.
Champaka Stavana.
Upasargahára Stotra.
Guru Stava.
Karma Stava.

LEGENDARY TALES AND HISTORIES.

Padma Puráńa. Bháshá.
Mahávira Charitra, which is called by others portion of the *Trishashtiśalákápurusha Charita*, or Legend of the sixty-three personages most eminent in *Jain* Tradition. *Sanskrit.*
Nemirájarshi Charitra.
Śalábhadra Charitra. Bháshá.
Chitrasena Charitra. Bháshá.
Gajasukumára Charitra. Bháshá.
Chandrarája Charitra. Bháshá.
Bhaktámara.
Śripála Charitra. Bháshá.
Kálikácharya Kathá.
Samyaktwa Kaumudi.
Vastradána Kathá.
Meghadútapáda Samasyá.
Avantiśakumára Charitra.
Ratnachúropákhyána.
Mŕigávati Charitra.
Ratnachúra Muni Chaupai. Bháshá.
Mŕigavati Chaupai. Bháshá.
Sádhu Charitra.
Śatrunjaya Máhátmya.
Gajasinha Charitra.
Daśadŕishtánta Kathá.

liarity of the system which he taught, and may be regarded as a safe guide. In his vocabulary* he specifies what appear to be the *Jaina* scriptures, at least in the estimation of the *Śvetámbara* sect, to which he belonged, and in a valuable Commentary on his own work he has further particularised the works named in his text. From this it appears that the principal authorities of a sacred character were termed *Angas*, and were eleven in number or, with a supplementary division, twelve. They are thus enumerated and described: *Áchárángam*, a book teaching sacred observances after the practice of *Váśishṫha* and other saints. *Sútrakṙitángam*, a work on acts imposed by positive precepts. *Sthánángam*, on the organs in which life abides, or the ten acts essential to purity. *Samaváyángam*, on the hundred *Padárthas* or categories. *Bhagavatyangam*, on the ritual, or rules for worship. *Jnátádharmakathá*, an account of the acquisition of knowledge by holy personages. *Upásakadaśá*, rules for the conduct of *Śrávakas*, or secular *Jains*, appa-

---

MISCELLANEOUS.

Vṙiddhayavana, *Astronomy. Sanskrit.*
Chaturdaśasvapanavichára.
Trailokya Dípiká.
Setunjoddhar.
Páṫhanárambhapíṫhiká.
Hastarekhávivaraṅa. Prákrit.
Námávali.
Páṫávali.

Many of these are of small extent, but others are exceedingly voluminous, as the *Bhagavatyanga*, *Padma Puráṅa*, *Śatrunjaya Máhátmya*, and others.

* [243 – 8.]

rently in ten lectures. *Antakríddaśá*, on the actions of the *Tírthankaras*, in ten lectures. *Anuttaropapátikadaśá*, on the principal or final births of the *Tírthankaras*, in ten lectures. *Praśnavyákarańam*, Grammar of questions, probably on the Code of the *Jains*. *Vipákaśrutam*, on the fruits or consequences of actions.

With these are connected inferior *Angas* or *Upángas*, the names of which are not specified—whilst the *Dŕishťiváda*, the twelfth *Anga*, which seems to be a supplementary authority, is divided into five portions entitled: *Parikarma*, on moral acts; *Sútra*, precepts for conduct and life; *Púrvánuyoga*, on the doctrines and practice of the *Tírthankaras* before attaining perfection; *Púrvagata*, on the same after perfection! *Chúliká*, on doctrines and practice not comprised in the two preceding.

These different works profess to be derived from the oral instructions of MAHÁVÍRA himself to his disciples, especially to GAUTAMA; but besides these a class of works is enumerated by HEMACHANDRA, entitled *Púrvas*, because they were drawn up by the *Gańadharas* before the *Angas*[1]. There are fourteen of them treating of the chief tenets of the sect, apparently sometimes controversially, as the *Astipraváda*, the doctrine of existence and non-existence; *Jnánapraváda*, the doctrine of holy knowledge; *Satyapra-*

1 सूत्रितानि गणधरैरङ्गेभ्यः पूर्वमेव यत् ।
पूर्वाणीत्यभिधीयन्ते तेनैतानि चतुर्दश ॥
Mahá Vira Char. Section 5.

váda, discussion of truth; *Átmapraváda*, investigation of spirit; *Práńáváya*, nature of corporeal life; *Kriyá-viśála*, consequences of acts, and others[1]. They are held to be the works of MAHÁVÍRA's *Gańas*, or of that *Tírthankara* and his predecessors, or to have emanated from them originally, although committed to writing by other hands. Some of them still exist, it appears[2], although in general their places have been assumed by a list of more recent compositions.

From this brief statement it will be evident that there is no want of original authorities with regard to the belief, the practices, or the legends of the *Jaina* sect. There is indeed more than a sufficiency, and the vast extent of the materials is rather prejudicial to the enquiry, it being impossible to consult any extensive proportion of what has been written, and it being equally impossible without so doing to know that the best guides have been selected. For such accounts as are here given, the Vocabulary of HEMACHANDRA, with his own Commentary, the *Mahávíra Charitra* of the same author, the *Kalpa Sútra*, the *Avaśyakavŕihad Vŕitta*, the *Bhagavatyanga Vŕitta*, *Nava Tattwabodha*, and *Jíva Vichára* have chiefly been consulted.

The leading tenets of the *Jains*, and those which

---

[1] A similar enumeration of these Works occurs in the *Mahávíra Charitra*.

[2] Thus the *Thánángisútra* and *Upásakadaśa*, of HAMILTON, are no doubt the *Sthánánga* and *Upásakadaśa* of *Hemachandra*'s text; the *Bhagavatyanga* is in the *Sanskrit* College Library.

chiefly distinguish them from the rest of the *Hindus*, are well known—they are, first, the denial of the divine origin and infallible authority of the *Vedas*; secondly, the reverence of certain holy mortals who acquired, by practices of self-denial and mortification, a station superior to that of the gods; and thirdly, extreme and even ludicrous tenderness of animal life.

The disregard of the authority of the *Vedas* is common to the *Jains* and the *Bauddhas*, and involves a neglect of the rites which they prescribe: in fact, it is in a great degree from those rites that an inference unfavourable to the sanctity of the *Vedas* is drawn; and not to speak of the sacrifices of animals which the *Vedas* occasionally enjoin, the *Homa*, or burnt offering, which forms a part of every ceremonial in those works, is an abomination, as insects crawling amongst the fuel, bred by the fermented butter, or falling into the flame, cannot fail to be destroyed by every oblation. As far however as the doctrines they teach are conformable to *Jain* tenets, the *Vedas* are admitted and quoted as authority.

The veneration and worship of mortals is also common to the *Jains* and *Bauddhas*, but the former have expanded and methodised the notions of the latter. The *Bauddhas*, although they admit an endless number of earthly *Buddhas* to have existed, and specify more than a century of names[1], confine their reverence to a comparatively small number—to seven. The *Jainas*

---

[1] Asiat. Researches, Vol. XVI, pages 446 to 449.

extend this number to twenty-four for a given period, and enumerate by name the twenty-four of their past age, or *Avasarpiṅí*, the twenty-four of the present, and the twenty-four of the age to come. The statues of these, either all or in part, are assembled in their temples, sometimes of colossal dimensions, and usually of black or white marble. The objects held in highest esteem in *Hindustan* are PÁRŚVANÁTH and MAHÁVÍRA, the twenty-third and twenty-fourth *Jinas* of the present era, who seem to have superseded all their predecessors.

The generic names of a *Jaina* saint express the ideas entertained of his character by his votaries. He is *Jagatprabhu*, lord of the world; *Kshíṅakarmá*, free from bodily or ceremonial acts; *Sarvajna*, omniscient; *Adhíśvara*, supreme lord; *Devádhideva*, god of gods; and similar epithets of obvious purport; whilst others are of a more specific character, as *Tírthakara*, or *Tírthankara*, *Kevalí*, *Arhat*, and *Jina*. The first implies one who has crossed over *(Tíryate anena)*, that is the world, compared to the ocean; *Kevalí* is the possessor of *Kevala*, or spiritual nature, free from its investing sources of error; *Arhat* is one entitled to the homage of gods and men, and *Jina* is the victor over all human passions and infirmities[1].

---

[1] तीर्यते संसारसमुद्रोऽनेनेति तीर्थं तत्करोतीति तीर्थकरः। सर्वथावरणविलये चेतनस्वरूपाविर्भावः केवलं तदस्यास्ति केवली। सुरेन्द्रादिकृतां पूजामर्हतीत्यर्हन्। जयति रागद्वेषमोहानिति जिनः॥
These Etymologies are from *Hemachandra*'s Commentary [to śl. 24. 25., p. 292, ed. Boehtlingk and Rieu].

Besides these epithets, founded on attributes of a generic character, there are other characteristics common to all the *Jinas* of a more specific nature. These are termed *Atiśayas*, or super-human attributes, and are altogether thirty-six; four of them, or rather four classes, regard the person of a *Jina*, such as the beauty of his form, the fragrance of his body, the white colour of his blood, the curling of his hair, its non-increase, and that of the beard and nails, his exemption from all natural impurities, from hunger and thirst, from infirmity and decay: these properties are considered to be born with him. He can collect around him millions of beings, gods, men, and animals, in a comparatively small space, his voice is audible to a great distance, and his language, which is *Arddha Mágadhi*, is intelligible to animals, men and gods, the back of his head is surrounded with a halo of light brighter than the disk of the sun, and for an immense interval around him, wherever he moves, there is neither sickness nor enmity, storm nor dearth, neither plague portents, nor war. Eleven *Atiśayas* of this kind are ascribed to him. The remaining nineteen are of celestial origin, as the raining of flowers and perfumes, the sound of heavenly drums, and the menial offices rendered by *Indra* and the gods*.

Notwithstanding the sameness of the general character and identity of generic attributes, the twenty-four *Jinas* are distinguished from each other in colour,

* [Hemachandra I. 1. 62–88.]

stature, and longevity. Two of them are red, two white, two blue, two black, the rest are of a golden hue, or a yellowish brown. The other two peculiarities are regulated with very systematic precision, and observe a series of decrement from *Ŕishabha*, the first *Jina*, who was five hundred poles in stature, and lived 8,400,000 great years, to *Mahávíra*, the 24th, who had degenerated to the size of man, and was not more than forty years on earth. These peculiarities have been detailed by Mr. COLEBROOKE, in the ninth volume of the Researches, and he draws a probable inference from the return to reason in the stature and years of the two last *Jinas*, that they alone are to be considered as historical personages. The rest are the creatures of fiction. The notion of decreasing longevity, like that of the existence of human beings, superior to the gods, is common to the *Bauddhas*[1].

There is also great similarity in the general tenor

---

[1] A comparison of the *Jain* and *Bauddha* series suggests strong confirmation of the opinion that the *Jain* legends are only *Bauddha* notions exaggerated. The ages of the seven *Buddhas* run thus:

run thus:	*Vipaśyi*, ...	80,000 Years.
	Śikhí, ...	70,000 ditto.
	Viśvabhú, ...	60,000 ditto.
	Krakuchchhanda, ...	40,000 ditto.
	Kanaka, ...	30,000 ditto.
	Káśyapa, ...	20,000 ditto.
	Śákya, ...	100 ditto.

A. R. Vol. XVI, p. 453. The last *Jina* but one, or *Párśvanáth*, lived, like *Śákya*, 100 years. [See also A. Weber, Ueber das Śatrunjaya Máhátmyam. Leipzig: 1858, p. 3, and C. F. Koeppen, die Religion des Buddha, I, p. 314 ff.]

of the legends related of each of the *Jinas*. They are all born a number of times, and in a variety of characters, before they arrive at the state of a *Tírthankara*: after which, as their attainment of divine knowledge is the work of self-denial and ascetic meditation, we need not expect much varied incident in their adventures. A sketch of the life of MAHÁVÍRA, from the *Mahávíra Charitra*, will convey some notion of their ordinary history, whilst further illustration may be derived from an abstract of the *Párśvanátha Charitra*, or life of PÁRŚVANÁTH, in the Royal Asiatic Society's Transactions*.

LIFE OF MAHÁVÍRA.

The twenty-fourth *Tírthankara* MAHÁVÍRA's first birth, which occurred at a period indefinitely remote, was as NAYASÁRA, head man of a village, in the country of *Vijaya*, subject to ŚATRUMARDANA. His piety and humanity elevated him next to the heaven called *Saudharma*, where he enjoyed happiness for some oceans of years. He was next born as MARÍCHI, the grandson of the first *Tírthankara* ŔISHABHA, then transferred to the *Brahmaloka*, whence he returned to earth as a worldly-minded and sensual *Brahman*, the consequence of which was his repeated births in the same caste, each birth being separated by an interval passed in one of the *Jain* heavens, and each period of life extending to many *lakhs* of years. He then became VIŚVABHÚTA, prince of *Rájagŕiha*, and next a *Vásu-*

* [I, 428.]

deva, named TRIPŔISHŤHA, from having three back bones: his uncle and foe in a former life, *Visabhánandi*, was born as his *Protagonist*, or *Prativásudeva*, named AŚVAGRÍVA or HAYAGRÍVA, and was, in the course of events, destroyed by the *Vásudeva*, a palpable adaptation of the *Pauráńic* legend of VISHŃU and HAYAGRÍVA. TRIPŔISHŤHA having put his Chamberlain cruelly to death was condemned to hell, and again born as a lion: he migrated through various forms, until he became the *Chakravartti* PRIYAMITRA, in the division of the world *Mahávideha*. After a victorious reign of eighty-four *lakhs* of years he became an ascetic for a further period of a hundred *lakhs*, and was then translated to one of the higher heavens. Thence he returned to earth in the *Bharata* division as NANDANA, the son of JITAŚATRU, who adopted a life of devotion and diligently adored the *Jinas*. After an existence of twenty-five *lakhs* of years he was raised to the dignity of king of the gods in the *Pushpottara* heaven, in which capacity he preserved his ancient faith, offering flowers to, and bathing daily the one hundred and eight images of the *Arhats*. Such exalted piety was now to meet with its reward, and the pains of existence were to be terminated in the person of the *Tírthankara* MAHÁVÍRA, or VARDDHAMÁNA.

On the return of the spirit of NANDANA to earth it first animated the womb of the wife of a *Brahman*, but MAHENDRA disapproving of the receptacle as of low caste transferred it to the womb of TRIŚALÁ, wife of SIDDHÁRTHA, of the family of *Ikshváku*, and prince of *Pavana*, in *Bharatakshetra*. Mahávíra was born on the thirteenth of the light fortnight of *Chaitra*: the fifty-six nymphs of the universe assisted at his birth, and his consecration was performed by Śakra, and the other sixty-three *Indras*. The name given by his father was Varddhamána, as causing increase of riches and prosperity, but Śakra gave him also the appellation of Mahávíra as significant of his power and supremacy over men and gods.

When arrived at maturity, Mahávíra was prevailed upon by his parents to marry Yaśodá, daughter of the prince Samaravíra. By her he had a daughter, Priyadarśaná, who was married to Jamálí, a prince, one of the Saint's pupils, and founder of a schism. Siddhártha and his wife died when their son was twenty-eight years old, on which Mahávíra adopted an ascetic life, the government devolving on his elder brother Nandivarddhana. After two years of abstinence and self-denial at home he commenced an erratic life, and the attainment of the degree of a *Jina*.

During the first six years of his peregrination, Mahávíra observed frequent fasts of several months' duration, during each of which he kept his eyes fixed upon the tip of his nose, and maintained perpetual silence. He was invisibly attended by a *Yaksha*, named Siddhártha, who, at the command of Indra, watched over his personal security, and where speech was necessary acted as spokesman. At *Nálańdá*, a village near *Rájagŕiha*, Mahávíra acquired a follower named Gośála, so called from his birth in a cow-house, a man of low caste and vulgar propensities, and who acts as a sort of buffoon [1]. He is involved in repeated difficulties and not unfrequently receives a beating, but when free from fault, the *Yakshas,* who attend on SIDDHÁRTHA, come to his aid, and destroy with fire the houses and property of his assailants. Amongst other enemies he provokes the followers of VARDDHANA SÚRI, the disciple of CHANDRA-ÁCHÁRYA, a teacher of the *Jain* faith, according to the doctrines of PÁRŚVANÁTH. In the course of the dispute it appears that the followers of PÁRŚVANÁTH wore clothes, whilst MAHÁVÍRA was indifferent to vesture, and the latter consequently belonged to the division of the *Jains* called *Digambaras*, or those who go naked, whilst PÁRŚVANÁTH's disciples were *Śvetámbaras*, dressed in garments [2].

---

[1] Some curious and unintelligible things are related of this individual, which suggest a suspicion that the author had in view some of the oriental legends relating to *Mani* or *Manes.* The birth of GOŚÁLA in a cow-house may or may not refer to Christianity; but it is also observed that his father and mother carried about a *Chitra paṭṭiká,* a painted cloth or picture, which GOŚÁLA stole from them, and that when he adopted the service of MAHÁVÍRA, he abandoned the heresy of the picture. चित्रफलकपाषण्डं विहाय.

[2] They reply to GOŚÁLA's enquiry: निर्ग्रन्थाः पार्श्वशिष्याः वयं "We are the pupils of PÁRŚVA, free from restraint"—to which he rejoins कथन्नु यूयं निर्ग्रन्था वस्त्रादिग्रन्थधारिणः । केवलं जीविकाहेतोरियं पाषण्डकल्पना ॥ वस्त्रादिसंगरहितो निरपेक्षो वपुष्यपि । धर्माचार्यो हि यादृग्मे निर्ग्रन्थास्तादृशाः खलु ॥ "How can you be free from restraint, encumbered with clothes and the like? these heretical practices are adopted merely for a livelihood: wholly unfettered by clothes and such things, and disregarding the body,

During the six years expended in this manner MAHÁVÍRA visits a number of places, most of which appear to be in *Behár* and the adjacent provinces, as *Rájagríha*, *Śrávasti* near *Oude*, *Vaiśálí*, which is identified with the capital of *Behár*, and others.

Proceeding on his peregrinations MAHÁVÍRA voluntarily exposed himself to be maltreated by the *Mlechchha* tribes of *Vajrabhúmi*, *Śuddhibhúmi*, and *Lát*, or *Lár*, the countries apparently of the *Gońds*, who abused and beat him, and shot at him with arrows, and baited him with dogs, to all which he offered no resistance, and indeed rejoiced in his sufferings; for, however necessary to personal purification, it is not the duty of a *Jain* ascetic to inflict tortures upon himself—his course of penance is one of self-denial, fasting and silence, and pain, however meritorious its endurance, must be inflicted by others, not himself. At the end of the ninth year MAHÁVÍRA relinquished his silence in answer to a question put by GOŚÁLA, but continued engaged in the practice of mortification and in an erratic life. His squire having learned from him the possession of the *Tejalesya*, or power of ejecting flame, and having learned from certain of the disciples of PÁRŚVANÁTH, what is technically termed

---

the followers of such a teacher as mine is are the only persons exempt from restraint." Further confirmation of MAHÁVÍRA and his followers being *Digambaras* occurs in various places, especially in a passage where GOŚÁLA gets beaten, and almost killed by the women of a village in *Magadha*, because he is a naked *Śramańa*, or mendicant.

the *Mahánimitta* of the eight *Angas*, intending probably their scriptural doctrines, set up for himself as a *Jina*, and quitted his master.

Indra having declared that Mahávíra's meditations could not be disturbed by men or gods, one of the inferior spirits of heaven, indignant at the assertion, assailed the Sage with a variety of horrors and temptations, but in vain. Mahávíra's pious abstraction was unbroken. He then wandered about and visited *Kauśámbí*, the capital of *Śatáníka*, where he was received with great veneration, and where his period of self-denial ended in perfect exemption from human infirmities. The whole of the time expended by him in these preparatory exercises was twelve years and six months, and of this he had fasted nearly eleven years. His various fasts are particularised with great minuteness, as one of six months, nine of four months each, twelve of one month, and seventy-two of half a month each, making altogether ten years and three hundred and forty-nine days.

The bonds of action were snapped like an old rope, and the *Kevala*, or *only knowledge* attained by Mahávíra on the north bank of the *Ṛijupáliká*, under a *Sál* tree, on the tenth of the light fortnight *Vaiśákha*, in the fourth watch of the day, whilst the moon was in the asterism *Hasta*. Indra instantly hastened to the spot, attended by thousands of deities, who all did homage to the Saint, and attended him on his progress to *Apápapuri*, in *Behár*, where he commenced his instructions on a stage erected for the purpose by the deities, a model of which is not uncommonly represented in *Jain* temples. The following is the introductory lecture ascribed to Mahávíra by his biographer.

"The world is without bounds, like a formidable ocean; its cause is action *(Karma)* which is as the seed of the tree. The being *(Jíva)* invested with body, but devoid of judgment, goes like a well-sinker ever downwards by the acts it performs, whilst the embodied being which has attained purity goes ever upwards by its own acts, like the builder of a palace. Let not any one injure life, whilst bound in the bonds of action; but be as assiduous in cherishing the life of another as his own. Never let any one speak falsehood, but always speak the truth. Let every one who has a bodily form avoid giving pain to others as much as to himself. Let no one take property not given to him, for wealth is like the external life of men, and he who takes away such wealth commits as it were murder. Associate not with women, for it is the destruction of life: let the wise observe continence, which binds them to the Supreme. Be not encumbered with a family, for by the anxiety it involves the person separated from it falls like an ox too heavily laden. If it be not in their power to shun these more subtle destroyers of life, let those who desire so to do avoid at least the commission of all gross offences."

When Mahávíra's fame began to be widely diffused, it attracted the notice of the *Brahmans* of *Magadha*, and several of their most eminent teachers undertook to refute his doctrines. Instead of effecting their purpose, however, they became converts, and constituted his *Gańadharas*, heads of schools, the disciples of Mahávíra and teachers of his doctrines, both orally and scripturally. It is of some interest to notice them in detail, as the epithets given to them are liable to be misunderstood, and to lead to erroneous notions respecting their character and history.

This is particularly the case with the first, Indrabhúti, or Gautama, who has been considered as the same with the Gautama of the *Bauddhas*, the son of Máyádeví, and author of the Indian metaphysics[1]. That any connexion exists between the *Jain* and the *Bráhmańa* Sage is, at least, very doubtful; but the Gautama of the *Bauddhas*, the son of Śuddhodana and Máyá, was a *Kshattriya*, a prince of the royal or warrior caste. All the *Jain* traditions make their Gautama a *Brahman*, originally of the *Gotra*, or tribe of Gotama *Ŕishi*, a division of the *Brahmans* well known, and still existing in the South of India. These two persons therefore cannot be identified, whether they be historical or fictitious personages.

Indrabhúti, Agnibhúti, and Váyubhúti are described as the sons of Vasubhúti, a *Brahman* of the *Gotama* tribe, residing at *Govara*, a village in *Magadha*: from their race, Hemachandra, in the Commentary on the Vocabulary*, observes, they are all

[1] R. A. S. Transactions, Vol. I, p. 538.

* [Śl. 31. Weber, Ueber das Śatrunjaya Máhátmyam, p. 3–5.]

called GAUTAMAS. VYAKTA and SUDHARMÁ were the sons of DHANAMITRA and DHAMMILLA, two *Brahmans* of *Kollaka*, the former of the *Bharadwája*, and the latter of the *Agnivaiśya* tribe. MAṄḌITA and MAURYAPUTRA were half-brothers, the sons of VIJAYADEVÍ by DHANADEVA and MAURYA, two *Brahmans* of the *Vásishṫha* and *Káśyapa* races, but cousins by the mother's side, and consequently, according to the custom of the country, it is stated, the one took the other's widow to wife upon his decease. AKAMPITA was the son of a *Maithilí Brahman*, of the *Gautama* tribe; ACHALABHRÁTÁ, of a *Brahman* of *Oude*, of the *Hárita* family; METÁRYA was a *Brahman* of *Vatsa*, of the *Kauṅḋinya* tribe; and PRABHÁSA, a *Brahman* of the same race, but a native of *Rájagṙiha* in Behár. These are the eleven *Gaṅadharas*, or *Gaṅádhipas*, holders or masters of *Jain* schools, although, before their conversion, learned in the four *Vedas*, and teaching the doctrines contained in them.

These converts to *Jain* principles are mostly made in the same manner: each comes to the Saint, prepared to overwhelm him with shame, when he salutes them mildly by name, tells them the subject that excites their unuttered doubts and solves the difficulty, not always very satisfactorily or distinctly, it must be admitted; but the whole is an epitome of the *Jain* notions on those subjects which chiefly engage the attention of the Hindu philosophers.

INDRABHÚTI doubts whether there be life *(Jíva)* or not—MAHÁVÍRA says there is, and that it is the vessel of virtue and vice, or where would be the use of acts of virtue or piety.

Agnibhúti questions if there be acts *(Karma)* or not, to which Mahávíra replies in the affirmative, and that from them proceed all bodily pleasure and pain, and the various migrations of the living principle through different forms.

Váyubhúti doubts if life be not body, which the Sage denies, as the objects of the senses may be remembered after the senses cease to act, even after death, that is, in a succeeding state of existence occasionally.

Vyakta questions the reality of elementary matter, referring it with the *Vedántis* to illusion; the Sage replies that the doctrine of vacuity is false, illustrating his position rather obscurely by asking if there are no other worlds than the *Gandharva*, cities of dreams, or castles in the air.

Sudharmá imagines that the same kind of bodies which are worn in one life will be assumed in another, or that a human being must be born again amongst mankind; for as the tree is always of the same nature as the seed, so must the consequences of acts, in a peculiar capacity, lead to results adapted to a similar condition. This Mahávíra contradicts, and says that causes and effects are not necessarily of the same nature, as horn, and similar materials are convertible into arrow-barbs, and the like.

Mańdita has not made up his mind on the subjects of bondage and liberation, *(Bandha* and *Moksha)*; the *Jina* explains the former to be connexion with and dependence on worldly acts, whilst the latter is total detachment from them, and independence of them effected by knowledge.

Mauryaputra doubts of the existence of gods, to which Mahávíra opposes the fact of the presence of Indra, and the rest around his throne. They cannot bear the odour of mere mortality, he adds; but they never fail to attend at the birth, inauguration, and other passages of the life of a *Jina*.

Akampita is disposed to disbelieve the existence of the spirits of hell, because he cannot see them; but the Sage says that they are visible to those possessing certain knowledge, of whom *he* is one.

Achalabhrátá is sceptical as to the distinction between vice and virtue, for which Mahávíra rebukes him, and desires him to judge of them by their fruits: length of days, honorable birth, health, beauty and prosperity being the rewards in this life of virtue; and the reverse of these the punishments of vice.

Metárya questions a future existence, because life having no certain form must depend on elementary form, and consequently perish with it; but Mahávíra replies, that life is severally present in various elementary aggregates to give them consciousness, and existing independent of them, may go elsewhere when they are dissolved. He adds, in confirmation of the doctrine, that the *Śrutis* and *Smŕitis*, that is, the scriptural writings of the *Bráhmańas*, assert the existence of other worlds.

The last of the list is Prabhása, who doubts if there

be such a thing as *Nirváń*, that state of non-entity which it is the object of a *Jaina* saint to attain. The solution is not very explicit. *Nirváń* is declared to be the same with *Moksha*, liberation, and *Karma-kshaya*, abrogation of acts, and that this is real is proved by the authority of the *Veda*, and is visibly manifested in those who acquire true knowledge.

According to this view of the *Jain* system, therefore, we find the vital principle recognised as a real existence animating in distinct portions distinct bodies, and condemned to suffer the consequences of its actions by migrations through various forms. The reality of elementary matter is also asserted, as well as of gods, demons, heaven, and hell. The final state of the vital and sentient principle is left rather obscure, but as its actual and visible exemption from human acts is taught, it follows that it is exempt from their consequences or repeated births in various shapes, and therefore ceases to be in any sensible or suffering form. It is unnecessary to dwell longer on the subject here, as we shall have occasion to recur to it.

After the conversion of these *Brahmans* and their disciples, MAHÁVÍRA instructed them further in his doctrines, and they again taught them to others, becoming the heads of separate schools. AKAMPITA and ACHALABHRÁTÁ, however, and METÁRYA and PRABHÁSA taught in common, so that the eleven *Gańádhipas* established but nine *Gańas* or classes*.

---

* [Schol. ad śl. 31, p. 292. Weber, l. l., p. 4.]

Having thus attained the object of his penance and silence, MAHÁVÍRA, attended by his disciples, wandered about to different places, disseminating the *Jain* belief, and making numerous converts. The scene of his labours is mostly along the Ganges, in the modern districts of *Behár* and *Alláhábád*, and principally at the cities of *Kauśámbi* and *Rájagŕiha*, under the kings ŚASÁNÍKA and ŚREŃIKA, both of whom are *Jains*. The occurrences described relate more to the disciples of the Saint than to himself, and there are some curious matters of an apparently historical character. There is also a prophetic account of HEMACHANDRA himself, and his patron KUMÁRA PÁLA of *Guzerat*, put into the mouth of MAHÁVÍRA; but these are foreign to our present purpose, which is confined to the progress of the *Jain* sage.

MAHÁVÍRA having completed the period of his earthly career, returned to *Apápapuri*, whither he was attended by a numerous concourse of followers of various designations. However fanciful the enumeration, the list is not uninstructive, as it displays the use of various terms to signify different orders of one sect, and not, as has been sometimes erroneously supposed, the sect itself. *Śramańas, Sádhus* and *Śrávaks* may be *Jains*, but they are not necessarily so, nor do they singly designate all the individuals of that persuasion. *Vira*'s train consists of *Sádhus*, holy men, fourteen thousand; *Sádhwis*, holy women, thirty-six thousand; *Śramańas*, or ascetics, versed in the fourteen *Púrvas*, three hundred; *Avadhijnánis*, those knowing the limits or laws, one thousand and three hundred; *Kevalís*, or detached from acts, seven hundred; *Manovits*, possessors of intellectual wisdom, five hundred; *Vádís*, controversialists, four hundred; *Śrávakas*, the male laity, one *lakh* and fifty-nine thousand; and *Śrávikás*, female hearers of the word, double that number, or three *lakhs* and eighteen thousand. The only *Gańadharas* present were GAUTAMA and SUDHARMÁ, the other nine having attained felicity, or having died before their master.

The period of his liberation having arrived, MAHÁVÍRA resigned his breath, and his body was burned by ŚAKRA and other deities, who divided amongst them such parts as were not destroyed by the flames, as the teeth and bones, which they preserved as relics; the ashes of the pile were distributed amongst the assistants: the gods erected a splendid monument on the spot, and then returned to their respective heavens. These events occurred on the day of new moon, in the month *Kártik*, when MAHÁVÍRA was seventy-two years of age, thirty of which were spent in social duties, and the rest in religious avocations, and he died two hundred and fifty years after the preceding *Jina*, PÁRŚVANÁTH: no other date is given, but in the passage, in the prophetic strain above alluded to, it is mentioned that KUMÁRA PÁLA will found *Anahilla Pattan**, and become the disciple of HEMACHANDRA, one thousand six hundred and sixty-nine years after the death of MAHÁVÍRA.

* [formerly called *Analaváta*.]

The conversion of KUMÁRA PÁLA occurred about A. D. 1174*, and consequently the last *Jina* expired about five hundred years before the Christian era. According to other authorities the date assigned to this event is commonly about a century and a half earlier, or before Christ six hundred and sixty-three[1], but HEMACHANDRA is a preferable guide, although, in point of actual chronology, his date is probably not more to be depended upon than those derived from other sources.

The doctrines of the *Jains*, which constitute the philosophy of their system, it is not part of the present plan to discuss: but a few of the leading tenets, as derived from original authorities, may be here briefly adverted to. It is the more necessary to dwell on the subject, as the chief opinions of the sect of *Jina*, as described elsewhere, have for the most part been taken from verbal communication, or the controversial writings of the *Brahmans*.

An eternal and presiding first cause forms no part of the *Jain* creed, nor do the *Jains* admit of soul or spirit as distinct from the living principle. All existence is divisible into two heads—*Life* (*Jiva*) or the

---

* [See Lassen, Ind. Alt. III, 567. Weber, l. l., p. 46.]

[1] Colonel MACKENZIE, on the information of the *Belligola Jains*, says *Varddhamána* attained beatitude 2464 years before the year 1801, which is 663 years before Christ. Mr. COLEBROOKE observes, that the *Jains* of Bengal reckon *Varddhamána* to have lived 580 years before *Vikramáditya*, which is A. C. 636.

living and sentient principle; and *Inertia* or *Ajíva,* the various modifications of inanimate matter. Both these are uncreated and imperishable. Their forms and conditions may change, but they are never destroyed; and with the exception of the unusual cases in which a peculiar living principle ceases to be subject to bodily acts, both life and matter proceed in a certain course, and at stated periods the same forms, the same characters, and the same events are repeated.

To proceed, however; according to the original authorities, all objects, sensible or abstract, are arranged under nine categories, termed *Tattwas,* truths or existences, which we shall proceed to notice in some detail*.

I. *Jíva,* Life, or the living and sentient principle, as existing in various forms, but especially reducible to two classes, those with, and those without mobility. The first comprises animals, men, demons, and gods— the second, all combinations of the four elements, earth, water, fire, air, as minerals, vapours, meteors, and tempests—and all the products of the vegetable kingdom. They are again arranged in five classes according to their possession of as many *Indriyas*, or sensible properties. The wholly unconscious bodies to ordinary apprehension, but which have a subtle vitality perceptible to saintly and super-human beings, have the property of form: such are minerals, and the like. Snails, worms, and insects, in general, have

* [Sarvadarśana Sangraha, p. 35 ff. Stevenson, the Kalpa Sútra, p. 116 ff. Colebrooke, Essays, p. 245 ff. 296.]

two properties—form and face. Lice, fleas, and the like have three properties, or form, face, and the organ of smell. Bees, gnats, and the rest have, in addition to these, vision; whilst animals, men, demons, and gods have form, vision, hearing, smell, and taste. To these five predicates of vital beings two others are sometimes added, and they are said to be *Sanjninaḱ* and *Asanjninaḱ*, or, born by procreation, or spontaneously generated. Again, these seven orders are distinguished as complete or incomplete, making altogether fourteen classes of living things. According to the acts done or suffered in each condition, the vital principle migrates to an inferior or superior grade, until it is emancipated from bodily acts altogether. It is a peculiarity of the *Jain* notions of life, that it is always adapted to the body it animates, and diminishes with the gnat, and expands to the elephant, a notion that is treated with just ridicule by the *Brahmans*. Generically, it is defined to be without beginning or end, endowed with attributes of its own, agent and enjoyer, conscious, subtle, proportionate to the body it animates; through sin it passes into animals, or goes to hell; through virtue and vice combined it passes into men, and through virtue alone ascends to heaven; through the annihilation of both vice and virtue it obtains emancipation.

II. *Ajíva*, the second predicate of existence, comprises objects or properties devoid of consciousness and life. These seem to be vaguely and variously classed, and to be in general incapable of interpretation; but the enumeration is commonly fourteen, like the modification of vitality. They are *Dharmástikáya*, *Adharmástikáya*, and *Ákáśástikáya*, each comprehending three varieties. *Kála*, or time, is the tenth; and *Pudgala*, or elementary matter, in four modifications, completes the series.

It is not very easy to understand these technicalities, for the etymology of the words is of little avail. *Astikáya* indicates the existence of body, "*Body is*"; whilst *Dharma* signifies virtue, and *Adharma*, vice; but *Dharma* means also peculiar function or office, in which sense it seems to be here intended, thus—*Dharmástikáya* is defined to be that which facilitates the motion of animate or inanimate bodies, as water for fish. *Adharmástikáya* is that which impedes or stops their motion. *Ákáśástikáya* is the principle of repulsion, that which keeps bodies separate, or space: the varieties of these are only in degree, of little, more, and complete. Time is sufficiently intelligible, but the *Jains* indulge in modifications of it infinitely more extravagant than those for which the Hindus are reproached; thus after enumerating days, weeks, months, and years, we have the *Palya**, or *Palyopama*, a period measured by the time in which a vast well, one hundred *Yojans* every way, filled with minute hairs so closely packed that a river might be hurried over them without penetrating the interstices, could be emptied at the rate of one hair in a century. A

* [See Hemachandra's Abhidh. 132, and p. 304.]

Ságaropama is one hundred million millions of *Palyas*, and an *Avasarpińí* and *Utsarpińí*, which make up a great age, consists each of one hundred million millions of *Ságaras*. *Pudgala* is atomic matter, distinguished like the first three categories, by being combined in three degrees—little, much, and most, whilst it adds a fourth state, or that of *Paramáńu*, primitive, subtle, indivisible, and uncombined.

III. The third *Tattwa* is *Puńya, Good*, or whatever is the cause of happiness to living beings: the subdivisions of this category are forty-two: it will be sufficient here to enumerate a few of the principal.

1. *Uchchhairgotra*, high birth, rank, or the respect of mankind.

2. *Manushyagati*, the state of man, either as obtained from some other form of being or continuance in it.

3. *Suragati*, the state of divinity, Godhead.

4. *Panchendriya*, the state of superior vitality, or possession of five organs of sense.

5. *Panchadeha*, the possession of body, or form of one of five kinds:

Audárika, elementary—that arising from the aggregation of elements, as the bodies of men and beasts.

Vaikriya, transmigrated—that assumed in consequence of acts, as the forms of spirits and gods.

Áhárika, adventitious, one assumed, such as that of the *Púrvadharas*, of one cubit in stature, when they went to see the *Tírthankaras* in *Mahávidehakshetra*.

Taijasa, the form obtained by suppressing mortal wants, in which state fire can be ejected from the body.

Kármańa, the form which is the necessary consequence of acts. These two last are necessarily connected from all time, and can only be disunited by final liberation, or *Moksha*.

Other varieties of '*Good*' are colour, odour, flavour, touch, warmth, coolness, and the like.

IV. *Pápa*, or '*Ill*', in contradistinction to the preceding, and implying that which is the cause of unhappiness to mankind: there are eighty-two kinds;

As the five *Ávarańas*, or difficulties in acquiring as many gradations of holy or divine wisdom. Five *Antaráyas*, disappointments, or impediments, as not obtaining what is about to be presented, not being able to enjoy an object of fruition when in possession of it, and want of vigour though in bodily health. Four *Darśanávasánas*, obstructions, or impediments to information derivable from the senses, or the understanding or to the acquirement of divine knowledge. Five states of sleep, inferior birth, pain, as a condition of existence, as when condemned to purgatory, belief in false gods, defect of size or shape, and all the human passions and infirmities—as anger, pride, covetousness, &c., including, amongst the ills of life, laughter and love.

V. *Ásrava* is that source from which the evil acts of living beings proceed. The varieties are the five *Indriyas*, or organs of sense; the four *Kasháyas*, or passions, as wrath, pride, covetousness, and deceit; the five *Avratas*, non-observance of positive commands, as lying, stealing, &c. and three *Yogas*, addiction or attachment of the mind, speech, and body to any act; *Kriyás*, or acts, of which twenty-six varieties are specified as those performed with any part of the body, or with the instrumentality of a weapon, or the like—those prompted by feelings of hate or wrath—those which are inceptive, progressive, or conclusive—those performed by oneself, or through another creature—those which are suggested by impiety, or unbelief in the doctrine of the *Tírthankaras*.

VI. The sixth *Tattwa* is termed *Samvara*, and is that by which acts are collected or impeded. There are fifty-seven varieties classed under six heads.

1. *Samiti*, keeping the attention properly alive, so as to see immediately if an insect is in the way, to refrain from uttering what should not be said, to distinguish any of the forty-two defects in food given as alms, taking or relinquishing any thing indifferently, and avoiding or abandoning unfit things.

2. *Gupti*, secrecy, or reserve of three kinds, or in mind, speech and person.

3. *Parishahá*, endurance or patience, as when a person has taken a vow of abstemiousness he must bear hunger and thirst; so he must endure heat and cold, when he practices the immoveable posture of *Jain* abstraction; if he is disappointed in what he has laboured or begged for, he must not murmur; and if he is reviled or even beaten, he must patiently submit.

4. *Yatidharma*, the duties of an ascetic; these are ten in number: patience, gentleness, integrity, and

disinterestedness, abstraction, mortification, truth, purity, poverty, and continence.

5. *Bhávaná*, conviction or conclusion, such as that worldly existences are not eternal, that there is no refuge after death, that life is perpetually migrating through the eighty-four *lakhs* of living forms, that life is one or many: it also includes perception of the source whence evil acts proceed, and the like.

The sixth division of this class is *Cháritra*, practice or observance, of five sorts: *Sámáyika*, conventional, or the practice and avoidance of such actions as are permitted or prescribed; *Chhedopasthápaníya*, prevention of evil, as of the destruction of animal life; *Parihára viśuddhi*, purification by such mortification and penance as are enjoined by the example of ancient saints and sages. *Sulakshmasamparáya*, the practices of those pious men who have attained a certain degree of eminence; and *Yathákhyátam*, the same after all the impediments and impurities of human nature are overcome or destroyed.

VII. *Nirjará*, the seventh *Tattwa*, is the religious practice that destroys mortal impurities, or, in other words, penance: it is of two kinds, external and internal; the first comprehends fasting, continence, silence, and bodily suffering; the second, repentance, piety, protection of the virtuous, study, meditation, and disregard, or rejection of both virtue and vice.

VIII. *Bandha* is the integral association of life with acts, as of milk with water, fire with a red hot iron ball; it is of four kinds: *Prakŕiti*, the natural disposition or nature of a thing; *Sthiti*, duration, or measure of time, through which life continues; *Anubhága*, feeling, or sensible quality; *Pradeśa*, atomic individuality. The characters of this principle are illustrated by a *confection*: 1. According to its natural properties it cures phlegm, bile, &c.; 2. it remains efficient but for a given period; 3. it is sweet, bitter, sour, &c.; and 4. it is divisible into large or small proportions, retaining each the properties of the whole mass.

XI. The last of the nine principles is *Moksha*, or liberation of the vital spirit from the bonds of action; it is of nine sorts:

1. *Satpadaprarúpańa.* The determination of the real nature of things, the consequence of a finite course of progress through different stages of being and purification. It is attainable only by living creatures of the highest order, or those having the five organs of sense; by those possessed of the *Trasakáya*, or a body endowed with consciousness and mobility; by those beings which are engendered, not self-produced; by those which have reached the fifth *Cháritra*, or exemption from human infirmity; by those which are in the *Ksháyika Samyaktwa*, or that state of perfection in which elementary or material existence is destroyed; by those no longer requiring material existence; by those who have acquired the *Kevalajnána*, the only knowledge, and the *Kevaladarśana*, or only vision.

2. *Dravyapramáńa*, as regulated by the fitness of the things or persons to be emancipated.

3. *Kshetrapramáńa*, depending on the essentiality

of certain holy places at which only it can be obtained.

4. *Sparśana*, contact, or identity of the individuated living principle with that of the universe, or any part of it.

5. *Kála*, the times or ages at which emancipation is attainable; or the periods spent in various transmigrations.

6. *Antara*, the difference of temperaments or dispositions.

7. *Bhága*, the existence of the imperishable part of all living bodies in which the purified essences or *Siddhas* reside.

8. *Bháva*, the nature or property of that pure existence which has attained the *Kevalajnána*, and other perfections essential to final liberation.

9. *Alpabahutwa*, the degree or ratio in which different classes of beings obtain emancipation[1].

From the details of these nine *Tattwas* the sum of the whole *Jain* system may be collected, but they form only the text on which further subtilties are founded, and they leave the end and scope of all the doctrine or the attainment of ultimate liberation singularly indistinct.

The *Moksha* of the *Jains* is exemption from the incidents of life, and above all from the necessity of

---

[1] Although termed मोक्षभेदाः in the original authorities, these varieties are rather in the requisite conditions for attaining *Moksha*, than in the kind or sort of emancipation attained.

being born again; but in what state the living principle subsists after it is so exempted, does not very satisfactorily appear. In one state indeed the bodily individuality remains, or that of *Jívanmukti*, liberation during life, whilst from most of the subdivisions of *Moksha*, it follows that the *Siddhas*, the pure existences, correspond with our notions of spiritual beings, having an impassive and inappreciable form, variable at will, capable of infinite contraction or dilation, and wholly void of feeling or passion. This is not incompatible with their enjoyment of *Nirván*, another term for *Moksha*, and which, as Mr. COLEBROOKE observes, meaning literally, extinct or gone out as a fire, set as a heavenly luminary, defunct as a saint who has passed away, implies profound calm. "It is not annihilation," he concludes*, "but unceasing apathy which they, 'the *Jains* and *Buddhas*,' understand to be the extinction of their saints, and which they esteem to be supreme felicity worthy to be sought by practice of mortification as well as by acquisition of knowledge."

Besides the notions exhibited in the detail of the nine *Tattwas*, the *Jains* are known in controversial writings** by the title *Saptavádís*, or *Saptabhangís*, the *disputers* or *refuters* of seven positions: more correctly speaking, they are reconcilers, or could be so, of seven contradictory assertions, evincing a sceptical

* [Essays, p. 259.]

** [e. g. Sarvadarśana Saṅgr. pp. 41. 42.]

character which justifies another epithet which they acknowledge, of *Syádvádís*, or assertors of possibilities; the seven positions are the following:

1. A thing is; 2. it is not; 3. it is and it is not; 4. it is not definable; 5. it *is*, but is not definable; 6. it is not, neither is it definable; 7. it is and it is not, and is not definable. Now these positions imply the doctrines of the different schools, the *Sánkhya*, *Vedánta*, and others, with regard to the world, to life, and to spirit, and are met in every case by the *Jains* with the reply, *Syádvá*, *It may be so sometimes;* that is, whatever of these dogmas is advanced will be true in some respects, and not in others; correct under some circumstances, and not under others; and they are therefore not entitled to implicit trust, nor are they irreconcileable. There is one inference to be drawn from this attempt to reconcile the leading doctrines of the principal schools, of some importance to the history of the *Jain* doctrines, and it renders it probable that they were posterior to all the rest. As this reasoning however has been opposed by Rámánuja, it dates earlier than the twelfth century.

Liberation during life and, as a necessary consequence, exemption after it from future birth implies the abandonment of eight classes of *Karmas*, or acts, four of which are noxious and four innoxious; they are all included under the *Tattwa Pápa*, Ill, as above noticed, but are also more especially detailed. To the first order belong the following:

Jnánávaraňa, disregard of the various stages of

knowledge, from simple comprehension to the only true wisdom, as so many steps to final liberation;

Darśanávaraṅa, disbelief in the doctrines of the *Jain* Saints;

Mohaníya, hesitation in obeying the injunctions of the *Jain* code, or doubt as to their importance and the consequences of their neglect;

Antaráya, impeding or vexing those engaged in seeking liberation.

The second class comprises:

Vedaníya, self-consciousness or sufficiency;

Náma, pride of name; *Gotra*, pride of birth; and *Áyushka*, attachment to bodily existence.

These essential principles of the faith are common to all classes of *Jains*, but some differences occur in their *Duties* as they are divided into religious or lay orders, *Yatís* and *Śrávakas*. Implicit belief in the doctrines and actions of the *Tírthankaras* is, of course, obligatory on both; but the former are expected to follow a life of abstinence, taciturnity, and continence, whilst the latter add to their moral and religious code the practical worship of the *Tírthankaras*, and profound reference for their more pious brethren. The moral code of the *Jains* is expressed in five *Mahávratas*, or great duties: Refraining from injury to life, truth, honesty, chastity, and freedom from worldly desires. There are four *Dharmas*, or merits—liberality, gentleness, piety, and penance; and three sorts of restraint—government of the mind, the tongue, and the person. To these are superadded a number of minor instructions or prohibitions, sometimes of a beneficial and sometimes of a trivial, or even ludicrous tendency, such as to abstain, at certain seasons, from salt, flowers, green fruit, and roots, honey, grapes, and tobacco; to drink water thrice strained: never to leave a liquid uncovered, lest an insect should be drowned in it; not to deal in soap, natron, indigo, and iron; and never to eat in the dark lest a fly should be swallowed. Religious characters wear a piece of cloth over their mouths to prevent insects from flying into them, and carry a brush under their arms to sweep the place on which they are about to sit, to remove any ants or other living creatures out of the way of danger. Upon the whole, the doctrine of the *Jainas* is a system of quietism calculated to render those who follow it perfectly innoxious, and to inspire them with apathetic indifference towards both this world and the next.

The ritual of the *Jains* is as simple as their moral code. The *Yatí*, or devotee, dispenses with acts of worship at his pleasure, and the lay votary is only bound to visit daily a temple where some of the images of the *Tírthankaras* are erected, walk round it three times, make an obeisance to the images, with an offering of some trifle, usually fruit or flowers, and pronounce some such *Mantra*, or prayer, as the following: "*Namo Arihantánam, Namo Siddhánam, Namo Aryánam, Namo Upájyánam; Namo Löe Sabba Sahúnam*—Salutation to the *Arhats*, to the Pure Existences, to the Sages, to the Teachers, to all the Devout in the world." A morning prayer is also repeated: "*Ichchhámi khamá Śamaño bandiyon, jo man jáye nisiáye; máthena vandámi*—I beg forgiveness, oh Lord, for your slave, whatever evil thoughts the night may have produced—I bow with my head." The worshipper then perhaps remains to hear read part of the *Kalpasútra* or *Bhaktámara*, or some narrative of one or other of the *Tírthankaras*, and the devotion of their followers, and proceeds to his daily occupations.

The reader in a *Jain* temple is a *Yati*, or religious character; but the ministrant priest, the attendant on the images, the receiver of offerings, and conductor of all usual ceremonies is a *Brahman*. It is a curious peculiarity in the *Jain* system, that they should have no priests of their own, but it is the natural consequence of the doctrine and example of the *Tírthankaras*, who performed no rites, either vicariously or for themselves, and gave no instruction as to their observance. It shews also the true character of this form of faith, that it was a departure from established practices, the observance of which was held by the *Jain* teachers to be matter of indifference, and which none of any credit would consent to regulate; the laity were, therefore, left to their former priesthood, as far as outward ceremonies were concerned.

The objects of worship are properly only the *Tírthankaras*, but the *Jains* do not deny the existence of the Hindu gods, and admit such of them as they have chosen to connect with the adventures of their saints, according to a classification of their own, to a share in the worship offered to their human superiors.

According to the Mythology which they have adopted and modified the *Jains* reckon four classes of divine beings whom they name *Bhuvanapatis*, *Vyantaras*, *Jyotishkas*, and *Vaimánikas*; the first comprises ten orders: the progeny of the *Asuras*, Serpents, *Garuḍa*, the *Dikpálas*, Fire, Air, the Ocean, Thunder and Lightning,—who are supposed to reside in the several hells or regions below the Earth. The second has eight orders: the *Piśáchas*, *Bhútas*, *Kinnaras, Gandharvas*, and other monstrous or terrestrial divinities inhabiting mountains, woods, and forests, as well as the lower regions, or air. The third has five orders: the Sun, Moon, Planets, Asterisms, and other heavenly bodies. The fourth includes the Gods of present and past*Kalpas*. Of the first kind are those born in the Heavens, *Saudharma*, *Íśána*, *Mahendra, Brahmá*, *Sanatkumára*, *Śukra*, and others to the number of twelve, or in the *Kalpas*, when SUDHARMÁ and the rest were severally presiding Deities. The last class reside in two divisions of five and of nine heavens—the five termed *Vijaya*, *Vaijayantí*, &c.; the second termed *Anuttara*, because there are none beyond them, as they crown the triple construction of the universe. In the sovereignty of the hosts of heaven a great number of *Indras* are recognised, but of these two are always specified as the chief, ŚUKRA and ÍŚÁNA, one regent of the north, the other of the south heaven: the former alone has eighty-four thousand fellow gods, each of whom has myriads of associates and attendants.

Above all these rank in dignity, and as objects of worship, the twenty-four *Tírthankaras*, or with those of the past and of the future periods seventy-two. Allusion is made by Hemachandra, in his life of Mahávíra, to a hundred and one, and the same work specifies four *Śáśvat* or eternal *Jinas*, Ŕishabhánana, Chandránana, Várisena, and Varddhamána. What is meant by them is not explained, and they are not recognised by all *Jains*.

The presence of Brahman ministrants, or the lapse of time and the tendency of the native mind to multiply objects of veneration, seems to have introduced different innovations into the worship of the *Jainas* in different parts of Hindustan; and in upper India the ritual in use is often intermixed with formulæ derived from the *Tantras*, and belonging more properly to the *Śaiva* and *Śákta* worship. Images of the *Bhairavas* and *Bhairavis*, the fierce attendants on Śiva and Kálí, take their place in *Jain* temples, and at suitable seasons the *Jains* equally with the Hindus address their adoration to Sarasvatí and Deví[1].

---

[1] Thus in a *Pújápaddhati* procured at *Mainpuri*, where a *Jain* temple of considerable size stands, the *Tírthankaras*, as they are severally presented with offerings, are addressed; *Om Śrí Ŕishabháya Svasti — Om Hrím húm:* and *Om Hrím Śrí Sudharmáchárya, Ádigurubhyo Namaḣ, Om Hrím Hrám, Samajinachaityálayebhyo Śrí Jinendrebhyo namaḣ.* There are also observances for regular Hindu festivals, as the *Śripanchamí, Akshayatritiyá*, &c., when Sarasvati and other goddesses are invoked. Rules are given for the *Ghaṫa Sthápana*, when Śakti or Deví is supposed to be present in a water jar erected as her receptacle and em-

In the South of India, from the account given by Colonel MACKENZIE, it appears that the *Jains* observe all the Brahmanical *Sanskáras*, or essential ceremonies. This is not the case in Upper India, and the only rites followed are the Initiation of the infant, twelve days after birth, by repeating a *Mantra* over it, making a circular mark with the sandal and perfumes on the top of the head: Marriage and Cremation, which are much the same as those of the Brahmans, omitting the *Mantras* of the *Vedas*. *Śráddhas*, obsequial ceremonies at stated periods, are not performed by the *Jains* in Upper Hindustan.

The festivals of the *Jains* are peculiar to themselves, and occur especially on days consecrated by the birth or death of some of the principal *Tírthankaras*, especially the two last, *Párśvanáth* and *Varddhamána*. The places where these events occurred are also objects of pilgrimage, and very numerous assemblages of devout pilgrims occur at them at different seasons: thus, in Behár, a very celebrated place of resort is the scene of *Párśvanáth*'s liberation; the mountain *Samet Śikhara*, or *Parasnáth*, near *Pachete*[1]; and another of equal sanctity, the scene of *Varddhamána*'s departure from earth, is at *Pápapurí*[2], in the

---

blem, and the *Shodaśa Karańa Pújá* ends with a *Lakshmí Stotra*, or Hymn, addressed to the Goddess of Prosperity.

[1] Described very fully, as previously noticed, in the Quarterly Magazine for December, 1827.

[2] It is also written *Apápapurí* and *Pávapurí*, under which

same province. Pilgrims come from all parts of India to these places at all seasons, but the principal *Melás* are held at the former in *Mágh*, and in *Kártik* at the latter. On the western side of India the mountains of *Abú*[1] and *Girinár* are the great scenes of pilgrimage, being covered with *Jain* temples and remains. Ŕishabha Deva and Nemináth seem to be the favourite divinities in that quarter.

Besides these particular festivals, the *Jains* observe several that are common to the Hindus, as the *Vasantayátrá*, or spring festival, the *Śrípanchamí*, and others; they also hold in veneration certain of the Lunar days, as the 2d, 5th, 8th, 11th and 12th; on these no new work should be undertaken, no journey commenced, and fasting, or abstinence at least, and continence should be observed.

The origin of the *Jain* faith is immersed in the obscurity which invests all remote history amongst the Hindus. That it is the most recent of all the systems pursued in Hindustan is rendered highly probable by the extravagances in which it deals, by the doctrines it opposes to those of all other schools, and by the comparatively recent date of many *Jain* authors of celebrity and of numerous monumental relics; but

---

latter name, it and other celebrated *Jaina* shrines in Behár are described by a Native traveller, a *Jain*, in the service of Colonel Mackenzie, in the Calcutta Magazine for June, 1823.

[1] See Asiatic Researches, Vol. XVI. *Jain* Inscriptions at Abú.

at what period it actually took its rise it is not easy to determine[1]. Mr. COLEBROOKE has suggested the probability of the *Jain* religion being the work of PÁRŚVANÁTH, in the account of whom there is a nearer approach to sober history and credible chronology than in the narratives of his predecessors. This would throw back the origin of the *Jain* faith to the ninth century before the Christian era, admitting the *Jain* chronology of VARDDHAMÁNA's existence; but it is difficult to concur in the accuracy of so remote a date, and whatever indirect evidence on the subject is procurable is opposed to such a belief.

It has been supposed that we have notices of the *Jaina* sect as far back as the time of the Macedonian

[1] Major DELAMAINE observes, "the usual idea of the *Jains* being a modern sect may not be erroneous: the doctrines originating with *Ŕishabha*, and continued by *Arhanta*, dividing at periods of schism into more distinct classes, of which the *Jains* or *Śrávaks*, as now established, form one, and the modern *Buddhas*, as in *Burma*, *Siam*, *Ceylon*, *Tibet*, &c. another." T. R. A. S. I, 427.—"Were I disposed to speculate on the origin of the *Jains* from the striking coincidences of doctrine and religious usages between them and the *Buddhists*, I should be led to conjecture that they were originally a sect of Buddhists." Mr. Erskine, Bombay Trans. III, 502.—"It is certainly probable, as remarked by Dr. HAMILTON and Major DELAMAINE, that the *Gautama* of the *Jinas* and of the *Bauddhas* is the same personage, and this leads to the further surmise that both these sects are branches of one stock.—Both have adopted the Hindu Pantheon, or assemblage of subordinate deities, both disclaim the authority of the *Vedas*, and both elevate their pre-eminent saints to divine supremacy." Mr. Colebrooke, Trans. R. A. S. I, 521.

invasion of India, or at least at the period at which MEGASTHENES was sent ambassador to SANDRACOPTUS, and that these notices are recorded by STRABO and ARRIAN. The nature of the expressions which those and other writers have employed has been canvassed by Mr. COLEBROOKE *, and shewn satisfactorily to establish the existence at that time of the regular Brahmans, as well as of other sects: what those sects were, however, it was no part of his object to enquire, and he has left it still to be ascertained how far it can be concluded that the *Jainas* were intended.

Much perplexity in the Greek accounts of the Brahmans Gymnosophists has, no doubt, occurred from their not having been acquainted with the subdivision of the priestly caste into the four orders of student, householder, hermit, and mendicant, and therefore they describe the Brahman sometimes as living in towns, sometimes in woods, sometimes observing celibacy, and sometimes married, sometimes as wearing clothes, and sometimes as going naked; contradictions which, though apparently irreconcileable if the same individuals or classes be meant, were appreciated by the shrewdness of BAYLE more justly than he was himself aware of[1], and are all explained by the *Ácháras*,

* [and by Lassen, Ind. Alt., II, 700 ff., 710.]

[1] "It may be that they (the Brachmanes) did not follow the same institutes in all ages, and that with a distinction of time one might reconcile some of the variations of the authors who have spoken of them."—Article Brachmans, Note C. Harris (I, 454) also has rightly estimated the real character of the Ger-

or institutes of the Hindus, as affecting the various periods of life and corresponding practices of Brahmanical devotion.

As far, therefore, as the customs or observances of the Gymnosophists are described, we have no reason to conclude that any but the followers of the *Vedas* are intended, and the only part of the account applicable to any other sect is the term *Germanes,* or *Sermanes,* or *Samanæans*, applied to one division of the Sophists or Sages. This name, as Mr. Colebrooke observes, seems to bear some affinity to the *Śramańas,* or ascetics of the *Jains* or *Bauddhas*, but we can derive no positive conclusion from a resemblance, which may possibly be rather imaginary than real, and the object of which, after all, is far from being the individual property of any sect, but is equally applicable to the ascetic of every religious system. As distinct from the Brahmans, the *Sarmanes* will be equally distinct from the *Jains*; for the Brahmans, it is said by Porphyry, are of one race; and the *Samanæans* are selected from all the tribes, and consist of persons choosing to prosecute divine studies,—precisely the independent *Sannyási* or *Gosáin* of modern times, few persons of which description belong to the order of the *Brahmans*, or are united with the rest by any community of origin or peculiarity of faith.

Again, another *word* has been adduced in corrobo-

---

manes, and concluded that they were nothing but Gioghis, from Pietro della Valle's description of the latter.

ration of the existence of the *Jains*, and it may be admitted that this is a better proof than the preceding, as the *Pramnæ** are declared to be the opposers of the Brahmans, which is no where mentioned of the *Sarmanes*. This expression is said to designate the *Jains*, but this is far from certain: the term is probably derived from *Pramáńa*, proof, evidence, and is especially the right of the followers of the logical school, who are usually termed *Prámáńikas*: it is applicable, however, to any sect which advocates positive or ocular proof in opposition to written dogmas, or belief in scriptural authority, and is in that sense more correctly an epithet of the *Bauddha* sectaries than of the *Jains*, who admit the legends and worship the deities of the *Puráńas*, and who hold it the height of impiety to question the written doctrines of their own teachers. The proofs from classical writers, therefore, are wholly inadequate to the decision of the antiquity of the *Jains*, and we are still entirely left to sources of a less satisfactory description.

All writers on the *Jains* entitled to our attention agree in admitting an intimate connexion between them and the *Bauddhas*; the chief analogies have been above adverted to, and the inference of later origin is justly founded on the extravagant exaggerations of the system adopted by the *Jains*. Their identity of origin rests chiefly upon the name of GAUTAMA, which appears as that of VARDDHAMÁNA's chief pupil,

* [See Lassen, Ind. Alt. I, 835, Weber, Ind. Lit. 27.]

and as the legislator of the *Bauddha* nations in the east. The dates also assigned to both are not far removed; the apotheosis of the *Buddha* GAUTAMA occurring five hundred and forty-three years before Christ, and the death of MAHÁVÍRA, the preceptor of the *Jain* GAUTAMA, about the same time. That there is some connexion may be conceded, but for reasons already assigned it is not likely that the persons are the same; the *Jains* have not improbably derived their GAUTAMA from that of their predecessors*.

No argument for the antiquity of the *Jains* is derivable from the account given of ŔISHABHA in the *Bhágavata Puráńa***. He was not a seceder from the true faith, although the mistaken imitation of his practices is said to have led others into errors, evidently intending the *Jain* heresy. He is scarcely identifiable, in consequence, with the *Jain* ŔISHABHA, the first of the *Tírthankaras*; but even if that were the case, no confidence could be placed in the authority, as the work is a modern compilation not exceeding, at the most, twelve centuries of antiquity. The refutation of *Jain* doctrines in the *Brahma Sútras**** is a less questionable testimony of their early existence; but the date of that work is to be yet ascertained. ŚANKARA ÁCHÁRYA, the commentator on the texts of VYÁSA, affords a more definite approximation; but he

---

* [Weber, Ueber das Śatrunjaya Máhátmyam, p. 2–6.]

** [V. 5, 28 ff. Vishńu Pur., p. 164, Note.]

*** [II, 2, 6.]

will not carry us back above ten centuries. It is also to be observed, that the objects of the attacks of the *Sútras* and of Śankara are philosophical and speculative tenets, and these may have been current long before they formed part of a distinct practical system of faith, as promulgated by a class of *Bauddhas*, the germ of the *Jains*.

However, we may admit from these authorities the existence of the *Jains* as a distinct sect, above ten or twelve centuries ago; we have reason to question their being of any note or importance much earlier. The *Bauddhas*, we know from Clemens of Alexandria, existed in India in the second century of the Christian æra, and we find them not only the principal objects of Hindu confutation and anathema, but they are mentioned in works of lighter literature referable to that period, in which the *Jains* are not noticed, nor alluded to: the omission is the more worthy of notice, because, since the *Bauddhas* disappeared from India, and the *Jains* only have been known, it will be found that the Hindu writers, whenever they speak of *Bauddhas*, shew, by the phraseology and practices ascribed to them, that they really mean *Jains*: the older writers do not make the same mistake, and the usages and expressions which they give to *Bauddha* personages are not *Jain*, but *Bauddha*; with the one they were familiar, the other were yet unknown.

The literature of the *Jains* themselves is unfavourable to the notion of high antiquity. Hemachandra, one of their greatest writers, flourished in the end of the twelfth century, and the compiler of the *Jain Puráńas* of the *Dekhan* is said to have written at the end of the ninth. The *Kalpa Sútra* professes to have been composed nine hundred and eighty years after the death of MAHÁVÍRA, or fifteen centuries ago; but from internal evidence* it could not have been composed earlier than the twelfth or thirteenth century. Various eminent *Jain* authors were cotemporary also with MUNJA and BHOJA, princes of *Dhár*, in the ninth and tenth century**, and a number of works seem to have been compiled in the sixteenth century during the tolerant reign of AKBAR.

Of the progress of the *Jain* faith in the Gangetic provinces of Upper India we have no very satisfactory traces. It may be doubted if they ever extended themselves in Bengal. Behár, according to their own traditions, was the birth-place of VARDDHAMÁNA, and Benares of PÁRŚVANÁTH; and temples and monuments of their teachers are common in both, particularly the former; but all those now existing are of very recent dates[1], and there are no vestiges referable to an inter-

* [Weber, Ueber das Śatrunjaya Máhátmyam, p. 7–12, fixes the year 632 p. Chr. as the date of its composition.]

** [in the tenth and eleventh, according to Lassen, Ind. Alt., III, 843–54.]

[1] As late even as the eighteenth and nineteenth centuries. [See, however, Journal of the Bombay Br. R. A. S., III, p. 88 ff.]— These dates are sometimes said to indicate the periods at which the temples were repaired, but the intelligent author of the 'Visit to Mount *Párśvanáth*' observes, "only in one instance is

mediate period between the last *Tírthankara,* and the eighteenth century. At Benares its princes professed the faith of *Bauddha* as late as the eleventh century, whilst during the same period, as is proved by inscriptions and the historical work of CHANDRAKAVI, the sovereigns of Kanoj and Dehli were of the orthodox persuasion. It is very doubtful, therefore, if the *Jains* ever formed a leading sect in this part of Hindustan. They were more successful in the west and south.

In Western Márwáŕ, and the whole of the territory subject to the *Chálukya* princes of Guzerat, the *Jain* faith became that of the ruling dynasty; but this occurred at no very remote period. The Mohammedan Geographer EDRISI states that the king of *Nehrwálá**, the capital of Guzerat, worshipped BUDDHA; and we know from the writings of HEMACHANDRA, that he was the apostle of the *Jain* faith in that kingdom—converting KUMÁRA PÁLA, the monarch of Guzerat, to his creed. This is also an occurrence of the twelfth century, or about 1174. The consequences of this conversion are still apparent in the abundant relics of the *Jain* faith, and the numbers by whom it is professed in Márwáŕ, Guzerat, and the upper part of the Malabar Coast.

---

there reason to suspect that the buildings are much older than the inscriptions announce. The most ancient Mundir at that place is reckoned to be but fifty years old."—Calcutta Magazine, December, 1827.

* [i. e. Analavâta, see p. 304 Note, and Lassen, Ind. Alt., III, 546.]

On the Coromandel side of the Peninsula the *Jains* were introduced upon the downfall of the *Bauddhas*, in the reign of AMOGHAVARSHA, king of *Tońdai Mań-ḍalam*, in the ninth century or, according to some traditions, in the eighth. Farther south, in Madurá, the date of their introduction is not known, but they were in power in the eleventh century under KUŃA PÁŃḌYA. In this, and in the twelfth, they seem to have reached their highest prosperity, and from that period to have declined. KUŃA PÁŃḌYA became a *Śaiva*. VISHŃU VARDDHANA, Rájá of Mysore, was converted from the *Jain* to the *Vaishńava* faith in the twelfth century, and about the same time the *Lingavant Śaivas* deposed and murdered VIJALA, the *Jain* king of *Kalyáń**. The sect, however, continued to meet with partial countenance from the kings of *Vijayanagar* until a comparatively modern date.

The conclusions founded on traditionary or historical records are fully supported by the testimony of monuments and inscriptions—the latter of which are exceedingly numerous in the south and west of India. Most of these are very modern—none are earlier than the ninth century. An exception is said to exist in an inscription on a rock at *Belligola*, recording a grant of land by *Chámuńḍa Ráya* to the shrine of GOMATÍŚVARA, in the year 600 of the *Kali* age, meaning the *Kali* of the *Jains*, which began three years after the death of VARDDHAMÁNA. This inscription, therefore,

---

* [Lassen, Ind. Alt., IV, 119 ff., 237 ff.]

if it exists, was written about fifty or sixty years before the Christian æra—but it is not clear that any such record is in existence, the fact resting on the oral testimony of the head Pontiff at *Belligola*: even, if it be legible on the face of the rock, it is of questionable authenticity, as it is perfectly solitary, and no other document of like antiquity has been met with.

The MACKENZIE Collection contains many hundred *Jain* inscriptions. Of these the oldest record grants made by the princes of *Homchi**, a petty state in *Mysore*. None of them are older than the end of the ninth century. Similar grants, extending through the eleventh and twelfth centuries by the VEĹLÁĹA sovereigns of *Mysore*, are also numerous, whilst they continue with equal frequency to the sixteenth and seventeenth centuries, during the existence of the sovereignty of *Vijayanagar*. Again, at *Abú*, under the patronage of the Guzerat princes, we have a number of *Jain* inscriptions, but the oldest of them bears date *Samvat* 1245 (A. D. 1189)[1]; they multiply in the thirteenth and fourteenth centuries, and are found as late as the middle of the eighteenth—and, finally, in *Magadha*, the scene of VARDDHAMÁNA's birth and apotheosis, the oldest inscriptions found date no further back than the beginning of the sixteenth century[2].

---

* [See Journal R. As. Soc., III, 217, compared with Lassen, Ind. Alt., IV, 239, Note.]

[1] Asiatic Researches, Vol. XVI, p. 317.

[2] Dr. HAMILTON's Description of Jain Temples in Behár.—

From all credible testimony, therefore, it is impossible to avoid the inference that the *Jains* are a sect of comparatively recent institution, who first came into power and patronage about the eighth and ninth century: they probably existed before that date as a division of the *Bauddhas*, and owed their elevation to the suppression of that form of faith to which they contributed. This is positively asserted by the traditions of the south in several instances: the *Bauddhas* of *Kánchí* were confuted by Akalanka, a *Jain* priest, and thereupon expelled the country *. Vara Páńḋya, of *Madurá*, on becoming a *Jain*, is said to have persecuted the *Bauddhas*, subjecting them to personal tortures, and banishing them from the country. In *Guzerat Bauddha* princes were succeeded by the *Jains*. There is every reason to be satisfied, therefore, that the total disappearance of the *Bauddhas* in India proper is connected with the influence of the *Jains*, which may have commenced in the sixth or seventh centuries, and continued till the twelfth.

The inveteracy prevalent between kindred schisms is a sufficient reason for any enmity felt by the *Jains* towards the *Bauddhas*, rather than towards the Brahmanical Hindus. There is, indeed, a political leaning to the latter, observable in their recognition of the

---

Trans. R. A. S., I, 525. To these may be added the inscriptions at *Párśvanáth*, and a number of inscriptions a *Gwalior*, copies of which were sent to Mr. Fraser, and which are all dated in the middle of the 15th century.

* [Journal As. Soc. Bengal, VII, 122. Lassen, IV, 239.]

orthodox Pantheon, in the deference paid to the *Vedas*, and to the rites derivable from them, to the institution of castes, and to the employment of Brahmans as ministrant priests. They appear also to have adapted themselves to the prevailing form of Hinduism in different places: thus at *Abú* several *Jain* inscriptions commence with invocations of Śiva[1], and in the *Dekhan* an edict promulgated by Bukka Ráya, of *Vijayanagar*, declares there is no real difference between the *Jains* and *Vaishńavas*[2]. In some places the same temples are resorted to by *Jains* and *Rámánujíya Vaishńavas*, and, as observed by Mr. Colebrooke, a *Jain* on renouncing the heretical doctrines of his sect takes his place amongst the orthodox Hindus as a *Kshatriya* or *Vaiśya*, which would not be the case with a convert, who has not already caste as a Hindu[3]. In the South of India, indeed, the *Jains* preserve the distinction of castes: in Upper India they profess to be of one caste, or *Vaiśyas*. It is very clear, however, that admission to the *Jain* communion was originally independent of caste[4], and the partial adoption of it

---

[1] Major Delamaine notices that the mountain *Girnár* is equally sacred to *Hindus* as to *Jains*, and that an ancient temple of Mahádeva is erected there.

[2] Asiatic Researches, Vol. IX, p. 270 [Lassen, Ind. Alt., IV, 174].

[3] Transactions Royal Asiatic Society, I, 549.

[4] Maháv́ira himself was the son of a king, and should therefore be a *Kshatriya*. His chief disciples, Indrabhúti, and the rest, were *Brahmans*. His especial attendant, Gośála, was an outcast, and his followers, of both sexes, were of every caste.

or pretension to it, is either a spontaneous or politic conformity to the strong feeling on the subject which prevails amongst all Hindus.

These are the great outlines of the rise and progress of the sect as derivable from sources entitled to credit; but the *Jains* have amongst themselves records of sectarial value detailing the succession of different teachers, and the origin of various heresies. Some extracts from one of these attached to a copy of the *Kalpa Sútra* may be acceptable.

The succession of teachers is always deduced from Mahávíra, through his disciple Sudharmá. Of the rest all but Gautama died before their Master, as has been observed above, and Gautama survived him but a month, which he spent in penance and fasting. Sudharmá, therefore, was the only one who remained competent to impart instruction. His pupil was Jambusvámí, the last of the *Kevalís*, or possessors of true wisdom: six teachers follow, termed *Śrutakevalís*, or hearers of the first masters, and then seven others, *Daśapúrvís*, from having been taught the works so named[1].

---

[1] The following are the names of the individuals alluded to in the text:

Śrutakevalís.	Daśapúrvís.
Prabhava Svámí.	*Árya Mahágiri Súri.*
Śayyambhadra Súri.	*Árya Suhastí Súri.*
Yaśobhadra Súri.	*Árya Susthita Súri.*
Sambhúti Vijaya Súri.	*Indradinna Súri.*
Bhadrabáhu Súri.	*Dinna Súri.*
Sthúlabhadra Súri.	*Sinhagiri Súri.*
	Vajrasvámí Súri.

These are common to all the lists when correct. In the *Belligola* list they are omitted, and the successor of JAMBUSVÁMÍ is there named VERAŚÍNA, who may have been, as Mr. COLEBROOKE remarks, a hundred degrees removed. The lists, subsequently, vary according to the particular line of descent to which they belong.

Of these persons the second *Śrutakevali* is reputed to be the author of the *Daśavaikaliká*, one of the standard works of the sect. SUHASTÍ, the second *Daśapúrvi*, was the preceptor of SAMPRATÍ RÁJÁ, and the third, SUSTHITA, founded the *Kote gachcha*, or tribe. VAJRASVÁMÍ, the last, established a particular division called the *Vajra Śákhá*.

Of the succeeding teachers, or *Súris*, the title borne by the spiritual preceptors of the *Jains*, CHANDRASÚRI, the second, is the founder of the family of that name, eight hundred and nine years, it is said, after the emancipation of MAHÁVÍRA. In his time, it is stated, the *Digambaras* arose; but we have seen that they were at least cotemporary with MAHÁVÍRA.

The 38th on the list, from MAHÁVÍRA inclusive, UDYOTANA SÚRI, first classed the *Jains* under eighty-nine Gachchas. The 40th JINEŚVARÍ who lived A. D. 1024, founded the *Khartara* family[1]. With the 44th,

[A few variations occur in Hemachandra's Abhidh., śl. 33 and 34, and in the list of Sthaviras, translated by J. Stevenson. See the Kalpa Sútra and Nava Tatva, p. 100 f.]

[1] Major TOD gives a somewhat different account of the origin of this tribe. *Khartra*, he says, means true, an epithet of dis-

JINADATTA, originated the *Oświál* family, and the *Madhyakhartara* branch; he was a teacher of great celebrity, and impressions of his feet in plaster or on stone are preserved in some temples, as at *Bhelupur* in Benares; he lived in 1148. Other divisions, either of a religious or civil nature, are attributed to various teachers, as the *Chitrabala Gachcha* to JINAPATI SÚRI, in A. D. 1149; the *Anchalika* doctrine to JINEŚVARA in 1160; the *Laghu Khartara* family to JINACHANDRA in 1265; another JINACHANDRA, the 61st in the list, was cotemporary with AKBAR. The list closes with the 70th *Jina*, HARSHA SÚRI, with whom, or his pupils, several works originated in the end of the seventeenth century[1].

Admitting this record to have been carefully preserved, we have seventy-one persons from MAHÁVÍRA, to whom a period of less than fourteen centuries can scarcely be assigned, and whose series would, therefore, have begun in the third century. It is not at all unlikely that such was the case, but no positive con-

---

tinction which was bestowed by that great supporter of the *Buddhists* or *Jains*, SIDRÁJ, King of *Anhalvára Pattan*, on one of the branches *(Gachch)* in a grand religious disputation at the capital, in the eleventh century. The accounts are by no means incompatible, and my authority represents *Jineśvari* victorious in a controversy.

[1] HEMACHANDRA, at the end of the *Mahávíra Charitra*, after stating that VAJRASVÁMÍ founded the VAJRAŚÁKHÁ, which was established in the *Chandra Gachcha*, gives the teachers of that family down to himself, YAŚOBHADRA, PRADYUMNA, VIŚVASENA, DEVACHANDRA, and HEMACHANDRA.

clusion can be drawn from a single document of this nature: a comparison with other lists is necessary, to determine the weight to be attached to it as an authority.

The *Jains* are divided into two principal divisions, *Digambaras* and *Śvetámbaras*; the former of which appears to have the best pretensions to antiquity, and to have been most widely diffused[1]. The discriminating difference is implied in these terms, the former meaning the *Sky-clad*, that is, naked, and the latter the white-robed, the teachers being so dressed. In the present day, however, the *Digambara* ascetics do not go naked, but wear coloured garments; they confine the disuse of clothes to the period of their meals, throwing aside their wrapper when they receive the food given them by their disciples: the points of difference between the two sects are far from restricted to that of dress, and comprehend a list of no fewer than seven hundred, of which eighty-four are regarded as of infinite importance: a few of these may be here noticed.

The *Śvetámbaras* decorate the images of the *Tirthankaras* with earrings, necklaces, armlets, and tiaras

---

[1] All the *Dakhini Jains* appear to belong to the *Digambara* division. So it is said do the majority of the *Jains* in Western India. In the early philosophical writings of the Hindus the *Jains* are usually termed *Digambaras*, or *Nagnas*, naked. The term *Jain* rarely occurs, and *Śvetámbara* still more rarely if ever, as observed in the text; also VARDHAMÁNA, practically at least, was a *Digambara*.

of gold and jewels: the *Digambaras* leave their images without the foreign aid of ornament.

The *Śvetámbaras* assert that there are twelve heavens, and sixty-four *Indras*: the *Digambaras* maintain that there are sixteen heavens, and one hundred Olympian monarchs.

The *Śvetámbaras* permit their *Gurus* to eat out of vessels: the *Digambaras* receive the food in their open hands from their disciples.

The *Śvetámbaras* consider the accompaniments of the brush, waterpot, &c., as essential to the character of an ascetic: the *Digambaras* deny their importance.

The *Śvetámbaras* assert that the *Angas*, or scriptures, are the work of the immediate disciples of the *Tírthankaras*: the *Digambaras*, with more reason, maintain that the leading authorities of the *Jain* religion are the composition of subsequent teachers or *Ácháryas*.

The advantage gained by the *Digambaras* in the last debateable matter, they lose, it is to be apprehended, in the next, when they assert that no woman can obtain *Nirváń*, in opposition to the more gallant doctrine of their rivals, which admits the fair sex to the enjoyment of final annihilation.

These will be sufficient specimens of the causes of disagreement that divide the *Jainas* into two leading branches, whose mutual animosity is, as usual, of an intensity very disproportionate to the sources from whence it springs.

Besides these two great divisions, several minor sects are particularised as existing amongst the *Jains*. They appear, however, to be of no importance, as it has been found impossible to obtain any satisfactory account of the heresies they have adopted, or of their origin and present condition. Schism was contemporary even with MAHÁVÍRA, and his son-in-law, JAMÁLI, founded a dissentient order. His follower, GOŚÁLA, was also the institutor of a sect, and an impostor into the bargain, pretending to be the twenty-fourth *Tírthankara*. VAJRABANDA, the pupil of a very celebrated *Digambara* teacher, KUNDA KUŃḋ ÁCHÁRYA, founded the *Dráviḋa* sect, according to some in the fifth, and to the others, in the seventh century. VAJRASVÁMÍ instituted the *Mahániśitha* sect, and JINENDRA SÚRI founded the *Lampaka* sect, by which images were discarded. The sects now most often heard of, although little known, are the *Múla Sanghís*, who use brushes of peacock's feathers, wear red garments, and receive alms in their hands: the *Káshṫa Sanghís*, who make their images of wood and employ brushes of the tail of the *Yak*: the *Terah Panthís* and *Bís Panthís*, or followers of thirteen and of twenty, said sometimes to refer to the number of objects which are most essential to salvation, and at others, explained by a legend of the foundation of the heresy by a number of persons, such as the denomination implies. Both these are said to deny the supremacy of a *Guru*, to dispense with the ministration of a *Brahman*, and to present no perfumes, flowers, nor fruits to the images of the

Tírthankaras[1]. The *Bhíshańa Panthís* carry their aversion to external emblems still farther, and discard the use of images altogether. The *Duńdiyas* and *Samvegís* are religious orders: the former affect rigorous adherence to the moral code, but disregard all set forms of prayer or praise, and all modes of external worship: the *Samvegís* follow the usual practices, but subsist upon alms, accepting no more than is indispensable for present wants.

The whole of the *Jains* are again distinguished into clerical and lay, or into *Yatís* and *Śrávakas*: the former lead a religious life, subsisting upon the alms supplied by the latter. According to the greater or less degree of sanctity to which they pretend are their seeming purity and outward precision, shewn especially in their care of animal life: they carry a brush to sweep the ground before they tread upon it; never eat nor drink in the dark, lest they should inadvertently swallow an insect, and sometimes wear a thin cloth over their mouths lest their breath should demolish some of the atomic ephemera that frolic in the sun-beams; they wear their hair cut short, strictly they should pluck it out by the roots; they profess continence and poverty, and pretend to observe frequent fasts and exercise profound abstraction. Some of them may be simple enthusiasts; many of them, however, are knaves, and the reputation which they

[1] The *Bis Panthís* are said to be, in fact, the orthodox *Digambaras*, of whom the *Terah Panthís* are a dissenting branch.

enjoy all over India as skilful magicians is not very favourable to their general character: they are, in fact, not unfrequently *Charlatans* pretending to skill in palmistry and necromancy, dealing in empirical therapeutics, and dabbling in chemical, or rather alchemical manipulations. Some of them are less disreputably engaged in traffic, and they are often the proprietors of *Maths* and temples, and derive a very comfortable support from the offerings presented by the secular votaries of *Jina*. The *Yatis*, as above remarked, never officiate as priests in the temples, the ceremonies being conducted by a member of the orthodox priesthood, a *Brahman*, duly trained for the purpose. The *Yatis* are sometimes collected in *Maths* called by them *Pośálas*, and even when abroad in the world, they acknowledge a sort of obedience to the head of the *Pośála* of which they were once members.

The secular members of the *Jaina* religion, or *Śrávakas*, follow the usual practices of the other Hindus, but give alms only to the *Yatis*, and present offerings and pay homage only to the *Tírthankaras*; the present worship, indeed, is almost restricted to the two last of these personages, to Párśvanáth, as commonly named *Páriśnáth*, the twenty-third, and to Varddhamána or Mahávíra Svámí, the twenty-fourth *Tírthankara* of the present age. The temples of these divinities are, in general, much handsomer buildings than those of the orthodox Hindus: they consist of a square or oblong room, large enough to admit a tolerably numerous assemblage, surrounded by an open portico:

on one side is a sort of altar-piece of several stages; on the centre of the upper tier sits the chief deity of the temple supported by two other *Arhats*, whilst the rest, or a portion of them, are ranged upon the inferior tiers: the steeple is also distinguishable from that of other temples, being formed of departments, which are intended, apparently, to represent leaves, and surmounted by a pole resembling a flag-staff terminating in a gilt knob: there are several of these temples in the chief cities along the Ganges, and no fewer than a dozen in *Murshidábád*, to which the circumstance of the *Śet* family being of the *Jaina* persuasion attracted a number of fellow worshippers. In Calcutta there are four temples, two belonging to each sect. In Behár are the temples of Páriśnáth and the *Pádukas*, or feet of Varddhamána, and Vásupújya. Benares possesses several temples, one of which, in the suburb, called *Belupura*, is honoured as the birthplace of Párśvanáth. The shrine comprises two temples, one belonging to the *Śvetámbaras*, and one to the *Digambaras*. A temple of some size and celebrity occurs at *Mainpuri*, in the Doab, and most of the towns in that direction present *Jain* spires. The chief temples, however, are to the westward, and especially at *Jaypur*. The whole of *Mewár* and *Márwár* is strewed with remains of the sacred edifices of this sect.

The *Jains* of the South of India, as has been observed, are divided into castes: this is not the case in Upper Hindustan, where they are all of one caste, or, which is the same thing, of none. They are nevertheless equally tenacious of similar distinctions, and not only refuse to mix with other classes, but recognise a number of orders amongst themselves, between which no intermarriages can take place, and many of whom cannot eat together. This classification is the *Gachcha* or *Got*, the family or race, which has been substituted for the *Varńa*, the *Játi*, or caste. Of these *Gachchas*, or family divisions, they admit eighty-four[1],

---

[1] The following are the appellations of the eighty-four *Gachchas*:

Khandewál.
Porwál.
Agarwál.
Jaiswál.
Barihiya.
Golál.
Gajapúrví.
Śrímál.
Vanśwál, or Oświl.
Porwár.
Palliwál.
Danderwál.
Himmdrgujaráti.
Baramora.
Kharawa.
Labechu.
Khandoya.
Kathnora.
Kabliya.
Kapola.
Nadila.
Natila.
Moihiya.
Tattora.
Bágerwál.
Harsola.
Śriguru.
Jolura.
Gahakhanduja.
Chordiya.
Bhungeriwál.
Brahmatá.
Beduja.
Báhariya.
Goguwál.
Ańdáluja.
Gogayya.
Mańdaluja.
Pancham.
Somacanśibogar.
Chaturtha.
Hardar.
Ḍhaktha.
Vaiśya.
Nágdhár.
Por.
Surendra.
Kadaya.
Káhari.
Sońiya.
Soráṭhiya.
Rájiya.
Maya.
Kammeha.
Bhangela.
Gangarda.
Márkeya.
Moiwál.
Śvetwál.
Chakkichap.
Khandarya.
Narischya.
Bimongai.
Vikriya.
Vidyavya.
Bersári.
Astaki.
Ashṭadhár.
Páwarábhi.
Ḍhakkachála.
Bogośrí.
Naraya.
Korgháriya.
Bamáriya.
Séksantánya.
Ánándi.
Nágora.
Tattora.
Pákhastya.
Sachhora.
Jannorá.
Nemilára.
Gandoriya.
Dhawaljóti.

and these again appear to comprehend a variety of subdivisions: some of the *Gachchas* comprehend a portion of *Śrí Vaishńavas*, between which sect and the *Jains* in Upper India a singular alliance seems sometimes to prevail.

The condition of *Jaina* worship may be inferred from the above notices of its temples. Its professors are to be found in every province of Hindustan, collected chiefly in towns, where, as merchants and bankers, they usually form a very opulent portion of the community. In Calcutta there are said to be five hundred families; but they are much more numerous at *Murshidábád*. In *Behár* they have been estimated at between three and four hundred families. They are in some numbers in *Benares*, but become more numerous ascending the *Doáb*. It is, however, to the westward that they abound: the provinces of *Mewár* and *Máŕwáŕ* being apparently the cradle of the sect[1]. They are also numerous in *Guzerat*, in the upper part of the Malabar coast, and are scattered throughout

---

Some of these are well known, but many of the others are never met with. The list was furnished by a respectable *Yatí*—but how far it is throughout genuine, I cannot pretend to say. It omits several *Gachchas* of celebrity, particularly the *Chandra* and *Khartara*.

[1] According to Major Tod, the Pontiff of the *Kharatra Gachcha* has eleven thousand clerical disciples scattered over India, and the single community of *Ośwál* numbers one hundred thousand families. In the West of India, the officers of the state and revenue, the bankers, the civil magistrates, and the heads of corporations, are mostly *Jains*.—Trans. R. As. Soc., Vol. II, 1, p. 263.

the Peninsula. They form, in fact, a very large and, from their wealth and influence, a most important division of the population of India.

BÁBÁ LÁLÍS.

The followers of BÁBÁ LÁL are sometimes included amongst the *Vaishńava* sects, and the classification is warranted by the outward seeming of these sectaries, who streak the forehead with *Gopíchandana*, and profess a veneration for RÁMA: in reality, however, they adore but one God, dispensing with all forms of worship, and directing their devotion by rules and objects derived from a medely of *Vedánta* and *Ssúfí* tenets.

BÁBÁ LÁL was a *Kshatriya*, born in *Málvá*, about the reign of JEHÁNGÍR: he early adopted a religious life under the tuition of CHETANA SVÁMÍ, whose fitness as a teacher had been miraculously proved. This person soliciting alms of BÁBÁ LÁL received some raw grain, and wood to dress it with: lighting the wood, he confined the fire between his feet, and supported the vessel in which he boiled the grain upon his insteps. BÁBÁ LÁL immediately prostrated himself before him as his *Guru*, and receiving from him a grain of the boiled rice to eat, the system of the universe became immediately unfolded to his comprehension. He followed CHETANA to *Lahore*, whence being dispatched to *Dwáraká* by his *Guru*, to procure some of the earth called *Gopíchandana*, he effected his mission in less than an hour: this miraculous rapidity, the distance being some hundred miles, attesting his proficiency, he was dismissed by his *Guru*, in order to become a teacher. He settled at *Dehanpur*, near *Sirhind*, where he erected a *Math*, comprehending a handsome temple, and where he initiated a number of persons in the articles of his faith.

Amongst the individuals attracted by the doctrines of Bábá Lál, was the liberal-minded and unfortunate Dárá Shukoh: he summoned the sage to his presence to be instructed in his tenets, and the result of seven interviews was committed to writing, in the form of a dialogue between the Prince and the *Pír*, by two literary Hindus attached to the Prince's train, one Yadu Dás, a *Kshatriya*, and the other Raichand *Brahman*, the latter the *Mírmúnshí*; the interview took place in the garden of Jaffar Khán Sáduh, in the 21st year of Sháh Jehán's reign, or 1649: the work is entitled *Nádir un nikát*, and is written, as the name implies, in the Persian language. Some miscellaneous extracts from it may not be unacceptable, as they may not only explain the tenets of Bábá Lál, and something of the *Vedánta* and *Ssúfí* doctrines, but may illustrate better than any description the notions generally prevailing of the duties of a religious and mendicant life. The interrogator is the Prince, Bábá Lál himself the respondent.

What is the passion of a Fakír? —Knowledge of God.
What is the power of an Ascetic?—Impotence.
What is Wisdom?—Devotion of the heart to the Heart's Lord.
How are the hands of a Fakír employed?—To cover his ears.

Where are his feet?—Hidden, but not hampered by his garments.

What best becomes him?—Vigilance night and day.

In what should he be unapt?—Immoderate diet.

In what should he repose?—In a corner, seclusion from mankind, and meditation on the only True.

What is his dwelling?—God's creatures.

His Kingdom?—God.

What are the lights of his mansion?—The Sun and Moon.

What is his couch?—The Earth.

What is his indispensable observance?—Praise and glorification of the Cherisher of all things, and the needer of none.

What is suitable for a Fakír?—*Lá*, none; as *Lá Allah*, &c. there is no God but God.

How passes the existence of a Fakír?—Without desire, without restraint, without property.

What are the duties of a Fakír?—Poverty and faith.

Which is the best religion?—Verse, "The Creed of the lover differs from other Creeds. God is the faith and creed of those who love him, but to do good is best for the follower of every faith." Again, as HÁFIZ says:

> The object of all religions is alike,
> All men seek their beloved,—
> What is the difference between prudent and wild?
> All the world is love's dwelling,
> Why talk of a Mosque or a Church?

With whom should the Fakír cultivate intimacy?—With the Lord of loveliness.

To whom should he be a stranger?—To covetousness, anger, envy, falsehood, and malice.

Should he wear garments or go naked?—The loins should be covered by those who are in their senses; nudity is excusable in those who are insane. The love of God does not depend upon a cap or a coat.

How should a *Fakír* conduct himself?—He should perform what he promises, and not promise what he cannot perform.

Should evil be done to evil doers?—The *Fakír* is to do evil to none, he is to consider good and ill alike, so HÁFIZ says:

"The repose of the two worlds depends upon two rules, kindness to friends and gentleness to foes."

What is the nature of the *Takia* (the pillow or abbacy?)—To commence with a seat upon it is improper, and at all times an erratic life is preferable; when the body is weakened by age or sickness, the *Fakir* may then repose upon his pillow: so situated, he should welcome every *Fakir* as his guest, and consider nothing but God to be his own.

Is it necessary for a *Fakir* to withdraw from the world?—It is prudent, but not necessary: the man in society who fixes his heart on God is a *Fakir*, and the *Fakir* who takes an interest in the concerns of men is a man of the world, so MAULÁNÁ RÚMÍ observes: "What is the world? forgetfulness of God, not clothes, nor wealth, nor wife, nor offspring."

What is the difference between nature and created things?—Some compare them to the seed and the tree. The seed and the tree are equivalent though related; although the same in substance, they are not necessarily co-existent nor co-relative. They may be also compared to the waves and the sea; the first cannot be without the second, but the sea may be without waves, wind is necessary to their product: so, although nature and created things are of one essence, yet the evolution of the latter from the former requires the interference of an evolving cause, or the interposition of a Creator.

Are the soul, life, and body merely shadows?—The soul is of the same nature as God, and one of the many properties of universal life, like the sea, and a drop of water; when the latter joins the former, it also is sea.

How do the *Paramátmá* (supreme soul) and *Jivátmá* (living soul) differ?—They do not differ, and pleasure and pain ascribable to the latter arises from its imprisonment in the body: the water of the Ganges is the same whether it run in the river's bed or be shut up in a decanter.

What difference should that occasion?—Great: a drop of wine added to the water in the decanter will impart its flavor to the whole, but it would be lost in the river. The *Paramátmá*, therefore, is beyond accident, but the *Jivátmá* is afflicted by sense and passion. Water cast loosely on a fire will extinguish the fire; put that water over the fire in a boiler, and the fire will evaporise the water, so the body being the confining caldron, and passion the fire, the soul, which is compared to the water, is dispersed abroad;—the one great supreme soul is incapable of these properties, and happiness is therefore only obtained in re-union with it, when the dispersed and individualized portions combine again with it, as the drops of water with the parent stream; hence, although God needs not the service of his slave, yet the slave should remember that he is separated from God by the body alone, and may exclaim perpetually: Blessed be the moment when I shall lift the veil from off that face. The veil of the face of my beloved is the dust of my body.

What are the feelings of the perfect *Fakír*?—They have not been, they are not to be, described, as it is said: a person asked me what are the sensations of a lover? I replied, when you are a lover, you will know.

PRÁṄ NÁTHÍS.

These are also called *Dhámís*: they owe their origin to PRÁṄ NÁTH, a *Kshatriya*, who being versed in Mohammedan learning, as well as in his own, attempted to reconcile the two religions: with this view he composed a work called the *Mahitáriyal*, in which texts from the *Korán*, and the *Vedas* are brought together, and shewn not to be essentially different. PRÁṄ NÁTH flourished about the latter part of AURANGZEB's reign, and is said to have acquired great influence with CHATTRASÁL, *Rájá* of *Búndelkhaṅd*, by effecting the discovery of a diamond mine. *Búndelkhaṅd* is the chief seat of his followers, and in *Punna* is a building consecrated to the use of the sect, in one apartment of which, on a table covered with gold cloth, lies the volume of the founder.

As a test of the disciple's consent to the real identity of the essence of the Hindu and Mohammedan creeds, the ceremony of initiation consists of eating in the society of members of both communions: with this exception, and the admission of the general principle, it does not appear that the two classes confound their civil or even religious distinctions: they continue to observe the practices and ritual of their forefathers, whether Musalman or Hindu, and the union, beyond that of community of eating, is no more than any rational individual of either sect is fully prepared for, or the admission, that the God of both, and of all religions, is one and the same.

SÁDHS.

A full account of this sect of Hindu Unitarians, by the Reverend Mr. FISHER, was published in the Missionary Intelligencer some years ago, and some further notice of them is inserted in the Transactions of the Royal Asiatic Society[1], by Mr. TRANT. They are distinguished from other Hindus by professing the adoration of one Creator, and by personal and moral observances which entitle them, in their own estimation, to the appellation of *Sádhs*, *Sádhus*, Pure or Puritans.

The *Sádhs* are found chiefly in the upper part of the *Doáb*, from *Farúkhábád* to beyond *Dehli*. In the

---

* [1, 251 ff.]

former they occupy a suburb called *Sádhwára*, and are more numerous there than in any other town; their numbers are estimated at two thousand. There are said to be some at *Mirzapore*, and a few more to the South; their numbers, however, are limited, and they are chiefly from the lower classes.

The sect originated in the year of VIKRAMÁDITYA 1714 (A. D. 1658), according to Mr. TRANT, with a person named BÍRBHÁN, who received a miraculous communication from one UDAYA DÁS, and in consequence taught the *Sádh* doctrines. Mr. FISHER calls BÍRBHÁN the disciple of JOGÍ DÁS, who commanding a body of troops in the service of the *Rájá* of *Dholpur* was left as slain on the field of battle, but restored to life by a stranger in the guise of a mendicant, who carried him to a mountain, taught him the tenets of the faith, and having bestowed upon him the power of working miracles sent him to disseminate his doctrines. These circumstances are rather obscurely alluded to in the original authorities consulted on the present occasion, but they agree with the above in considering BÍRBHÁN an inhabitant of *Brijhasir*, near *Nárnaul*, in the province of *Dehli*, as the founder of the sect, at the date above mentioned. BÍRBHÁN received his knowledge from the SAT GURU, the pure teacher, also called *Úda ká Dás*, the servant of the one God, and particularly described as the *Málek ká Hukm*, the order of the Creator, the personified word of God.

The doctrines taught by the super-human instructor of BÍRBHÁN were communicated in *Śabdas* and *Sákhis*, detached Hindí stanzas like those of Kabír. They are collected into manuals, and read at the religious meetings of the *Sádhs*: their substance is collected into a tract entitled *Ádi Upadeś*, first precepts, in which the whole code is arranged under the following twelve *Hukms*, or Commandments.

1. Acknowledge but one God who made and can destroy you, to whom there is none superior, and to whom alone therefore is worship due, not to earth, nor stone, nor metal, nor wood, nor trees, nor any created thing. There is but one Lord, and the word of the Lord. He who meditates on falsehoods, practices falsehood, and commits sin, and he who commits sin falls into Hell.

2. Be modest and humble, set not your affections on the world, adhere faithfully to your creed, and avoid intercourse with all not of the same faith, eat not of a stranger's bread.

3. Never lie nor speak ill at any time to, or of any thing, of earth or water, of trees or animals. Let the tongue be employed in the praise of God. Never steal, nor wealth, nor land, nor beasts, nor pasture: distinguish your own from another's property, and be content with what you possess. Never imagine evil. Let not your eyes rest on improper objects, nor men, nor women, nor dances, nor shows.

4. Listen not to evil discourse, nor to any thing but the praises of the Creator, nor to tales, nor gossip, nor calumny, nor music, nor singing, except hymns; but then the only musical accompaniment must be in the mind.

5. Never covet any thing, either of body or wealth: take not of another. God is the giver of all things, as your trust is in him so shall you receive.

6. When asked what you are, declare yourself a *Sádh*, speak not of caste, engage not in controversy, hold firm your faith, put not your hope in men.

7. Wear white garments, use no pigments, nor collyrium, nor dentifrice, nor *Menhdí*, nor mark your person, nor your

forehead with sectarial distinctions, nor wear chaplets, or rosaries, or jewels.

8. Never eat nor drink intoxicating substances, nor chew *pán*, nor smell perfumes, nor smoke tobacco, nor chew nor smell opium, hold not up your hands, bow not down your head in the presence of idols or of men.

9. Take no life away, nor offer personal violence, nor give damnatory evidence, nor seize any thing by force.

10. Let a man wed one wife, and a woman one husband, let not a man eat of a woman's leavings, but a woman may of a man's, as may be the custom. Let the woman be obedient to the man.

11. Assume not the garb of a mendicant, nor solicit alms, nor accept gifts. Have no dread of necromancy, neither have recourse to it. Know before you confide. The meetings of the Pious are the only places of pilgrimage, but understand who are the Pious before you so salute them.

12. Let not a *Sádh* be superstitious as to days, or to lunations, or to months, or the cries or appearances of birds or animals; let him seek only the will of the Lord.

These injunctions are repeated in a variety of forms, but the purport is the same, and they comprise the essence of the *Sádh* doctrine which is evidently derived from the unitarianism of KABÍR, NÁNAK, and similar writers, with a slight graft from the principles of Christianity. In their notions of the constitution of the universe, in the real, although temporary existence of inferior deities and their incarnations, and in the ultimate object of all devotion, liberation from life on earth, or *Mukti*, the *Sádhs* do not differ from other *Hindus*.

The *Sádhs* have no temples, but assemble at stated periods in houses, or courts adjoining set apart for this purpose. According to Mr. FISHER, their meetings are held every full moon, when men and women collect at an early hour, all bringing such food as they are able, the day is spent in miscellaneous conversation, or in the discussion of matters of common interest. In the evening they eat and drink together, and the night is passed in the recitation of the stanzas attributed to BÍRBHÁN, or his preceptor, and the poems of DÁDÚ, NÁNAK, or KABÍR.

From the term they apply to the deity, SATNÁM, the *true* name, the *Sádhs* are also called *Satnámís*; but this appellation more especially indicates a different, although kindred, sect.

SATNÁMÍS.

These profess to adore the true name alone, the one God, the cause and creator of all things, *Nirguń*, or void of sensible qualities, without beginning or end. They borrow, however, their notions of creation from the *Vedánta* philosophy, or rather from the modified form in which it is adapted to vulgar apprehension. Worldly existence is illusion, or the work of MÁYÁ, the primitive character of BHAVÁNÍ, the wife of ŚIVA. They recognise accordingly the whole Hindu Pantheon—and, although they profess to worship but one God, pay reverence to what they consider manifestations of his nature visible in the *Avatárs*, particularly RÁMA and KŔISHŃA.

Unlike the *Sádhs* also, they use distinctive marks, and wear a double string of silk bound round the right wrist. Frontal lines are not invariably employed, but some make a perpendicular streak with ashes of a burnt offering made to HANUMÁN.

Their moral code is something like that of all *Hindu* quietists, and enjoins indifference to the world, its pleasures or its pains, implicit devotion to the spiritual guide, clemency and gentleness, rigid adherence to truth, the discharge of all ordinary, social, or religious obligations, and the hope of final absorption into the one spirit which pervades all things.

There is little or no difference therefore in essentials between the *Satnámís* and some of the *Vaishńava* unitarians, but they regard themselves as a separate body, and have their own founder JAGJÍVAN DÁS. He was a *Kshatriya* by birth, and continued in the state of *Gŕihastha*, or house-holder, through life: he was a native of *Oude*, and his *Samádh*, or shrine, is shewn at *Katwa*, a place between *Lucknow* and *Ajúdhyá*. He wrote several tracts, as the *Jnán Prakáś*, *Mahá-pralaya*, and *Prathama Grantha*: they are in *Hindí* couplets; the first is dated in *Samvat* 1817, or A. D. 1761, the last is in the form of a dialogue between ŚIVA and PÁRVATÍ. The following is from the *Mahápralaya*.

"The pure man lives amidst all, but away from all: his affections are engaged by nothing: what he may know he knows, but he makes no enquiry: he neither goes nor comes, neither learns nor teaches, neither cries nor sighs, but discusses himself with himself. There is neither pleasure nor pain, neither clemency nor wrath, neither fool nor sage to him. JAGJÍVANDÁS asks, does any one know a man so exempt from infirmity who lives apart from mankind and indulges not in idle speech?"

ŚIVA NÁRÁYAŃÍS.

This is another sect professing the worship of one God, of whom no attributes are predicated. Their unitarianism is more unqualified than that of either of the preceding, as they offer no worship, pay no regard whatever to any of the objects of Hindu or Mohammedan veneration. They also differ from all in admitting proselytes alike from Hindus or Mohammedans, and the sect comprises even professed Christians from the lower classes of the mixed population.

Admission into the sect is not a matter of much ceremony, and a *Guru*, or spiritual guide, is not requisite; a few *Śiva Náráyańís* assemble at the requisition of a novice, place one of their text books in the midst of them, on which betel and sweetmeats have previously been arranged. After a while these are distributed amongst the party, a few passages are read from the book, and the sect has acquired a new member.

Truth, temperance, and mercy are the cardinal virtues of this sect, as well as of the *Sádhs*; polygamy is prohibited, and sectarial marks are not used: conformity to the external observances of the Hindus or Mohammedans, independently of religious rites, is recommended, but latitude of practice is not unfrequent; and the *Śiva Náráyańis*, of the lower orders, are occasionally addicted to strong potations.

The sect derives its appellation from that of its founder Śivanáráyań, a *Rájput*, of the *Nerivána* tribe, a native of *Chandávan*, a village near *Gházípur*: he flourished in the reign of Mohammed Sháh, and one of his works is dated *Samvat*, 1791, or A. D. 1735. He was a voluminous writer in the inculcation of his doctrines, and eleven books, in Hindí verse, are ascribed to him. They are entitled: *Lao* or *Lava Granth*, *Śántvilás*, *Vajan Granth*, *Śántsundara*, *Gurunyás*, *Śántáchárí*, *Śántopadeśa*, *Śabdávalí*, *Śántparváńa*, *Śántmahimá*, *Śántságar*.

There is also a twelfth, the Seal of the whole, but it has not yet been divulged, remaining in the exclusive charge of the head of the sect. This person resides at *Balsande*, in the *Gházípur* district, where there is a college and establishment.

The *Śivanáráyańis* are mostly *Rájputs*, and many are *Sipáhis*: many of the Up-country Bearers also belong to the sect. The members are said to be numerous about *Gházípur*, and some are to be met with in Calcutta.

ŚÚNYAVÁDÍS.

The last sect which it has been propose to noticed is one of which the doctrines are atheistical. There is no novelty in this creed, as it was that of the *Chárvákas* and *Nástikas*, and is, to a great extent, that of the *Bauddhas* and *Jains*; but an attempt has been recently made to give it a more comprehensive and universal character, and to bring it within the reach of popular attraction.

A distinguished Patron of the *Śúnyavádís* was DÁYARÁM, the *Rájá* of *Hatras*, when that fortress was destroyed by the Marquis of HASTINGS. Under his encouragement a work in Hindí verse was composed by BAKHTÁVAR, a religious mendicant, entitled the *Śúnísár*, the essence of emptiness, the purport of which is to shew that all notions of man and God are fallacies, and that nothing is. A few passages from this book will convey an idea of the tenets of the sect.

"Whatever I behold is Vacuity. Theism and Atheism—MÁYÁ and BRAHM—all is false, all is error; the globe itself, and the egg of BRAHMÁ, the seven *Dwípas* and nine *Khańdas*, heaven and earth, the sun and moon, BRAHMÁ, VISHŃU and ŚIVA, KÚRMA and ŚESHA, the *Guru* and his pupil, the individual and the species, the temple and the god, the observance of ceremonial rites, and the muttering of prayers, all is emptiness. Speech, hearing and discussion are emptiness, and substance itself is no more."

"Let every one meditate upon himself, nor make known his self-communion to another; let him be the worshipper and the worship, nor talk of a difference between this and that; look into yourself and not into another, for in yourself that other will be found. There is no other but myself, and I talk of another from ignorance. In the same way as I see my face in a glass I see myself in others; but it is error to think that what I see is not my face, but that of another—whatever you see is but yourself, and father and mother are non-entities; you are the infant and the old man, the wise man and the fool, the male and the female: it is you who are drowned in the stream, you who pass over, you are the killer, and the slain, the slayer and the eater, you are the king and the subject. You seize yourself and let go, you sleep, and you wake, you dance for yourself and sing for yourself. You are the sensualist and the ascetic, the sick man and the strong. In short, whatever you see, that is you, as bubbles, surf, and billows are all but water."

"When we are visited in sleep by visions, we think in our sleep that those visions are realities—we wake, and find them falsehoods, and they leave not a wreck behind. One man in his sleep receives some information, and he goes and tells it to his neighbour: from such idle narrations what benefit is obtained? what will be left to us when we have been winnowing chaff?"

"I meditate upon the *Śúni* Doctrine alone, and know neither virtue nor vice—many have been the princes of the earth, and nothing did they bring and nothing took they away; the good name of the liberal survived him, and disrepute covered the niggard with its shadow. So let men speak good words, that none may speak ill of them afterwards. Take during the few days of your life what the world offers you. Enjoy your own share, and give some of it to others: without liberality, who shall acquire reputation? Give ever after your means, such is the established rule. To some give money, to some respect, to some kind words, and to some delight. Do good to all the world, that all the world may speak good of you. Praise the name of the liberal when you rise in the morning, and throw dust upon the name of the niggard. Evil and good are attributes of the body; you have the choice of two sweetmeats in your hands. KARŃA was a giver of gold, and JANAKA as liberal as wise. ŚIVI, HARIŚCHANDRA, DADHÍCHA, and many others, have acquired by their bounty fame throughout the world."

"Many now are, many have been, and many will be—the world is never empty; like leaves upon the trees, new ones blossom as the old decay. Fix not your heart upon a withered leaf, but seek the shade of the green foliage: a horse of a thousand rupees is good for nothing when dead, but a living tattoo will carry you along the road. Have no hope in the man that is dead, trust but in him that is living. He that is dead will be alive no more: a truth that all men do not know; of all those that have died, has any business brought any one back again, or has any one brought back tidings of the rest? A rent garment cannot be spun anew, a broken pot cannot be pieced again. A living man has nothing to do with heaven and hell, but when the body has become dust, what is the difference between a Jackass and a dead Saint?"

"Earth, water, fire, and wind blended together constitute the body—of these four elements the world is composed, and there is nothing else. This is BRAHMÁ, this is a pismire, all consists of these elements, and proceeds from them through separate receptacles."

"Beings are born from the womb, the egg, the germ, and vapour."

"*Hindus* and *Musalmans* are of the same nature, two leaves of one tree—these call their teachers *Mullás*, those term them *Pańdits*; two pitchers of one clay: one performs *Namáz*, the other offers *Pújá*: where is the difference? I know of no dissimilarity—they are both followers of the doctrine of Duality—they have the same bone, the same flesh, the same blood, and the same marrow. One cuts off the foreskin, the other puts on a sacrificial thread. Ask of them the difference, enquire the importance of these distinctions, and they will quarrel with you: dispute not, but know them to be the same; avoid all idle wrangling and strife, and adhere to the truth, the doctrine of Dáyarám."

"I fear not to declare the truth; I know no difference between a subject and a king; I want neither homage nor respect, and hold no communion with any but the good: what I can obtain with facility that will I desire, but a palace or a thicket are to me the same—the error of *mine* and *thine* have I cast away, and know nothing of loss or gain. When a man can meet with a preceptor to teach him these truths, he will destroy the errors of a million of births. Such a teacher is now in the world, and such a one is Dáyarám."

The survey that has thus been taken of the actual state of the Hindu religion will shew, that its internal constitution has not been exempt from those varieties, to which all human systems of belief are subject, and that it has undergone great and frequent modifications, until it presents an appearance which, there is great reason to suppose, is very different from that which it originally wore.

The precise character of the primitive Hindu system will only be justly appreciated, when a considerable portion of the ritual of the *Vedas* shall have been translated, but some notion of their contents and purport may be formed from Mr. COLEBROOKE's account of them[1], as well as from his description of the religious ceremonies of the Hindus[2]. It is also probable that the Institutes of MANU, in a great measure, harmonise with the *Vaidik* Code.

From these sources then it would seem, that some of the original rites are still preserved in the *Homa*, or fire offerings, and in such of the *Sanskáras*, or purificatory ceremonies, as are observed at the periods of birth, tonsure, investiture, marriage and cremation. Even in these ceremonies, however, formulæ borrowed from the *Tantras* assume the place of the genuine texts, whilst on many occasions the observances of the *Vedas* are wholly neglected. Nor is this inconsistent with the original system, which was devised

---

[1] Asiatic Researches Vol. VIII. [Essays, p. 1–69.]

[2] Asiatic Researches Vol. VII. [Essays, p. 76–142.]

for certain recognised classes into which the Hindu community was then divided, and of which three out of four parts no longer exist—the Hindus being now distinguished into Brahmans and mixed castes alone—and the former having almost universally deviated from the duties and habits to which they were originally devoted. Neither of these classes, therefore, can with propriety make use of the *Vaidik* ritual, and their manual of devotion must be taken from some other source.

How far the preference of any individual Divinity as an especial object of veneration is authorised by the *Vedas*, remains yet to be determined; but there is no reason to doubt that most of the forms to which homage is now paid are of modern canonization. At any rate such is the highest antiquity of the most celebrated Teachers and Founders of the popular sects; and Basava in the *Dekhan*, Vallabha Svámí in *Hindustan*, and Chaitanya in *Bengal*, claim no earlier a date than the eleventh and sixteenth centuries.

Consistent with the introduction of new objects of devotion is the elevation of new races of individuals to the respect or reverence of the populace as their ministers and representatives. The Brahmans retain, it is true, a traditional sanctity; and when they cultivate pursuits suited to their character, as the Law and Literature of their sacred language, they receive occasional marks of attention, and periodical donations from the most opulent of their countrymen. But a very mistaken notion prevails generally amongst Europeans of the position of the Brahmans in Hindu society, founded on the terms in which they are spoken of by MANU, and the application of the expression 'Priesthood' to the Brahmanical Order by Sir WILLIAM JONES. In the strict sense of the phrase it never was applicable to the Brahmans; for although some amongst them acted in ancient times as family priests, and conducted the fixed or occasional ceremonials of household worship, yet even MANU* holds the Brahman, who ministers to an idol, infamous during life, and condemned to the infernal regions after death, and the Sanskrit language abounds with synonymes for the priest of a temple, significant of his degraded condition both in this world and the next. Ministrant Priests in temples, therefore, the Brahmans, collectively speaking, never were—and although many amongst them act in that capacity, it is no more their appropriate province than any other lucrative occupation. In the present day, however, they have ceased to be in a great measure the ghostly advisers of the people, either individually or in their households. This office is now filled by various persons, who pretend to superior sanctity, as *Gosáins*, *Vairágis*, and *Sannyásis*. Many of these are Brahmans, but they are not necessarily so, and it is not as Brahmans that they receive the veneration of their lay followers. They derive it, as we have seen, from individual repute, or more frequently from their descent from the founder of some particular division, as is the case with the

* [III, 152. See also Lassen, Ind. Alt., I, 794.]

Gokulastha Gosáins and the *Gosvámis* of Bengal. The Brahmans as a caste exercise little real influence on the minds of the Hindus beyond what they obtain from their numbers, affluence and rank. As a hierarchy they are null, and as a literary body they are few, and meet with but slender countenance from their countrymen or their foreign rulers. That they are still of great importance 'in the social system of British India, is unquestionable, but it is not as a priesthood. They bear a very large proportion to all the other tribes; they are of more respectable birth, and in general of better education; a prescriptive reverence for the order improves these advantages, and Brahmans are accordingly numerous amongst the most affluent and distinguished members of every Hindu state. It is only, however, as far as they are identified with the *Gurus* of the popular sects, that they can be said to hold any other than secular consideration.

Aware apparently of the inequality upon which those *Gurus* contended with the long established claims of the Brahmanical tribe, the new teachers of the people took care to invest themselves with still higher pretensions. The *Áchárya* or *Guru* of the three first classes is no doubt described by MANU* as entitled to the most profound respect from his pupil during pupilage, but the *Guru* of the present day exacts implicit devotion from his disciples during life**. It is

* [II, 192 ff.]

** [Many passages from modern Tantras, such as the Rudra

unnecessary here to repeat what there has been previous occasion to notice with respect to the extravagant obedience to be paid by some sectarians to the *Guru*, whose favour is declared to be of much more importance than that of the god whom he represents.

Another peculiarity in the modern systems which has been adverted to in the preceding pages is the paramount value of *Bhakti*—faith—implicit reliance on the favour of the Deity worshipped. This is a substitute for all religious or moral acts, and an expiation for every crime. Now, in the *Vedas*, two branches are distinctly marked, the practical and speculative. The former consists of prayers and rules for oblations to any or all of the gods—but especially to INDRA and AGNI, the rulers of the firmament and of fire, for positive worldly goods, health, posterity and affluence. The latter is the investigation of matter and spirit, leading to detachment from worldly feelings and interests, and final liberation from bodily existence. The first is intended for the bulk of mankind, the second for philosophers and ascetics. There is not a word of faith, of implicit belief or passionate devotion in all this, and they seem to have been as little essential to the primitive Hindu worship as they were to the religious systems of Greece and Rome. *Bhakti* is an invention, and apparently a modern one*, of the

---

Yámala, Gupta Sádhana Tantra, Vŕihan Níla Tantra, and others, are quoted in the Práńatoshańí, fol. 49–55.]

* [See, however, Burnouf, Bhág. Pur. I, p. CXI. Lassen, Ind. Alt, II, 1096 ff.]

Institutors of the existing sects, intended, like that of the mystical holiness of the *Guru*, to extend their own authority. It has no doubt exercised a most mischievous influence upon the moral principles of the Hindus.

Notwithstanding the provisions with which the sectarian *Gurus* fortified themselves, it is clear that they were never able to enlist the whole of Hinduism under their banners, or to suppress all doubt and disbelief. It has been shewn in the introductory pages of this essay, that great latitude of speculation has always been allowed amongst the Brahmans themselves, and it will have been seen from the notices of different sects, that scepticism is not unfrequent amongst the less privileged orders. The tendency of many widely diffused divisions is decidedly monotheistical, and we have seen that both in ancient and modern times attempts have been made to inculcate the doctrines of utter unbelief. It is not likely that these will ever extensively spread, but there can be little doubt that with the diffusion of education independent enquiry into the merits of the prevailing systems and their professors will become more universal, and be better directed. The germ is native to the soil: it has been kept alive for ages under the most unfavourable circumstances, and has been apparently more vigorous than ever during the last century. It only now requires prudent and patient fostering to grow into a stately tree, and yield goodly fruit.

INDEX.

ERRATA.

Page 10 l. 8 read: taken.
- 12 - 28 - *Brahma.*
- — - — - caste.
- 18 - 3 - Śiva.
- — - 6 - by.
- — - 8 - *Rahasya.*
- 22 - 8 - *Śúnya.*
- — - 10 - *Chárvákas.*
- 28 - 8 - *Kánchí.*
- — - 13 - *Śákta.*
- 32 - 13 - Úrddhabáhus.
- — - 14 - Gúdaras.
- — - 21 - Kánchuliyas.
- 34 - 3 - less.
- 35 - 16 - Brahmá.
- 36 - 3 - *Kánchí.*
- 37 - 3 - *Rájá.*
- — - 31 - *Rámeśvara.*
- — - — - *Kánchí.*
- 51 - 1 - control.
- 56 - 29 - Anantánand.
- 60 - 22 - *Máŕwáŕ.*

p. 62 l. 22 read: good.
- 68 - 22 - Sítá.
- 96 - 18 - *Śáli.*
- 114 - 1 - Śikhs.
- 139 - 21 - Madhiga.
- 141 - 17 - superintendence.
- 149 - 17 - initiated.
- 181 - 8 - outcast.
- 197 - 13 - descendants.
- 199 - 3 - have.
- — - — - Notwithstanding.
- 215 - 12 - *Tretá.*
- 216 - 20 - caste.
- 235 - 20. 21 - Gúdaras.
- 246 - 16 - *Sattwa.*
- 249 - 3 - *Puráńa.*
- — - 5 - *Tantras.*
- 264 - 1 - Karárís.
- 268 - 30 - *Prasáda.*
- 275 - 22 - *Prasáda.*
- 298 - 16 - *Kshatriya.*
- 379 - 7 - *Gúdaras.*

LINGUISTIC PUBLICATIONS

OF

TRÜBNER & CO.,

57 AND 59, LUDGATE HILL, LONDON, E.C.

Adi Granth (The); OR, THE HOLY SCRIPTURES OF THE SIKHS, translated from the original Gurmukhī, with Introductory Essays, by Dr. ERNEST TRUMPP, Professor Regius of Oriental Languages at the University of Munich, etc. Roy. 8vo. cloth, pp. 866. £2 12*s*. 6*d*.

Ahlwardt.—THE DIVÁNS OF THE SIX ANCIENT ARABIC POETS, Ennábiga, 'Antara, Tarafa, Zubair, 'Algama, and Imruolgais; chiefly according to the MSS. of Paris, Gotha, and Leyden, and the collection of their Fragments: with a complete list of the various readings of the Text. Edited by W. AHLWARDT, 8vo. pp. xxx. 340, sewed. 1870. 12*s*.

Aitareya Brahmanam of the Rig Veda. 2 vols. See under HAUG.

Alabaster.—THE WHEEL OF THE LAW: Buddhism illustrated from Siamese Sources by the Modern Buddhist, a Life of Buddha, and an account of H.M. Consulate-General in Siam; M.R.A.S. Demy 8vo. pp. lviii. and 324. 1871. 14*s*.

Alif Lailat wa Lailat.—THE ARABIAN NIGHTS. 4 vols. 4to. pp. 495, 493, 442, 434. Cairo, A.H. 1279 (1862). £3 3*s*.

This celebrated Edition of the Arabian Nights is now, for the first time, offered at a price which makes it accessible to Scholars of limited means.

Amberley.—AN ANALYSIS OF RELIGIOUS BELIEF. By VISCOUNT AMBERLEY. 2 vols. 8vo. cl., pp. xvi. 496 and 512. 1876. 30*s*.

American Oriental Society, Transactions of. Subscription, £1 5*s*. per volume.

Andrews.—A DICTIONARY OF THE HAWAIIAN LANGUAGE, to which is appended an English-Hawaiian Vocabulary, and a Chronological Table of Remarkable Events. By LORRIN ANDREWS. 8vo. pp. 560, cloth. £1 11*s*. 6*d*.

Anthropological Institute of Great Britain and Ireland (The Journal of the). Published Quarterly.

Vol I., No. 1. January–July, 1871. 8vo. pp. 120–clix, sewed. Illustrated with 11 full page Plates, and numerous Woodcuts; and accompanied by several folding plates of Tables, etc. 7*s*.
Vol. I., No. 2. October, 1871. 8vo. pp. 121–264, sewed. 4*s*.
Vol. I., No. 3. January, 1872. 8vo. pp. 265–427, sewed. 16 full-page Plates. 4*s*.
Vol. II., No. 1. April, 1872. 8vo. pp. 136, sewed. Eight two-page plates and two four-page plates. 4*s*.
Vol. II., No. 2. July and Oct., 1872. 8vo. pp. 137–312. 9 plates and a map. 6*s*.
Vol. II., No. 3. January, 1873. 8vo. pp. 143. With 4 plates. 4*s*.
Vol. III., No. 1. April, 1873. 8vo. pp. 136. With 8 plates and two maps. 4*s*.
Vol. III., No. 2. July and October, 1873. 8vo. pp. 168, sewed. With 9 plates. 4*s*.
Vol. III., No. 3. January, 1874. 8vo. pp. 238, sewed. With 8 plates, etc. 6*s*.
Vol. IV., No. 1. April and July, 1874. 8vo. pp. 308, sewed. With 22 plates. 8*s*.
Vol. IV., No. 2. April, 1875. 8vo. pp. 200, sewed. With 11 plates. 6*s*.
Vol. V., No. 1. July, 1875. 8vo. pp. 120, sewed. With 3 plates. 4*s*.
Vol. V., No. 2. October, 1875. 8vo. pp. 132, sewed. With 8 plates. 4*s*.
Vol. V., No. 3. January, 1876. 8vo. pp. 156, sewed. With 8 plates. 5*s*.
Vol. V., No. 4. April, 1876. 8vo. pp. 128, sewed. With 2 plates. 5*s*.

1000
3,10,79

Anthropological Institute—*continued.*
Vol. VI., No. 1. July, 1876. 8vo. pp. 100, sewed. With 5 plates. 5*s.*
Vol. VI., No. 2. October, 1876. 8vo. pp. 98, sewed. With 4 plates and a map. 5*s.*
Vol. VI., No. 3. January, 1877. 8vo. pp. 146, sewed. With 11 plates. 5*s.*
Vol. VI., No. 4. May, 1877. 8vo. pp. iv. and 184, sewed. With 7 plates. 5*s.*
Vol. VII., No. 1. August, 1877. 8vo. pp. 116, sewed. With three plates. 5*s.*
Vol. VII., No. 2. November, 1877. 8vo. pp. 84, sewed. With one plate. 5*s.*
Vol., VII., No. 3. February, 1878. 8vo. pp. 193, sewed. With three plates. 5*s.*
Vol. VII., No. 4. May, 1878. 8vo. pp. iv. and 158, sewed. With nine plates. 5*s.*
Vol. VIII., No. 1. August, 1878. 8vo. pp. 103, sewed. With one plate. 5*s.*
Vol. VIII., No. 2. November, 1878. 8vo. pp. 126, sewed. With three plates. 5*s.*

Apastambíya Dharma Sutram.—Aphorisms of the Sacred Laws of the Hindus, by Apastamba. Edited, with a Translation and Notes, by G. Bühler. By order of the Government of Bombay. 2 parts. 8vo. cloth, 1868–71. £1 4*s.* 6*d.*

Arabic and Persian Books (A Catalogue of). Printed in the East. Constantly for sale by Trübner and Co., 57 and 59, Ludgate Hill, London. 16mo. pp. 46, sewed. 1*s.*

Archæological Survey of India.—See under Burgess and Cunningham.

Arden.—A Progressive Grammar of the Telugu Language, with Copious Examples and Exercises. In Three Parts. Part I. Introduction.—On the Alphabet and Orthography.—Outline Grammar, and Model Sentences. Part II. A Complete Grammar of the Colloquial Dialect. Part III. On the Grammatical Dialect used in Books. By A. H. Arden, M.A., Missionary of the C. M. S. Masulipatam. 8vo. sewed, pp. xiv. and 380. 14*s.*

Arnold.—The Iliad and Odyssey of India. By Edwin Arnold, M.A., C.S.I., F.R.G.S., etc. Fcap. 8vo. sd., pp. 24. 1*s.*

Arnold.—The Indian Song of Songs. From the Sanskrit of the Gita Govinda of Jayadeva. By Edwin Arnold, M.A., C.S.I., F.R.G.S. (of University College, Oxford), formerly Principal of Poona College, and Fellow of the University of Bombay. Cr. 8vo. cl., pp. xvi. and 144. 1875. 5*s.*

Arnold.—A Simple Transliteral Grammar of the Turkish Language. Compiled from various sources. With Dialogues and Vocabulary. By Edwin Arnold, M.A., C.S.I., F.R.G.S. Pott 8vo. cloth, pp. 80. 2*s.* 6*d.*

Asher.—On the Study of Modern Languages in General, and of the English Language in particular. An Essay. By David Asher, Ph.D. 12mo. pp. viii. and 80, cloth. 2*s.*

Asiatic Society.—Journal of the Royal Asiatic Society of Great Britain and Ireland, from the Commencement to 1863. First Series, complete in 20 Vols. 8vo., with many Plates. Price £10; or, in Single Numbers, as follows:—Nos. 1 to 14, 6*s.* each; No. 15, 2 Parts, 4*s.* each; No. 16, 2 Parts, 4*s.* each; No. 17, 2 Parts, 4*s.* each, No. 18, 6*s.* These 18 Numbers form Vols. I. to IX.—Vol. X., Part 1, op.; Part 2, 5*s.*; Part 3, 5*s.*—Vol. XI., Part 1, 6*s.*; Part 2 not published.—Vol. XII., 2 Parts, 6*s.* each.—Vol. XIII., 2 Parts, 6*s.* each.—Vol. XIV., Part 1, 5*s.*; Part 2 not published.—Vol. XV., Part 1, 6*s.*; Part 2, with 3 Maps, £2 2*s.*—Vol. XVI., 2 Parts, 6*s.* each.—Vol. XVII., 2 Parts, 6*s.* each.—Vol. XVIII., 2 Parts, 6*s.* each.—Vol. XIX., Parts 1 to 4, 16*s.*—Vol. XX., Parts 1 and 2, 4*s.* each. Part 3, 7*s.* 6*d.*

Asiatic Society.—Journal of the Royal Asiatic Society of Great Britain and Ireland. *New Series.* Vol. I. In Two Parts. pp. iv. and 490, sewed. 1864–5. 16*s.*

Contents.—I. Vajra-chhedika, the "Kin Kong King," or Diamond Sútra. Translated from the Chinese by the Rev. S. Beal, Chaplain, R.N.—II. The Páramitá-hridaya Sútra, or, in Chinese, "Mo-ho-pô-ye-po-lo-mih-to-sin-king," *i.e.* "The Great Páramitá Heart Sútra." Translated from the Chinese by the Rev. S. Beal, Chaplain, R.N.—III. On the Preservation of National Literature in the East. By Colonel F. J. Goldsmid.—IV. On the Agricultural, Commercial, Financial, and Military Statistics of Ceylon. By E. R. Power, Esq.—V. Contributions to a Knowledge of the Vedic Theogony and Mythology. By J. Muir, D.C.L., LL.D.—VI. A Tabular List of Original Works and Translations, published by the late Dutch Government of Ceylon at their Printing Press at Colombo. Compiled by Mr. Mat. P. J. Ondaatje, of Colombo.—VII. Assyrian and Hebrew Chronology compared, with a view of showing the extent to which the Hebrew Chronology of Ussher must be modified, in conformity with the Assyrian Canon. By J. W. Bosanquet, Esq.—VIII. On the existing Dictionaries of the Malay Language. By Dr. H. N. van der Tuuk.—IX. Bilingual Readings: Cuneiform and Phœnician. Notes on some Tablets in the British Museum, containing Bilingual Legends (Assyrian and Phœnician). By Major-General Sir H. Rawlinson, K.C.B., Director R.A.S.—X. Translations of Three Copper-plate Inscriptions of the Fourth Century A.D., and Notices of the Châlukya and Gurjjara Dynasties By Professor J. Dowson, Staff College, Sandhurst.—XI. Yama and the Doctrine of a Future Life, according to the Rig-Yajur-, and Atharva-Vedas. By J. Muir, Esq., D.C.L., LL.D.—XII. On the Jyotisha Observation of the Place of the Colures, and the Date derivable from it. By William D. Whitney, Esq., Professor of Sanskrit in Yale College, New Haven, U.S.—Note on the preceding Article. By Sir Edward Colebrooke, Bart., M.P., President R.A.S.—XIII. Progress of the Vedic Religion towards Abstract Conceptions of the Deity. By J. Muir, Esq., D.C.L., LL.D.—XIV. Brief Notes on the Age and Authenticity of the Work of Aryabhata, Varâhamihira, Brahmagupta, Bhattotpala, and Bhâskarâchârya. By Dr. Bhâu Dâjî, Honorary Member R.A.S.—XV. Outlines of a Grammar of the Malagasy Language. By H. N. Van der Tuuk.—XVI. On the Identity of Xandrames and Krananda. By Edward Thomas, Esq.

Vol. II. In Two Parts. pp. 522, sewed. 1866–7. 16*s.*

CONTENTS.—I. Contributions to a Knowledge of Vedic Theogony and Mythology. No. 2. By J. Muir, Esq.—II. Miscellaneous Hymns from the Rig- and Atharva-Vedas. By J. Muir, Esq.—III. Five hundred questions on the Social Condition of the Natives of Bengal. By the Rev. J. Long.—IV. Short account of the Malay Manuscripts belonging to the Royal Asiatic Society. By Dr. H. N. van der Tuuk.—V. Translation of the Amitâbha Sûtra from the Chinese. By the Rev. S. Beal, Chaplain Royal Navy.—VI. The initial coinage of Bengal. By Edward Thomas, Esq.—VII. Specimens of an Assyrian Dictionary. By Edwin Norris, Esq.—VIII. On the Relations of the Priests to the other classes of Indian Society in the Vedic age By J. Muir, Esq.—IX. On the Interpretation of the Veda. By the same.—X. An attempt to Translate from the Chinese a work known as the Confessional Services of the great compassionate Kwan Yin, possessing 1000 hands and 1000 eyes. By the Rev. S. Beal, Chaplain Royal Navy. —XI. The Hymns of the Gaupâyanas and the Legend of King Asamâti. By Professor Max Müller, M.A., Honorary Member Royal Asiatic Society.—XII. Specimen Chapters of an Assyrian Grammar. By the Rev. E. Hincks, D.D., Honorary Member Royal Asiatic Society.

Vol. III. In Two Parts. pp. 516, sewed. With Photograph. 1868. 22*s.*

CONTENTS.—I. Contributions towards a Glossary of the Assyrian Language. By H. F. Talbot. —II. Remarks on the Indo-Chinese Alphabets. By Dr. A. Bastian.—III. The poetry of Mohamed Rabadan, Arragonese. By the Hon. H. E. J. Stanley.—IV. Catalogue of the Oriental Manuscripts in the Library of King's College, Cambridge. By Edward Henry Palmer, B.A, Scholar of St. John's College, Cambridge; Member of the Royal Asiatic Society, Membre de la Société Asiatique de Paris.—V. Description of the Amravati Tope in Guntur. By J. Fergusson, Esq., F.R.S.—VI. Remarks on Prof. Brockhaus' edition of the Kathâsarit-sâgara, Lambaka IX. XVIII. By Dr. H. Kern, Professor of Sanskrit in the University of Leyden.—VII. The source of Colebrooke's Essay "On the Duties of a Faithful Hindu Widow." By Fitzedward Hall, Esq., M.A., D.C.L. Oxon. Supplement: Further detail of proofs that Colebrooke's Essay, "On the Duties of a Faithful Hindu Widow," was not indebted to the Vivâdabhangârnava. By Fitzedward Hall, Esq.—VIII. The Sixth Hymn of the First Book of the Rig Veda. By Professor Max Müller, M.A. Hon. M.R.A.S.—IX. Sassanian Inscriptions. By E. Thomas, Esq.—X. Account of an Embassy from Morocco to Spain in 1690 and 1691. By the Hon. H. E. J. Stanley.—XI. The Poetry of Mohamed Rabadan, of Arragon. By the Hon. H. E. J. Stanley.—XII. Materials for the History of India for the Six Hundred Years of Mohammadan rule, previous to the Foundation of the British Indian Empire. By Major W. Nassau Lees, LL.D., Ph.D.—XIII. A Few Words concerning the Hill people inhabiting the Forests of the Cochin State. By Captain G. E. Fryer, Madras Staff Corps, M.R.A.S.—XIV. Notes on the Bhojpurî Dialect of Hindî, spoken in Western Behar. By John Beames, Esq., B.C.S., Magistrate of Chumparun.

Vol. IV. In Two Parts. pp. 521, sewed. 1869–70. 16*s.*

CONTENTS.—I. Contribution towards a Glossary of the Assyrian Language. By H. F. Talbot. Part II.—II. On Indian Chronology. By J. Fergusson, Esq., F.R.S.—III. The Poetry of Mohamed Rabadan of Arragon. By the Hon. H. E. J. Stanley.—IV. On the Magar Language of Nepal. By John Beames, Esq., B.C.S.—V. Contributions to the Knowledge of Parsee Literature. By Edward Sachau, Ph.D.—VI. Illustrations of the Lamaist System in Tibet, drawn from Chinese Sources. By Wm. Frederick Mayers, Esq., of H.B.M. Consular Service, China.—VII. Khuddaka Pâtha, a Pâli Text, with a Translation and Notes. By R. C. Childers, late of the Ceylon Civil Service.—VIII. An Endeavour to elucidate Rashiduddin's Geographical Notices of India. By Col. H. Yule, C.B.—IX. Sassanian Inscriptions explained by the Pahlavi of the Pârsis. By E. W. West, Esq.—X. Some Account of the Senbyû Pagoda at Mengûn, near the Burmese Capital, in a Memorandum by Capt. E. H. Sladan, Political Agent at Mandalé; with Remarks on the Subject by Col. Henry Yule, C.B.—XI. The Brhat-Sanhitâ; or, Complete System of Natural Astrology of Varâha-Mihira. Translated from Sanskrit into English by Dr. H. Kern.—XII. The Mohammedan Law of Evidence, and its influence on the Administration of

Justice in India. By N. B. E. Baillie, Esq.—XIII. The Mohammedan Law of Evidence in connection with the Administration of Justice to Foreigners. By N. B. E. Baillie, Esq.—XIV. A Translation of a Bactrian Pâli Inscription. By Prof. J. Dowson.—XV. Indo-Parthian Coins By E. Thomas, Esq.

Vol. V. In Two Parts. pp. 463, sewed. With 10 full-page and folding Plates. 1871-2. 18*s.* 6*d.*

CONTENTS.—I. Two Jâtakas. The original Pâli Text, with an English Translation. By V. Fausböll.—II. On an Ancient Buddhist Inscription at Keu-yung kwan, in North China. By A. Wylie.—III. The Brhat Sanhitâ; or, Complete System of Natural Astrology of Varâha-Mihira Translated from Sanskrit into English by Dr. H. Kern.—IV. The Pongol Festival in Southern India. By Charles E. Gover.—V. The Poetry of Mohamed Rabadan, of Arragon. By the Right Hon. Lord Stanley of Alderley.—VI. Essay on the Creed and Customs of the Jangams. By Charles P. Brown.—VII. On Malabar, Coromandel, Quilon, etc. By C. P. Brown.—VIII. On the Treatment of the Nexus in the Neo-Aryan Languages of India. By John Beames, B.C.S.—IX. Some Remarks on the Great Tope at Sânchi. By the Rev. S. Beal.—X. Ancient Inscriptions from Mathura. Translated by Professor J. Dowson.—Note to the Mathura Inscriptions. By Major-General A. Cunningham.—XI. Specimen of a Translation of the Adi Granth. By Dr. Ernest Trumpp.—XII. Notes on Dhammapada, with Special Reference to the Question of Nirvâna. By R. C. Childers, late of the Ceylon Civil Service.—XIII. The Brhat-Sanhitâ; or, Complete System of Natural Astrology of Varâha-mihira. Translated from Sanskrit into English by Dr. H. Kern.—XIV. On the Origin of the Buddhist Arthakathâs. By the Mudliar L. Comrilla Vijasinha, Government Interpreter to the Ratnapura Court, Ceylon. With an Introduction by R. C. Childers, late of the Ceylon Civil Service.—XV. The Poetry of Mohamed Rabadan, of Arragon. By the Right Hon. Lord Stanley of Alderley.—XVI. Proverbia Communia Syriaca. By Captain R. F. Burton. XVII. Notes on an Ancient Indian Vase, with an Account of the Engraving thereupon. By Charles Horne, M.R.A.S., late of the Bengal Civil Service.—XVIII. The Bhar Tribe. By the Rev. M. A. Sherring, LL.D., Benares. Communicated by C. Horne, M.R.A.S., late B.C.S.—XIX. Of *Jihad* in Mohammedan Law, and its application to British India. By N. B. E. Baillie.—XX. Comments on Recent Pehlvi Decipherments. With an Incidental Sketch of the Derivation of Aryan Alphabets. And Contributions to the Early History and Geography of Tabaristán. Illustrated by Coins. By E. Thomas, F.R.S.

Vol. VI., Part 1, pp. 212, sewed, with two plates and a map. 1872. 8*s.*

CONTENTS.—The Ishmaelites, and the Arabic Tribes who Conquered their Country. By A. Sprenger.—A Brief Account of Four Arabic Works on the History and Geography of Arabia. By Captain S. B. Miles.—On the Methods of Disposing of the Dead at Llassa, Thibet, etc. By Charles Horne, late B.C.S. The Brhat-Sanhitâ; or, Complete System of Natural Astrology of Varâha-mihira, Translated from Sanskrit into English by Dr. H. Kern.—Notes on Hwen Thsang's Account of the Principalities of Tokhâristân, in which some Previous Geographical Identifications are Reconsidered. By Colonel Yule, C.B.—The Campaign of Ælius Gallus in Arabia. By A. Sprenger.—An Account of Jerusalem, Translated for the late Sir H. M. Elliott from the Persian Text of Nâsir ibn Khusrû's Safanâmah by the late Major A. R. Fuller.—The Poetry of Mohamed Rabadan, of Arragon. By the Right Hon. Lord Stanley of Alderley.

Vol. VI., Part II., pp. 213 to 400 and lxxxiv., sewed. Illustrated with a Map, Plates, and Woodcuts. 1873. 8*s.*

CONTENTS.—On Hiouen-Thsang's Journey from Patna to Ballabhi. By James Fergusson, D.C.L., F.R.S.—Northern Buddhism. [Note from Colonel H. Yule, addressed to the Secretary.]—Hwen Thsang's Account of the Principalities of Tokhâristân, etc. By Colonel H. Yule, C.B.—The Brhat-Sanhitâ; or, Complete System of Natural Astrology of Varâha-mihira. Translated from Sanskrit into English by Dr. H. Kern.—The Initial Coinage of Bengal, under the Early Muhammadan Conquerors. Part II. Embracing the preliminary period between A.H. 614-634 (A.D. 1217-1236-7). By Edward Thomas, F.R.S.—The Legend of Dipañkara Buddha. Translated from the Chinese (and intended to illustrate Plates xxix. and L., 'Tree and Serpent Worship'). By S. Beal.—Note on Art. IX., antè pp. 213-274, on Hiouen-Thsang's Journey from Patna to Ballabhi. By James Fergusson D.C.L., F.R.S.—Contributions towards a Glossary of the Assyrian Language. By H. F. Talbot.

Vol. VII., Part I., pp. 170 and 24, sewed. With a plate. 1874. 8*s.*

CONTENTS.—The *Upasampadâ-Kammavâcâ*, being the Buddhist Manual of the Form and Manner of Ordering of Priests and Deacons. The Pâli Text, with a Translation and Notes. By J. F. Dickson, B.A., sometime Student of Christ Church, Oxford, now of the Ceylon Civil Service.—Notes on the Megalithic Monuments of the Coimbatore District, Madras. By M. J. Walhouse, late Madras C.S.—Notes on the Sinhalese Language. No. I. On the Formation of the Plural of Neuter Nouns. By R. C. Childers, late of the Ceylon Civil Service.—The Pali Text of the *Mahâparinibbâna Sutta* and Commentary, with a Translation. By R. C. Childers, late of the Ceylon Civil Service.—The Brihat-Sanhitâ; or, Complete System of Natural Astrology of Varâha-mihira. Translated from Sanskrit into English by Dr. H. Kern.—Note on the Valley of Choombi. By Dr. A. Campbell, late Superintendent of Darjeeling.—The Name of the Twelfth Imâm on the Coinage of Egypt. By H. Sauvaire and Stanley Lane Poole.—Three Inscriptions of Parâkrama Bâhu the Great from Pulastipura, Ceylon (date circa 1180 A.D.). By T. W. Rhys Davids.—Of the Kharâj or Muhammadan Land Tax; its Application to British India, and Effect on the Tenure of Land. By N. B. E. Baillie.—Appendix: A Specimen of a Syriac Version of the Kalilah wa-Dimnah, with an English Translation. By W. Wright.

Vol. VII., Part II., pp. 191 to 394, sewed. With seven plates and a map. 1875. 8*s*.

CONTENTS.—Sigiri, the Lion Rock, near Pulastipura, Ceylon; and the Thirty-ninth Chapter of the Mahâvamsa. By T. W. Rhys Davids.—The Northern Frontagers of China. Part I. The Origines of the Mongols. By H. H. Howorth.—Inedited Arabic Coins. By Stanley Lane Poole.—Notice on the Dinârs of the Abbasside Dynasty. By Edward Thomas Rogers.—The Northern Frontagers of China. Part II. The Origines of the Manchus. By H. H. Howorth.—Notes on the Old Mongolian Capital of Shangtu. By S. W. Bushell, B.Sc., M.D.—Oriental Proverbs in their Relations to Folklore, History, Sociology; with Suggestions for their Collection, Interpretation, Publication. By the Rev. J. Long.—Two Old Simhalese Inscriptions. The Sahasa Malla Inscription, date 1200 A.D., and the Ruwanwæli Dagaba Inscription, date 1191 A.D. Text, Translation, and Notes. By T. W. Rhys Davids.—Notes on a Bactrian Pali Inscription and the Samvat Era. By Prof. J. Dowson.—Note on a Jade Drinking Vessel of the Emperor Jahângîr. By Edward Thomas, F.R.S.

Vol. VIII., Part I., pp. 156, sewed, with three plates and a plan. 1876. 8*s*.

CONTENTS.—Catalogue of Buddhist Sanskrit Manuscripts in the Possession of the Royal Asiatic Society (Hodgson Collection). By Professors E. B. Cowell and J. Eggeling.—On the Ruins of Sigiri in Ceylon. By T. H. Blakesley, Esq., Public Works Department, Ceylon.—The Pâtimokkha, being the Buddhist Office of the Confession of Priests. The Pali Text, with a Translation, and Notes. By J. F. Dickson, M.A., sometime Student of Christ Church, Oxford, now of the Ceylon Civil Service.—Notes on the Sinhalese Language. No. 2. Proofs of the Sanskritic Origin of Sinhalese. By R. C. Childers, late of the Ceylon Civil Service.

Vol. VIII., Part II., pp. 157-308, sewed. 1876. 8*s*.

CONTENTS.—An Account of the Island of Bali. By R. Friederich.—The Pali Text of the Mahâparinibbâna Sutta and Commentary, with a Translation. By R. C. Childers, late of the Ceylon Civil Service.—The Northern Frontagers of China. Part III. The Kara Khitai. By H. H. Howorth.—Inedited Arabic Coins. II. By Stanley Lane Poole.—On the Form of Government under the Native Sovereigns of Ceylon. By A. de Silva Ekanâyaka, Mudaliyar of the Department of Public Instruction, Ceylon.

Vol. IX., Part I., pp. 156, sewed, with a plate. 1877. 8*s*.

CONTENTS.—Bactrian Coins and Indian Dates. By E. Thomas, F.R.S.—The Tenses of the Assyrian Verb. By the Rev. A. H. Sayce, M.A.—An Account of the Island of Bali. By R. Friederich (continued from Vol. VIII. N.S. p. 218).—On Ruins in Makran. By Major Mockler.—Inedited Arabic Coins. III. By Stanley Lane Poole.—Further Note on a Bactrian Pali Inscription and the Samvat Era. By Prof. J. Dowson.—Notes on Persian Belûchistan. From the Persian of Mirza Mehdy Khân. By A. H. Schindler.

Vol IX., Part II., pp. 292, sewed, with three plates. 1877. 10*s*. 6*d*.

CONTENTS.—The Early Faith of Asoka. By E. Thomas, F.R.S.—The Northern Frontagers of China. Part II. The Manchus (Supplementary Notice). By H. H. Howorth.—The Northern Frontagers of China. Part IV. The Kin or Golden Tatars. By H. H. Howorth.—On a Treatise on Weights and Measures by Eliyâ, Archbishop of Nisîbîn. By M. H. Sauvaire.—On Imperial and other Titles. By Sir T. E. Colebrooke, Bart., M.P.—Affinities of the Dialects of the Chepang and Kusundah Tribes of Nipâl with those of the Hill Tribes of Arracan. By Captain C. J. F. Forbes, F.R.G.S., M.A.S. Bengal, etc.—Notes on Some Antiquities found in a Mound near Damghan. By A. H. Schindler.

Vol. X., Part I., pp. 156, sewed, with two plates and a map. 1878. 8*s*.

CONTENTS.—On the Non-Aryan Languages of India. By E. L. Brandreth, Esq.—A Dialogue on the Vedantic Conception of Brahma. By Pramadâ Dâsa Mittra, late Officiating Professor of Anglo-Sanskrit, Government College, Benares.—An Account of the Island of Bali. By R. Friederich (continued from Vol. IX. N. S. p. 120).—Unpublished Glass Weights and Measures. By Edward Thomas Rogers.—China viâ Tibet. By S. C. Boulger.—Notes and Recollections on Tea Cultivation in Kumaon and Garhwâl. By J. H. Batten, F.R.G.S., Bengal Civil Service Retired, formerly Commissioner of Kumaon.

Vol. X., Part II., pp. 146, sewed. 1878. 6*s*.

CONTENTS.—Note on Pliny's Geography of the East Coast of Arabia. By Major-General S. B. Miles, Bombay Staff Corps. The Maldive Islands; with a Vocabulary taken from François Pyrard de Laval, 1602—1607. By A. Gray, late of the Ceylon Civil Service.—On Tibeto-Burman Languages. By Captain C. J. F. S. Forbes, of the Burmese Civil Service Commission.—Burmese Transliteration. By H. L. St. Barbe, Esq., Resident at Mandelay.—On the Connexion of the Mônš of Pegu with the Koles of Central India. By Captain C. J. F. S. Forbes, of the Burmese Civil Commission.—Studies on the Comparative Grammar of the Semitic Languages, with Special Reference to Assyrian. By Paul Haupt. The Oldest Semitic Verb-Form.—Arab Metrology. II. El-Djabarty. By M. H. Sauvaire.—The Migrations and Early History of the White Huns; principally from Chinese Sources. By Thomas W. Kingsmill.

Vol. X., Part III., pp. 204, sewed. 1878. 8*s*.

CONTENTS.—On the Hill Canton of Sâlár,—the most Easterly Settlement of the Turk Race. By Robert B. Shaw.—Geological Notes on the River Indus. By Griffin W. Vyse, B.A., M.R.A.S., etc., Executive Engineer P.W.D. Panjab.—Educational Literature for Japanese Women. By Basil Hall Chamberlain, Esq., M.R.A.S.—On the Natural Phenomenon Known in the East by the Names Sub-hi-Käzib, etc., etc. By J. W. Redhouse, M.R.A.S., Hon. Memb. R.S.L.—On a Chinese Version of the Sánkhya Káriká, etc., found among the Buddhist Books comprising the Tripitaka and two other works. By the Rev. Samuel Beal, M.A.—The Rock-cut Phrygian Inscriptions at Doganlu. By Edward Thomas, F.R.S.—Index.

Vol. XI., Part. I., pp. 128, sewed. *5s.*

CONTENTS.—On the Position of Women in the East in the Olden Time. By Edward Thomas, F.R.S.—Notice of the Scholars who have Contributed to the Extension of our Knowledge of the Languages of British India during the last Thirty Years. By Robert N. Cust, Hon. Librarian R.A.S.—Ancient Arabic Poetry: its Genuineness and Authenticity. By Sir William Muir, K.C.S.I., LL.D.—Note on Manrique's Mission and the Catholics in the time of Sháh Jahán. By H. G. Keene, Esq.—On Sandhi in Pali. By the late R. C. Childers.—On Arabic Amulets and Mottoes. By E. T. Rogers, M.R.A.S.

Asiatic Society.—TRANSACTIONS OF THE ROYAL ASIATIC SOCIETY OF GREAT BRITAIN AND IRELAND. Complete in 3 vols. 4to., 80 Plates of Facsimiles, etc., cloth. London, 1827 to 1835. Published at £9 *5s.*; reduced to £5 *5s.*

The above contains contributions by Professor Wilson, G. C. Haughton, Davis, Morrison, Colebrooke, Humboldt, Dorn, Grotefend, and other eminent Oriental scholars.

Asiatic Society of Bengal.—JOURNAL OF THE ASIATIC SOCIETY OF BENGAL. Edited by the Honorary Secretaries. 8vo. 8 numbers per annum, *4s.* each number.

Asiatic Society of Bengal.—PROCEEDINGS OF THE ASIATIC SOCIETY OF BENGAL. Published Monthly. *1s.* each number.

Asiatic Society.—THE JOURNAL OF THE BOMBAY BRANCH OF THE ROYAL ASIATIC SOCIETY. Edited by the Secretary. Nos. 1 to 35. *7s. 6d.* to *10s. 6d.* each number.

Asiatic Society.—JOURNAL OF THE CEYLON BRANCH OF THE ROYAL ASIATIC SOCIETY. 8vo. Published irregularly. *7s. 6d.* each part.

Asiatic Society of Japan.—TRANSACTIONS OF THE ASIATIC SOCIETY OF JAPAN. Vol. I. From 30th October, 1872, to 9th October, 1873. 8vo. pp. 110, with plates. 1874. Vol. II. From 22nd October, 1873, to 15th July, 1874. 8vo. pp. 249. 1874. Vol. III. Part I. From 16th July, 1874, to December, 1874, 1875. Vol. III. Part II. From 13th January, 1875, to 30th June, 1875. Vol. IV. From 20th October, 1875, to 12th July, 1876. Each Part *7s. 6d.*

Asiatic Society.—JOURNAL OF THE NORTH CHINA BRANCH OF THE ROYAL ASIATIC SOCIETY. New Series. Parts 1 to 11.

Aston.—A GRAMMAR OF THE JAPANESE WRITTEN LANGUAGE. By W. G. ASTON, M.A., Assistant Japanese Secretary, H B.M.'s Legation, Yedo, Japan. Second edition, Enlarged and Improved. Royal 8vo. pp. 306. *28s.*

Aston.—A SHORT GRAMMAR OF THE JAPANESE SPOKEN LANGUAGE. By W. G. ASTON, M.A., H. B. M.'s Legation, Yedo, Japan. Third edition. 12mo. cloth, pp. 96. *12s.*

Athar-ul-Adhâr—TRACES OF CENTURIES; or, Geographical and Historical Arabic Dictionary, by SELIM KHURI and SELIM SH-HADE. Geographical Parts I. to IV., Historical Parts I. and II. 4to. pp. 788 and 384. Price *7s. 6d.* each part. [*In course of publication.*

Atharva Veda Prátiçákhya.—See under WHITNEY.

Auctores Sanscriti. Edited for the Sanskrit Text Society, under the supervision of THEODOR GOLDSTÜCKER. Vol. I., containing the Jaiminîya-Nyâya-Mâlâ-Vistara. Parts I. to VII., pp. 582, large 4to. sewed. *10s.* each part. Complete in one vol., cloth, £3 *13s. 6d.* Vol. II. The Institutes of Gautama. Edited with an Index of Words, by A. F. STENZLER, Ph.D., Professor of Oriental Languages in the University of Breslau. 8vo. cloth, pp. iv. 78. *4s. 6d.* Vol. III. Vaitâna Sûtra. The Ritual of the Atharva Veda. Edited with Critical Notes and Indices, by DR. RICHARD GARBE. 8vo. sewed, pp. 119. *5s.*

Axon.—The Literature of the Lancashire Dialect. A Bibliographical Essay. By William E. A. Axon, F.R.S.L. Fcap. 8vo. sewed. 1870. 1*s.*

Baba.—An Elementary Grammar of the Japanese Language, with Easy Progressive Exercises. By Tatui Baba. Crown 8vo. cloth, pp. xii. and 92. 5*s.*

Bachmaier.—Pasigraphical Dictionary and Grammar. By Anton Bachmaier, President of the Central Pasigraphical Society at Munich. 18mo. cloth, pp. viii.; 26; 160. 1870. 3*s.*

Bachmaier.—Pasigraphisches Wörterbuch zum Gebrauche für die deutsche Sprache. Verfasst von Anton Bachmaier, Vorsitzendem des Central-Vereins für Pasigraphie in München. 18mo. cloth, pp. viii.; 32; 128; 120. 1870. 2*s.* 6*d*

Bachmaier.— Dictionnaire Pasigraphique, précédé de la Grammaire. Redigé par Antoine Bachmaier, Président de la Société Centrale de Pasigraphie à Munich. 18mo. cloth, pp. vi. 26; 168; 150. 1870. 2*s.* 6*d.*

Baldwin.—A Manual of the Foochow Dialect. By Rev. C. C. Baldwin, of the American Board Mission. 8vo. pp. viii.-256. 18*s.*

Balfour.—Waifs and Strays from the Far East; being a Series of Disconnected Essays on Matters relating to China. By Frederic Henry Balfour. 1 vol. demy 8vo. cloth, pp. 224. 10*s.* 6*d.*

Ballad Society (The).—Subscription—Small paper, one guinea, and large paper, three guineas, per annum. List of publications on application.

Ballantyne.—A Grammar of the Mahratta Language. For the use of the East India College at Haileybury. By James R. Ballantyne, of the Scottish Naval and Military Academy. 4to. cloth, pp. 56. 5*s.*

Ballantyne.—Elements of Hindí and Braj Bháká Grammar. By the late James R. Ballantyne, LL.D. Second edition, revised and corrected Crown 8vo., pp. 44, cloth. 5*s.*

Ballantyne.—First Lessons in Sanskrit Grammar; together with an Introduction to the Hitopadésa. Second edition. Second Impression. By James R. Ballantyne, LL.D., Librarian of the India Office. 8vo. pp. viii. and 110, cloth. 1873. 3*s.* 6*d.*

Ballantyne.—Hindustani Selections in the Naskhi and Devanagari Character. With a Vocabulary of the Words. Prepared for the use of the Scottish Naval and Military Academy, by James R. Ballantyne. Royal 8vo. cloth, pp. 74. 3*s.* 6*d.*

Ballantyne.—Principles of Persian Caligraphy, illustrated by Lithographic Plates of the TA"LIK characters, the one usually employed in writing the Persian and the Hindūstānī. Second edition. Prepared for the use of the Scottish Naval and Military Academy, by James R. Ballantyne. 4to. cloth, pp. 14, 6 plates. 2*s.* 6*d.*

Banerjea.—The Arian Witness, or the Testimony of Arian Scriptures in corroboration of Biblical History and the Rudiments of Christian Doctrine. Including Dissertations on the Original Home and Early Adventures of Indo-Arians. By the Rev. K. M. Banerjea. 8vo. sewed, pp. xviii. and 236. 8*s.* 6*d.*

Bate.—A Dictionary of the Hindee Language. Compiled by J. D. Bate. 8vo. cloth, pp. 806. £2 12*s.* 6*d.*

Beal.—Travels of Fah Hian and Sung-Yun, Buddhist Pilgrims from China to India (400 A.D. and 518 A.D.) Translated from the Chinese, by S. Beal (B.A. Trinity College, Cambridge), a Chaplain in Her Majesty's Fleet, a Member of the Royal Asiatic Society, and Author of a Translation of the Pratimôksha and the Amithâba Sûtra from the Chinese. Crown 8vo. pp. lxxiii. and 210, cloth, ornamental, with a coloured map. 10*s.* 6*d.*

Beal.—A CATENA OF BUDDHIST SCRIPTURES FROM THE CHINESE. By S. BEAL, B.A., Trinity College, Cambridge; a Chaplain in Her Majesty's Fleet, etc. 8vo. cloth, pp. xiv. and 436. 1871. 15*s.*

Beal.—THE ROMANTIC LEGEND OF SÂKHYA BUDDHA. From the Chinese-Sanscrit by the Rev. SAMUEL BEAL, Author of "Buddhist Pilgrims," etc. Crown 8vo. cloth, pp. 400. 1875. 12*s.*

Beal.—THE BUDDHIST TRIPITAKA, as it is known in China and Japan. A Catalogue and Compendious Report. By SAMUEL BEAL, B.A. Folio, sewed, pp. 117. 7*s.* 6*d.*

Beal.—TEXTS FROM THE BUDDHIST CANON, commonly known as DHAMMAPADA. Translated from the Chinese by S. BEAL, B.A., Professor of Chinese, University of London. With accompanying Narrative. Post 8vo. pp. viii. and 176, cloth. 7*s.* 6*d.*

Beames.—OUTLINES OF INDIAN PHILOLOGY. With a Map, showing the Distribution of the Indian Languages. By JOHN BEAMES. Second enlarged and revised edition. Crown 8vo. cloth, pp. viii. and 96. 5*s.*

Beames.—NOTES ON THE BHOJPURÍ DIALECT OF HINDÍ, spoken in Western Behar. By JOHN BEAMES, Esq., B.C.S., Magistrate of Chumparun. 8vo. pp. 26, sewed. 1868. 1*s.* 6*d.*

Beames.—A COMPARATIVE GRAMMAR OF THE MODERN ARYAN LANGUAGES OF INDIA (to wit), Hindi, Panjabi, Sindhi, Gujarati, Marathi, Uriya, and Bengali. By JOHN BEAMES, Bengal C.S., M.R.A.S., &c.

Vol. I. On Sounds. 8vo. cloth, pp. xvi and 360. 16*s.*

Vol. II. The Noun and the Pronoun. 8vo. cloth, pp. xii. and 348. 16*s.*

Vol III. The Verb. 8vo. cloth, pp. xii. and 316. [*Just ready.*

Bede.—VENERABILIS BEDÆ HISTORIA ECCLESIASTICA GENTIS ANGLORUM. Ad Fidem Codd. MSS. recensuit JOSEPHUS STEVENSON. With plan of the English Historical Society, by the late John Miller 8v. pp. xxxv., xxi. and 424, and 2 facsimiles. 7*s.* 6*d.*

The same, in royal 8vo., uniform with the publications of the Master of the Rolls. 10*s.* 6*d.*

Bellairs.—A GRAMMAR OF THE MARATHI LANGUAGE. By H. S. K. BELLAIRS, M.A., and LAXMAN Y. ASHKEDKAR, B.A. 12mo. cloth, pp. 90. 5*s.*

Bellew.—A DICTIONARY OF THE PUKKHTO, OR PUKSHTO LANGUAGE, on a New and Improved System. With a reversed Part, or English and Pukkhto, By H. W. BELLEW, Assistant Surgeon, Bengal Army. Super Royal 8vo. op. xii. and 356, cloth. 42*s.*

Bellew.—A GRAMMAR OF THE PUKKHTO OR PUKSHTO LANGUAGE, on a New and Improved System. Combining Brevity with Utility, and Illustrated by Exercises and Dialogues. By H. W. BELLEW, Assistant Surgeon, Bengal Army. Super-royal 8vo., pp. xii. and 156, cloth. 21*s.*

Bellew.—FROM THE INDUS TO THE TIGRIS: a Narrative of a Journey through the Countries of Balochistan, Afghanistan, Khorassan, and Iran, in 1872; together with a Synoptical Grammar and Vocabulary of the Brahoe Language, and a Record of the Meteorological Observations and Altitudes on the March from the Indus to the Tigris. By H. W. BELLEW, C.S.I., Surgeon Bengal Staff Corps, Author of "A Journal of a Mission to Afghanistan in 1857–58," and "A Grammar and Dictionary of the Pukkhto Language." Demy 8vo. cloth. 14*s.*

Bellew.—KASHMIR AND KASHGHAR. A Narrative of the Journey ot the Embassy to Kashghar in 1873–74. By H. W. BELLEW, C.S.I. Demy 8vo. cl., pp. xxxii. and 420. 16*s.*

Bellows.—ENGLISH OUTLINE VOCABULARY, for the use of Students of the Chinese, Japanese, and other Languages. Arranged by JOHN BELLOWS. With Notes on the writing of Chinese with Roman Letters.By Professor SUMMERS, King's College, London. Crown 8vo., pp. 6 and 368, cloth. 6*s.*

Bellows.—OUTLINE DICTIONARY, FOR THE USE OF MISSIONARIES, Explorers, and Students of Language. By MAX MÜLLER, M.A., Taylorian Professor in the University of Oxford. With an Introduction on the proper use of the ordinary English Alphabet in transcribing Foreign Languages. The Vocabulary compiled by JOHN BELLOWS. Crown 8vo. Limp morocco, pp. xxxi. and 368. 7s. 6d.

Bellows.—DICTIONARY FOR THE POCKET, French and English, English and French. Both Divisions on same page. By JOHN BELLOWS. Masculine and Feminine Words shown by Distinguishing Types. Conjugations of all the Verbs; Liaison marked in French Part, and Hints to aid Pronunciation. Together with Tables and Maps. Revised by ALEXANDRE BELJAME, M.A., and Fellow of the University, Paris. Second Edition. 32mo. roan, with tuck, gilt edges. 10s. 6d. Persian, 10s. 6d. Morocco, 12s. 6d.

Benfey.—A GRAMMAR OF THE LANGUAGE OF THE VEDAS. By Dr. THEODOR BENFEY. In 1 vol. 8vo., of about 650 pages. [*In preparation.*

Benfey.—A PRACTICAL GRAMMAR OF THE SANSKRIT LANGUAGE, for the use of Early Students. By THEODOR BENFEY, Professor of Sanskrit in the University of Göttingen. Second, revised and enlarged, edition Royal 8vo. pp. viii. and 296, cloth. 10s. 6d.

Benfey.—VEDICA UND VERWANDTES. Von THEODOR BENFEY. Cr. 8vo. 7s. 6d.

Beschi.—CLAVIS HUMANIORUM LITTERARUM SUBLIMIORIS TAMULICI IDIOMATIS. Auctore R. P. CONSTANTIO JOSEPHO BESCHIO, Soc. Jesu. in Madurensi Regno Missionario. Edited by the Rev. K. IHLEFELD, and printed for A. Burnell, Esq., Tranquebar. 8vo. sewed, pp. 171. 10s. 6d.

Beveridge.—THE DISTRICT OF BAKARGANJ; its History and Statistics. By H. BEVERIDGE, B.C.S. 8vo. cloth, pp. xx. and 460. 21s.

Bhagavat-Geeta.—See under WILKINS.

Bibliotheca Indica. A Collection of Oriental Works published by the Asiatic Society of Bengal. Old Series. Fasc. 1 to 235. New Series. Fasc. 1 to 408. (Special List of Contents to be had on application.) Each Fsc in 8vo., 2s.; in 4to., 4s.

Bibliotheca Orientalis: or, a Complete List of Books, Pamphlets, Essays, and Journals, published in France, Germany, England, and the Colonies, on the History and the Geography, the Religions, the Antiquities, Literature, and Languages of the East. Edited by CHARLES FRIEDERICI. Part I., 1876, sewed, pp. 86, 2s. 6d. Part II., 1877, sewed, pp. 100, 2s. 6d.

Bibliotheca Sanskrita.—See TRÜBNER.

Bickell.—OUTLINES OF HEBREW GRAMMAR. By GUSTAVUS BICKELL, D.D. Revised by the Author; Annotated by the Translator, SAMUEL IVES CURTISS, junior, Ph.D. With a Lithographic Table of Semitic Characters by Dr. J. EUTING. Cr. 8vo. sd., pp. xiv. and 140. 1877. 3s. 6d.

Bigandet.—THE LIFE OR LEGEND OF GAUDAMA, the Buddha of the Burmese, with Annotations. The ways to Neibban, and Notice on the Phongyies, or Burmese Monks. By the Right Reverend P. BIGANDET, Bishop of Ramatha, Vicar Apostolic of Ava and Pegu. 8vo. pp. xi., 538, and v. £1 11s. 6d.

Bleek.—A COMPARATIVE GRAMMAR OF SOUTH AFRICAN LANGUAGES. By W. H. I. BLEEK, Ph.D. Volume I. I. Phonology. II. The Concord. Section 1. The Noun. 8vo. pp. xxxvi. and 322, cloth. £1 16s.

Bleek.—A BRIEF ACCOUNT OF BUSHMAN FOLK LORE AND OTHER TEXTS. By W. H. I. BLEEK, Ph.D., etc., etc. Folio sd., pp. 21. 1875. 2s. 6d.

Bleek.—REYNARD IN SOUTH AFRICA; or, Hottentot Fables. Translated from the Original Manuscript in Sir George Grey's Library. By Dr. W. H. I. BLEEK, Librarian to the Grey Library, Cape Town, Cape of Good Hope. In one volume, small 8vo., pp. xxxi. and 94, cloth. 3s. 6d.

Blochmann.—THE PROSODY OF THE PERSIANS, according to Saifi, Jami, and other Writers. By H. BLOCHMANN, M.A. Assistant Professor, Calcutta Madrasah. 8vo. sewed, pp. 166. 10*s.* 6*d.*

Blochmann.—SCHOOL GEOGRAPHY OF INDIA AND BRITISH BURMAH. By H. BLOCHMANN, M.A. 12mo. pp. vi. and 100. 2*s.* 6*d.*

Blochmann.—A TREATISE ON THE RUBA'I entitled Risalah i Taranah. By AGHA AHMAD 'ALI. With an Introduction and Explanatory Notes, by H. BLOCHMANN, M.A. 8vo. sewed, pp. 11 and 17. 2*s.* 6*d.*

Blochmann.—THE PERSIAN METRES BY SAIFI, and a Treatise on Persian Rhyme by Jami. Edited in Persian, by H. BLOCHMANN, M.A. 8vo. sewed pp. 62. 3*s.* 6*d.*

Bombay Sanskrit Series. Edited under the superintendence of G. BÜHLER, Ph. D., Professor of Oriental Languages, Elphinstone College, and F. KIELHORN, Ph. D., Superintendent of Sanskṛit Studies, Deccan College. 1868–70.

1. PANCHATANTRA IV. AND V. Edited, with Notes, by G. BÜHLER, Ph. D. Pp. 84, 16. 6*s.*
2. NÁGOJÍBHAṬṬA'S PARIBHÁSHENDUŚEKHARA. Edited and explained by F. KIELHORN, Ph. D. Part I., the Sanskṛit Text and Various Readings. pp. 116. 10*s.* 6*d.*
3. PANCHATANTRA II. AND III. Edited, with Notes, by G. BÜHLER, Ph. D. Pp. 86, 14, 2. 7*s.* 6*d.*
4. PANCHATANTRA I. Edited, with Notes, by F. KIELHORN, Ph.D. Pp. 114, 53. 7*s.* 6*d.*
5. KÁLIDÁSA'S RAGHUVAÑŚA. With the Commentary of Mallinátha. Edited, with Notes, by SHANKAR P. PAṆḌIT, M.A. Part I. Cantos I.–VI. 10*s.* 6*d.*
6. KÁLIDÁSA'S MÁLAVIKÁGNIMITRA. Edited, with Notes, by SHANKAR P. PAṆḌIT, M.A. 10*s.* 6*d.*
7. NÁGOJÍBHAṬṬA'S PARIBHÁSHENDUŚEKHARA Edited and explained by F. KIELHORN, Ph.D. Part II. Translation and Notes. (Paribhâshâs, i.–xxxvii.) pp. 184. 10*s.* 6*d.*
8. KÁLIDÁSA'S RAGHUVAÑŚA. With the Commentary of Mallinátha. Edited, with Notes, by SHANKAR P. PAṆḌIT, M.A. Part II. Cantos VII.–XIII. 10*s.* 6*d.*
9. NÁGOJÍBHAṬṬA'S PARIBHÁSHENDUṢEKHARA. Edited and explained by F. KIELHORN. Part II. Translation and Notes. (Paribhâshâs xxxviii.–lxix.) 7*s.* 6*d.*
10. DANDIN'S DASAKUMARACHARITA. Edited with critical and explanatory Notes by G. Bühler. Part I. 7*s.* 6*d.*
11. BHARTRIHARI'S NITISATAKA AND VAIRAGYASATAKA, with Extracts from Two Sanskrit Commentaries. Edited, with Notes, by KASINATH T. TELANG. 9*s.*
12. NAGOJIBHATTA'S PARIBHÁSHENDUSEKHARA. Edited and explained by F. KIELHORN. Part II. Translation and Notes. (Paribhâshâs lxx.–cxxii.) 7*s.* 6*d.*
13. KALIDASA'S RAGHUVAÑṢA, with the Commentary of Mallinátha. Edited, with Notes, by SHANKAR P. PAṆḌIT. Part III. Cantos XIV.–XIX. 10*s.* 6*d.*
14. VIKRAMÂNKADEVACHARITA. Edited, with an Introduction, by G. BÜHLER. 7*s.* 6*d.*
15. BHAVABHÛTI'S MÂLATÎ-MÂDHAVA. With the Commentary of Jagaddhara, edited by RAMKRISHNA GOPAL BHANDARKAR. 14*s.*

Borooah.—A Practical English-Sanskrit Dictionary. By Anundoram Borooah, B.A., B.C.S., of the Middle Temple, Barrister-at-Law. Vol. I. A to Falseness. pp. xx.-580-10. £1 11*s*. 6*d*.

Borooah.—A Companion to the Sanskrit-Reading Undergraduates of the Calcutta University, being a few notes on the Sanskrit Texts selected for examination, and their Commentaries. By Anundoram Borooah. 8vo. pp. 64. 3*s*. 6*d*.

Borooah.—Bhavabhuti and his Place in Sanskrit Literature. By Anundoram Borooah. 8vo. sewed, pp. 70. 5*s*.

Bottrell.—Traditions and Hearthside Stories of West Cornwall. By W. Bottrell (an old Celt). Demy 12mo. pp. vi. 292, cloth. 1870. Scarce.

Bottrell.—Traditions and Hearthside Stories of West Cornwall. By William Bottrell. With Illustrations by Mr. Joseph Blight. Second Series. Crown 8vo. cloth, pp. iv. and 300. 6*s*.

Bowditch.—Suffolk Surnames. By N. I. Bowditch. Third Edition, 8vo. pp. xxvi. and 758, cloth. 7*s*. 6*d*.

Bretschneider.—On the Knowledge Possessed by the Ancient Chinese of the Arabs and Arabian Colonies, and other Western Countries mentioned in Chinese Books. By E. Bretschneider, M.D., Physician of the Russian Legation at Peking. 8vo. pp. 28, sewed. 1871. 1*s*.

Bretschneider.—Notes on Chinese Mediæval Travellers to the West. By E. Bretschneider, M.D. Demy 8vo. sd., pp. 130. 5*s*.

Bretschneider.—Archæological and Historical Researches on Peking and its Environs. By E. Bretschneider, M.D., Physician to the Russian Legation at Peking. Imp. 8vo. sewed, pp. 64, with 4 Maps. 5*s*.

Bretschneider.—Notices of the Mediæval Geography and History of Central and Western Asia. Drawn from Chinese and Mongol Writings, and Compared with the Observations of Western Authors in the Middle Ages. By E. Bretschneider, M.D. 8vo. sewed, pp. 233, with two Maps. 12*s*. 6*d*.

Brhat-Sanhita (The).—See under Kern.

Brinton.—The Myths of the New World. A Treatise on the Symbolism and Mythology of the Red Race of America. By Daniel G. Brinton, A.M., M.D. Second Edition, revised. Cr. 8vo. cloth, pp. viii. and 331. 12*s*. 6*d*.

British Museum.—Catalogue of Sanskrit and Pali Books in the British Museum. By Dr. Ernst Haas. Printed by permission of the Trustees of the British Museum. 4to pp. viii. and 188, boards. £1 1*s*.

British Museum Publications (List of) on Sale by Trübner & Co. [*On application.*

British Archæological Association (Journal of The). Volumes 1 to 31, 1844 to 1876, £1 11*s*. 6*d*. each. General Index to vols. 1 to 30. 8vo. cloth. 15*s*. Parts Quarterly, 8*s*. each.

Brockie.—Indian Philosophy. Introductory Paper. By William Brockie, Author of "A Day in the Land of Scott," etc., etc. 8vo. pp. 26, sewed. 1872. 6*d*.

Bronson.—A Dictionary in Assamese and English. Compiled by M. Bronson, American Baptist Missionary. 8vo. calf, pp. viii. and 609. £2 2*s*.

Brown.—The Dervishes; or, Oriental Spiritualism. By John P. Brown, Secretary and Dragoman of the Legation of the United States of America at Constantinople. With twenty-four Illustrations. 8vo. cloth, pp. viii. and 415. 14*s*.

Brown.—Sanskrit Prosody and Numerical Symbols Explained. By Charles Philip Brown, Author of the Telugu Dictionary, Grammar, etc., Professor of Telugu in the University of London. Demy 8vo. pp. 64, cloth. 3*s*. 6*d*.

Bühler.—ELEVEN LAND-GRANTS OF THE CHAULUKYAS OF AṆHILVÂḌ. A Contribution to the History of Gujarât. By G. BÜHLER. 16mo. sewed, pp. 126, with Facsimile. *3s. 6d.*

Bühler.—THREE NEW EDICTS OF AŚOKA. By G. BÜHLER. 16mo. sewed, with Two Facsimiles. *2s. 6d.*

Burgess.—ARCHÆOLOGICAL SURVEY OF WESTERN INDIA. Vol. 1. Report of the First Season's Operations in the Belgâm and Kaladgi Districts. Jan. to May, 1874. By JAMES BURGESS. With 56 photographs and lith. plates. Royal 4to. pp. viii. and 45. *£2 2s.*

Vol. 2. Report of the Second Season's Operations. Report on the Antiquities of Kâthiâwâd and Kachh. 1874–5. By JAMES BURGESS, F.R.G.S., M.R.A.S., etc. With Map, Inscriptions, Photographs, etc. Roy. 4to. half bound, pp. x. and 242. *£3 3s.*

Vol. 3. Report of the Third Season's Operations. 1875–76. Report on the Antiquities in the Bidar and Aurangabad District. Royal 4to. half bound pp. viii. and 138, with 66 photographic and lithographic plates. *£2 2s.*

Burnell.—CATALOGUE OF A COLLECTION OF SANSKRIT MANUSCRIPTS. By A. C. BURNELL, M.R.A.S., Madras Civil Service. PART 1. *Vedic Manuscripts.* Fcap. 8vo. pp. 64, sewed. 1870. *2s.*

Burnell.—DAYADAÇAÇLOKI. TEN SLOKAS IN SANSKRIT, with English Translation. By A. C. BURNELL. 8vo. pp. 11. 2s.

Burnell.—ELEMENTS OF SOUTH INDIAN PALÆOGRAPHY. From the Fourth to the Seventeenth Century A.D. By A. C. BURNELL. Second Corrected and Enlarged Edition, 34 Plates and Map, in One Vol. 4to. pp. xiv.–148. *£2 12s. 6d.*

Burnell.—ON THE AINDRA SCHOOL OF SANSKRIT GRAMMARIANS. Their Place in the Sanskrit and Subordinate Literatures. By A. C. BURNELL. 8vo. pp. 120. *10s. 6d.*

Burnell.—THE SÂMAVIDHÂNABRÂHMAṆA (being the Third Brâhmaṇa) of the Sâma Veda. Edited, together with the Commentary of Sâyaṇa, an English Translation, Introduction, and Index of Words, by A. C. BURNELL. Volume I.—Text and Commentary, with Introduction. 8vo. pp. xxxviii. and 104. *12s. 6d.*

Burnell.—THE ARSHEYABRAHMAṆA (being the fourth Brâhmana) OF THE SAMA VEDA. The Sanskrit Text. Edited, together with Extracts from the Commentary of Sayana, etc. An Introduction and Index of Words. By A. C. BURNELL, Ph.D. 8vo, pp. 51 and 109. *10s. 6d.*

Burnell.—THE DEVATÂDHYÂYABRÂHMAṆA (being the Fifth Brâhmaṇa) of the Sama Veda. The Sanskrit Text edited, with the Commentary of Sâyaṇa, an Index of Words, etc., by A. C. BURNELL, M.R.A.S. 8vo. and Trans., pp. 34. *5s.*

Burnell.—THE JAIMINÎYA TEXT OF THE ARSHEYABRÂHMAṆA OF THE Sâma Veda. Edited in Sanskrit by A. C. BURNELL, Ph. D. 8vo. sewed, pp. 56. *7s. 6d.*

Burnell. — THE SAṂHITOPANISHADBRÂHMAṆA (Being the Seventh Brâhmaṇa) of the Sâma Veda. The Sanskrit Text. With a Commentary, an Index of Words, etc. Edited by A. C. BURNELL, Ph.D. 8vo. stiff boards, pp. 86. *7s. 6d.*

Burnell.—THE VAṂÇABRÂHMAṆA (being the Eighth Brâhmaṇa) of the Sâma Veda. Edited, together with the Commentary of Sâyaṇa, a Preface and Index of Words, by A. C. BURNELL, M.R.A.S., etc. 8vo. sewed, pp. xliii., 12, and xii., with 2 coloured plates. *10s. 6d.*

Butler.—HUNGARIAN POEMS AND FABLES FOR ENGLISH READERS. Selected and translated by E. D. BUTLER, of the British Museum. With Illustrations by A. G. BUTLER. Fcap. limp cloth, pp. vi.-88. 1877. 2*s*.

Buttmann.—A GRAMMAR OF THE NEW TESTAMENT GREEK. By A. BUTTMANN. Authorized translation by Prof J. H. Thayer, with numerous additions and corrections by the author. Demy 8vo. cloth, pp. xx. and 474. 1873. 14*s*.

Butrus-al-Bustâny.—كتاب دائرة المعارف An Arabic Encylopædia of Universal Knowledge, by BUTRUS-AL-BUSTÂNY, the celebrated compiler of Mohît ul Mohît (محيط المحيط), and Katr el Mohît (قطر المحيط). This work will be completed in from 12 to 15 Vols., of which Vols. I. to III. are ready, Vol. I. contains letter ا to اب; Vol. II. اب to ار; Vol. III. ار to اغ. Small folio, cloth, pp. 800 each. £1 11*s*. 6*d*. per Vol.

Byington.—GRAMMAR OF THE CHOCTAW LANGUAGE. By the Rev. CYRUS BYINGTON. Edited from the Original MSS. in Library of the American Philosophical Society, by D. G. BRINTON, M.D. Cr. 8vo. sewed, pp. 56. 7*s*. 6*d*.

Calcutta Review (THE).—Published Quarterly. Price 8*s*. 6*d*. per number.

Caldwell.—A COMPARATIVE GRAMMAR OF THE DRAVIDIAN, OR SOUTH-INDIAN FAMILY OF LANGUAGES. By the Rev. R. CALDWELL, LL.D. A Second, corrected, and enlarged Edition. Demy 8vo. pp. 805. 1875. 28*s*.

Callaway.—IZINGANEKWANE, NENSUMANSUMANE, NEZINDABA, ZABANTU (Nursery Tales, Traditions, and Histories of the Zulus). In their own words, with a Translation into English, and Notes. By the Rev. HENRY CALLAWAY, M.D. Volume I., 8vo. pp. xiv. and 378, cloth. Natal, 1866 and 1867. 16*s*.

Callaway.—THE RELIGIOUS SYSTEM OF THE AMAZULU.

Part I.—Unkulunkulu; or, the Tradition of Creation as existing among the Amazulu and other Tribes of South Africa, in their own words, with a translation into English, and Notes. By the Rev. Canon CALLAWAY, M.D. 8vo. pp. 128, sewed. 1868. 4s.

Part II.—Amatongo; or, Ancestor Worship, as existing among the Amazulu, in their own words, with a translation into English, and Notes. By the Rev. CANON CALLAWAY, M.D. 1869. 8vo. pp. 127, sewed. 1869. 4*s*.

Part III.—Izinyanga Zokubula; or, Divination, as existing among the Amazulu, in their own words. With a Translation into English, and Notes. By the Rev. Canon CALLAWAY, M.D. 8vo. pp. 150, sewed. 1870. 4*s*.

Part IV.—Abatakati, or Medical Magic and Witchcraft. 8vo. pp. 40, sewed. 1*s*. 6*d*.

Calligaris.—LE COMPAGNON DE TOUS, OU DICTIONNAIRE POLYGLOTTE. Par le Colonel LOUIS CALLIGARIS, Grand Officier, etc. (French—Latin—Italian—Spanish—Portuguese—German—English—Modern Greek—Arabic—Turkish.) 2 vols. 4to., pp. 1157 and 746. Turin. £4 4*s*.

Campbell.—SPECIMENS OF THE LANGUAGES OF INDIA, including Tribes of Bengal, the Central Provinces, and the Eastern Frontier. By Sir G. CAMPBELL, M.P. Folio, paper, pp. 308. 1874. £1 11*s*. 6*d*.

Carletti.—IDH-HAR-UL-HAQQ, Ou Manifestation de la Vérité de El-hage Rahmat-ullah Effendi de Delhi (un des Descendants du Califfe Osman-ben-'Affan). Traduit de l'Arabe, par un éminent, quoique très-jeune, Orientaliste de Tunis. Revu sur le texte, retouché en plusieurs endroits et augmenté d'une preface et d'un appendixe. Par P. V. Carletti. In Two Vols. 8vo. [*In the press.*

Carpenter.—THE LAST DAYS IN ENGLAND OF THE RAJAH RAMMOHUN ROY. By MARY CARPENTER, of Bristol. With Five Illustrations. 8vo. pp. 272, cloth. 7*s*. 6*d*.

Carr.—ఆంధ్రలోకోక్తి చంద్రిక. A Collection of Telugu Proverbs, Translated, Illustrated, and Explained; together with some Sanscrit Proverbs printed in the Devnâgarî and Telugu Characters. By Captain M. W. Carr, Madras Staff Corps. One Vol. and Supplemnt, royal 8vo. pp. 488 and 148. 31*s*. 6*d*

Catlin.—O-Kee-Pa. A Religious Ceremony of the Mandans. By George Catlin. With 13 Coloured Illustrations. 4to pp. 60, bound in cloth, gilt edges. 14*s*.

Chalmers.—A Concise Khang-hsi Chinese Dictionary. By the Rev. J. Chalmers, LL.D., Canton. Three Vols. Royal 8vo. bound in Chinese style, pp. 1000. 21*s*.

Chalmers.—The Origin of the Chinese; an Attempt to Trace the connection of the Chinese with Western Nations in their Religion, Superstitions, Arts, Language, and Traditions. By John Chalmers, A.M. Foolscap 8vo. cloth, pp. 78. 5*s*.

Chalmers.—The Speculations on Metaphysics, Polity, and Morality of "The Old Philosopher" Lau Tsze. Translated from the Chinese, with an Introduction by John Chalmers, M.A. Fcap. 8vo. cloth, xx. and 62. 4*s*. 6*d*.

Charnock.—Ludus Patronymicus; or, the Etymology of Curious Surnames. By Richard Stephen Charnock, Ph.D., F.S.A., F.R.G.S. Crown 8vo., pp. 182, cloth. 7*s*. 6*d*.

Charnock.—Verba Nominalia; or Words derived from Proper Names. By Richard Stephen Charnock, Ph. Dr. F.S.A., etc. 8vo. pp. 326, cloth. 14*s*.

Charnock.—The Peoples of Transylvania. Founded on a Paper read before The Anthropological Society of London, on the 4th of May, 1869. By Richard Stephen Charnock, Ph.D., F.S.A., F.R.G.S. Demy 8vo. pp. 36, sewed. 1870. 2*s*. 6*d*.

Chaucer Society's (The).—Subscription, two guineas per annum. List of Publications on application.

Childers.—A Pali-English Dictionary, with Sanskrit Equivalents, and with numerous Quotations, Extracts, and References. Compiled by the late Prof. R. C. Childers, late of the Ceylon Civil Service. Imperial 8vo. Double Columns. Complete in 1 Vol., pp. xxii. and 622, cloth. 1875. £3 3*s*.

The first Pali Dictionary ever published.

Childers.—Notes on the Sinhalese Language. No. 1. On the Formation of the Plural of Neuter Nouns. By the late Prof. R. C. Childers. Demy 8vo. sd., pp. 16. 1873. 1*s*.

Childers.—On Sandhi in Pali. By the late Prof. R. C. Childers. 8vo. sewed, pp. 22. 1*s*.

Childers.—The Mahâparinibbânasutta of the Sutta-Pitaka. The Pali Text. Edited by the late Professor R. C. Childers. 8vo. cloth, pp. 72. 5*s*.

China Review; or, Notes and Queries on the Far East. Published bi-monthly. Edited by E. J. Eitel. 4to. Subscription, £1 10*s*. per volume.

Chintamon.—A Commentary on the Text of the Bhagavad-Gítá; or, the Discourse between Krishna and Arjuna of Divine Matters. A Sanscrit Philosophical Poem. With a few Introductory Papers. By Hurrychund Chintamon, Political Agent to H. H. the Guicowar Mulhar Rao Maharajah of Baroda. Post 8vo. cloth, pp. 118. 6*s*.

Christaller.—A Dictionary, English, Tshi, (Asante), Akra; Tshi (Chwee), comprising as dialects Akán (Asànté, Akém, Akuapém, etc.) and Fànté; Akra (Accra), connected with Adangme; Gold Coast, West Africa.

Enyiresi, Twi né Ṅkraṅ nsẹm - asekyerẹ - ṅhõma.	Eṅliši, Otšũi kẹ Gã wiemọi - ašišitšõmọ- wolo.

By the Rev. J. G. Christaller, Rev. C. W. Locher, Rev. J. Zimmermann. 16mo. 7*s*. 6*d*.

Christaller.—A Grammar of the Asante and Fante Language, called Tshi (Chwee, Twi): based on the Akuapem Dialect, with reference to the other (Akan and Fante) Dialects. By Rev. J. G. Christaller. 8vo. pp. xxiv. and 203. 1875. 10*s*. 6*d*.

Clarke.—Ten Great Religions: an Essay in Comparative Theology. By James Freeman Clarke. 8vo. cloth, pp. x. and 528. 1871. 15*s*.

Clarke.—Memoir on the Comparative Grammar of Egyptian, Coptic, and Ude. By Hyde Clarke, Cor. Member American Oriental Society; Mem. German Oriental Society, etc., etc. Demy 8vo. sd., pp. 32. 2*s*.

Clarke.—Researches in Pre-historic and Proto-historic Comparative Philology, Mythology, and Archæology, in connexion with the Origin of Culture in America and the Accad or Sumerian Families. By Hyde Clarke. Demy 8vo. sewed, pp. xi. and 74. 1875. 2*s*. 6*d*.

Clarke.—Serpent and Siva Worship, and Mythology in Central America, Africa and Asia. By Hyde Clarke, Esq. 8vo. sewed. 1*s*.

Cleasby.—An Icelandic-English Dictionary. Based on the MS. Collections of the late Richard Cleasby. Enlarged and completed by G. Vigfússon. With an Introduction, and Life of Richard Cleasby, by G. Webbe Dasent, D.C.L. 4to. £3 7*s*.

Cleasby.—Appendix to an Icelandic-English Dictionary. *See* Skeat.

Colebrooke.—The Life and Miscellaneous Essays of Henry Thomas Colebrooke. The Biography by his Son, Sir T. E. Colebrooke, Bart., M.P., The Essays edited by Professor Cowell. In 3 vols.

Vol. I. The Life. With Portrait and Map. Demy 8vo. cloth, pp. xii. and 492. 14*s*.

Vols. II. and III. The Essays. A New Edition, with Notes by E. B. Cowell, Professor of Sanskrit in the University of Cambridge. Demy 8vo. cloth, pp. xvi.-544, and x.-520. 1873. 28*s*.

Colleccao de Vocabulos e Frases usados na Provincia de S. Pedro, do Rio Grande do Sul, no Brasil. 12mo. pp. 32, sewed. 1*s*.

Contopoulos.—A Lexicon of Modern Greek-English and English Modern Greek. By N. Contopoulos. In 2 vols. 8vo. cloth. Part I. Modern Greek-English, pp. 460. Part II. English-Modern Greek, pp. 582. £1 7*s*.

Conway.—The Sacred Anthology. A Book of Ethnical Scriptures. Collected and edited by M. D. Conway. 4th edition. Demy 8vo. cloth, pp. xvi. and 480. 12*s*.

Coomára Swamy.—The Dathávansa; or, the History of the Tooth-Relic of Gotama Buddha. The Pali Text and its Translation into English, with Notes. By Sir M. Coomára Swámy, Mudeliár. Demy 8vo. cloth, pp. 174. 1874. 10*s*. 6*d*.

Coomára Swamy.—The Dathávansa; or, the History of the Tooth-Relic of Gotama Buddha. English Translation only. With Notes. Demy 8vo. cloth, pp. 100. 1874. 6*s*.

Coomára Swamy.—Sutta Nipáta; or, the Dialogues and Discourses of Gotama Buddha. Translated from the Pali, with Introduction and Notes. By Sir M. Coomára Swamy. Cr. 8vo. cloth, pp. xxxvi. and 160. 1874. 6*s*.

Cotton.—Arabic Primer. Consisting of 180 Short Sentences containing 30 Primary Words prepared according to the Vocal System of Studying Language. By General Sir Arthur Cotton, K.C.S.I. Cr. 8vo. cloth, pp. 38. 2*s*.

Cowell and Eggeling.—Catalogue of Buddhist Sanskrit Manuscripts in the Possession of the Royal Asiatic Society (Hodgson Collection). By Professors E. B. Cowell and J. Eggeling. 8vo. sd., pp. 56. 2*s.* 6*d.*

Cowell.—A short Introduction to the Ordinary Prakrit of the Sanskrit Dramas. With a List of Common Irregular Prakrit Words. By Prof. E. B. Cowell. Cr. 8vo. limp cloth, pp. 40. 1875. 3*s.* 6*d.*

Cunningham.—The Ancient Geography of India. I. The Buddhist Period, including the Campaigns of Alexander, and the Travels of Hwen-Thsang. By Alexander Cunningham, Major-General, Royal Engineers (Bengal Retired). With thirteen Maps. 8vo. pp. xx. 590, cloth. 1870. 28*s.*

Cunningham.—The Bhilsa Topes; or, Buddhist Monuments of Central India: comprising a brief Historical Sketch of the Rise, Progress, and Decline of Buddhism; with an Account of the Opening and Examination of the various Groups of Topes around Bhilsa. By Brev.-Major Alexander Cunningham, Bengal Engineers. Illustrated with thirty-three Plates. 8vo. pp. xxxvi. 370, cloth. 1854. £2 2*s.*

Cunningham.—Archæological Survey of India. Four Reports, made during the years 1862-63-64-65. By Alexander Cunningham, C.S.I., Major-General, etc. With Maps and Plates. Vols. 1 to 5. 8vo. cloth. £6.

Cust.—A Sketch of the Modern Languages of the East Indies. Accompanied by Two Language Maps. By R. Cust. Post 8vo. pp. xii. and 198, cloth. 12*s.*

Da Cunha.—Memoir on the History of the Tooth-Relic of Ceylon; with an Essay on the Life and System of Gautama Buddha. By J. Gerson da Cunha. 8vo. cloth, pp. xiv. and 70. With 4 photographs and cuts. 7*s.* 6*d.*

Da Cunha.—The Sahyadri Khaṇḍa of the Skanda Purana; a Mythological, Historical and Geographical Account of Western India. First edition of the Sanskrit Text, with various readings. By J. Gerson da Cunha, M.R.C.S. and L.M. Eng., L.R.C.P. Edinb., etc. 8vo. bds. pp. 580. £1 1*s.*

Da Cunha.—Notes on the History and Antiquities of Chaul and Bassein. By J. Gerson da Cunha, M.R.C.S. and L.M. Eng., etc. 8vo. cloth, pp. xvi. and 262. With 17 photographs, 9 plates and a map. £1 5*s.*

Dalton.—Descriptive Ethnology of Bengal. By Edward Tuite Dalton, C.S.I., Colonel, Bengal Staff Corps, etc. Illustrated by Lithograph Portraits copied from Photographs. 33 Lithograph Plates. 4to. half-calf, pp. 340. £6 6*s.*

D'Alwis.—A Descriptive Catalogue of Sanskrit, Pali, and Sinhalese Literary Works of Ceylon. By James D'Alwis, M.R.A.S., Advocate of the Supreme Court, &c., &c. In Three Volumes. Vol. I., pp. xxxii. and 244, sewed. 1870. 8*s.* 6*d.*

Davids.—Three Inscriptions of Parâkrama Bâhu the Great, from Pulastipura, Ceylon. By T. W. Rhys Davids. 8vo. pp. 20. 1*s.* 6*d.*

Davids.—Sigiri, the Lion Rock, near Pulastipura, and the 39th Chapter of the Mahâvamsa. By T. W. Rhys Davids. 8vo. pp. 30. 1*s.* 6*d.*

Delepierre.—Supercheries Litteraires, Pastiches Suppositions d'Auteur, dans les Lettres et dans les Arts. Par Octave Delepierre. Fcap. 4to. paper cover, pp. 328. 14*s.*

Delepierre.—Tableau de la Littérature du Centon, chez les Anciens et chez les Modernes. Par Octave Delepierre. 2 vols. small 4to. paper cover, pp. 324 and 318. 21*s.*

Delepierre.—Essai Historique et Bibliographique sur les Rébus. Par Octave Delepierre. 8vo. pp. 24, sewed. With 15 pages of Woodcuts. 1870. 3*s.* 6*d.*

Dennys.—CHINA AND JAPAN. A complete Guide to the Open Ports of those countries, together with Pekin, Yeddo, Hong Kong, and Macao; forming a Guide Book and Vade Mecum for Travellers, Merchants, and Residents in general; with 56 Maps and Plans. By WM. FREDERICK MAYERS, F.R.G.S. H.M.'s Consular Service; N. B. DENNYS, late H.M.'s Consular Service; and CHARLES KING, Lieut. Royal Marine Artillery. Edited by N. B. DENNYS. In one volume. 8vo. pp. 600, cloth. £2 2*s.*

Dennys.—A HANDBOOK OF THE CANTON VERNACULAR OF THE CHINESE LANGUAGE. Being a Series of Introductory Lessons, for Domestic and Business Purposes. By N. B. DENNYS, M.R.A.S., Ph.D. 8vo. cloth, pp. 4, 195, and 31. £1 10*s.*

Dennys.—A HANDBOOK OF MALAY COLLOQUIAL, as spoken in Singapore, Being a Series of Introductory Lessons for Domestic and Business Purposes. By N. B. DENNYS, Ph.D., F.R.G.S., M.R.A.S., etc., Author of "The Folklore of China," "Handbook of Cantonese," etc., etc. 8vo. cloth, pp. 204. £1 1*s.*

Dennys.—THE FOLK-LORE OF CHINA, and its Affinities with that of the Aryan and Semitic Races. By N. B. DENNYS, Ph.D., F.R.G.S., M.R.A.S., author of "A Handbook of the Canton Vernacular," etc. 8vo. cloth, pp. 168. 10*s.* 6*d.*

De Vere.—STUDIES IN ENGLISH; or, Glimpses of the Inner Life of our Language. By M. SCHELE DE VERE, LL.D., Professor of Modern Languages in the University of Virginia. 8vo. cloth, pp vi. and 365. 12*s.* 6*d.*

De Vere.—AMERICANISMS: THE ENGLISH OF THE NEW WORLD. By M. SCHELE DE VERE, LL.D., Professor of Modern Languages in the University of Virginia. 8vo. pp. 685, cloth. 12*s.*

Dickson.—THE PÂTIMOKKHA, being the Buddhist Office of the Confession of Priests. The Pali Text, with a Translation, and Notes, by J. F. DICKSON, M.A. 8vo. sd., pp. 69. 2*s.*

Dinkard (The).—The Original Pehlwi Text, the same transliterated in Zend Characters. Translations of the Text in the Gujrati and English Languages; a Commentary and Glossary of Select Terms. By PESHOTUN DUSTOOR BEHRAMJEE SUNJANA. Vols. I. and II. 8vo. cloth. £2 2*s.*

Döhne.—A ZULU-KAFIR DICTIONARY, etymologically explained, with copious Illustrations and examples, preceded by an introduction on the Zulu-Kafir Language. By the Rev. J. L. DÖHNE. Royal 8vo. pp. xlii. and 418, sewed. Cape Town, 1857. 21*s.*

Döhne.—THE FOUR GOSPELS IN ZULU. By the Rev. J. L. DÖHNE, Missionary to the American Board, C.F.M. 8vo. pp. 208, cloth. Pietermaritzburg, 1866. 5*s.*

Doolittle.—A VOCABULARY AND HANDBOOK OF THE CHINESE LANGUAGE. Romanized in the Mandarin Dialect. In Two Volumes comprised in Three arts. By Rev. JUSTUS DOOLITTLE, Author of "Social Life of the Chinese." Vol. I. 4to. pp. viii. and 548. Vol. II. Parts II. and III., pp. vii. and 695. £1 11*s.* 6*d.* each vol.

Douglas.—CHINESE-ENGLISH DICTIONARY OF THE VERNACULAR OR SPOKEN LANGUAGE OF AMOY, with the principal variations of the Chang-Chew and Chin-Chew Dialects. By the Rev. CARSTAIRS DOUGLAS, M.A., LL.D., Glasg., Missionary of the Presbyterian Church in England. 1 vol. High quarto, cloth, double columns, pp. 632. 1873. £3 3*s.*

Douglas.—CHINESE LANGUAGE AND LITERATURE. Two Lectures delivered at the Royal Institution, by R. K. DOUGLAS, of the British Museum, and Professor of Chinese at King's College. Cr. 8vo. cl., pp. 118. 1875. 5*s.*

Douglas.—THE LIFE OF JENGHIZ KHAN. Translated from the Chinese, with an Introduction, by ROBERT KENNAWAY DOUGLAS, of the British Museum, and Professor of Chinese, King's College, London. Cr. 8vo. cloth, pp. xxxvi.-106. 1877. 5*s.*

Douse.—Grimm's Law; A Study: or, Hints towards an Explanation of the so-called "Lautverschiebung." To which are added some Remarks on the Primitive Indo-European *K*, and several Appendices. By T. Le Marchant Douse. 8vo. cloth, pp. xvi. and 230. 10*s*. 6*d*.

Dowson.—A Grammar of the Urdu or Hindustani Language. By John Dowson, M.R.A.S. 12mo. cloth, pp. xvi. and 264. 10*s*. 6*d*.

Dowson.—A Hindustani Exercise Book. Containing a Series of Passages and Extracts adapted for Translation into Hindustani. By John Dowson, M.R.A.S., Professor of Hindustani, Staff College. Crown 8vo. pp. 100. Limp cloth, 2*s*. 6*d*.

Dwight.—Modern Philology: Its Discovery, History, and Influence. New edition, with Maps, Tabular Views, and an Index. By Benjamin W. Dwight. In two vols. cr. 8vo. cloth. First series, pp. 360; second series, pp. xi. and 554. £1.

Early English Text Society's Publications. Subscription, one guinea per annum.

1. Early English Alliterative Poems. In the West-Midland Dialect of the Fourteenth Century. Edited by R. Morris, Esq., from an unique Cottonian MS. 16*s*.
2. Arthur (about 1440 A.D.). Edited by F. J. Furnivall, Esq., from the Marquis of Bath's unique MS. 4*s*.
3. Ane Compendious and Breue Tractate concernyng ye Office and Dewtie of Kyngis, etc. By William Lauder. (1556 A.D.) Edited by F. Hall, Esq., D.C.L. 4*s*.
4. Sir Gawayne and the Green Knight (about 1320-30 A.D.). Edited by R. Morris, Esq., from an unique Cottonian MS. 10*s*.
5. Of the Orthographie and Congruitie of the Britan Tongue; a treates, noe shorter than necessarie, for the Schooles, be Alexander Hume. Edited for the first time from the unique MS. in the British Museum (about 1617 A.D.), by Henry B. Wheatley, Esq. 4*s*.
6. Lancelot of the Laik. Edited from the unique MS. in the Cambridge University Library (ab. 1500), by the Rev. Walter W. Skeat, M.A. 8*s*.
7. The Story of Genesis and Exodus, an Early English Song, of about 1250 A.D. Edited for the first time from the unique MS. in the Library of Corpus Christi College, Cambridge, by R. Morris, Esq. 8*s*.
8. Morte Arthure; the Alliterative Version. Edited from Robert Thornton's unique MS. (about 1440 A.D.) at Lincoln, by the Rev. George Perry, M.A., Prebendary of Lincoln. 7*s*.
9. Animadversions uppon the Annotacions and Corrections of some Imperfections of Impressiones of Chaucer's Workes, reprinted in 1598; by Francis Thynne. Edited from the unique MS. in the Bridgewater Library. By G. H. Kingsley, Esq., M.D., and F. J. Furnivall, Esq., M.A. 10*s*.
10. Merlin, or the Early History of King Arthur. Edited for the first time from the unique MS. in the Cambridge University Library (about 1450 A.D.), by Henry B. Wheatley, Esq. Part I. 2*s*. 6*d*.
11. The Monarche, and other Poems of Sir David Lyndesay. Edited from the first edition by Johne Skott, in 1552, by Fitzedward Hall, Esq., D.C.L. Part I. 3*s*.
12. The Wright's Chaste Wife, a Merry Tale, by Adam of Cobsam (about 1462 A.D.), from the unique Lambeth MS. 306. Edited for the first time by F. J. Furnivall, Esq., M.A. 1*s*.

Early English Text Society's Publications—*continued.*

13. Seinte Marherete, þe Meiden ant Martyr. Three Texts of ab. 1200, 1310, 1330 A.D. First edited in 1862, by the Rev. Oswald Cockayne, M.A., and now re-issued. 2*s.*

14. Kyng Horn, with fragments of Floriz and Blauncheflur, and the Assumption of the Blessed Virgin. Edited from the MSS. in the Library of the University of Cambridge and the British Museum, by the Rev. J. Rawson Lumby. 3*s.* 6*d*

15. Political, Religious, and Love Poems, from the Lambeth MS. No. 306, and other sources. Edited by F. J. Furnivall, Esq., M.A. 7*s.* 6*d.*

16. A Tretice in English breuely drawe out of þ book of Quintis essencijs in Latyn, þ Hermys þ prophete and king of Egipt after þ flood of Noe, fader of Philosophris, hadde by reuelacioun of an aungil of God to him sente. Edited from the Sloane MS. 73, by F. J. Furnivall, Esq., M.A. 1*s.*

17. Parallel Extracts from 29 Manuscripts of Piers Plowman, with Comments, and a Proposal for the Society's Three-text edition of this Poem. By the Rev. W. Skeat, M.A. 1*s.*

18. Hali Meidenhead, about 1200 A.D. Edited for the first time from the MS. (with a translation) by the Rev. Oswald Cockayne, M.A. 1*s.*

19. The Monarche, and other Poems of Sir David Lyndesay. Part II., the Complaynt of the King's Papingo, and other minor Poems. Edited from the First Edition by F. Hall, Esq., D.C L. 3*s.* 6*d.*

20. Some Treatises by Richard Rolle de Hampole. Edited from Robert of Thornton's MS. (ab. 1440 A.D.), by Rev. George G. Perry, M.A. 1*s.*

21. Merlin, or the Early History of King Arthur. Part II. Edited by Henry B. Wheatley, Esq. 4*s.*

22. The Romans of Partenay, or Lusignen. Edited for the first time from the unique MS. in the Library of Trinity College, Cambridge, by the Rev. W. W. Skeat. M.A. 6*s.*

23. Dan Michel's Ayenbite of Inwyt, or Remorse of Conscience, in the Kentish dialect, 1340 A.D. Edited from the unique MS. in the British Museum, by Richard Morris, Esq. 10*s.* 6*d.*

24. Hymns of the Virgin and Christ; The Parliament of Devils, and Other Religious Poems. Edited from the Lambeth MS. 853, by F. J. Furnivall, M.A. 3*s.*

25. The Stacions of Rome, and the Pilgrim's Sea-Voyage and Sea-Sickness, with Clene Maydenhod. Edited from the Vernon and Porkington MSS., etc., by F. J. Furnivall, Esq., M.A. 1*s.*

26. Religious Pieces in Prose and Verse. Containing Dan Jon Gaytrigg's Sermon; The Abbaye of S. Spirit; Sayne Jon, and other pieces in the Northern Dialect. Edited from Robert of Thorntone's MS. (ab. 1460 A.D.), by the Rev. G. Perry, M.A. 2*s.*

27. Manipulus Vocabulorum: a Rhyming Dictionary of the English Language, by Peter Levins (1570). Edited, with an Alphabetical Index, by Henry B. Wheatley. 12*s.*

28. The Vision of William concerning Piers Plowman, together with Vita de Dowel, Dobet et Dobest. 1362 A.D., by William Langland. The earliest or Vernon Text; Text A. Edited from the Vernon MS., with full Collations, by Rev. W. W. Skeat, M.A. 7*s.*

Early English Text Society's Publications—*continued.*

29. Old English Homilies and Homiletic Treatises. (Sawles Warde and the Wohunge of Ure Lauerd: Ureisuns of Ure Louerd and of Ure Lefdi, etc.) of the Twelfth and Thirteenth Centuries. Edited from MSS. in the British Museum, Lambeth, and Bodleian Libraries; with Introduction, Translation, and Notes. By Richard Morris. *First Series.* Part I. 7*s.*

30. Piers, the Ploughman's Crede (about 1394). Edited from the MSS. by the Rev. W. W. Skeat, M.A. 2*s.*

31. Instructions for Parish Priests. By John Myrc. Edited from Cotton MS. Claudius A. II., by Edward Peacock, Esq., F.S.A., etc., etc. 4*s.*

32. The Babees Book, Aristotle's A B C, Urbanitatis, Stans Puer ad Mensam, The Lytille Childrenes Lytil Boke. The Bokes of Nurture of Hugh Rhodes and John Russell, Wynkyn de Worde's Boke of Kervynge, The Booke of Demeanor, The Boke of Curtasye, Seager's Schoole of Vertue, etc., etc. With some French and Latin Poems on like subjects, and some Forewords on Education in Early England. Edited by F. J. Furnivall, M.A., Trin. Hall, Cambridge. 15*s.*

33. The Book of the Knight de la Tour Landry, 1372. A Father's Book for his Daughters, Edited from the Harleian MS. 1764, by Thomas Wright Esq., M.A., and Mr. William Rossiter. 8*s.*

34. Old English Homilies and Homiletic Treatises. (Sawles Warde, and the Wohunge of Ure Lauerd: Ureisuns of Ure Louerd and of Ure Lefdi, etc.) of the Twelfth and Thirteenth Centuries. Edited from MSS. in the British Museum, Lambeth, and Bodleian Libraries; with Introduction, Translation, and Notes, by Richard Morris. *First Series.* Part 2. 8*s.*

35. Sir David Lyndesay's Works. Part 3. The Historie of ane Nobil and Wailzeand Sqvyer, William Meldrum, umqvhyle Laird of Cleische and Bynnis, compylit be Sir Dauid Lyndesay of the Mont *alias* Lyoun King of Armes. With the Testament of the said Williame Meldrum, Squyer, compylit alswa be Sir Dauid Lyndesay, etc. Edited by F. Hall, D.C.L. 2*s.*

36. Merlin, or the Early History of King Arthur. A Prose Romance (about 1450–1460 A.D.), edited from the unique MS. in the University Library, Cambridge, by Henry B. Wheatley. With an Essay on Arthurian Localities, by J. S. Stuart Glennie, Esq. Part III. 1869. 12*s.*

37. Sir David Lyndesay's Works. Part IV. Ane Satyre of the thrie estaits, in commendation of vertew and vituperation of vyce. Maid be Sir David Lindesay, of the Mont, *alias* Lyon King of Armes. At Edinbvrgh. Printed be Robert Charteris, 1602. Cvm privilegio regis. Edited by F. Hall, Esq., D.C.L. 4*s.*

38. The Vision of William concerning Piers the Plowman, together with Vita de Dowel, Dobet, et Dobest, Secundum Wit et Resoun, by William Langland (1377 A.D.). The "Crowley" Text; or Text B. Edited from MS. Laud Misc. 581, collated with MS. Rawl. Poet. 38, MS. B. 15. 17. in the Library of Trinity College, Cambridge, MS. Dd. 1. 17. in the Cambridge University Library, the MS. in Oriel College, Oxford, MS. Bodley 814, etc. By the Rev. Walter W. Skeat, M.A., late Fellow of Christ's College, Cambridge. 10*s.* 6*d.*

39. The "Gest Hystoriale" of the Destruction of Troy. An Alliterative Romance, translated from Guido De Colonna's "Hystoria Troiana." Now first edited from the unique MS. in the Hunterian Museum, University of Glasgow, by the Rev. Geo. A. Panton and David Donaldson. Part I. 10*s.* 6*d.*

Early English Text Society's Publications—*continued.*

40. English Gilds. The Original Ordinances of more than One Hundred Early English Gilds: Together with the olde usages of the cite of Wynchestre; The Ordinances of Worcester; The Office of the Mayor of Bristol; and the Customary of the Manor of Tettenhall-Regis. From Original MSS. of the Fourteenth and Fifteenth Centuries. Edited with Notes by the late Toulmin Smith, Esq., F.R.S. of Northern Antiquaries (Copenhagen). With an Introduction and Glossary, etc., by his daughter, Lucy Toulmin Smith. And a Preliminary Essay, in Five Parts, On the History and Development of Gilds, by Lujo Brentano, Doctor Juris Utriusque et Philosophiæ. 21*s.*

41. The Minor Poems of William Lauder, Playwright, Poet, and Minister of the Word of God (mainly on the State of Scotland in and about 1568 A.D., that year of Famine and Plague). Edited from the Unique Originals belonging to S. Christie-Miller, Esq., of Britwell, by F. J. Furnivall, M.A., Trin. Hall, Camb. 3*s.*

42. Bernardus de Cura rei Famuliaris, with some Early Scotch Prophecies, etc. From a MS., KK 1. 5, in the Cambridge University Library. Edited by J. Rawson Lumby, M.A., late Fellow of Magdalen College, Cambridge. 2*s.*

43. Ratis Raving, and other Moral and Religious Pieces, in Prose and Verse. Edited from the Cambridge University Library MS. KK 1. 5, by J. Rawson Lumby, M.A., late Fellow of Magdalen College, Cambridge. 3*s.*

44. Joseph of Arimathie: otherwise called the Romance of the Seint Graal, or Holy Grail: an alliterative poem, written about A.D. 1350, and now first printed from the unique copy in the Vernon MS. at Oxford. With an appendix, containing "The Lyfe of Joseph of Armathy," reprinted from the black-letter copy of Wynkyn de Worde; "De sancto Joseph ab Arimathia," first printed by Pynson, A.D. 1516; and "The Lyfe of Joseph of Arimathia," first printed by Pynson, A.D. 1520. Edited, with Notes and Glossarial Indices, by the Rev. Walter W. Skeat, M.A. 5*s.*

45. King Alfred's West-Saxon Version of Gregory's Pastoral Care. With an English translation, the Latin Text, Notes, and an Introduction Edited by Henry Sweet, Esq., of Balliol College, Oxford. Part I. 10*s.*

46. Legends of the Holy Rood; Symbols of the Passion and Cross-Poems. In Old English of the Eleventh, Fourteenth, and Fifteenth Centuries. Edited from MSS. in the British Museum and Bodleian Libraries; with Introduction, Translations, and Glossarial Index. By Richard Morris, LL.D. 10*s.*

47. Sir David Lyndesay's Works. Part V. The Minor Poems of Lyndesay. Edited by J. A. H. Murray, Esq. 3*s.*

48. The Times' Whistle: or, A Newe Daunce of Seven Satires, and other Poems: Compiled by R. C., Gent. Now first Edited from MS. Y. 8. 3. in the Library of Canterbury Cathedral; with Introduction, Notes, and Glossary, by J. M. Cowper. 6*s.*

49. An Old English Miscellany, containing a Bestiary, Kentish Sermons, Proverbs of Alfred, Religious Poems of the 13th century. Edited from the MSS. by the Rev. R. Morris, LL.D. 10*s.*

50. King Alfred's West-Saxon Version of Gregory's Pastoral Care. Edited from 2 MSS., with an English translation. By Henry Sweet, Esq., Balliol College, Oxford. Part II. 10*s.*

51. Þe Liflade of St. Juliana, from two old English Manuscripts of 1230 A.D. With renderings into Modern English, by the Rev. O. Cockayne and Edmund Brock. Edited by the Rev. O. Cockayne, M.A. Price 2*s.*

Early English Text Society's Publications—*continued.*

52. PALLADIUS ON HUSBONDRIE, from the unique MS., ab. 1420 A.D., ed. Rev. B. LODGE. Part I. 10*s.*

53. OLD ENGLISH HOMILIES, Series II., from the unique 13th-century MS. in Trinity Coll. Cambridge, with a photolithograph; three Hymns to the Virgin and God, from a unique 13th-century MS. at Oxford, a photolithograph of the music to two of them, and transcriptions of it in modern notation by Dr. RIMBAULT, and A. J. ELLIS, Esq., F.R.S.; the whole edited by the Rev. RICHARD MORRIS, LL.D. 8*s.*

54. THE VISION OF PIERS PLOWMAN, Text C (completing the three versions of this great poem), with an Autotype; and two unique alliterative Poems: Richard the Redeles (by WILLIAM, the author of the *Vision*); and The Crowned King; edited by the Rev. W. W. SKEAT, M.A. 18*s.*

55. GENERYDES, a Romance, edited from the unique MS., ab. 1440 A.D., in Trin. Coll. Cambridge, by W. ALDIS WRIGHT, Esq., M.A., Trin. Coll. Cambr. Part I. 3*s.*

56. THE GEST HYSTORIALE OF THE DESTRUCTION OF TROY, translated from Guido de Colonna, in alliterative verse; edited from the unique MS. in the Hunterian Museum, Glasgow, by D. DONALDSON, Esq., and the late Rev. G. A. Panton. Part II. 10*s.* 6*d.*

57. THE EARLY ENGLISH VERSION OF THE "CURSOR MUNDI," in four Texts, from MS. Cotton, Vesp. A. iii. in the British Museum; Fairfax MS. 14. in the Bodleian; the Göttingen MS. Theol. 107; MS. R. 3, 8, in Trinity College, Cambridge. Edited by the Rev. R. Morris, LL.D. Part I. with two photo-lithographic facsimiles by Cooke and Fotheringham. 10*s.* 6*d.*

58. THE BLICKLING HOMILIES, edited from the Marquis of Lothian's Anglo-Saxon MS. of 971 A.D., by the Rev. R. MORRIS, LL.D. (With a Photolithograph). Part I. 8*s.*

59. THE EARLY ENGLISH VERSION OF THE "CURSOR MUNDI;" in four Texts, from MS. Cotton Vesp. A. iii. in the British Museum; Fairfax MS. 14. in the Bodleian; the Göttingen MS. Theol. 107; MS. R. 3, 8, in Trinity College, Cambridge. Edited by the Rev. R. MORRIS, LL.D. Part II. 15*s.*

60. MEDITACYUNS ON THE SOPER OF OUR LORDE (perhaps by ROBERT OF BRUNNE). Edited from the MSS. by J. M. COWPER, Esq. 2*s.* 6*d.*

61. THE ROMANCE AND PROPHECIES OF THOMAS OF ERCELDOUNE, printed from Five MSS. Edited by Dr. JAMES A. H. MURRAY. 10*s.* 6*d.*

62. THE EARLY ENGLISH VERSION OF THE "CURSOR MUNDI," in Four Texts. Edited by the Rev. R. MORRIS, M.A., LL.D. Part III. 15*s.*

63. THE BLICKLING HOMILIES. Edited from the Marquis of Lothian's Anglo-Saxon MS. of 971 A.D., by the Rev. R. MORRIS, LL.D. Part II. 4*s.*

64. FRANCIS THYNNE'S EMBLEMES AND EPIGRAMS, A.D. 1600, from the Earl of Ellesmere's unique MS. Edited by F. J. FURNIVALL, M.A. 4*s.*

65. BE DOMES DÆGE (Bede's De Die Judicii) and other short Anglo-Saxon Pieces. Edited from the unique MS. by the Rev. J. RAWSON LUMBY, B.D. 2*s.*

66. THE EARLY ENGLISH VERSION OF THE "CURSOR MUNDI," in Four Texts. Edited by Rev. R. MORRIS, M.A., LL.D. Part IV. 10*s.*

67. NOTES ON PIERS PLOWMAN. By the Rev. W. W. SKEAT, M.A. Part I. 21*s.*

68. The Early English Version of the "CURSOR MUNDI," in Four Texts. Edited by Rev. R. MORRIS, M.A., LL.D. Part V. 25*s.*

Early English Text Society's Publications—*continued.*

69. ADAM DAVY'S FIVE DREAMS ABOUT EDWARD II. THE LIFE OF SAINT ALEXIUS. Solomon's Book of Wisdom. St. Jerome's 15 Tokens before Doomsday. The Lamentation of Souls. Edited from the Laud MS. 622, in the Bodleian Library, by F. J. FURNIVALL, M.A. *5s.*

Extra Series. Subscriptions—Small paper, one guinea; large paper two guineas, per annum.

1. THE ROMANCE OF WILLIAM OF PALERNE (otherwise known as the Romance of William and the Werwolf). Translated from the French at the command of Sir Humphrey de Bohun, about A.D. 1350, to which is added a fragment of the Alliterative Romance of Alisaunder, translated from the Latin by the same author, about A.D. 1340; the former re-edited from the unique MS. in the Library of King's College, Cambridge, the latter now first edited from the unique MS. in the Bodleian Library, Oxford. By the Rev. WALTER W. SKEAT, M.A. 8vo. sewed, pp. xliv. and 328. £1 *6s.*

2. ON EARLY ENGLISH PRONUNCIATION, with especial reference to Shakspere and Chaucer; containing an investigation of the Correspondence of Writing with Speech in England, from the Anglo-Saxon period to the present day, preceded by a systematic Notation of all Spoken Sounds by means of the ordinary Printing Types; including a re-arrangement of Prof. F. J. Child's Memoirs on the Language of Chaucer and Gower, and reprints of the rare Tracts by Salesbury on English, 1547, and Welsh, 1567, and by Barcley on French, 1521 By ALEXANDER J. ELLIS, F.R.S. Part I. On the Pronunciation of the XIVth, XVIth, XVIIth, and XVIIIth centuries. 8vo. sewed, pp. viii. and 416. *10s.*

3. CAXTON'S BOOK OF CURTESYE, printed at Westminster about 1477–8, A.D., and now reprinted, with two MS. copies of the same treatise, from the Oriel MS. 79, and the Balliol MS. 354. Edited by FREDERICK J. FURNIVALL, M.A. 8vo. sewed, pp. xii. and 58. *5s.*

4. THE LAY OF HAVELOK THE DANE; composed in the reign of Edward I., about A.D. 1280. Formerly edited by Sir F. MADDEN for the Roxburghe Club, and now re-edited from the unique MS. Laud Misc. 108, in the Bodleian Library, Oxford, by the Rev. WALTER W. SKEAT, M.A. 8vo. sewed, pp. lv. and 160. *10s.*

5. CHAUCER'S TRANSLATION OF BOETHIUS'S "DE CONSOLATIONE PHILOSOPHIE." Edited from the Additional MS. 10,340 in the British Museum. Collated with the Cambridge Univ. Libr. MS. Ii. 3. 21. By RICHARD MORRIS. 8vo. *12s.*

6 THE ROMANCE OF THE CHEVELERE ASSIGNE. Re-edited from the unique manuscript in the British Museum, with a Preface, Notes, and Glossarial Index, by HENRY H. GIBBS, Esq., M.A. 8vo. sewed, pp. xviii. and 38. *3s.*

7. ON EARLY ENGLISH PRONUNCIATION, with especial reference to Shakspere and Chaucer. By ALEXANDER J. ELLIS, F.R.S., etc., etc. Part II. On the Pronunciation of the XIIIth and previous centuries, of Anglo-Saxon, Icelandic, Old Norse and Gothic, with Chronological Tables of the Value of Letters and Expression of Sounds in English Writing. *10s.*

8. QUEENE ELIZABETHES ACHADEMY, by Sir HUMPHREY GILBERT. A Booke of Precedence, The Ordering of a Funerall, etc. Varying Versions of the Good Wife, The Wise Man, etc., Maxims, Lydgate's Order of Fools, A Poem on Heraldry, Occleve on Lords' Men, etc., Edited by F. J. FURNIVALL, M.A., Trin. Hall, Camb. With Essays on Early Italian and German Books of Courtesy, by W. M. ROSSETTI, Esq., and E. OSWALD, Esq. 8vo. *13s.*

Early English Text Society's Publications—*continued.*

9. The Fraternitye of Vacabondes, by John Awdeley (licensed in 1560-1, imprinted then, and in 1565), from the edition of 1575 in the Bodleian Library. A Caueat or Warening for Commen Cursetors vulgarely called Vagabones, by Thomas Harman, Esquiere. From the 3rd edition of 1567, belonging to Henry Huth, Esq., collated with the 2nd edition of 1567, in the Bodleian Library, Oxford, and with the reprint of the 4th edition of 1573. A Sermon in Praise of Thieves and Thievery, by Parson Haben or Hyberdyne, from the Lansdowne MS. 98, and Cotton Vesp. A. 25. Those parts of the Groundworke of Conny-catching (ed. 1592), that differ from *Harman's Caueat.* Edited by Edward Viles & F. J. Furnivall. 8vo. 7*s.* 6*d.*

10. The Fyrst Boke of the Introduction of Knowledge, made by Andrew Borde, of Physycke Doctor. A Compendyous Regyment of a Dyetary of Helth made in Mountpyllier, compiled by Andrewe Boorde, of Physycke Doctor. Barnes in the Defence of the Berde: a treatyse made, answerynge the treatyse of Doctor Borde upon Berdes. Edited, with a life of Andrew Boorde, and large extracts from his Breuyary, by F. J Furnivall, M.A., Trinity Hall, Camb 8vo. 18*s.*

11. The Bruce; or, the Book of the most excellent and noble Prince, Robert de Broyss, King of Scots: compiled by Master John Barbour, Archdeacon of Aberdeen. A.D. 1375. Edited from MS. G 23 in the Library of St. John's College, Cambridge, written A.D. 1487; collated with the MS. in the Advocates' Library at Edinburgh, written A.D. 1489, and with Hart's Edition, printed A.D. 1616; with a Preface, Notes, and Glossarial Index, by the Rev. Walter W. Skeat, M.A. Part I 8vo. 12*s.*

12. England in the Reign of King Henry the Eighth. A Dialogue between Cardinal Pole and Thomas Lupset, Lecturer in Rhetoric at Oxford. By Thomas Starkey, Chaplain to the King. Edited, with Preface, Notes, and Glossary, by J. M. Cowper. And with an Introduction, containing the Life and Letters of Thomas Starkey, by the Rev. J. S. Brewer, M.A. Part II. 12*s.* (*Part I., Starkey's Life and Letters, is in preparation.*

13. A Supplicacyon for the Beggars. Written about the year 1529, by Simon Fish. Now re-edited by Frederick J. Furnivall. With a Supplycacion to our moste Soueraigne Lorde Kynge Henry the Eyght (1544 A.D.), A Supplication of the Poore Commons (1546 A.D.), The Decaye of England by the great multitude of Shepe (1550-3 A.D.). Edited by J. Meadows Cowper. 6*s.*

14. On Early English Pronunciation, with especial reference to Shakspere and Chaucer. By A. J. Ellis, F.R.S., F.S.A. Part III. Illustrations of the Pronunciation of the xivth and xvith Centuries. Chaucer, Gower, Wycliffe, Spenser, Shakspere, Salesbury, Barcley, Hart, Bullokar, Gill. Pronouncing Vocabulary. 10*s.*

15. Robert Crowley's Thirty-one Epigrams, Voyce of the Last Trumpet, Way to Wealth, etc., 1550-1 A.D. Edited by J. M. Cowper, Esq. 12*s.*

16. A Treatise on the Astrolabe; addressed to his son Lowys, by Geoffrey Chaucer, A.D. 1391. Edited from the earliest MSS. by the Rev. Walter W. Skeat, M.A., late Fellow of Christ's College, Cambridge. 10*s.*

17. The Complaynt of Scotlande, 1549, A.D., with an Appendix of four Contemporary English Tracts. Edited by J. A. H. Murray, Esq. Part I. 10*s.*

18. The Complaynt of Scotlande, etc. Part II. 8*s.*

19. Oure Ladyes Myroure, A.D. 1530, edited by the Rev. J. H. Blunt, M.A., with four full-page photolithographic facsimiles by Cooke and Fotheringham. 24*s.*

Early English Text Society's Publications—*continued.*

20. LONELICH'S HISTORY OF THE HOLY GRAIL (ab. 1450 A.D.), translated from the French Prose of SIRES ROBIERS DE BORRON. Re-edited from the Unique MS. in Corpus Christi College, Cambridge, by F. J. Furnivall, Esq. M.A. Part I. 8*s.*

21. BARBOUR'S BRUCE. Edited from the MSS. and the earliest printed edition by the Rev. W. W. SKEAT, M.A. Part II. 4*s.*

22. HENRY BRINKLOW'S COMPLAYNT OF RODERYCK MORS, somtyme a gray Fryre, unto the Parliament Howse of Ingland his naturall Country, for the Redresse of certen wicked Lawes, euel Customs, and cruel Decreys (ab. 1542); and THE LAMENTACION OF A CHRISTIAN AGAINST THE CITIE OF LONDON, made by Roderigo Mors, A.D. 1545. Edited by J. M. COWPER, Esq. 9*s.*

23. ON EARLY ENGLISH PRONUNCIATION, with especial reference to Shakspere and Chaucer. By A. J. ELLIS, Esq., F.R.S. Part IV. 10*s.*

24. LONELICH'S HISTORY OF THE HOLY GRAIL (ab. 1450 A.D.), translated from the French Prose of SIRES ROBIERS DE BORRON. Re-edited from the Unique MS. in Corpus Christi College, Cambridge, by F. J. FURNIVALL, Esq., M.A. Part II. 10*s.*

25. THE ROMANCE OF GUY OF WARWICK. Edited from the Cambridge University MS. by Prof. J. ZUPITZA, Ph.D. Part I. 20*s.*

26. THE ROMANCE OF GUY OF WARWICK. Edited from the Cambridge University MS. by Prof. J. ZUPITZA, Ph.D. (The 2nd or 15th century version.) Part II. 14*s.*

27. THE ENGLISH WORKS OF JOHN FISHER, Bishop of Rochester (died 1535). Edited by Professor J. E. B. MAYOR, M.A. Part I., the Text. 16*s.*

28. LONELICH'S HISTORY OF THE HOLY GRAIL. Edited by F. J. FURNIVALL, M.A. Part III. 10*s.*

29. BARBOUR'S BRUCE. Edited from the MSS. and the earliest Printed Edition, by the Rev. W. W. SKEAT, M.A. Part III. 21*s.*

30. LONELICH'S HISTORY OF THE HOLY GRAIL. Edited by F. J. FURNIVALL, ESQ., M.A. Part IV. 15*s.*

31. ALEXANDER AND DINDIMUS. Translated from the Latin about A.D. 1340–50. Re-edited by the Rev. W. W. SKEAT, M.A. 6*s.*

Edda Saemundar Hinns Froda—The Edda of Saemund the Learned. From the Old Norse or Icelandic. By BENJAMIN THORPE. Part I. with a Mythological Index. 12mo. pp. 152, cloth, 3*s.* 6*d.* Part II. with Index of Persons and Places. 12mo. pp. viii. and 172, cloth. 1866. 4*s.*; or in 1 Vol. complete, 7*s.* 6*d.*

Edkins.—INTRODUCTION TO THE STUDY OF THE CHINESE CHARACTERS. By J. EDKINS, D.D , Peking, China. Roy. 8vo. pp. 340, paper boards. 18*s.*

Edkins.—CHINA'S PLACE IN PHILOLOGY. An attempt to show that the Languages of Europe and Asia have a common origin. By the Rev. JOSEPH EDKINS. Crown 8vo , pp. xxiii.—403, cloth. 10*s.* 6*d.*

Edkins.—A VOCABULARY OF THE SHANGHAI DIALECT. By J. EDKINS. 8vo. half-calf, pp. vi. and 151. Shanghai, 1869. 21*s.*

Edkins.—A GRAMMAR OF COLLOQUIAL CHINESE, as exhibited in the Shanghai Dialect. By J. EDKINS, B.A. Second edition, corrected. 8vo. half-calf, pp. viii. and 225. Shanghai, 1868. 21*s.*

Edkins.—A GRAMMAR OF THE CHINESE COLLOQUIAL LANGUAGE, commonly called the Mandarin Dialect. By JOSEPH EDKINS. Second edition. 8vo. half-calf, pp. viii. and 279. Shanghai, 1864. £1 10*s.*

Edkins.—PROGRESSIVE LESSONS IN THE CHINESE SPOKEN LANGUAGE. With Lists of Common Words and Phrases. By J. EDKINS, B.A. Third edition, 8vo. pp. 120. 1869. 14*s.*

Edkins.—RELIGION IN CHINA. A Brief Account of the Three Religions of the Chinese. By JOSEPH EDKINS, D.D. Post 8vo. cloth. 7*s.* 6*d.*

Eger and Grime; an Early English Romance. Edited from Bishop Percy's Folio Manuscript, about 1650 A.D. By JOHN W. HALES, M.A., Fellow and late Assistant Tutor of Christ's College, Cambridge, and FREDERICK J. FURNIVALL, M.A., of Trinity Hall, Cambridge. 1 vol. 4to., pp. 64, (only 100 copies printed), bound in the Roxburghe style. 10*s.* 6*d.*

Egyptian Calendar for the Year 1295 A.H (1878 A.D.), corresponding with the years 1594, 1595, of the Koptic Era. Demy 8vo. sewed, pp. 98. 5*s.*

Eitel.—A CHINESE DICTIONARY IN THE CANTONESE DIALECT. By ERNEST JOHN EITEL, Ph.D. Tubing. Will be completed in four parts. Part I. (A—K). 8vo. sewed, pp. 202. 12*s.* 6*d.* Part II. (K—M). pp. 202. 12*s.* 6*d.*

Eitel.—HANDBOOK FOR THE STUDENT OF CHINESE BUDDHISM. By the Rev. E. J. EITEL, of the London Missionary Society. Crown 8vo. pp. viii., 224, cl., 18*s*

Eitel.—FENG-SHUI: or, The Rudiments of Natural Science in China. By Rev. E. J. EITEL, M.A., Ph.D. Demy 8vo. sewed, pp. vi. and 84. 6*s.*

Eitel.—BUDDHISM: its Historical, Theoretical, and Popular Aspects. In Three Lectures. By Rev. E. J. EITEL, M.A. Ph.D. Second Edition. Demy 8vo. sewed, pp. 130. 5*s.*

Elliot.—THE HISTORY OF INDIA, as told by its own Historians. The Muhammadan Period. Complete in Eight Vols. Edited from the Posthumous Papers of the late Sir H. M. ELLIOT, K.C.B., East India Company's Bengal Civil Service, by Prof. JOHN DOWSON, M.R.A.S., Staff College, Sandhurst.

Vols. I. and II. With a Portrait of Sir H. M. Elliot. 8vo. pp xxxii. and 542, x. and 580, cloth. 18*s.* each.
Vol. III. 8vo. pp. xii. and 627, cloth. 24*s.*
Vol. IV. 8vo. pp. x. and 563 cloth 21*s*
Vol. V. 8vo. pp. xii. and 576, cloth. 21*s.*
Vol. VI. 8vo. pp. viii. and 574, cloth. 21*s.*
Vol. VII. 8vo. pp. viii. and 574, cloth. 21*s.*
Vol. VIII. 8vo. pp. xxxii., 444, and lxviii. cloth. 24*s.*

Elliot.—MEMOIRS ON THE HISTORY, FOLKLORE, AND DISTRIBUTION OF THE RACES OF THE NORTH WESTERN PROVINCES OF INDIA; being an amplified Edition of the original Supplementary Glossary of Indian Terms. By the late Sir HENRY M. ELLIOT, K.C.B., of the Hon. East India Company's Bengal Civil Service. Edited, revised, and re-arranged, by JOHN BEAMES, M.R.A.S., Bengal Civil Service; Member of the German Oriental Society, of the Asiatic Societies of Paris and Bengal, and of the Philological Society of London. In 2 vols. demy 8vo., pp. xx., 370, and 396, cloth. With two Lithographic Plates, one full-page coloured Map, and three large coloured folding Maps. 36*s.*

Ellis.—ON NUMERALS, as Signs of Primeval Unity among Mankind. By ROBERT ELLIS, B.D., Late Fellow of St. John's College, Cambridge. Demy 8vo. cloth, pp. viii. and 94. 3*s.* 6*d.*

Ellis.—THE ASIATIC AFFINITIES OF THE OLD ITALIANS. By ROBERT ELLIS, B.D., Fellow of St. John's College, Cambridge, and author of "Ancient Routes between Italy and Gaul." Crown 8vo. pp. iv. 156, cloth. 1870. 5*s.*

Ellis.—PERUVIA SCYTHICA. The Quichua Language of Peru: its derivation from Central Asia with the American languages in general, and with the Turanian and Iberian languages of the Old World, including the Basque, the Lycian, and the Pre-Aryan language of Etruria. By ROBERT ELLIS, B.D. 8vo. cloth, pp. xii. and 219. 1875. 6*s.*

Ellis.—ETRUSCAN NUMERALS. By ROBERT ELLIS, B.D. 8vo. sewed, pp. 52. 2*s.* 6*d.*

English and Welsh Languages.—THE INFLUENCE OF THE ENGLISH AND Welsh Languages upon each other, exhibited in the Vocabularies of the two Tongues. Intended to suggest the importance to Philologers, Antiquaries, Ethnographers, and others, of giving due attention to the Celtic Branch of the Indo-Germanic Family of Languages. Square, pp. 30, sewed. 1869. 1*s.*

English Dialect Society's Publications. Subscription, 1873 to 1876, 10*s.* 6*d.* per annum; 1877 and following years, 20*s.* per annum.

1873.

1. Series B. Part 1. Reprinted Glossaries. Containing a Glossary of North of England Words, by J. H.; five Glossaries, by Mr. MARSHALL; and a West-Riding Glossary, by Dr. WILLAN. 7*s.* 6*d.*
2. Series A. Bibliographical. A List of Books illustrating English Dialects. Part I. Containing a General List of Dictionaries, etc.; and a List of Books relating to some of the Counties of England. 4*s.*
3. Series C. Original Glossaries. Part I. Containing a Glossary of Swaledale Words. By Captain HARLAND. 4*s.*

1874.

4. Series D. The History of English Sounds. By H. SWEET, Esq. 4*s.* 6*d.*
5. Series B. Part II. Reprinted Glossaries. Containing seven Provincial English Glossaries, from various sources. 7*s.*
6. Series B. Part III. Ray's Collection of English Words not generally used, from the edition of 1691; together with Thoresby's Letter to Ray, 1703. Re-arranged and newly edited by Rev. WALTER W. SKEAT. 8*s.*

6*. Subscribers to the English Dialect Society for 1874 also receive a copy of 'A Dictionary of the Sussex Dialect.' By the Rev. W. D. PARISH.

1875.

7. Series D. Part II. The Dialect of West Somerset. By F. T. ELWORTHY, Esq. 3*s.* 6*d.*
8. Series A. Part II. Containing a List of Books Relating to some of the Counties of England. 6*s.*
9. Series C. A Glossary of Words used in the Neighbourhood of Whitby. By F. K. ROBINSON. Part I. 7*s.* 6*d.*
10. Series C. A Glossary of the Dialect of Lancashire. By J. H. NODAL and G. MILNER. Part I. 3*s.* 6*d.*

1876.

11. On the Survival of Early English Words in our Present Dialects. By Dr. R. MORRIS. 6*d.*
12. Series C. Original Glossaries. Part III. Containing Five Original Provincial English Glossaries. 7*s.*
13. Series C. A Glossary of Words used in the Neighbourhood of Whitby. By F. K. Robinson. Part II. 6*s* 6*d.*
14. A Glossary of Mid-Yorkshire Words, with a Grammar. By C. CLOUGH ROBINSON. 9*s.*

1877.

15. A Glossary of Words used in the Wapentakes of Manley and Corringham, Lincolnshire. By Edward Peacock, F.S.A. 9*s.* 6*d.*

16. A Glossary of Holderness Words. By F. Ross, R. Stead, and T. Holderness. With a Map of the District. 4*s.*

17. On the Dialects of Eleven Southern and South-Western Counties, with a new Classification of the English Dialects. By Prince Louis Lucien Bonaparte. With Two Maps. 1*s.*

18. Bibliographical List. Part III. completing the Work, and containing a List of Books on Scottish Dialects, Anglo-Irish Dialect, Cant and Slang, and Americanisms, with additions to the English List and Index. Edited by J. H. Nodal. 4*s.* 6*d.*

19. An Outline of the Grammar of West Somerset. By F. T. Elworthy, Esq. 5*s.*

1878.

20. A Glossary of Cumberland Words and Phrases. By William Dickinson, F.L.S. 6*s.*

21. Tusser's Five Hundred Pointes of Good Husbandrie. Edited with Introduction, Notes and Glossary, by W. Paine and Sidney J. Herrtage, B.A. 12*s.* 6*d.*

22. A Dictionary of English Plant Names. By James Britten, F.L.S., and Robert Holland. Part I. (A to F). 8*s.* 6*d.*

1879.

23. Five Reprinted Glossaries, including Wiltshire, East Anglian, Suffolk, and East Yorkshire Words, and Words from Bishop Kennett's Parochial Antiquities. Edited by the Rev. Professor Skeat, M.A. 7*s.*

24. Supplement to the Cumberland Glossary (No. 20). By W. Dickinson, F.L.S. 1*s.*

Etherington.—The Student's Grammar of the Hindí Language. By the Rev. W. Etherington, Missionary, Benares. Second edition. Crown 8vo. pp. xiv., 255, and xiii., cloth. 1873. 12*s.*

Faber.—A systematical Digest of the Doctrines of Confucius, according to the Analects, Great Learning, and Doctrine of the Mean, with an Introduction on the Authorities upon Confucius and Confucianism. By Ernst Faber, Rhenish Missionary. Translated from the German by P. G. von Möllendorff. 8vo. sewed, pp. viii. and 131. 1875. 12*s.* 6*d.*

Facsimiles of Two Papyri found in a Tomb at Thebes. With a Translation by Samuel Birch, LL.D., F.S.A., Corresponding Member of the Institute of France, Academies of Berlin, Herculaneum, etc., and an Account of their Discovery. By A. Henry Rhind, Esq., F.S.A., etc. In large folio, pp. 30 of text, and 16 plates coloured, bound in cloth. 21*s.*

Fallon.—A New Hindustani-English Dictionary. With Illustrations from Hindustani Literature and Folk-lore. By S. W. Fallon, Ph.D. Halle. Parts I. to XIX. Roy. 8vo. Price 4*s.* 6*d.* each Part.

To be completed in about 25 Parts of 48 pages each Part, forming together One Volume.

Farley.—Egypt, Cyprus, and Asiatic Turkey. By J. Lewis Farley, Author of "The Resources of Turkey," etc. Demy 8vo. cl., pp. xvi.–270. 10*s.* 6*d.*

Fausböll.—The Dasaratha-Játaka, being the Buddhist Story of King Ráma. The original Páli Text, with a Translation and Notes by V. Fausböll. 8vo. sewed, pp. iv. and 48. 2*s.* 6*d.*

Fausböll.—Five Játakas, containing a Fairy Tale, a Comical Story, and Three Fables. In the original Páli Text, accompanied with a Translation and Notes. By V. Fausböll. 8vo. sewed, pp. viii. and 72. 6*s.*

Fausböll.—Ten Játakas The Original Páli Text, with a Translation and Notes. By V. Fausböll. 8vo. sewed, pp. xiii. and 128. 7*s*. 6*d*.

Fausböll.—Játaka. See under Játaka.

Fiske.—Myths and Myth-Makers: Old Tales and Superstitions interpreted by Comparative Mythology. By John Fiske, M.A., Assistant Librarian, and late Lecturer on Philosophy at Harvard University. Crown 8vo. cloth, pp. viii. and 252. 10*s*. 6*d*.

Fornander.—An Account of the Polynesian Race: Its Origin and Migrations. By A. Fornander. Vol. I. Post 8vo., cloth. 7*s*. 6*d*.

Forsyth.—Report of a Mission to Yarkund in 1873, under Command of Sir T. D. Forsyth, K.C.S.I., C.B., Bengal Civil Service, with Historical and Geographical Information regarding the Possessions of the Ameer of Yarkund. With 45 Photographs, 4 Lithographic Plates, and a large Folding Map of Eastern Turkestan. 4to. cloth, pp. iv. and 573. £5 5*s*.

Foss.—Norwegian Grammar, with Exercises in the Norwegian and and English Languages, and a List of Irregular Verbs. By Frithjof Foss, Graduate of the University of Norway. Crown 8vo., pp. 50, cloth limp. 2*s*.

Foster.—Pre-Historic Races of the United States of America. By J. W. Foster, LL.D., Author of the "Physical Geography of the Mississippi Valley," etc. With 72 Illustrations. 8vo. cloth, pp. xvi. and 416. 14*s*.

Fryer.—Vuttodaya. (Exposition of Metre.) By Sangharakkhita Thera. A Pali Text, Edited, with Translation and Notes, by Major G. E. Fryer. 8vo. pp. 44. 2*s*. 6*d*.

Furnivall.—Education in Early England. Some Notes used as Forewords to a Collection of Treatises on "Manners and Meals in the Olden Time," for the Early English Text Society. By Frederick J. Furnivall, M.A., Trinity Hall, Cambridge, Member of Council of the Philological and Early English Text Societies. 8vo. sewed, pp. 74. 1*s*.

Garrett.—A Classical Dictionary of India, illustrative of the Mythology, Philosophy, Literature, Antiquities, Arts, Manners, Customs, etc., of the Hindus. By John Garrett. 8vo. pp. x. and 798. cloth. 28*s*.

Garrett.—Supplement to the above Classical Dictionary of India. By John Garrett, Director of Public Instruction at Mysore. 8vo. cloth, pp. 160. 7*s*. 6*d*.

Gautama.—The Institutes of Gautama. *See Auctores Sanscriti.*

Gesenius.—Hebrew and English Lexicon of the Old Testament, including the Biblical Chaldee, from the Latin. By Edward Robinson. Fifth Edition. 8vo. cloth, pp. xii. and 1160. £1 16*s*.

Gesenius.—Hebrew Grammar. Translated from the Seventeenth Edition. By Dr. T. J. Conant. With Grammatical Exercises, and a Chrestomathy by the Translator. 8vo. cloth, pp. xvi.-364. £1.

Giles.—Chinese Sketches. By Herbert A. Giles, of H.B.M.'s China Consular Service. 8vo. cl., pp. 204. 10*s*. 6*d*.

Giles.—A Dictionary of Colloquial Idioms in the Mandarin Dialect. By Herbert A. Giles. 4to. pp. 65. £1 8*s*.

Giles.—Synoptical Studies in Chinese Character. By Herbert A. Giles. 8vo. pp. 118. 15*s*.

Giles.—Chinese without a Teacher. Being a Collection of Easy and Useful Sentences in the Mandarin Dialect. With a Vocabulary. By Herbert A. Giles. 12mo. pp 60. 5*s*.

Giles.—Record of the Buddhist Kingdoms. Translated from the Chinese by H. A. Giles, of H.M. Consular Service. 8vo. sewed, pp. x.-129. 5*s*.

Giles.—THE SAN TZU CHING; or, Three Character Classic; and the Ch'Jen Tsu Wen; or, Thousand Character Essay. Metrically Translated by HERBERT A. GILES. 12mo. pp. 28. 2*s.* 6*d.*

Giles.—A GLOSSARY OF REFERENCE ON SUBJECTS CONNECTED WITH THE Far East. By H. A. GILES, of H.M. China Consular Service. 8vo. sewed, pp. v.-183. 7*s.* 6*d.*

Giles.—HEBREW AND CHRISTIAN RECORDS. An Historical Enquiry concerning the Age and Authorship of the Old and New Testaments. By the Rev. Dr. GILES, Rector of Sutton, Surrey, and formerly Fellow of Corpus Christi College, Oxford. Now first published complete, 2 Vols. Vol. I., Hebrew Records; Vol. II., Christian Records. 8vo. cloth, pp. 442 and 440. 1877. 24*s.*

Gliddon.—ANCIENT EGYPT, Her Monuments, Hieroglyphics, History, Archæology, and other subjects connected with Hieroglyphical Literature. By GEORGE R. GLIDDON, late United States Consul, at Cairo. 15th Edition. Revised and Corrected, with an Appendix. 4to. sewed, pp. 68. 2*s.* 6*d.*

God.—BOOK OF GOD. By ⊙. 8vo. cloth. Vol. I.: The Apocalypse. pp. 647. 12*s.* 6*d.*—Vol. II. An Introduction to the Apocalypse, pp. 752. 14*s.*—Vol. III. A Commentary on the Apocalypse, pp. 854. 16*s.*

Goldstücker.—A DICTIONARY, SANSKRIT AND ENGLISH, extended and improved from the Second Edition of the Dictionary of Professor H. H. WILSON, with his sanction and concurrence. Together with a Supplement, Grammatical Appendices, and an Index, serving as a Sanskrit-English Vocabulary. By THEODOR GOLDSTÜCKER. Parts I. to VI. 4to. pp. 400. 1856-1863. 6*s.* each.

Goldstücker.—PANINI: His Place in Sanskrit Literature. An Investigation of some Literary and Chronological Questions which may be settled by a study of his Work. A separate impression of the Preface to the Facsimile of MS. No. 17 in the Library of Her Majesty's Home Government for India, which contains a portion of the MANAVA-KALPA-SUTRA, with the Commentary of KUMARILA-SWAMIN. By THEODOR GOLDSTÜCKER. Imperial 8vo. pp. 268, cloth. £2 2*s.*

Goldstücker.—ON THE DEFICIENCIES IN THE PRESENT ADMINISTRATION OF HINDU LAW; being a paper read at the Meeting of the East India Association on the 8th June, 1870. By THEODOR GOLDSTÜCKER, Professor of Sanskrit in University College, London, &c. Demy 8vo. pp. 56, sewed. 1*s.* 6*d.*

Gover.—THE FOLK-SONGS OF SOUTHERN INDIA. By CHARLES E. GOVER. 8vo. pp. xxiii. and 299, cloth 10*s.* 6*d.*

Grammatography.—A MANUAL OF REFERENCE to the Alphabets of Ancient and Modern Languages. Based on the German Compilation of F. BALLHORN. Royal 8vo. pp. 80, cloth. 7*s.* 6*d.*

The "Grammatography" is offered to the public as a compendious introduction to the reading of the most important ancient and modern languages. Simple in its design, it will be consulted with advantage by the philological student, the amateur linguist, the bookseller, the corrector of the press, and the diligent compositor.

ALPHABETICAL INDEX.

Afghan (or Pushto).	Czechian (or Bohemian).	Hebrew (current hand).	Polish.
Amharic.	Danish.	Hebrew (Judæo-German).	Pushto (or Afghan).
Anglo-Saxon.	Demotic.	Hungarian.	Romaic (Modern Greek
Arabic.	Estrangelo.	Illyrian.	Russian.
Arabic Ligatures.	Ethiopic.	Irish.	Runes.
Aramaic.	Etruscan.	Italian (Old).	Samaritan.
Archaic Characters.	Georgian.	Japanese.	Sanscrit.
Armenian.	German.	Javanese.	Servian.
Assyrian Cuneiform.	Glagolitic.	Lettish.	Slavonic (Old).
Bengali.	Gothic.	Mantshu.	Sorbian (or Wendish).
Bohemian (Czechian).	Greek.	Median Cuneiform.	Swedish.
Búgis.	Greek Ligatures.	Modern Greek (Romaic)	Syriac.
Burmese.	Greek (Archaic).	Mongolian.	Tamil.
Canarese (or Carnâtaca).	Gujerati (or Guzzeratte).	Numidian.	Telugu.
Chinese.	Hieratic.	Old Slavonic (or Cyrillic).	Tibetan.
Coptic.	Hieroglyphics.	Palmyrenian.	Turkish.
Croato-Glagolitic.	Hebrew.	Persian.	Wallachian.
Cufic.	Hebrew (Archaic).	Persian Cuneiform.	Wendish (or Sorbian).
Cyrillic (or Old Slavonic).	Hebrew (Rabbinical).	Phœnician.	Zend.

Grassmann.—WÖRTERBUCH ZUM RIG-VEDA. Von HERMANN GRASSMANN, Professor am Marienstifts-Gymnasium zu Stettin. 8vo. pp. 1775. £1 10*s*.

Green.—SHAKESPEARE AND THE EMBLEM-WRITERS: an Exposition of their Similarities of Thought and Expression. Preceded by a View of the Emblem-Book Literature down to A.D. 1616. By HENRY GREEN, M.A. In one volume, pp. xvi. 572, profusely illustrated with Woodcuts and Photolith. Plates, elegantly bound in cloth gilt, large medium 8vo. £1 11*s*. 6*d*; large imperial 8vo. 1870. £2 12*s*. 6*d*.

Grey.—HANDBOOK OF AFRICAN, AUSTRALIAN, AND POLYNESIAN PHILOLOGY, as represented in the Library of His Excellency Sir George Grey, K.C.B., Her Majesty's High Commissioner of the Cape Colony. Classed, Annotated, and Edited by Sir GEORGE GREY and Dr. H. I. BLEEK.

Vol. I. Part 1.—South Africa. 8vo. pp. 186. 20*s*.
Vol. I. Part 2.—Africa (North of the Tropic of Capricorn). 8vo. pp. 70. 4*s*.
Vol. I. Part 3.—Madagascar. 8vo. pp. 24. 2*s*.
Vol. II. Part 1.—Australia. 8vo. pp. iv. and 44. 3*s*.
Vol. II. Part 2.—Papuan Languages of the Loyalty Islands and New Hebrides, comprising those of the Islands of Nengone, Lifu, Aneitum, Tana, and others. 8vo. p. 12. 1*s*.
Vol. II. Part 3.—Fiji Islands and Rotuma (with Supplement to Part II., Papuan Languages, and Part I., Australia). 8vo. pp. 34. 2*s*.
Vol. II. Part 4.—New Zealand, the Chatham Islands, and Auckland Islands. 8vo. pp. 76. 7*s*.
Vol. II. Part 4 (*continuation*).—Polynesia and Borneo. 8vo. pp. 77-154. 7*s*.
Vol. III. Part 1.—Manuscripts and Incunables. 8vo. pp. viii. and 24. 2*s*.
Vol. IV. Part 1.—Early Printed Books. England. 8vo. pp. vi. and 266. 12*s*.

Grey.—MAORI MEMENTOS: being a Series of Addresses presented by the Native People to His Excellency Sir George Grey, K.C.B., F.R.S. With Introductory Remarks and Explanatory Notes; to which is added a small Collection of Laments, etc. By CH. OLIVER B. DAVIS. 8vo. pp. iv. and 228, cloth. 12*s*.

Griffin.—THE RAJAS OF THE PUNJAB. Being the History of the Principal States in the Punjab, and their Political Relations with the British Government. By LEPEL H. GRIFFIN, Bengal Civil Service; Under Secretary to the Government of the Punjab, Author of "The Punjab Chiefs," etc. Second edition. Royal 8vo., pp. xiv. and 630. 21*s*.

Griffis.—THE MIKADO'S EMPIRE. Book I. History of Japan from 660 B.C. to 1872 A.D. Book II. Personal Experiences, Observations, and Studies in Japan, 1870-74. By W. E. GRIFFIS. Illustrated. 8vo cl., pp. 626. £1.

Griffith.—SCENES FROM THE RAMAYANA, MEGHADUTA, ETC. Translated by RALPH T. H. GRIFFITH, M.A., Principal of the Benares College. Second Edition. Crown 8vo. pp. xviii., 244, cloth. 6*s*.

CONTENTS.—Preface—Ayodhya—Ravan Doomed—The Birth of Rama—The Heir apparent—Manthara's Guile—Dasaratha's Oath—The Step-mother—Mother and Son—The Triumph of Love—Farewell?—The Hermit's Son—The Trial of Truth—The Forest—The Rape of Sita—Rama's Despair—The Messenger Cloud—Khumbakarna—The Suppliant Dove—True Glory—Feed the Poor—The Wise Scholar.

Griffith.—THE RÁMÁYAN OF VÁLMÍKI. Translated into English verse. By RALPH T. H. GRIFFITH, M.A., Principal of the Benares College. 5 vols.

Vol. I., containing Books I. and II. Demy 8vo. pp. xxxii. 440, cloth. 1870. 18*s*.
Vol. II., containing Book II., with additional Notes and Index of Names. Demy 8vo. pp. 504, cloth. 18*s*.
Vol. III. Demy 8vo. pp. v. and 371, cloth. 1872. 15*s*.
Vol. IV. Demy 8vo. pp. viii. and 432. 1873. 18*s*.
Vol. V. Demy 8vo. pp. 368, cloth. 1875. 15*s*.

Griffith.—THE BIRTH OF THE WAR GOD. A Poem by KÁLIDÁSA. Translated from the Sanskrit into English Verse. By RALPH T. H. GRIFFITH, M.A., Principal of Benares College. Second edition, post 8vo. cloth, pp. xii. and 116. 5*s*.

Grout.—The Isizulu: a Grammar of the Zulu Language; accompanied with an Historical Introduction, also with an Appendix. By Rev. Lewis Grout. 8vo. pp. lii. and 432, cloth. 21*s.*

Gubernatis.—Zoological Mythology; or, the Legends of Animals. By Angelo de Gubernatis, Professor of Sanskrit and Comparative Literature in the Instituto di Studii Superiori e di Perfezionamento at Florence, etc. In 2 vols. 8vo. pp. xxvi. and 432, vii. and 442. 28*s.*

Gundert.—A Malayalam and English Dictionary. By Rev. H. Gundert, D. Ph. Royal 8vo. pp. viii. and 1116. £2 10*s.*

Haas.—Catalogue of Sanskrit and Pali Books in the Library of the British Museum. By Dr. Ernst Haas. Printed by Permission of the Trustees of the British Museum. 4to. cloth, pp. 200. £1 1*s.*

Háfiz of Shíráz.—Selections from his Poems. Translated from the Persian by Herman Bicknell. With Preface by A. S. Bicknell. Demy 4to., pp. xx. and 384, printed on fine stout plate-paper, with appropriate Oriental Bordering in gold and colour, and Illustrations by J. R. Herbert, R.A. £2 2*s.*

Haldeman.—Pennsylvania Dutch: a Dialect of South Germany with an Infusion of English. By S. S. Haldeman, A.M., Professor of Comparative Philology in the University of Pennsylvania, Philadelphia. 8vo. pp. viii. and 70, cloth. 1872. 3*s.* 6*d.*

Hall.—Modern English. By Fitzedward Hall, M.A., Hon. D.C.L., Oxon. Cr. 8vo. cloth, pp. xvi. and 394. 10*s.* 6*d.*

Hall.—On English Adjectives in -Able, with Special Reference to Reliable. By Fitzedward Hall, C.E., M.A., Hon.D.C.L. Oxon.; formerly Professor of Sanskrit Language and Literature, and of Indian Jurisprudence, in King's College, London. Crown 8vo. cloth, pp. viii. and 238. 7*s.* 6*d.*

Hans Breitmann.—See under Leland.

Hardy.—Christianity and Buddhism Compared. By the late Rev. R. Spence Hardy, Hon. Member Royal Asiatic Society. 8vo. sd. pp. 138. 6*s.*

Hassoun.—The Diwan of Hatim Tai. An Old Arabic Poet of the Sixth Century of the Christian Era. Edited by R. Hassoun. With Illustrations. 4to. pp. 43. 3*s.* 6*d.*

Haswell.—Grammatical Notes and Vocabulary of the Peguan Language. To which are added a few pages of Phrases, etc. By Rev. J. M. Haswell. 8vo. pp. xvi. and 160. 15*s.*

Haug.—The Book of Arda Viraf. The Pahlavi text prepared by Destur Hoshangji Jamaspji Asa. Revised and collated with further MSS., with an English translation and Introduction, and an Appendix containing the Texts and Translations of the Gosht-i Fryano and Hadokht Nask. By Martin Haug, Ph.D., Professor of Sanskrit and Comparative Philology at the University of Munich. Assisted by E. W. West, Ph.D. Published by order of the Bombay Government. 8vo. sewed, pp. lxxx., v., and 316. £1 5*s.*

Haug.—A Lecture on an Original Speech of Zoroaster (Yasna 45), with remarks on his age. By Martin Haug, Ph.D. 8vo. pp. 28, sewed. Bombay, 1865. 2*s.*

Haug.—The Aitareya Brahmanam of the Rig Veda: containing the Earliest Speculations of the Brahmans on the meaning of the Sacrificial Prayers, and on the Origin, Performance, and Sense of the Rites of the Vedic Religion. Edited, Translated, and Explained by Martin Haug, Ph.D., Superintendent of Sanskrit Studies in the Poona College, etc., etc. In 2 Vols. Crown 8vo. Vol. I. Contents, Sanskrit Text, with Preface, Introductory Essay, and a Map of the Sacrificial Compound at the Soma Sacrifice, pp. 312. Vol. II. Translation with Notes, pp. 544. £2 2*s.*

Haug.—An Old Zand-Pahlavi Glossary. Edited in the Original Characters, with a Transliteration in Roman Letters. an English Translation, and an Alphabetical Index. By Destur Hoshengji Jamaspji, High-priest of the Parsis in Malwa, India. Rev. with Notes and Intro. by Martin Haug, Ph.D. Publ. by order of Gov of Bombay. 8vo. sewed, pp. lvi. and 132. 15*s.*

Haug.—An Old Pahlavi-Pazand Glossary. Ed., with Alphabetical Index, by Destur Hoshangji Jamaspji Asa, High Priest of the Parsis in Malwa. Rev. and Enl., with Intro. Essay on the Pahlavi Language, by M. Haug, Ph.D. Pub. by order of Gov. of Bombay. 8vo. pp. xvi. 152, 268, sd. 1870. 28*s.*

Haug.—Essays on the Sacred Language, Writings, and Religion of the Parsis. By Martin Haug, Ph D., late Professor of Sanskrit and Comparative Philology at the University of Munich. Second Edition. Edited by E. W. West, Ph.D. Post 8vo. pp. xvi. and 428, cloth, 16*s.*

Hawken.—Upa-Sastra: Comments, Linguistic and Doctrinal, on Sacred and Mythic Literature. By J. D. Hawken. 8vo. cloth, pp. viii.-288. 7*s.* 6*d.*

Heaviside.—American Antiquities; or, the New World the Old, and the Old World the New. By John T. C. Heaviside. 8vo. pp. 46, sewed. 1*s.* 6*d*

Hebrew Literature Society (Publications of). Subscription £1 1*s.* per Series. 1872-3. *First Series.*

Vol. I. Miscellany of Hebrew Literature. Demy 8vo. cloth, pp. viii. and 228. 10*s.*

Vol. II. The Commentary of Ibn Ezra on Isaiah Edited from MSS., and Translated with Notes, Introductions, and Indexes, by M. Friedländer, Ph.D. Vol. I. Translation of the Commentary. Demy 8vo. cloth, pp. xxviii. and 332. 10*s.* 6*d.*

Vol. III. The Commentary of Ibn Ezra. Vol. II. The Anglican Version of the Book of the Prophet Isaiah amended according to the Commentary of Ibn Ezra. Demy 8vo. cloth, pp. 112. 4*s.* 6*d.*

1877. *Second Series.*

Vol. I. Miscellany of Hebrew Literature. Vol. II. Edited by the Rev. A. Löwy. Demy 8vo. cloth, pp. vi. and 276. 10*s.* 6*d.*

Vol. II. The Commentary of Ibn Ezra. Vol. III. Demy 8vo. cloth, pp. 172. 7*s.*

Vol. III. Ibn Ezra Literature. Vol. IV. Essays on the Writings of Abraham Ibn Ezra. By M. Friedlände, Ph D. Demy 8vo. cloth, pp. x.-252 and 78. 12*s.* 6*d.*

Hepburn.—A Japanese and English Dictionary. With an English and Japanese Index. By J. C. Hepburn, M.D., LL.D. Second edition. Imperial 8vo. cloth, pp. xxxii., 632 and 201. £8 8*s.*

Hepburn.—Japanese-English and English-Japanese Dictionary. By J. C. Hepburn, M.D., LL.D. Abridged by the Author from his larger work. Small 4to. cloth, pp. vi. and 206. 1873. 18*s.*

Hernisz.—A Guide to Conversation in the English and Chinese Languages, for the use of Americans and Chinese in California and elsewhere. By Stanislas Hernisz. Square 8vo. pp. 274, sewed. 10*s.* 6*d.*

The Chinese characters contained in this work are from the collections of Chinese groups, engraved on steel, and cast into moveable types, by Mr. Marcellin Legrand, engraver of the Imperial Printing Office at Paris. They are used by most of the missions to China.

Hincks.—Specimen Chapters of an Assyrian Grammar. By the late Rev. E. Hincks, D.D., Hon. M.R.A.S. 8vo., pp. 44, sewed. 1*s.*

Hodgson.—Essays on the Languages, Literature, and Religion of Nepal and Tibet; together with further Papers on the Geography, Ethnology, and Commerce of those Countries. By B. H. Hodgson, late British Minister at Nepál. Royal 8vo. cloth, pp. 288. 14*s.*

Hoffmann.—Shopping Dialogues, in Japanese, Dutch, and English. By Professor J. Hoffmann. Oblong 8vo. pp. xiii. and 44, sewed. *5s.*

Hoffmann, J. J.—A Japanese Grammar. Second Edition. Large 8vo. cloth, pp. viii. and 368, with two plates. £1 1*s.*

Holbein Society.—Subscription £1 1s. per annum. A List of Publications to be had on application.

Hopkins.—Elementary Grammar of the Turkish Language. With a few Easy Exercises. By F. L. Hopkins, M.A., Fellow and Tutor of Trinity Hall, Cambridge. Cr. 8vo. cloth, pp. 48. 3*s.* 6*d.*

Howse.—A Grammar of the Cree Language. With which is combined an analysis of the Chippeway Dialect. By Joseph Howse, Esq., F.R.G.S. 8vo. pp. xx. and 324, cloth. 7*s.* 6*d.*

Hunter.—A Statistical Account of Bengal. By W. W. Hunter, B.A., LL.D. Director-General of Statistics to the Government of India; one of the Council of the Royal Asiatic Society; M.R.G.S.; and Honorary Member of various Learned Societies.

vol.
- I. 24 Parganás and Sundarbans.
- II. Nadiyá and Jessor.
- III. Midnapur, Húglí and Hourah.
- IV. Bardwán, Birbhúm and Bánkurá.
- V. Dacca, Bákarganj, Farídpur and Maimansinh.
- VI. Chittagong Hill Tracts, Chittagong, Noákhálí, Tipperah, and Hill Tipperah State.
- VII. Maldah, Rangpur and Dinájpur.
- VIII. Rájsháhí and Bográ.
- IX. Murshidábád and Pábná.

vol.
- X. Dárjíling, Jalpáigurí and Kuch Behar State.
- XI. Patná and Sáran.
- XII. Gayá and Sháhábád.
- XIII. Tirhut and Champáran.
- XIV. Bhágalpur and Santál Parganás.
- XV. Monghyr and Purniah.
- XVI. Hazáribágh and Lohárdagá.
- XVII. Singhbhúm, Chutiá, Nágpur Tributary States and Mánbhúm.
- XVIII. Cuttack and Balasor.
- XIX. Purí, and Orissa Tributary States.
- XX. Fisheries, Botany, and General Index.

Published by command of the Government of India. In 20 Vols. 8vo. half-morocco. £5.

Hunter (F. M.)—An Account of the British Settlement of Aden in Arabia. Compiled by Captain F. M. Hunter, F.R.G.S., F.R.A.S., Assistant Political Resident, Aden. Demy 8vo. half-morocco, pp. xii.-232. 7*s.* 6*d.*

Ikhwánu-s Safá; or, Brothers of Purity. Describing the Contention between Men and Beasts as to the Superiority of the Human Race. Translated from the Hindustání by Professor J. Dowson, Staff College, Sandhurst. Crown 8vo. pp. viii. and 156, cloth. 7*s.*

Indian Antiquary (The).—A Journal of Oriental Research in Archæology, History, Literature, Languages, Philosophy, Religion, Folklore, etc. Edited by James Burgess, M.R.A.S., F.R.G.S. 4to. Published 12 numbers per anuum. Subscription £2.

Ingleby.—Shakespeare: the Man and the Book. By C. M. Ingleby, M.A., LL.D. 8vo. boards, pp. 172. 6*s.*

Inman.—Ancient Pagan and Modern Christian Symbolism Exposed and Explained. By Thomas Inman, M.D. Second Edition. With Illustrations. Demy 8vo. cloth, pp. xl. and 148. 1874. 7*s.* 6*d.*

Jaiminîya-Nyâya-Mâlâ-Vistara.—See under Auctores Sanscriti.

Jami, Mulla.—Salámán U Absál. An Allegorical Romance; being one of the Seven Poems entitled the Haft Aurang of Mullā Jāmī, now first edited from the Collation of Eight Manuscripts in the Library of the India House, and in private collections, with various readings, by Forbes Falconer, M.A., M.R.A.S. 4to. cloth, pp. 92. 1850. 7*s.* 6*d.*

Jataka (The); together with its Commentary. Being Tales of the Anterior Birth of Gotama Buddha. For the first time Edited in the original Pali by V. FAUSBOLL, and Translated by T. W. RHYS DAVIDS. Vol. I. Text. Demy 8vo. cloth, pp. 512. 28*s*.

The "Jataka" is a collection of legends in Pali, relating the history of Buddha's transmigration before he was born as Gotama. The great antiquity of this work is authenticated by its forming part of the sacred canon of the Southern Buddhists, which was finally settled at the last Council in 246 B.C. The collection has long been known as a storehouse of ancient fables, and as the most original attainable source to which almost the whole of this kind of literature, from the Panchatantra and Pilpay's fables down to the nursery stories of the present day, is traceable; and it has been considered desirable, in the interest of Buddhistic studies as well as for more general literary purposes, that an edition and translation of the complete work should be prepared. The present publication is intended to supply this want.—*Athenæum*.

Jenkins's Vest-Pocket Lexicon.—AN ENGLISH DICTIONARY of all except Familiar Words; including the principal Scientific and Technical Terms, and Foreign Moneys, Weights and Masures. By JABEZ JENKINS. 64mo., pp. 564. cloth. 1*s*. 6*d*.

Johnson.—ORIENTAL RELIGIONS. *See* Trübner's Oriental Series.

Kalid-i-Afghani.—TRANSLATION OF THE KALID-I-AFGHANI, the Text-book for the Pakkhto Examination, with Notes, Historical, Geographical, Grammatical, and Explanatory. By TREVOR CHICHELE PLOWDEN. Imp. 8vo. pp. xx. and 406, with a Map. *Lahore*, 1875. £2 2*s*.

Káśikâ.—A COMMENTARY ON PÂNINI'S GRAMMATICAL APHORISMS. By PANDIT JAYÂDITYA. Edited by PANDIT BÂLA SÂSTRÎ, Prof. Sansk. Coll., Benares. First part, 8vo. pp. 490. 16*s*.

Kellogg.—A GRAMMAR OF THE HINDI LANGUAGE, in which are treated the Standard Hindî, Braj, and the Eastern Hindî of the Ramayan of Tulsi Das; also the Colloquial Dialects of Marwar, Kumaon, Avadh, Baghelkhand, Bhojpur, etc., with Copious Philological Notes. By the Rev. S. H. KELLOGG, M.A. Royal 8vo. cloth, pp. 400. 21*s*.

Kern.—THE ÂRYABHATIYA, with the Commentary Bhatadîpikâ of Paramadiçvara, edited by Dr. H. KERN. 4to. pp. xii. and 107. 9*s*.

Kern.—THE BRHAT-SANHITÁ; or, Complete System of Natural Astrology of Varâha-Mihira Translated from Sanskrit into English by Dr. H. KERN, Professor of Sanskrit at the University of Leyden. Part I. 8vo. pp. 50, stitched. Parts 2 and 3 pp. 51–154. Part 4 pp. 155–210. Part 5 pp. 211–266. Part 6 pp. 267–330. Price 2*s*. each part. [*Will be completed in Nine Parts*.

Khirad-Afroz (The Illuminator of the Understanding). By Maulaví Hafízu'd-dín. A new edition of the Hindústání Text, carefully revised, with Notes, Critical and Explanatory. By EDWARD B. EASTWICK, M.P., F.R.S., F.S.A., M.R.A.S., Professor of Hindústání at the late East India Company's College at Haileybury. 8vo. cloth, pp. xiv. and 321. 18*s*.

Kidd.—CATALOGUE OF THE CHINESE LIBRARY OF THE ROYAL ASIATIC SOCIETY. By the Rev. S. KIDD. 8vo. pp. 58, sewed. 1*s*.

Kielhorn.—A GRAMMAR OF THE SANSKRIT LANGUAGE. By F. KIELHORN, Ph.D., Superintendent of Sanskrit Studies in Deccan College. Registered under Act xxv. of 1867. Demy 8vo. pp. xvi. 260. cloth. 1870. 10*s*. 6*d*.

Kielhorn.—KÂTYÂYANA AND PATANJALI. Their Relation to each other and to Panini. By F. KIELHORN, Ph. D., Prof. of Orient. Lang. Poona. 8vo. pp. 64. 1876. 3*s*. 6*d*.

Kilgour.—THE HEBREW OR IBERIAN RACE, including the Pelasgians, the Phenicians, the Jews, the British, and others. By HENRY KILGOUR. 8vo. sewed, pp. 76. 1872. 2*s*. 6*d*.

Kistner.—BUDDHA AND HIS DOCTRINES. A Bibliographical Essay. By OTTO KISTNER. Imperial 8vo., pp. iv. and 32, sewed. 2*s*. 6*d*.

Koch.—A Historical Grammar of the English Language. By C. F. Koch. Translated into English. Edited, Enlarged, and Annotated by the Rev. R. Morris, LL.D., M.A. [*Nearly ready.*

Koran (The). Arabic text, lithographed in Oudh, A.H. 1284 (1867). 16mo. pp. 942. 7*s.* 6*d.*

Koran (The).—*See* Sale, and Trübner's Oriental Series.

Kramers' New Pocket Dictionary of the English and Dutch Languages. Royal 32mo. cloth, pp. xvi. and 714. 4*s.*

Kroeger.—The Minnesinger of Germany. By A. E. Kroeger. 12mo. cloth, pp. vi. and 284. 7*s.*

Contents.—Chapter I. The Minnesinger and the Minnesong.—II. The Minnelay.—III. The Divine Minnesong.—IV. Walther von der Vogelweide.—V. Ulrich von Lichtenstein.—VI. The Metrical Romances of the Minnesinger and Gottfried von Strassburg's ' Tristan and Isolde."

Lacombe.—Dictionnaire et Grammaire de la Langue des Cris, par le Rév. Père Alb. Lacombe. 8vo. paper, pp. xx. and 713, iv. and 190. 21*s.*

Laghu Kaumudí. A Sanskrit Grammar. By Varadarája. With an English Version, Commentary, and References. By James R. Ballantyne, LL.D., Principal of the Sanskrit College, Benares. 8vo. pp. xxxvi. and 424, cloth. £1 11*s.* 6*d.*

Land.—The Principles of Hebrew Grammar. By J. P. N. Land, Professor of Logic and Metaphysic in the University of Leyden. Translated from the Dutch by Reginald Lane Poole, Balliol College, Oxford. Part I. Sounds. Part II. Words. Crown 8vo. pp. xx. and 220, cloth. 7*s.* 6*d.*

Legge.—Confucianism in Relation to Christianity. A Paper Read before the Missionary Conference in Shanghai, on May 11, 1877. By Rev. James Legge, D.D., LL.D. 8vo. sewed, pp. 12. 1877. 1*s.* 6*d.*

Legge.—The Chinese Classics. With a Translation, Critical and Exegetical Notes, Prolegomena, and Copious Indexes. By James Legge, D.D., of the London Missionary Society. In seven vols.

Vol. I. containing Confucian Analects, the Great Learning, and the Doctrine of the Mean. 8vo. pp. 526, cloth. £2 2*s.*

Vol. II., containing the Works of Mencius. 8vo. pp. 634, cloth. £2 2*s.*

Vol. III. Part I. containing the First Part of the Shoo-King, or the Books of Tang, the Books of Yu, the Books of Hea, the Books of Shang, and the Prolegomena. Royal 8vo. pp. viii. and 280, cloth. £2 2*s.*

Vol. III. Part II. containing the Fifth Part of the Shoo-King, or the Books of Chow, and the Indexes. Royal 8vo. pp. 281—736, cloth. £2 2*s.*

Vol. IV. Part I. containing the First Part of the She-King, or the Lessons from the States; and the Prolegomena. Royal 8vo. cloth, pp. 182–244. £2 2*s.*

Vol. IV. Part II. containing the 2nd, 3rd and 4th Parts of the She-King, or the Minor Odes of the Kingdom, the Greater Odes of the Kingdom, the Sacrificial Odes and Praise-Songs, and the Indexes. Royal 8vo. cloth, pp. 540. £2 2*s.*

Vol. V. Part I. containing Dukes Yin, Hwan, Chwang, Min, He, Wan, Seuen, and Ch'ing; and the Prolegomena. Royal 8vo. cloth, pp. xii., 148 and 410. £2 2*s.*

Vol. V. Part II. Contents:—Dukes Seang, Ch'aon, Ting, and Gal, with Tso's Appendix, and the Indexes. Royal 8vo. cloth, pp. 526. £2 2*s.*

Legge.—The Chinese Classics. Translated into English. With Preliminary Essays and Explanatory Notes. By James Legge, D.D., LL.D.

Vol. I. The Life and Teachings of Confucius. Crown 8vo. cloth, pp. vi. and 338. 10*s.* 6*d.*

Vol. II. The Life and Works of Mencius. Crown 8vo. cloth, pp. 412. 12*s.*

Vol. III. The She King, or The Book of Poetry. Crown 8vo., cloth, pp. viii. and 432. 12*s.*

Legge.—INAUGURAL LECTURE ON THE CONSTITUTING OF A CHINESE CHAIR in the University of Oxford. Delivered in the Sheldonian Theatre, Oct. 27th, 1876, by Rev. JAMES LEGGE, M.A., LL.D., Professor of the Chinese Language and Literature at Oxford. 8vo. pp. 28, sewed. 6*d.*

Leigh.—THE RELIGION OF THE WORLD. By H. STONE LEIGH. 12mo. pp. xii. 66, cloth. 1869. 2*s.* 6*d.*

Leitner.—INTRODUCTION TO A PHILOSOPHICAL GRAMMAR OF ARABIC. Being an Attempt to Discover a Few Simple Principles in Arabic Grammar. By G. W. LEITNER. 8vo. sewed, pp. 52. *Lahore.* 4*s.*

Leitner.—SININ-I-ISLAM. Being a Sketch of the History and Literature of Muhammadanism and their place in Universal History. *For the use of Maulvis.* By G. W. LEITNER. Part I. The Early History of Arabia to the fall of the Abassides. 8vo. sewed. *Lahore.* 6*s.*

Leland.—THE ENGLISH GIPSIES AND THEIR LANGUAGE. By CHARLES G. LELAND. Second Edition. Crown 8vo. cloth, pp. 276. 7*s.* 6*d.*

Leland.—THE BREITMANN BALLADS. THE ONLY AUTHORIZED EDITION. Complete in 1 vol., including Nineteen Ballads illustrating his Travels in Europe (never before printed), with Comments by Fritz Schwackenhammer. By CHARLES G. LELAND. Crown 8vo. handsomely bound in cloth, pp. xxviii. and 292. 6*s.*

HANS BREITMANN'S PARTY. With other Ballads. By CHARLES G. LELAND. Tenth Edition. Square, pp. xvi. and 74, cloth. 2*s.* 6*d.*

HANS BREITMANN'S CHRISTMAS. With other Ballads. By CHARLES G. LELAND. Second edition. Square, pp. 80, sewed. 1*s.*

HANS BREITMANN AS A POLITICIAN. By CHARLES G. LELAND. Second edition. Square, pp. 72, sewed. 1*s.*

HANS BREITMANN IN CHURCH. With other Ballads. By CHARLES G. Leland. With an Introduction and Glossary. Second edition. Square, pp. 80, sewed. 1*s.*

HANS BREITMANN AS AN UHLAN. Six New Ballads, with a Glossary. Square, pp. 72, sewed. 1*s.*

Leland.—FUSANG; or, the Discovery of America by Chinese Buddhist Priests in the Fifth Century. By CHARLES G. LELAND. Cr. 8vo. cloth, pp. xix. and 212. 7*s.* 6*d.*

Leland.—ENGLISH GIPSY SONGS. In Rommany, with Metrical English Translations. By CHARLES G. LELAND, Author of "The English Gipsies," etc.; Prof. E. H. PALMER; and JANET TUCKEY. Crown 8vo. cloth, pp. xii. and 276. 7*s.* 6*d.*

Leland.—PIDGIN-ENGLISH SING-SONG; or Songs and Stories in the China-English Dialect. With a Vocabulary. By CHARLES G. LELAND. Fcap, 8vo. cl., pp. viii. and 140. 1876. 5*s.*

Leo.—FOUR CHAPTERS OF NORTH'S PLUTARCH. Containing the Lives of Caius Marcius Coriolanus, Julius Cæsar, Marcus Antoninus, and Marcus Brutus, as Sources to Shakespeare's Tragedies, Coriolanus, Julius Cæsar, and Antony and Cleopatra; and partly to Hamlet and Timon of Athens. Photolithographed in the size of the Edition of 1595. With Preface, Notes comparing the Text of the Editions of 1579, 1595, 1603, and 1612; and Reference Notes to the Text of the Tragedies of Shakespeare. Edited by Prof. F. A. LEO, Ph.D. In one volume, folio, elegantly bound, pp. 22 of letterpress and 130 pp. of facsimiles. £1 11*s.* 6*d.*

The Library Edition is limited to 250 copies, at the price £1 11*s.* 6*d.*

Of the Amateur Edition 50 copies have been struck off on a superior large hand-made paper, price £3 3*s.* per copy.

Leonowens.—The English Governess at the Siamese Court—being Recollections of six years in the Royal Palace at Bangkok. By Anna Harriette Leonowens. With Illustrations from Photographs presented to the Author by the King of Siam. 8vo. cloth, pp. x. and 332. 1870 12*s.*

Leonowens.—The Romance of Siamese Harem Life. By Mrs. Anna H. Leonowens, Author of "The English Governess at the Siamese Court." With 17 Illustrations, principally from Photographs, by the permission of J. Thomson, Esq. Crown 8vo. cloth, pp. viii. and 278. 14*s.*

Literature.—Transactions of the Royal Society of Literature of the United Kingdom. First Series, 6 parts in 3 vols. 4to. plates; 1827–39. Second Series, 10 vols. or 30 parts, and vol. xi. parts 1 and 2, 8vo. plates, 1843-76. A complete set, as far as published, £10 10*s.* A list of the contents of the volumes and parts on application.

Lobscheid.—English and Chinese Dictionary, with the Punti and Mandarin Pronunciation. By the Rev. W. Lobscheid, Knight of Francis Joseph, C.M.I.R.G.S.A., N.Z.B.S.V., etc. Folio, pp. viii. and 2016. In Four Parts. £8 8*s.*

Lobscheid.—Chinese and English Dictionary, Arranged according to the Radicals. By the Rev. W. Lobscheid, Knight of Francis Joseph, C.M.I.R.G.S.A., N.Z.B.S.V., &c. 1 vol. imp. 8vo. double columns, pp. 600, bound. £2 8*s.*

Ludewig.—The Literature of American Aboriginal Languages. By Herman E. Ludewig With Additions and Corrections by Professor Wm. W. Turner. Edited by Nicolas Trübner. 8vo. fly and general Title, 2 leaves; Dr. Ludewig's Preface, pp. v.—viii.; Editor's Preface, pp. iv.—xii; Biographical Memoir of Dr. Ludewig, pp. xiii.—xiv.; and Introductory Biographical Notices, pp. xiv.—xxiv., followed by List of Contents. Then follow Dr. Ludewig's Bibliotheca Glottica, alphabetically arranged, with Additions by the Editor, pp. 1—209; Professor Turner's Additions, with those of the Editor to the same, also alphabetically arranged, pp. 210—246; Index, pp. 247—256; and List of Errata, pp. 257, 258. Handsomely bound in cloth. 10*s.* 6*d.*

Luzzatto.—Grammar of the Biblical Chaldaic Language and the Talmud Babylonical Idioms. By S. D. Luzzatto. Translated from the Italian by J. S. Goldammer. Cr. 8vo. cl., pp. 122. 7*s.* 6*d.*

Macgowan.—A Manual of the Amoy Colloquial. By Rev. J. Macgowan, of the London Missionary Society. 8vo. sewed, pp. xvii. and 200. Amoy, 1871. £1 1*s.*

Mackay.—The Gaelic Etymology of the Languages of Western Europe, and more especially of the English and Lowland Scotch, and of their Slang, Cant, and Colloquial Dialects. By Charles Mackay, LL.D. Royal 8vo. cloth, pp. xxxii. and 604. 42*s.*

McClatchie. — A Translation of Section Forty-nine of the "Complete Works" of the Philosopher Choo-Foo-Tze, with Explanatory Notes. By the Rev. Thomas McClatchie, M.A. Small 4to. pp. xviii. and 162. 12*s.* 6*d.*

Maclay and Baldwin.—An Alphabetic Dictionary of the Chinese Language in the Foochow Dialect. By Rev. R. S. Maclay, D.D., of the Methodist Episcopal Mission, and Rev. C. C. Baldwin, A.M., of the American Board of Mission. 8vo. half-bound, pp. 1132. Foochow, 1871. £4 4*s.*

Mahabharata. Translated into Hindi for Madan Mohun Bhatt, by Krishnachandradharmadhikarin of Benares. (Containing all but the Harivansá.) 3 vols. 8vo. cloth, pp. 574, 810, and 1106. £3 3*s.*

Maha-Vira-Charita; or, the Adventures of the Great Hero Rama. An Indian Drama in Seven Acts. Translated into English Prose from the Sanskrit of Bhavabhûti. By JOHN PICKFORD, M.A. Crown 8vo. cloth. 5*s*.

Maino-i-Khard (The Book of the).—The Pazand and Sanskrit Texts (in Roman characters) as arranged by Neriosengh Dhaval, in the fifteenth century. With an English translation, a Glossary of the Pazand texts, containing the Sanskrit, Rosian, and Pahlavi equivalents, a sketch of Pazand Grammar, and an Introduction. By E. W. WEST. 8vo. sewed, pp. 484. 1871. 16*s*.

Maltby.—A PRACTICAL HANDBOOK OF THE URIYA OR ODIYA LANGUAGE. By THOMAS J. MALTBY, Esq., Madras C.S. 8vo. pp. xiii. and 201. 1874. 10*s*. 6*d*.

Manava-Kalpa-Sutra; being a portion of this ancient Work on Vaidik Rites, together with the Commentary of KUMARILA-SWAMIN. A Facsimile of the MS. No. 17, in the Library of Her Majesty's Home Government for India. With a Preface by THEODOR GOLDSTÜCKER. Oblong folio, pp. 268 of letter-press and 121 leaves of facsimiles. Cloth. £4 4*s*.

Manipulus Vocabulorum; A Rhyming Dictionary of the English Language. By Peter Levins (1570) Edited, with an Alphabetical Index, by HENRY B. WHEATLEY. 8vo. pp. xvi. and 370, cloth. 14*s*.

Manning.—AN INQUIRY INTO THE CHARACTER AND ORIGIN OF THE POSSESSIVE AUGMENT in English and in Cognate Dialects. By the late JAMES MANNING, Q.A.S., Recorder of Oxford. 8vo. pp. iv. and 90. 2*s*.

March.—A COMPARATIVE GRAMMAR OF THE ANGLO-SAXON LANGUAGE; in which its forms are illustrated by those of the Sanskrit, Greek, Latin, Gothic, Old Saxon, Old Friesic, Old Norse, and Old High-German. By FRANCIS A. MARCH, LL.D. Demy 8vo. cloth, pp. xi. and 253. 1877. 10*s*.

Mariette.—THE MONUMENTS OF UPPER EGYPT. A Translation of the Itineraire de la Haute Egypte, of Auguste Mariette Bey. By ALPHONSE MARRIETTE. Fcap. 8vo. cloth, pp. vii.-261. 7*s*. 6*d*.

Markham.—QUICHUA GRAMMAR and DICTIONARY. Contributions towards a Grammar and Dictionary of Quichua, the Language of the Yncas of Peru; collected by CLEMENTS R. MARKHAM, F.S.A., Corr. Mem. of the University of Chile. Author of "Cuzco and Lima," and "Travels in Peru and India." In one vol. crown 8vo., pp. 223, cloth. £1. 11*s*. 6*d*.

Markham.—OLLANTA: A DRAMA IN THE QUICHUA LANGUAGE. Text, Translation, and Introduction. By CLEMENTS R. MARKHAM, F.R.G.S. Crown 8vo., pp. 128, cloth. 7*s*. 6*d*.

Markham.—A MEMOIR OF THE LADY ANA DE OSORIO, Countess of Chinchon, and Vice-Queen of Peru, A.D. 1629–39. With a Plea for the Correct Spelling of the Chinchona Genus. By CLEMENTS R. MARKHAM, C.B., F.R.S., Commendador da Real Ordem de Christo, Socius Academiæ Cæsareæ Naturæ Curiosorum Cognomen Chinchon. Small 4to, pp. 112. With a Map, 2 Plates, and numerous Illustrations. Roxburghe binding. 28*s*.

Markham.—THE NARRATIVES OF THE MISSION OF GEORGE BOGLE, B.C.S., to the Teshu Lama, and of the Journey of Thomas Manning to Lhasa. Edited, with Notes and Introduction, and lives of Mr. Bogle and Mr. Manning, by CLEMENTS R MARKHAM, C.B., F.R.S. Demy 8vo., with Maps and Illustrations, pp. clxi. 314, cl. 21*s*.

Marsden's Numismata Orientalia. New International Edition. *See* under NUMISMATA ORIENTALIA.

Mason.—THE PALI TEXT OF KACHCHAYANO'S GRAMMAR, WITH ENGLISH ANNOTATIONS. By FRANCIS MASON, D.D. I. The Text Aphorisms, 1 to 673. II. The English Annotations, including the various Readings of six independent Burmese Manuscripts, the Singalese Text on Verbs, and the Cambodian Text on Syntax. To which is added a Concordance of the Aphorisms. In Two Parts. 8vo. sewed, pp. 208, 75, and 28. Toongoo, 1871. £1 11*s*. 6*d*.

Mathews.—ABRAHAM BEN EZRA'S UNEDITED COMMENTARY ON THE CANTICLES, the Hebrew Text after two MS., with English Translation by H. J. MATHEWS, B.A., Exeter College, Oxford. 8vo. cl. limp, pp. x., 34, 24. 2*s*. 6*d*.

Mathuráprasáda Misra.—A TRILINGUAL DICTIONARY, being a comprehensive Lexicon in English, Urdú, and Hindí, exhibiting the Syllabication, Pronunciation, and Etymology of English Words, with their Explanation in English, and in Urdú and Hindí in the Roman Character. By MATHURÁPRASÁDA MISRA, Second Master, Queen's College, Benares. 8vo. pp. xv. and 1330, cloth. Benares, 1865. £2 2*s*.

Matthews.—ETHNOLOGY AND PHILOLOGY OF THE HIDATSA INDIANS. By WASHINGTON MATTHEWS, Assistant Surgeon, U.S. Army. *Contents*:—Ethnography, Philology, Grammar, Dictionary, and English-Hidatsa Vocabulary. 8vo. cloth. £1 11*s*. 6*d*.

Mayers.—ILLUSTRATIONS OF THE LAMAIST SYSTEM IN TIBET, drawn from Chinese Sources. By WILLIAM FREDERICK MAYERS, Esq., of Her Britannic Majesty's Consular Service, China. 8vo. pp. 24, sewed. 1869. 1*s*. 6*d*.

Mayers.—THE CHINESE READER'S MANUAL. A Handbook of Biographical, Historical, Mythological, and General Literary Reference. By W. F. MAYERS, Chinese Secretary to H. B. M.'s Legation at Peking, F.R.G.S., etc., etc. Demy 8vo. pp. xxiv. and 440. £1 5*s*.

Mayers.—TREATIES BETWEEN THE EMPIRE OF CHINA AND FOREIGN Powers, together with Regulations for the Conduct of Foreign Trade, etc. Edited by W. F. MAYERS, Chinese Secretary to H.B.M.'s Legation at Peking. 8vo. cloth, pp. 246. 1877. 25*s*.

Mayers.—THE CHINESE GOVERNMENT. A Manual of Chinese Titles, Categorically arranged, and Explained with an Appendix. By W. F. MAYERS, Chinese Secretary to H.B.M.'s Legation at Peking. Royal 8vo. cloth, pp. viii.–160. 1878. £1 8*s*.

Mayers.—THE ANGLO-CHINESE CALENDAR MANUAL. A Handbook of Reference for the Determination of Chinese Dates during the period from 1860 to 1879. With Comparative Tables of Annual and Mensual Designations, etc. Compiled by W. F. MAYERS, Chinese Secretary, H.B.M.'s Legation, Peking. 2nd Edition. Sewed, pp. 28. 7*s*. 6*d*.

Medhurst.—CHINESE DIALOGUES, QUESTIONS, and FAMILIAR SENTENCES, literally translated into English, with a view to promote commercial intercourse and assist beginners in the Language. By the late W. H. MEDHURST, D.D. A new and enlarged Edition. 8vo. pp. 226. 18*s*.

Megasthenês.—ANCIENT INDIA AS DESCRIBED BY MEGASTHENÊS AND ARRIAN. Being a Translation of the Fragments of the Indika of Megasthenês collected by Dr. SCHWANBEKK, and of the First Part of the Indika of Arrian. By J. W. MCCRINDLE, M.A., Principal of the Government College, Patna, etc. With Introduction, Notes, and Map of Ancient India. Post 8vo. cloth, pp. ii.–224. 1877. 7*s*. 6*d*.

Megha-Duta (The). (Cloud-Messenger.) By Kālidāsa. Translated from the Sanskrit into English verse, with Notes and Illustrations. By the late H. H. WILSON, M.A., F.R.S., Boden Professor of Sanskrit in the University of Oxford, etc., etc. The Vocabulary by FRANCIS JOHNSON, sometime Professor of Oriental Languages at the College of the Honourable the East India Company, Haileybury. New Edition. 4to. cloth, pp. xi. and 180. 10*s*. 6*d*.

Memoirs read before the ANTHROPOLOGICAL SOCIETY OF LONDON, 1863 1864. 8vo., pp. 542, cloth. 21*s*.

Memoirs read before the ANTHROPOLOGICAL SOCIETY OF LONDON, 1865-6. Vol. II. 8vo., pp. x. 464, cloth. 21*s*.

Mills.—THE INDIAN SAINT; or, Buddha and Buddhism.—A Sketch Historical and Critical. By C. D. B. MILLS. 8vo. cl., pp. 192. 7*s*. 6*d*.

Minocheherji.—PAHLAVI, GUJARÂTI, AND ENGLISH DICTIONARY. By JAMASPJI DASTUR MINOCHEHERJI JAMASP ASANA, Fellow of the University of Bombay, and Member of the Bombay Branch of the Royal Asiatic Society. Vol. I. (To be completed in three volumes.) Demy 8vo. pp. clxxix and 168, with Photographic Portrait of the Author. 14*s*.

Mírkhónd.—THE HISTORY OF THE ATÁBEKS OF SYRIA AND PERSIA. By MUHAMMED BEN KHÁWENDSHÁH BEN MAHMUD, commonly called MÍRKHÓND. Now first Edited from the Collation of Sixteen MSS., by W. H. MORLEY, Barrister-at-law, M.R.A.S. To which is added a Series of Facsimiles of the Coins struck by the Atâbeks, arranged and described by W. S. W. Vaux, M.A., M.R.A.S. Roy. 8vo. cloth, 7 plates, pp. 118. 1848. 7*s*. 6*d*.

Mitra.—THE ANTIQUITIES OF ORISSA. By RAJENDRALALA MITRA. Vol. I. Published under Orders of the Government of India. Folio, cloth, pp. 180. With a Map and 36 Plates. £4 4*s*.

Molesworth.—A DICTIONARY, MÁRATHI and ENGLISH. Compiled by J. T. MOLESWORTH, assisted by GEORGE and THOMAS CANDY. Second Edition, revised and enlarged. By J. T. MOLESWORTH. Royal 4to. pp. xxx and 922, boards. Bombay, 1857. £3 3*s*.

Molesworth.—A COMPENDIUM OF MOLESWORTH'S MARATHI AND ENGLISH DICTIONARY. By BABA PADMANJI. Second Edition. Revised and Enlarged. Demy 8vo. cloth, pp. xx. and 624. 21*s*.

Möllendorff.—MANUAL OF CHINESE BIBLIOGRAPHY, being a List of Works and Essays relating to China. By P. G. and O. F. VON MÖLLENDORFF, Interpreters to H.I.G.M.'s Consulates at Shanghai and Tientsin. 8vo. pp. viii. and 378. £1 10*s*.

Morley.—A DESCRIPTIVE CATALOGUE of the HISTORICAL MANUSCRIPTS in the ARABIC and PERSIAN LANGUAGES preserved in the Library of the Royal Asiatic Society of Great Britain and Ireland. By WILLIAM H. MORLEY, M.R.A.S. 8vo. pp. viii. and 160, sewed. London, 1854. 2*s*. 6*d*.

Morris.—A DESCRIPTIVE AND HISTORICAL ACCOUNT OF THE GODAVERY DISTRICT in the Presidency of Madras By HENRY MORRIS, formerly of the Madras Civil Service. Author of a "History of India for Use in Schools" and other works. 8vo. cloth (with a map), pp. xii. and 390. 1878. 12*s*.

Morrison.—A DICTIONARY OF THE CHINESE LANGUAGE. By the Rev. R. MORRISON, D.D. Two vols. Vol. I. pp. x. and 762; Vol. II. pp. 828, cloth. Shanghae, 1865. £6 6*s*.

Muhammed.—THE LIFE OF MUHAMMED. Based on Muhammed Ibn Ishak. By Abd El Malik Ibn Hisham. Edited by Dr. FERDINAND WÜSTENFELD. The Arabic Text. 8vo. pp. 1026, sewed. Price 21*s*. Introduction, Notes, and Index in German. 8vo. pp. lxxii. and 266, sewed. 7*s*. 6*d*. Each part sold separately.

The text based on the Manuscripts of the Berlin, Leipsic, Gotha and Leyden Libraries, has been carefully revised by the learned editor, and printed with the utmost exactness.

Muir.—ORIGINAL SANSKRIT TEXTS, on the Origin and History of the People of India, their Religion and Institutions. Collected, Translated, and Illustrated by JOHN MUIR, Esq., D.C.L., LL.D., Ph.D.

Vol. I. Mythical and Legendary Accounts of the Origin of Caste, with an Inquiry into its existence in the Vedic Age. Second Edition, re-written and greatly enlarged. 8vo. pp. xx. 532, cloth. 1868. 21*s*.

Vol. II. The Trans-Himalayan Origin of the Hindus, and their Affinity with the Western Branches of the Aryan Race. Second Edition, revised, with Additions. 8vo. pp. xxxii. and 512, cloth. 1871. 21*s*.

Vol. III. The Vedas: Opinions of their Authors, and of later Indian Writers, on their Origin, Inspiration, and Authority. Second Edition, revised and enlarged. 8vo. pp. xxxii. 312, cloth. 1868. 16*s*.

Vol. IV. Comparison of the Vedic with the later representations of the principal Indian Deities. Second Edition Revised. 8vo. pp. xvi. and 524, cloth. 1873. 21*s*.

Vol. V. Contributions to a Knowledge of the Cosmogony, Mythology, Religious Ideas, Life and Manners of the Indians in the Vedic Age. 8vo. pp. xvi. 492, cloth, 1870. 21*s*.

Müller.—The Sacred Hymns of the Brahmins, as preserved to us in the oldest collection of religious poetry, the Rig-Veda-Sanhita, translated and explained. By F. Max Müller, M.A., Fellow of All Souls' College; Professor of Comparative Philology at Oxford; Foreign Member of the Institute of France, etc., etc. Volume I. Hymns to the Maruts or the Storm Gods. 8vo. pp. clii. and 264. 12*s*. 6*d*.

Müller.—The Hymns of the Rig-Veda in the Samhita and Pada Texts. Reprinted from the Editio Princeps. By F. Max Müller, M.A., etc. Second edition. With the Two Texts on Parallel Pages. In 2 vols. 8vo., pp. 1700, sewed. 32*s*.

Müller.—Lecture on Buddhist Nihilism. By F. Max Müller, M.A., Professor of Comparative Philology in the University of Oxford; Member of the French Institute, etc. Delivered before the General Meeting of the Association of German Philologists, at Kiel, 28th September, 1869. (Translated from the German.) Sewed. 1869. 1*s*.

Nagananda; or the Joy of the Snake-World. A Buddhist Drama in Five Acts. Translated into English Prose, with Explanatory Notes, from the Sanskrit of Sri-Harsha-Deva. By Palmer Boyd, B.A., Sanskrit Scholar of Trinity College, Cambridge. With an Introduction by Professor Cowell. Crown 8vo., pp. xvi. and 100, cloth. 4*s*. 6*d*.

Nalopákhyánam.—Story of Nala; an Episode of the Mahá-Bhárata. The Sanskrit Text, with Vocabulary, Analysis, and Introduction. By Monier Williams, M.A. The Metrical Translation by the Very Rev. H. H. Milman, D.D. 8vo. cl. 15*s*.

Naradiya Dharma Sastram; or, the Institutes of Narada. Translated for the First Time from the unpublished Sanskrit original. By Dr. Julius Jolly, University, Wurzburg. With a Preface, Notes chiefly critical, an Index of Quotations from Narada in the principal Indian Digests, and a general Index. Crown 8vo., pp. xxxv. 144, cloth. 10*s*. 6*d*.

Newman.—A Dictionary of Modern Arabic—1. Anglo-Arabic Dictionary. 2. Anglo-Arabic Vocabulary. 3. Arabo-English Dictionary. By F. W. Newman, Emeritus Professor of University College, London. In 2 vols. crown 8vo., pp. xvi. and 376–464, cloth. £1 1*s*.

Newman.—A Handbook of Modern Arabic, consisting of a Practical Grammar, with numerous Examples, Dialogues, and Newspaper Extracts, in a European Type. By F. W. Newman, Emeritus Professor of University College, London; formerly Fellow of Balliol College, Oxford. Post 8vo. pp. xx. and 192, cloth. London, 1866. 6*s*.

Newman.—The Text of the Iguvine Inscriptions, with interlinear Latin Translation and Notes. By Francis W. Newman, late Professor of Latin at University College, London. 8vo. pp. xvi. and 54, sewed. 2*s*.

Newman.—Orthoëpy: or, a simple mode of Accenting English, for the advantage of Foreigners and of all Learners. By Francis W. Newman, Emeritus Professor of University College, London. 8vo. pp. 28, sewed. 1869. 1*s.*

Nodal.—Elementos de Gramática Quichua ó Idioma de los Yncas. Bajo los Auspicios de la Redentora, Sociedad de Filántropos para mejorar la suerte de los Aboríjenes Peruanos. Por el Dr. José Fernandez Nodal, Abogado de los Tribunales de Justicia de la República del Perú. Royal 8vo. cloth, pp. xvi. and 441. Appendix, pp. 9. £1 1*s.*

Nodal.—Los Vinculos de Ollanta y Cusi-Kcuyllor. Drama en Quichua. Obra Compilada y Espurgada con la Version Castellana al Frente de su Testo por el Dr. José Fernandez Nodal, Abogado de los Tribunales de Justicia de la República del Perú. Bajo los Auspicios de la Redentora Sociedad de Filántropos para Mejoror la Suerte de los Aboríjenes Peruanos. Roy. 8vo. bds. pp. 70. 1874. 7*s.* 6*d.*

Notley.—A Comparative Grammar of the French, Italian, Spanish, and Portuguese Languages. By Edwin A. Notley. Crown oblong 8vo. cloth, pp. xv. and 396. 7*s.* 6*d.*

Numismata Orientalia.—The International Numismata Orientalia. Edited by Edward Thomas, F.R.S., etc. Vol. I. Illustrated with 20 Plates and a Map. Royal 4to. cloth. £3 13*s.* 6*d.*

Also in 6 Parts sold separately, viz.:—

Part I.—Ancient Indian Weights. By E. Thomas, F.R.S., etc. Royal 4to. sewed, pp. 84, with a Plate and a Map of the India of Manu. 9*s.* 6*d.*

Part II.—Coins of the Urtuki Turkumans. By Stanley Lane Poole, Corpus Christi College Oxford. Royal 4to. sewed, pp. 44, with 6 Plates. 9*s.*

Part III. The Coinage of Lydia and Persia, from the Earliest Times to the Fall of the Dynasty of the Achæmenidæ. By Barclay V. Head, Assistant-Keeper of Coins, British Museum. Royal 4to. sewed, pp. viii. and 56, with three Autotype Plates. 10*s.* 6*d.*

Part IV. The Coins of the Tuluni Dynasty. By Edward Thomas. Rogers. Royal 4to. sewed, pp. iv. and 22, and 1 Plate. 5*s.*

Part V. The Parthian Coinage. By Percy Gardner, M.A. Royal 4to. sewed, pp. iv. and 65, with 8 Autotype Plates. 18*s.*

Part VI. On the Ancient Coins and Measures of Ceylon. With a Discussion of the Ceylon Date of the Buddha's Death. By T. W. Rhys Davids, Barrister-at-Law, late of the Ceylon Civil Service. Royal 4to. sewed, pp. 60, with Plate. 10*s.*

Nutt.—Fragments of a Samaritan Targum. Edited from a Bodleian MS. With an Introduction, containing a Sketch of Samaritan History, Dogma, and Literature. By J. W. Nutt, M.A. Demy 8vo. cloth, pp. viii., 172, and 84. With Plate. 1874. 15*s.*

Nutt.—A Sketch of Samaritan History, Dogma, and Literature. Published as an Introduction to "Fragments of a Samaritan Targum. By J. W. Nutt, M.A. Demy 8vo. cloth, pp. viii. and 172. 1874. 5*s.*

Nutt.—Two Treatises on Verbs containing Feeble and Double Letters by R. Jehuda Hayug of Fez, translated into Hebrew from the original Arabic by R. Moses Gikatilia, of Cordova; with the Treatise on Punctuation by the same Author, translated by Aben Ezra. Edited from Bodleian MSS. with an English Translation by J. W. Nutt, M.A. Demy 8vo. sewed, pp. 312. 1870. 7*s.* 6*d.*

Oera Linda Book, from a Manuscript of the Thirteenth Century, with the permission of the Proprietor, C. Over de Linden, of the Helder The Original Frisian Text, as verified by Dr. J. O. Ottema; accompanied by an English Version of Dr. Ottema's Dutch Translation, by William R. Sandbach. 8vo. cl. pp. xxvii. and 223. 5*s.*

Ollanta: A Drama in the Quichua Language. See under Markham and under Nodal.

Oriental Congress.—Report of the Proceedings of the Second International Congress of Orientalists held in London, 1874. Roy. 8vo. paper, pp. 76. 5*s*.

Oriental Congress—Transactions of the Second Session of the International Congress of Orientalists, held in London in September, 1874. Edited by Robert K. Douglas, Honorary Secretary. Demy 8vo. cloth, pp. viii. and 456. 21*s*.

Osburn.—The Monumental History of Egypt, as recorded on the Ruins of her Temples, Palaces, and Tombs. By William Osburn. Illustrated with Maps, Plates, etc. 2 vols. 8vo. pp. xii. and 461; vii. and 643, cloth. £2 2*s*.

Vol. I.—From the Colonization of the Valley to the Visit of the Patriarch Abram.
Vol II.—From the Visit of Abram to the Exodus.

Otté.—How to Learn Danish (Dano-Norwegian). A Manual for Students of Danish (Dano-Norwegian). Based on the Ollendorffian System of Teaching Languages, and adapted for Self-Instruction. By E. C. Otté. Crown 8vo cloth, pp. xix.–338. 7*s*. 6*d*.

Key to the Exercises. Cloth, pp. 84. 3*s*.

Palmer.—Egyptian Chronicles, with a harmony of Sacred and Egyptian Chronology, and an Appendix on Babylonian and Assyrian Antiquities. By William Palmer, M.A., and late Fellow of Magdalen College, Oxford. vols.. 8vo. cloth, pp. lxxiv. and 428, and viii. and 636. 1861. 12*s*.

Palmer.—A Concise Dictionary of the Persian Language. By E. H. Palmer, M.A., Professor of Arabic in the University of Cambridge. Square 16mo. pp. viii. and 364, cloth. 10*s* 6*d*.

Palmer.—Leaves from a Word Hunter's Note Book. Being some Contributions to English Etymology. By the Rev. A. Smythe Palmer, B.A., sometime Scholar in the University of Dublin. Cr. 8vo. cl. pp. xii.–316. 7*s*. 6*d*.

Palmer.—The Song of the Reed; and other Pieces. By E. H. Palmer, M.A., Cambridge. Crown 8vo. pp. 208, handsomely bound in cloth. 5*s*.

Among the Contents will be found translations from Hafiz, from Omer el Kheiyám, and from other Persian as well as Arabic poets.

Pand-Námah.—The Pand-Námah; or, Books of Counsels. By Ádarbád Máráspand. Translated from Pehlevi into Gujerathi, by Harbad Sheriarjee Dadabhoy. And from Gujerathi into English by the Rev. Shapurji Edalji. Fcap. 8vo. sewed. 1870. 6*d*.

Pandit's (A) Remarks on Professor Max Müller's Translation of the "Rig-Veda." Sanskrit and English. Fcap. 8vo. sewed. 1870. 6*d*.

Paspati.—Études sur les Tchinghianês (Gypsies) ou Bohémiens de L'Empire Ottoman. Par Alexandre G. Paspati, M.D. Large 8vo. sewed, pp. xii. and 652. Constantinople, 1871. 28*s*.

Patanjali.—The Vyâkarana-Mahâbhâshya of Patanjali. Edited by F. Kielhorn, Ph.D., Professor of Oriental Languages, Deccan College. Vol. I., Part I. pp. 200. 8*s*. 6*d*.

Patell.—Cowasjee Patell's Chronology, containing corresponding Dates of the different Eras used by Christians, Jews, Greeks, Hindús, Mohamedans, Parsees, Chinese, Japanese, etc. By Cowasjee Sorabjee Patell. 4to. pp. viii. and 184, cloth. 50*s*.

Peking Gazette.—Translation of the Peking Gazette for 1872, 1873, 1874, 1875, 1876, and 1877. 8vo. cloth. 10*s*. 6*d*. each.

Percy.—Bishop Percy's Folio Manuscripts—Ballads and Romances. Edited by John W. Hales, M.A., Fellow and late Assistant Tutor of Christ's College, Cambridge; and Frederick J. Furnivall, M.A., of Trinity Hall, Cambridge: assisted by Professor Child, of Harvard University, Cambridge, U.S.A., W. Chappell, Esq., etc. In 3 volumes. Vol. I., pp. 610; Vol. 2, pp. 681.; Vol. 3, pp. 640. Demy 8vo. half-bound, £4 4*s.* Extra demy 8vo. half-bound, on Whatman's ribbed paper, £6 6*s.* Extra royal 8vo., paper covers, on Whatman's best ribbed paper, £10 10*s.* Large 4to., paper covers, on Whatman's best ribbed paper, £12.

Pfoundes.—Fu So Mimi Bukuro.—A Budget of Japanese Notes. By Capt. Pfoundes, of Yokohama. 8vo. sewed, pp. 184. 7*s.* 6*d.*

Philological Society (Transactions of The). A Complete Set, including the Proceedings of the Philological Society for the years 1842-1853. 6 vols. The Philological Society's Transactions, 1854 to 1876. 15 vols. The Philological Society's Extra Volumes. 9 vols. In all 30 vols. 8vo. £19 13*s.* 6*d.*

Proceedings (The) of the Philological Society 1842-1853. 6 vols. 8vo. £3.

Transactions of the Philological Society, 1854-1876. 15 vols. 8vo. £10 16*s.*

*** The Volumes for 1867, 1868-9, 1870-2, and 1873-4, are only to be had in complete sets, as above.

Separate Volumes.

For 1854: containing papers by Rev. J. W. Blakesley, Rev. T. O. Cockayne, Rev. J. Davies, Dr. J. W. Donaldson, Dr. Theod. Goldstücker, Prof. T. Hewitt Key, J. M. Kemble, Dr. R. G. Latham, J. M. Ludlow, Hensleigh Wedgwood, etc. 8vo. cl. £1 1*s.*

For 1855: with papers by Dr. Carl Abel, Dr. W. Bleek, Rev. Jno. Davies, Miss A. Gurney, Jas. Kennedy, Prof. T. H. Key, Dr. R. G. Latham, Henry Malden, W. Ridley, Thos. Watts, Hensleigh Wedgwood, etc. In 4 parts. 8vo. £1 1*s.*

*** Kamilaroi Language of Australia, by W. Ridley; and False Etymologies, by H. Wedgwood, separately. 1*s.*

For 1856-7: with papers by Prof. Aufrecht, Herbert Coleridge, Lewis Kr. Daa, M. de Haan, W. C. Jourdain, James Kennedy, Prof. Key, Dr. G. Latham, J. M. Ludlow, Rev. J. J. S. Perowne, Hensleigh Wedgwood, R. F. Weymouth, Jos. Yates, etc. 7 parts. 8vo. (The Papers relating to the Society's Dictionary are omitted.) £1 1*s.* each volume.

For 1858: including the volume of Early English Poems, Lives of the Saints, edited from MSS. by F. J. Furnivall; and papers by Ern. Adams, Prof. Aufrecht, Herbert Coleridge, Rev. Francis Crawford, M. de Haan Hettema, Dr. R. G. Latham, Dr. Lottner, etc. 8vo. cl. 12*s.*

For 1859: with papers by Dr. E. Adams, Prof. Aufrecht, Herb. Coleridge, F. J. Furnivall, Prof. T. H. Key, Dr. C. Lottner, Prof. De Morgan, F. Pulszky, Hensleigh Wedgwood, etc. 8vo. cl. 12*s.*

For 1860-1: including The Play of the Sacrament; and Pascon agan Arluth, the Passion of our Lord, in Cornish and English, both from MSS., edited by Dr. Whitley Stokes; and papers by Dr. E. Adams, T. F. Barham, Rev. Derwent Coleridge, Herbert Coleridge, Sir John F. Davis, Danby P. Fry, Prof. T. H. Key, Dr. C. Lottner, Bishop Thirlwall, Hensleigh Wedgwood, R. F. Weymouth, etc. 8vo. cl. 12*s.*

For 1862-3: with papers by C. B. Cayley, D. P. Fry, Prof. Key, H. Malden, Rich. Morris, F. W. Newman, Robert Peacock, Hensleigh Wedgwood, R. F. Weymouth, etc. 8vo. cl. 12*s.*

For 1864: containing 1. Manning's (Jas.) Inquiry into the Character and Origin of the Possessive Augment in English, etc.; 2. Newman's (Francis W.) Text of the Iguvine Inscriptions, with Interlinear Latin Translation; 3. Barnes's (Dr.

Philological Society (Transactions of The)—*continued.*

W.) Grammar and Glossary of the Dorset Dialect; 4. Gwreans An Bys—The Creation: a Cornish Mystery, Cornish and English, with Notes by Whitley Stokes, etc. 8vo. cl. 12*s.*

*** Separately: Manning's Inquiry, 3*s.*—Newman's Iguvine Inscription, 3*s.*—Stokes's Gwreans An Bys, 8*s.*

For 1865: including Wheatley's (H. B.) Dictionary of Reduplicated Words in the English Language; and papers by Prof. Aufrecht, Ed. Brock, C. B. Cayley, Rev. A. J. Church, Prof. T. H. Key, Rev. E. H. Knowles, Prof. H. Malden, Hon. G. P. Marsh, John Rhys, Guthbrand Vigfusson, Hensleigh Wedgwood, H. B. Wheatley, etc. 8vo. cl. 12*s.*

For 1866: including 1. Gregor's (Rev. Walter) Banffshire Dialect, with Glossary of Words omitted by Jamieson; 2. Edmondston's (T.) Glossary of the Shetland Dialect; and papers by Prof. Cassal, C. B. Cayley, Danby P. Fry, Prof. T. H. Key, Guthbrand Vigfusson, Hensleigh Wedgwood, etc. 8vo. cl. 12*s.*

*** The Volumes for 1867, 1868–9, 1870–2, and 1873–4, are out of print. Besides contributions in the shape of valuable and interesting papers, the volume for 1867 also includes: 1. Peacock's (Rob. B.) Glossary of the Hundred of Lonsdale; and 2. Ellis (A. J.) On Palæotype representing Spoken Sounds; and on the Diphthong "Oy." The volume for 1868–9—1. Ellis's (A. J.) Only English Proclamation of Henry III. in Oct. 1258; to which are added "The Cuckoo's Song and "The Prisoner's Prayer," Lyrics of the XIII. Century, with Glossary; and 2. Stokes's (Whitley) Cornish Glossary. That for 1870-2—1. Murray's (Jas. A. H.) Dialect of the Southern Counties of Scotland, with a linguistical map. That for 1873–4—Sweet's (H.) History of English Sounds.

For 1875–6: containing the Rev. Richard Morris (President), Fourth and Fifth Annual Addresses. 1. Some Sources of Aryan Mythology by E. L. Brandreth; 2. C. B. Cayley on Certain Italian Diminutives; 3. Changes made by four young Children in Pronouncing English Words, by Jas. M. Menzies; 4. The Manx Language, by H. Jenner; 5. The Dialect of West Somerset, by F. T. Elworthy; 6. English Metre, by Prof. J. B. Mayor; 7. Words, Logic, and Grammar, by H. Sweet; 8. The Russian Language and its Dialects, by W. R. Morfill; 9. Relics of the Cornish Language in Mount's Bay, by H. Jenner. 10. Dialects and Prehistoric Forms of Old English. By Henry Sweet, Esq.; 11. On the Dialects of Monmouthshire, Herefordshire, Worcestershire, Gloucestershire, Berkshire, Oxfordshire, South Warwickshire, South Northamptonshire, Buckinghamshire, Hertfordshire, Middlesex, and Surrey, with a New Classification of the English Dialects. By Prince Louis Lucien Bonaparte (with Two Maps), Index, etc. Part I., 6*s.*; Part II., 6*s.*; Part III., 2*s.*

For 1877 8–9: containing the President's (Henry Sweet, Esq.) Sixth and Seventh Annual Addresses. 1. Accadian Phonology, by Professor A. H. Sayce; 2. On *Here* and *There* in Chaucer, by Dr. R. Weymouth; 3. The Grammar of the Dialect of West Somerset, by F. T. Elworthy, Esq.; 4. English Metre, by Professor J. B. Mayor; 5. The Malagasy Language, by the Rev. W. E. Cousins; 6. The Anglo-Cymric Score, by A. J. Ellis, Esq., F.R.S. 8vo. Part I., 3*s.*; Part II., 7*s.*

The Society's Extra Volumes.

Early English Volume, 1862-64, containing: 1. Liber Cure Cocorum, A.D. *c.* 1440. -2. Hampole's (Richard Rolle) Pricke of Conscience, A.D. *c.* 1340.—3. The Castell off Love, A.D. *c.* 1320. 8vo. cloth. 1865. £1.

Or separately: Liber Cure Cocorum, Edited by Rich. Morris, 3*s.*; Hampole's (Rolle) Pricke of Conscience, edited by Rich. Morris, 12*s.*; and The Castell off Love, edited by Dr. R. F. Weymouth, 6*s.*

Philological Society (Transactions of the)—*continued.*

Dan Michel's Ayenbite of Inwyt, or Remorse of Conscience, in the Kentish Dialect, A.D. 1340. From the Autograph MS. in Brit. Mus. Edited with Introduction, Marginal Interpretations, and Glossarial Index, by Richard Morris. 8vo. cloth. 1866. 12*s.*

Levins's (Peter, A.D. 1570) Manipulus Vocabulorum: a Rhyming Dictionary of the English Language. With an Alphabetical Index by H. B. Wheatley. 8vo. cloth. 1867. 16*s.*

Skeat's (Rev. W. W.) Mœso-Gothic Glossary, with an Introduction, an Outline of Mœso-Gothic Grammar, and a List of Anglo-Saxon and old and modern English Words etymologically connected with Mœso-Gothic. 1868. 8vo. cl. 9*s.*

Ellis (A. J.) on Early English Pronunciation, with especial Reference to Shakspere and Chaucer: containing an Investigation of the Correspondence of Writing with Speech in England from the Anglo-Saxon Period to the Present Day, etc. 4 parts. 8vo. 1869–75. £2.

Mediæval Greek Texts: A Collection of the Earliest Compositions in Vulgar Greek, prior to A.D. 1500. With Prolegomena and Critical Notes by W. Wagner. Part I. Seven Poems, three of which appear for the first time. 1870. 8vo. 10*s.* 6*d.*

Phillips.—THE DOCTRINE OF ADDAI THE APOSTLE Now first Edited in a Complete Form in the Original Syriac, with an English Translation and Notes. By GEORGE PHILLIPS, D.D., President of Queen's College, Cambridge. 8vo. pp. 122, cloth. 7*s.* 6*d.*

Picard.—A NEW POCKET DICTIONARY OF THE ENGLISH AND DUTCH LANGUAGES. By H. PICARD. Revised and augmented by A. B. MAATJES and H. J. VOGIN. Fifth edition. Small 4to. cloth, pp. xvi. and 1186. 1877. 10*s.*

Pimentel.—CUADRO DESCRIPTIVO Y COMPARATIVO DE LAS LENGUAS INDIGENAS DE MÉXICO, o Tratado de Filologia Mexicana. Par FRANCISCO PIMENTEL. 2 Edicion unica completa. 3 Volsume 8vo. *Mexico,* 1875. £2 2*s.*

Pischel.—HEMACANDRA'S GRAMMATIK DER PRÂKRITSPRACHEN (Siddhahemacandram Adhyâya VIII.) mit Kritischen und Erläuternden Anmerkungen. Herausgegeben von RICHARD PISCHEL. Part I. Text und Wörtverzeichniss. 8vo. pp. xiv. and 236. 8*s.*

Pope.—A TAMIL HANDBOOK; or, Full Introduction to the Common Dialect of that Language, on the plan of Ollendorff and Arnold. With copious Vocabularies, Appendices, containing Reading Lessons, Analyses of Letters, Deeds, Complaints, Official Documents, and a Key to the Exercises. By Rev. G. U. POPE. Third edition, 8vo. cloth, pp. iv. and 388. 21*s.*

Prakrita-Prakasa; or, The Prakrit Grammar of Vararuchi, with the Commentary (Manorama) of Bhamaha. The first complete edition of the Original Text with Various Readings from a Collation of Six Manuscripts in the Bodleian Library at Oxford, and the Libraries of the Royal Asiatic Society and the East India House; with copious Notes, an English Translation, and Index of Prakrit words, to which is prefixed an easy Introduction to Prakrit Grammar. By E. B. COWELL. Second issue, with new Preface, and corrections. 8vo. pp. xxxii. and 204. 14*s.*

Priaulx.—QUÆSTIONES MOSAICÆ; or, the first part of the Book of Genesis compared with the remains of ancient religions. By OSMOND DE BEAUVOIR PRIAULX. 8vo. pp. viii. and 548, cloth. 12*s.*

Rámáyan of Válmiki.—5 vols. See under GRIFFITH.

Ram Jasan.—A SANSKRIT AND ENGLISH DICTIONARY. Being an Abridgment of Professor Wilson's Dictionary. With an Appendix explaining the use of Affixes in Sanskrit. By Pandit RAM JASAN, Queen's College, Benares. Published under the Patronage of the Government, N.W.P. Royal 8vo. cloth, pp. ii. and 707. 28*s.*

Ram Raz.—ESSAY on the ARCHITECTURE of the HINDUS. By RAM RAZ, Native Judge and Magistrate of Bangalore. With 48 plates. 4to. pp. xiv. and 64, sewed. London, 1834. £2 2*s.*

Rask.—A GRAMMAR OF THE ANGLO-SAXON TONGUE. From the Danish of Erasmus Rask, Professor of Literary History in, and Librarian to, the University of Copenhagen, etc. By BENJAMIN THORPE. Second edition, corrected and improved. 18mo. pp. 200, cloth. 5*s.* 6*d.*

Rawlinson.—A COMMENTARY ON THE CUNEIFORM INSCRIPTIONS OF BABYLONIA AND ASSYRIA, including Readings of the Inscription on the Nimrud Obelisk, and Brief Notice of the Ancient Kings of Nineveh and Babylon, by Major H. C. RAWLINSON. 8vo. pp. 84, sewed. London, 1850. 2*s.* 6*d.*

Rawlinson.—OUTLINES OF ASSYRIAN HISTORY, from the Inscriptions of Nineveh. By Lieut. Col. RAWLINSON, C.B., followed by some Remarks by A. H. LAYARD, Esq., D.C.L. 8vo., pp. xliv., sewed. London, 1852. 1*s.*

Rawlinson.—INSCRIPTION OF TIGLATH PILESER I., KING OF ASSYRIA, B.C. 1150, as translated by Sir H. RAWLINSON, FOX TALBOT, Esq., Dr. HINCKS, and Dr. OPPERT. Published by the Royal Asiatic Society. 8vo. sd., pp. 74. 2*s.*

Rawlinson.—NOTES ON THE EARLY HISTORY OF BABYLONIA. By Colonel RAWLINSON, C.B. 8vo. sd., pp. 48. 1*s.*

Redhouse.—THE TURKISH CAMPAIGNER'S VADE-MECUM OF OTTOMAN COLLOQUIAL LANGUAGE; containing a concise Ottoman Grammar; a carefully selected Vocabulary, alphabetically arranged, in two parts, English and Turkish, and Turkish and English: also a few Familiar Dialogues; the whole in English characters. By J. W. REDHOUSE, F.R.A.S. Oblong 32mo. limp cloth, pp. iv. and 332. 6*s.*

Redhouse.—كتاب لهجة المعانى لجيمس رد حاوس الانكليزى. A Lexicon English and Turkish, showing in Turkish the Literal, Incidental, Figurative, Colloquial, and Technical Significations of the English Terms, indicating their pronunciation in a new and systematic manner, and preceded by a Sketch of English Etymology to facilitate to Turkish Students the acquisition of the English Language. By J. W. REDHOUSE, M.R.A.S. Second edition, pp. xvii. and 827. 15*s.*

Redhouse.—A VINDICATION OF THE OTTOMAN SULTAN'S TITLE TO "CALIPH," showing its Antiquity, Validity, and Universal Acceptance. By J. W. REDHOUSE. 8vo. paper, pp. 20. 3*d.*

Renan.—AN ESSAY ON THE AGE AND ANTIQUITY OF THE BOOK OF NABATHÆAN AGRICULTURE. To which is added an Inaugural Lecture on the Position of the Shemitic Nations in the History of Civilization. By M. ERNEST RENAN, Membre de l'Institut. Crown 8vo., pp. xvi. and 148, cloth. 3*s.* 6*d.*

Revue Celtique (The).—A Quarterly Magazine for Celtic Philology, Literature, and History. Edited with the assistance of the Chief Celtic Scholars of the British Islands and of the Continent, and Conducted by H. GAIDOZ. 8vo. Subscription, £1 per Volume.

Rhys.—LECTURES ON WELSH PHILOLOGY. By JOHN RHYS, M.A., Professor of Celtic at Oxford. Second edition, revised and enlarged. Crown 8vo. cloth, pp. viii. and 466. 15*s.*

Rig-Veda.—*See* Müller.

Rig-Veda-Sanhita: The Sacred Hymns of the Brahmans. Translated and explained by F. Max Müller, M.A., LL.D., Fellow of All Souls' College, Professor of Comparative Philology at Oxford, Foreign Member of the Institute of France, etc., etc. Vol. I. Hymns to the Maruts, or the Storm-Gods. 8vo. pp. clii. and 264. cloth. 1869. 12*s.* 6*d.*

Rig-Veda Sanhita.—A Collection of Ancient Hindu Hymns. Constituting the First Ashtaka, or Book of the Rig-veda; the oldest authority for the religious and social institutions of the Hindus. Translated from the Original Sanskrit by the late H. H. Wilson, M.A. 2nd Ed., with a Postscript by Dr. Fitzedward Hall. Vol. I. 8vo. cloth, pp. lii. and 348, price 21*s.*

Rig-Veda Sanhita.—A Collection of Ancient Hindu Hymns, constituting the Fifth to Eighth Ashtakas, or books of the Rig-Veda, the oldest Authority for the Religious and Social Institutions of the Hindus. Translated from the Original Sanskrit by the late Horace Hayman Wilson, M.A., F.R.S., etc. Edited by E. B. Cowell, M.A., Principal of the Calcutta Sanskrit College. Vol. IV., 8vo., pp. 214, cloth. 14*s.*

A few copies of Vols. II. and III. still left. [*Vols. V. and VI. in the Press.*

Riola.—How to Learn Russian. A Manual for Students of Russian, based upon the Ollendorfian system of teaching languages, and adapted for self instruction. By Henry Riola, Teacher of the Russian Language. With a Preface by W. R. S. Ralston, M.A. Crown 8vo. cloth, pp. 576. 1878. 12*s.*

Key to the above. Crown 8vo. cloth, pp. 126. 1878. 5*s.*

Roberts.—Aryan Philology, according to the most recent Researches (Glottologia Aria Recentissima), Remarks Historical and Critical. By Domenico Pezzi, Membro della Facolta de Filosofia e lettere della R. Universit. di Torino. Translated by E. S. Roberts, M.A., Fellow and Tutor of Gonville and Caius College. Crown 8vo. cloth, pp. xvi. and 199. 6*s.*

Roe and Fryer.—Travels in India in the Seventeenth Century. By Sir Thomas Roe and Dr. John Fryer. Reprinted from the "Calcutta Weekly Englishman." 8vo. cloth, pp. 474. 7*s.* 6*d.*

Rœhrig.—The Shortest Road to German. Designed for the use of both Teachers and Students. By F. L. O. Rœhrig. Cr. 8vo. cloth, pp. vii. and 225. 1874. 7*s.* 6*d.*

Rogers.—Notice on the Dinars of the Abbasside Dynasty. By Edward Thomas Rogers, late H.M. Consul, Cairo. 8vo. pp. 44, with a Map and four Autotype Plates. 5*s.*

Rosny.—A Grammar of the Chinese Language. By Professor Leon de Rosny. 8vo. pp. 48. 1874. 3*s.*

Ross.—A Mandarin Primer. Being Easy Lessons for Beginners, Transliterated according to the European mode of using Roman Letters. By Rev. John Ross, Newchang. 8vo. wrapper, pp. 122. 6*s.*

Ross—A Corean Primer. Being Lessons in Corean on all Ordinary Subjects. Transliterated on the principles of the Mandarin Primer by the same author. By the Rev. John Ross, Newchang. Demy 8vo. stitched. pp. 90. 10*s.*

Routledge.—English Rule and Native Opinion in India. From Notes taken in the years 1870–74. By James Routledge. Post 8vo. cloth, pp. 344. 10*s.* 6*d.*

Royal Society of Literature of the United Kingdom (Transactions of The). First Series, 6 Parts in 3 Vols., 4to., Plates; 1827–39. Second Series, 10 Vols. or 30 Parts, and Vol. XI. Parts 1 and 2, 8vo., Plates; 1843–76.

A complete set, as far as published, £10 10*s*. Very scarce. The first series of this important series of contributions of many of the most eminent men of the day has long been out of print and is very scarce. Of the Second Series, Vol. I.–IV., each containing three parts, are quite out of print, and can only be had in the complete series, noticed above. Three Numbers, price 4*s*. 6*d*. each, form a volume. The price of the volume complete, bound in cloth, is 13*s*. 6*d*.

Separate Publications.

I. Fasti Monastici Aevi Saxonici: or an Alphabetical List of the Heads of Religious Houses in England previous to the Norman Conquest, to which is prefixed a Chronological Catalogue of Contemporary Foundations. By Walter de Gray Birch. Royal 8vo. cloth. 1872. 7*s*. 6*d*.

II. Li Chantari di Lancellotto; a Troubadour's Poem of the XIV. Cent. Edited from a MS. in the possession of the Royal Society of Literature, by Walter de Gray Birch. Royal 8vo. cloth. 1874. 7*s*.

III. Inquisitio Comitatus Cantabrigiensis, nunc primum, è Manuscripto unico in Bibliothecâ Cottoniensi asservato, typis mandata: subjicitur Inquisitio Eliensis: curâ N. E. S. A. Hamilton. Royal 4to. With map and 3 facsimiles. 1876. £2 2*s*.

IV. A Commonplace-Book of John Milton. Reproduced by the autotype process from the original MS. in the possession of Sir Fred. U. Graham, Bart., of Netherby Hall. With an Introduction by A. J. Horwood. Sq. folio. Only one hundred copies printed. 1876. £2 2*s*.

V. Chronicon Adæ de Usk, A.D. 1377–1404. Edited, with a Translation and Notes, by Ed. Maunde Thompson. Royal 8vo. 1876. 10*s*. 6*d*.

Rudy.—The Chinese Mandarin Language, after Ollendorff's New Method of Learning Languages. By Charles Rudy. In 3 Volumes. Vol. I. Grammar. 8vo. pp. 248. £1 1*s*.

Sabdakalpadruma, the well-known Sanskrit Dictionary of Rajáh Radhakanta Deva. In Bengali characters. 4to. Parts 1 to 40. (In course of publication.) 3*s*. 6*d*. each part.

Sakuntala.—Kâlidâsa's Çakuntalâ. The Bengalí Recension. With Critical Notes. Edited by Richard Pischel. 8vo. cloth, pp. xi. and 210. 14*s*.

Sakuntala.—A Sanskrit Drama in Seven Acts. Edited by Monier Williams, M.A. Second Edition. 8vo. cl. £1 1*s*.

Sale.—The Koran; commonly called The Alcoran of Mohammed. Translated into English immediately from the original Arabic. By George Sale, Gent. To which is prefixed the Life of Mohammed. Crown 8vo. cloth, pp. 472. 7*s*.

Sâma-Vidhâna-Brâhmana. With the Commentary of Sâyana. Edited, with Notes, Translation, and Index, by A. C. Burnell, M.R.A.S. Vol. I. Text and Commentary. With Introduction. 8vo. cloth, pp. xxxviii. and 104. 12*s*. 6*d*.

Sanskrit Works.—A Catalogue of Sanskrit Works Printed in India, offered for Sale at the affixed nett prices by Trübner & Co. 16mo. pp. 52. 1*s*.

Sarva-Sabda-Sambodhini; or, The Complete Sanskrit Dictionary. In Telugu characters. 4to. cloth, pp. 1078. £2 15*s*.

Satow.—An English Japanese Dictionary of the Spoken Language. By Ernest Mason Satow, Japanese Secretary to H.M. Legation at Yedo, and Ishibashi Masakata, of the Imperial Japanese Foreign Office. Imp. 32mo., pp. xx. and 366, cloth. 12*s*.

Sayce.—AN ASSYRIAN GRAMMAR FOR COMPARATIVE PURPOSES. By A. H. SAYCE, M.A. 12mo. cloth, pp. xvi. and 188. 7*s*. 6*d*.

Sayce.—THE PRINCIPLES OF COMPARATIVE PHILOLOGY. By A. H. SAYCE, Fellow and Tutor of Queen's College, Oxford. Second Edition. Cr. 8vo. cl., pp. xxxii. and 416. 10*s*. 6*d*.

Scarborough.—A COLLECTION OF CHINESE PROVERBS. Translated and Arranged by WILLIAM SCARBOROUGH, Wesleyan Missionary, Hankow. With an Introduction, Notes, and Copious Index. Cr. 8vo. pp. xliv. and 278. 10*s*.6*d*.

Schleicher.—COMPENDIUM OF THE COMPARATIVE GRAMMAR OF THE INDO-EUROPEAN, SANSKRIT, GREEK, AND LATIN LANGUAGES. By AUGUST SCHLEICHER. Translated from the Third German Edition by HERBERT BENDALL, B.A., Chr. Coll. Camb. Part I. Grammar. 8vo. cloth, pp. 184. 7*s*. 6*d*.

Part II. Morphology. 8vo. cloth, pp. viii. and 104. 6*s*.

Schemeil.—EL MUBTAKER; or, First Born. (In Arabic, printed at Beyrout). Containing Five Comedies, called Comedies of Fiction, on Hopes and Judgments, in Twenty-six Poems of 1092 Verses, showing the Seven Stages of Life, from man's conception unto his death and burial. By EMIN IBRAHIM SCHEMEIL. In one volume, 4to. pp. 166, sewed. 1870. 5*s*.

Schlagintweit.—BUDDHISM IN TIBET. Illustrated by Literary Documents and Objects of Religious Worship. With an Account of the Buddhist Systems preceding it in India. By EMIL SCHLAGINTWEIT, LL.D. With a Folio Atlas of 20 Plates, and 20 Tables of Native Prints in the Text. Royal 8vo., pp. xxiv. and 404. £2 2*s*.

Schlagintweit.—GLOSSARY OF GEOGRAPHICAL TERMS FROM INDIA AND TIBET, with Native Transcription and Transliteration. By HERMANN DE SCHLAGINTWEIT. Forming, with a "Route Book of the Western Himalaya, Tibet, and Turkistan," the Third Volume of H., A., and R. DE SCHLAGINTWEIT'S "Results of a Scientific Mission to India and High Asia." With an Atlas in imperial folio, of Maps, Panoramas, and Views. Royal 4to., pp. xxiv. and 293. £4.

Semitic (Songs of The). In English Verse. By G. E. W. Cr. 8vo. cloth, pp. 140. 5*s*.

Shakspere Society (The New).—Subscription £1 1*s*. per annum. List of publications on application.

Shápurjí Edaljí.—A GRAMMAR OF THE GUJARÁTÍ LANGUAGE. By SHÁPURJÍ EDALJÍ. Cloth, pp. 127. 10*s*. 6*d*.

Shápurjí Edaljí.—A DICTIONARY, GUJRATI AND ENGLISH. By SHÁPURJÍ EDALJÍ. Second Edition. Crown 8vo. cloth, pp. xxiv. and 874. 21*s*.

Shaw.—A SKETCH OF THE TURKI LANGUAGE. As Spoken in Eastern Turkistan (Kàshghar and Yarkand). By ROBERT BARKLAY SHAW, F.R.G.S., Political Agent. In Two Parts. With Lists of Names of Birds and Plants by J. SCULLY, Surgeon, H.M. Bengal Army. 8vo. sewed, Part I., pp. 130. 7*s*. 6*d*.

Sherring—THE SACRED CITY OF THE HINDUS. An Account of Benares in Ancient and Modern Times. By the Rev. M. A. SHERRING, M.A., LL.D.; and Prefaced with an Introduction by FITZEDWARD HALL, Esq., D.C.L. 8vo. cloth, pp. xxxvi. and 388, with numerous full-page illustrations. 21*s*.

Sherring.—THE HINDOO PILGRIMS. By the Rev. M. A. SHERRING, Fcap. 8vo. cloth, pp. vi. and 125. 5*s*.

Singh.—SAKHEE BOOK; or, The Description of Gooroo Gobind Singh's Religion and Doctrines, translated from Gooroo Mukhi into Hindi, and afterwards into English. By SIRDAR ATTAR SINGH, Chief of Bhadour. With the author's photograph. 8vo. pp. xviii. and 205. 15*s*.

Skeat.—A List of English Words, the Etymology of which is illustrated by Comparison with Icelandic. Prepared in the form of an Appendix to Cleasby and Vigfusson's Icelandic-English Dictionary. By the Rev. Walter W. Skeat, M.A., English Lecturer and late Fellow of Christ's College, Cambridge; and M.A. of Exeter College, Oxford; one of the Vice-Presidents of the Cambridge Philological Society; and Member of the Council of the Philological Society of London. 1876. Demy 4to. sewed. 2*s*.

Smith.—A Vocabulary of Proper Names in Chinese and English. of Places, Persons, Tribes, and Sects, in China, Japan, Corea, Assam, Siam, Burmah, The Straits, and adjacent Countries. By F. Porter Smith, M.B., London, Medical Missionary in Central China. 4to. half-bound, pp. vi., 72, and x. 1870. 10*s*. 6*d*.

Smith.—Contributions towards the Materia Medica and Natural History of China. For the use of Medical Missionaries and Native Medical Students. By F. Porter Smith, M.B. London, Medical Missionary in Central China. Imp. 4to. cloth, pp. viii. and 240. 1870. £1 1*s*.

Sophocles.—A Glossary of Later and Byzantine Greek. By E. A. Sophocles. 4to., pp. iv. and 624, cloth. £2 2*s*.

Sophocles.—Romaic or Modern Greek Grammar. By E. A. Sophocles. 8vo. pp. xxviii. and 196.

Sophocles.—Greek Lexicon of the Roman and Byzantine Periods (from B.C. 146 to A.D. 1100). By E. A. Sophocles. Imp. 8vo. pp. xvi. 1188, cloth. 1870. £2 10*s*.

Spurrell.—A Grammar of the Welsh Language. By William Spurrell. 3rd Edition. Fcap. cloth, pp. viii.-206. 1870. 3*s*.

Spurrell.—A Welsh Dictionary. English-Welsh and Welsh-English. With Preliminary Observations on the Elementary Sounds of the English Language, a copious Vocabulary of the Roots of English Words, a list of Scripture Proper Names and English Synonyms and Explanations. By William Spurrell. Third Edition. Fcap. cloth, pp. xxv. and 732. 8*s*. 6*d*.

Steele.—An Eastern Love Story. Kusa Játakaya: a Buddhistic Legendary Poem, with other Stories. By Thomas Steele, Ceylon Civil Service. Crown 8vo. cloth, pp. xii. and 260. 1871. 6*s*.

Steere.—Short Specimens of the Vocabularies of Three Unpublished African Languages (Gindo, Zaramo, and Angazidja). Collected by Edward Steere, LL.D. 12mo. pp. 20. 6*d*.

Steere.—Collections for a Handbook of the Nyamwezi Language, as spoken at Unyanyembe. By Edward Steere, LL.D. Fcap. cloth, pp. 100. 1*s*. 6*d*.

Stent.—The Jade Chaplet, in Twenty-four Beads. A Collection of Songs, Ballads, etc. (from the Chinese). By George Carter Stent, M.N.C.B.R.A.S., Author of "Chinese and English Vocabulary," "Chinese and English Pocket Dictionary," "Chinese Lyrics," "Chinese Legends," etc. Cr. 8o. cloth, pp. 176. 5*s*.

Stent.—A Chinese and English Vocabulary in the Pekinese Dialect. By G. E. Stent. 8vo. pp. ix. and 677. 1871. £1 10*s*.

Stent.—A Chinese and English Pocket Dictionary. By G. E. Stent. 16mo. pp. 250. 1874. 10*s*. 6*d*.

Stoddard.—Grammar of the Modern Syriac Language, as spoken in Oroomiah, Persia, and in Koordistan. By Rev. D. T. Stoddard, Missionary of the American Board in Persia. Demy 8vo. bds., pp. 190. 10*s*. 6*d*.

Stokes.—Beunans Meriasek. The Life of Saint Meriasek, Bishop and Confessor. A Cornish Drama. Edited, with a Translation and Notes, by Whitley Stokes. Medium 8vo. cloth, pp. xvi., 280, and Facsimile. 1872. 15s.

Stokes.—Goidelica—Old and Early-Middle Irish Glosses: Prose and Verse. Edited by Whitley Stokes. Second edition. Medium 8vo. cloth, pp. 192. 18s.

Strangford.—Original Letters and Papers of the late Viscount Strangford, upon Philological and Kindred Subjects. Edited by Viscountess Strangford. Post 8vo. cloth, pp. xxii. and 284. 1878. 12s. 6d.

Stratmann.—A Dictionary of the Old English Language. Compiled from the writings of the xiiith, xivth, and xvth centuries. By Francis Henry Stratmann. Third Edition. 4to. In wrapper. £1 10s.

Stratmann.—An Old English Poem of the Owl and the Nightingale. Edited by Francis Henry Stratmann. 8vo. cloth, pp. 60. 3s.

Strong.—Selections from the Bostan of Sadi, translated into English Verse. By Dawsonne Melancthon Strong, Captain H.M. 10th Bengal Lancers. 12mo. cloth, pp. ii. and 56. 2s. 6d.

Sunjana.—A Grammar of the Pahlvi Language, with Quotations and Examples from Original Works and a Glossary of Words bearing affinity with the Semitic Languages. By Peshotun Dustoor Behramjee Sunjana, Principal of Sir Jamsetjee Jejeeboy Zurthosi Madressa. 8vo. cl., pp. 18–457. 25s.

Surya-Siddhanta (Translation of the).—*See* Whitney.

Sweet.—A History of English Sounds, from the Earliest Period, including an Investigation of the General Laws of Sound Change, and full Word Lists. By Henry Sweet. Demy 8vo. cloth, pp. iv. and 164. 4s. 6d.

Syed Ahmad.—A Series of Essays on the Life of Mohammed, and Subjects subsidiary thereto. By Syed Ahmad Khan Bahador, C.S.I., Author of the "Mohammedan Commentary on the Holy Bible," Honorary Member of the Royal Asiatic Society, and Life Honorary Secretary to the Allygurh Scientific Society. 8vo. pp. 532, with 4 Genealogical Tables, 2 Maps, and a Coloured Plate, handsomely bound in cloth. £1 10s.

Syro-Egyptian Society.—Original Papers read before the Syro-Egyptian Society of London. Volume I. Part 1. 8vo. sewed, 2 plates and a map, pp. 144. 3s. 6d.

Including, among other papers, Remarks on the Obelisks of Ancient Egypt. By W. H. Yates, M.D.—Notes on the Hieroglyphics of Horapollo Nilous. By S. Sharpe.—Remarks on the Wedge Inscription recently discovered on the Upper Euphrates. By G. F. Grotefend, Ph.D. (With a Copy of the Original Inscription).

Táittiríya-PrATIçakhya.—See Whitney.

Tarkavachaspati.—Vachaspatya, a Comprehensive Dictionary, in Ten Parts. Compiled by Taranatha Tarkavachaspati, Professor of Grammar and Philosophy in the Government Sanskrit College of Calcutta. An Alphabetically Arranged Dictionary, with a Grammatical Introduction and Copious Citations from the Grammarians and Scholiasts, from the Vedas, etc. Parts I. to VII. 4to. paper. 1873–6. 18s. each Part.

Technologial Dictionary.—Pocket Dictionary of Technical Terms used in Arts and Sciences. English-German-French. Based on the larger Work by Karmarsch. 3 vols. imp. 16mo. cloth. 12s.

Technological Dictionary of the terms employed in the Arts and Sciences; Architecture, Civil, Military and Naval; Civil Engineering, including Bridge Building, Road and Railway Making; Mechanics; Machine and Engine Making; Shipbuilding and Navigation; Metallurgy, Mining and Smelting; Artillery; Mathematics; Physics; Chemistry; Mineralogy, etc. With a Preface by Dr. K. Karmarsch. Second Edition. 3 vols.

Vol. I. English—German—French. 8vo. cloth, pp. 666. 12*s.*

Vol. II. German—English—French. 8vo. cloth, pp. 646. 12*s.*

Vol. III. French—German—English. 8vo. cloth, pp. 618. 12*s.*

The Boke of Nurture. By John Russell, about 1460–1470 Anno Domini. The Boke of Keruynge. By Wynkyn de Worde, Anno Domini 1513. The Boke of Nurture. By Hugh Rhodes, Anno Domini 1577. Edited from the Originals in the British Museum Library, by Frederick J. Furnivall, M.A., Trinity Hall, Cambridge, Member of Council of the Philological and Early English Text Societies. 4to. half-morocco, gilt top, pp. xix. and 146, 28, xxviii. and 56. 1867. 1*l.* 11*s.* 6*d.*

Thibaut.—The Súlvasútras. English Translation, with an Introduction. By G. Thibaut, Ph.D., Anglo-Sanskrit Professor Benares College. 8vo. cloth, pp. 47, with 4 Plates. 5*s.*

Thibaut.—Contributions to the Explanation of Jyotisha-Vedânga. By G. Thibaut, Ph.D. 8vo. pp. 27. 1*s.* 6*d.*

Thomas.—Early Sassanian Inscriptions, Seals and Coins, illustrating the Early History of the Sassanian Dynasty, containing Proclamations of Ardeshir Babek, Sapor I., and his Successors. With a Critical Examination and Explanation of the Celebrated Inscription in the Hájiábad Cave, demonstrating that Sapor, the Conqueror of Valerian, was a Professing Christian. By Edward Thomas, F.R.S. Illustrated. 8vo. cloth, pp. 148. 7*s.* 6*d.*

Thomas.—The Chronicles of the Pathán Kings of Dehli. Illustrated by Coins, Inscriptions, and other Antiquarian Remains. By Edward Thomas, F.R.S., late of the East India Company's Bengal Civil Service. With numerous Copperplates and Woodcuts. Demy 8vo. cloth, pp. xxiv. and 467. 1871. £1 8*s.*

Thomas.—The Revenue Resources of the Mughal Empire in India, from a.d. 1593 to a.d. 1707. A Supplement to "The Chronicles of the Pathán Kings of Delhi." By Edward Thomas, F.R.S. Demy 8vo., pp. 60, cloth. 3*s.* 6*d.*

Thomas.—Comments on Recent Pehlvi Decipherments. With an Incidental Sketch of the Derivation of Aryan Alphabets, and contributions to the Early History and Geography of Tabaristán. Illustrated by Coins. By Edward Thomas, F.R.S. 8vo. pp. 56, and 2 plates, cloth, sewed. 3*s.* 6*d.*

Thomas.—Sassanian Coins. Communicated to the Numismatic Society of London. By E. Thomas, F.R.S. Two parts. With 3 Plates and a Woodcut. 12mo, sewed, pp. 43. 5*s.*

Thomas.—Records of the Gupta Dynasty. Illustrated by Inscriptions, Written History, Local Tradition and Coins. To which is added a Chapter on the Arabs in Sind. By Edward Thomas, F.R.S. Folio, with a Plate, handsomely bound in cloth, pp. iv. and 64. Price 14*s.*

Thomas.—Jainism; or, The Early Faith of Asoka. With Illustrations of the Ancient Religions of the East, from the Pantheon of the Indo-Scythians. To which is added a Notice on Bactrian Coins and Indian Dates. By Edward Thomas, F.R.S. 8vo. pp. viii., 24 and 82. With two Autotype Plates and Woodcuts. 7*s.* 6*d.*

Thomas.—The Theory and Practice of Creole Grammar. By J. J. Thomas. Port of Spain (Trinidad), 1869. 1 vol. 8vo. bds. pp. viii. and 135. 12*s.*

Thorburn.—Bannú; or, Our Afghán Frontier. By S. S. Thorburn, I.C.S., Settlement Officer of the Bannú District. 8vo. cloth, pp. x. and 480. 18*s.*

Thorpe.—Diplomatarium Anglicum Ævi Saxonici. A Collection of English Charters, from the reign of King Æthelberht of Kent, A.D., DCV., to that of William the Conqueror. Containing: I. Miscellaneous Charters. II. Wills. III. Guilds. IV. Manumissions and Acquittances. With a Translation of the Anglo-Saxon. By the late Benjamin Thorpe, Member of the Royal Academy of Sciences at Munich, and of the Society of Netherlandish Literature at Leyden. 8vo. pp. xlii. and 682, cloth. 1865. £1 1*s.*

Tiele.—Outlines of the History of Religion to the Spread of the Universal Religions. By C. P. Tiele, Dr. Theol. Professor of the History of Religions in the University of Leiden. Translated from the Dutch by J. Estlin Carpenter, M.A. Post 8vo. cloth, pp. xix. and 249. 7*s.* 6*d.*

Tindall.—A Grammar and Vocabulary of the Namaqua-Hottentot Language. By Henry Tindall, Wesleyan Missionary. 8vo. pp. 124, sewed. 6*s.*

Trübner's Bibliotheca Sanscrita. A Catalogue of Sanskrit Literature, chiefly printed in Europe. To which is added a Catalogue of Sanskrit Works printed in India; and a Catalogue of Pali Books. Constantly for sale by Trübner & Co. Cr. 8vo. sd., pp. 84. 2*s.* 6*d.*

Trübner's Oriental Series.

I. Essays on the Sacred Language, Writings, and Religion of the Parsis. By Martin Haug, Ph.D. late Professor of Sanskrit and Comparative Philology at the University of Munich. Edited by Dr. E. W. West. Second Edition. Post 8vo. cloth, pp. xvi. and 428. 1878. 16*s.*

II. Texts from the Buddhist Canon, commonly known as Dhammapada. With accompanying Narratives. Translated from the Chinese by S. Beal, B.A., Professor of Chinese, University College, London. Post 8vo. cloth, pp. viii. and 176. 1878. 7*s.* 6*d.*

III. The History of Indian Literature. By Albrecht Weber. Translated from the German by John Mann, M.A., and Theodor Zachariae, Ph.D., with the sanction of the Author. Post 8vo. cloth, pp. xxiii. and 360. 1878. 18*s.*

IV. A Sketch of the Modern Languages of the East Indies. By Robert Cust. Accompanied by Two Language Maps. Post 8vo. cloth, pp. xii. and 198. 1878. 12*s.*

V. The Birth of the War God. A Poem by Kálidása. Translated from the Sanskrit into English Verse. By Ralph T. H. Griffith, M.A., Principal of Benares College. Second Edition. Post 8vo. cloth, pp. xii.-116. 1879. 5*s.*

The following Works are in Preparation.

A Classical Dictionary of Hindu Mythology and History, Geography and Literature. By John Dowson, M.R.A.S., late Professor in the Staff College. In One Volume, post 8vo., about 500 pages, price not to exceed 21*s.*

Selections from the Ku-ran. With a Commentary. Translated by the late Edward William Lane, Author of an "Arabic-English Lexicon," etc. A New Edition, Revised, with an Introduction on the History and Development of Islam, especially with reference to India. By Stanley Lane Poole. Post 8vo. cloth.

Passages Religious, Moral, Prudential, and Narrative, from the Mahabharata and other Sanskrit Works. Freely Translated or Paraphrased in English Verses. With an Appendix containing Prose Versions of the Original Texts. By John Muir, LL.D. Post 8vo. cloth.

Trübner's Oriental Series—*continued.*

ORIENTAL RELIGIONS in their Relation to Universal Religion. By SAMUEL JOHNSON. First Section—India. Second Section—China. In Two Volumes, post 8vo. cloth.

MISCELLANEOUS ESSAYS Relating to Indian Subjects. By B. H. HODGSON, late British Minister at Nepal. In Two Volumes, post 8vo. cloth.

THE GULISTAN; or, Rose Garden of Shekh Mushliu'd-din Sadi of Shiraz. Translated for the first time into Prose and Verse, with an Introductory Preface, and a Life of the Author, from the Ātish Kadah, by EDWARD B. EASTWICK, F.R.S., M.R.A.S., etc. Second Edition, post 8vo. cloth.

THE JATAKA STORIES. With the Commentary and Collection of Buddhist Fairy Tales, Fables, and Folk Lore. Translated from the original Pali by T. W. RHYS DAVIDS. (The first part of the Commentary contains the most complete account we yet have of the Life of Buddha.) Vol. I., post 8vo. cloth.

CHINESE BUDDHISM. A Volume of Sketches, Historical and Critical. By J. EDKINS, D.D, Author of "China's Place in Philology," "Religion in China," etc., etc. Post 8vo. cloth.

BUDDHIST RECORDS OF THE WESTERN WORLD. Being the SI-YU-KI by HYEN THSANG. Translated from the original Chinese, with Introduction, Index, etc. By SAMUEL BEAL, Trinity College, Cambridge; Professor of Chinese, University College, London. In Two Vols., post 8vo. cloth.

THE POEMS OF HAFIZ OF SHIRAZ. Translated from the Persian into English Verse by E. H. PALMER, M.A., Professor of Arabic in the University of Cambridge. Post 8vo. cloth.

HISTORY OF THE PORTUGUESE IN INDIA. Based upon Documentary Evidence, now for the first time made available. By J. GERSON DA CUNHA, M.D. Post 8vo. cloth.

INDIAN TALES FROM THIBETAN SOURCES. Translated from the Thibetan into German by ANTON SCHIEFNER. Rendered into English, with Notes, by W. R. S. RALSTON. In One Volume, post 8vo.

ON THE VICISSITUDES OF ARYAN CIVILISATION IN INDIA. One of the Florence Prize Essays. By Dr. J. GERSON DA CUNHA. In Two Volumes, post 8vo.

Trumpp.—GRAMMAR OF THE PAṢTO, or Language of the Afghans, compared with the Irānian and North-Indian Idioms. By Dr. ERNEST TRUMPP. 8vo. sewed, pp. xvi. and 412. 21*s*.

Trumpp.—GRAMMAR OF THE SINDHI LANGUAGE. Compared with the Sanskrit-Prakrit and the Cognate Indian Vernaculars. By Dr. ERNEST TRUMPP. Printed by order of Her Majesty's Government for India. Demy 8vo. sewed, pp. xvi. and 590. 15*s*.

Van der Tuuk.—OUTLINES OF A GRAMMAR OF THE MALAGASY LANGUAGE By H. N. VAN DER TUUK. 8vo., pp. 28, sewed. 1*s*.

Van der Tuuk.—SHORT ACCOUNT OF THE MALAY MANUSCRIPTS BELONGING TO THE ROYAL ASIATIC SOCIETY. By H. N. VAN DER TUUK. 8vo., pp. 52. 2*s*. 6*d*.

Vedarthayatna (The); or, an Attempt to Interpret the Vedas. A Marathi and English Translation of the Rig Veda, with the Original Saṁhitâ and Pada Texts in Sanskrit. Parts I. to XXVIII. 8vo. pp. 1—896. Price 3*s*. 6*d*. each.

Vishnu-Purana (The); a System of Hindu Mythology and Tradition. Translated from the original Sanskrit, and Illustrated by Notes derived chiefly from other Purāṇas. By the late H. H. WILSON, M.A., F.R.S., Boden Professor of Sanskrit in the University of Oxford, etc., etc. Edited by FITZEDWARD

HALL. In 6 vols. 8vo. Vol. I. pp. cxl. and 200; Vol. II. pp. 343; Vol. III., pp. 348; Vol IV. pp. 346, cloth; Vol. V. Part I. pp. 392, cloth. 10*s.* 6*d.* each. Vol. V., Part 2, containing the Index, compiled by Fitzedward Hall. 8vo. cloth, pp. 268. 12*s.*

Vissering, W.—ON CHINESE CURRENCY. Coin and Paper Money. With Facsimile of a Bank Note. Royal 8vo. cloth, pp. xv. and 219. *Leiden,* 1877. 18*s.*

Wade.—YÜ-YEN TZŬ-ERH CHI. A progressive course designed to assist the Student of Colloquial Chinese, as spoken in the Capital and the Metropolitan Department. In eight parts, with Key, Syllabary, and Writing Exercises. By THOMAS FRANCIS WADE, C.B., Secretary to Her Britannic Majesty's Legation, Peking. 3 vols. 4to. Progressive Course, pp. xx. 296 and 16; Syllabary, pp. 126 and 36; Writing Exercises, pp. 48; Key, pp. 174 and 140, sewed. £4.

Wade.—WÊN-CHIEN TZŬ-ERH CHI. A series of papers selected as specimens of documentary Chinese, designed to assist Students of the language, as written by the officials of China. In sixteen parts, with Key. Vol. I. By THOMAS FRANCIS WADE, C.B., Secretary to Her Britannic Majesty's Legation at Peking. 4to., half-cloth, pp. xii. and 455; and iv., 72, and 52. £1 16*s.*

Wake.—CHAPTERS ON MAN. With the Outlines of a Science of comparative Psychology. By C. STANILAND WAKE, Fellow of the Anthropological Society of London. Crown 8vo. pp. viii. and 344, cloth. 7*s.* 6*d.*

Wake.—THE EVOLUTION OF MORALITY. Being a History of the Development of Moral Culture. By C. STANILAND WAKE, author of "Chapters on Man," etc. Two vols. 8vo. cloth, pp. xvi. and 506, xii. and 474. 21*s.*

Watson.—INDEX TO THE NATIVE AND SCIENTIFIC NAMES OF INDIAN AND OTHER EASTERN ECONOMIC PLANTS AND PRODUCTS, originally prepared under the authority of the Secretary of State for India in Council. By JOHN FORBES WATSON, M.A., M.D., F.L.S., F.R.A.S., etc., Reporter on the Products of India. Imperial 8vo., cloth, pp. 650. £1 11*s.* 6*d.*

Weber.—ON THE RÂMÂYANA. By Dr. ALBRECHT WEBER, Berlin. Translated from the German by the Rev. D. C. Boyd, M.A. Reprinted from "The Indian Antiquary." Fcap. 8vo. sewed, pp. 130. 5*s.*

Weber.—THE HISTORY OF INDIAN LITERATURE. By ALBRECHT WEBER. Translated from the German by JOHN MANN, M.A., and Dr. THEODOR ZACHARIAE, with the Author's sanction. Post 8vo. pp. xxiii. and 360, cloth, 1878. 18*s.*

Wedgwood.—A DICTIONARY OF ENGLISH ETYMOLOGY. By HENSLEIGH WEDGWOOD. Third Edition, thoroughly revised and enlarged. With an Introduction on the Formation of Language. Imperial 8vo., double column, pp. lxxii. and 746. 21*s.*

Wedgwood.—ON THE ORIGIN OF LANGUAGE. By HENSLEIGH WEDGWOOD, late Fellow of Christ's College, Cambridge. Fcap. 8vo. pp. 172, cloth. 3*s.* 6*d.*

West.—GLOSSARY AND INDEX OF THE PAHLAVI TEXTS OF THE BOOK OF Arda Viraf, The Tale of Gosht-I Fryano, The Hadokht Nask, and to some extracts from the Din-Kard and Nirangistan; prepared from Destur Hoshangji Asa's Glossary to the Arda Viraf Namak, and from the Original Texts, with Notes on Pahlavi Grammar. By E. W. WEST, Ph.D. Revised by MARTIN HAUG, Ph.D. Published by order of the Government of Bombay. 8vo. sewed, pp. viii. and 352. 25*s.*

West and Buhler.—A DIGEST OF THE HINDU LAW OF INHERITANCE and Partition, from the Replies of the Sâstris in the several Courts of the Bombay Presidency. With Introduction, Notes and Appendix. Edited by RAYMOND WEST and J. G. BUHLER. Second Edition. Demy 8vo. sewed, pp. 674. £1 11*s.* 6*d.*

Wheeler.—THE HISTORY OF INDIA FROM THE EARLIEST AGES. By J. TALBOYS WHEELER, Assistant Secretary to the Government of India in the Foreign Department, Secretary to the Indian Record Commission, author of "The Geography of Herodotus," etc. etc. Demy 8vo. cl.

Vol. I. The Vedic Period and the Maha Bharata. pp. lxxv. and 576.

Vol. II., The Ramayana and the Brahmanic Period. pp. lxxxviii. and 680, with two Maps. 21*s.*

Vol. III. Hindu, Buddhist, Brahmanical Revival. pp. 484, with two maps. 18*s.*

Vol. IV. Part I. Mussulman Rule. pp. xxxii. and 320. 14*s.*

Vol. IV. Part II. In the press.

Wheeler.—EARLY RECORDS OF BRITISH INDIA. A History of the English Settlement in India, as told in the Government Records, the works of old travellers and other contemporary Documents, from the earliest period down to the rise of British Power in India. By J. TALBOYS WHEELER. Royal 8vo. cloth, pp. xxxii. and 392. 1878. 15*s.*

Whitmee.—A GRAMMAR AND DICTIONARY OF THE SAMOAN LANGUAGE. By Rev. GEORGE PRATT, forty years a Missionary of the London Missionary Society in Samoa. Second Edition. Edited by Rev. S. J. WHITMEE, F.R.G.S. Crown 8vo. cloth, pp. 388. 18*s.*

Whitney.—ORIENTAL AND LINGUISTIC STUDIES. By WILLIAM DWIGHT WHITNEY, Professor of Sanskrit and Comparative Philology in Yale College. First Series. The Veda; the Avesta; the Science of Language. Cr. 8vo. cl., pp. x. and 418. 12*s.*

Second Series.—The East and West—Religion and Mythology—Orthography and Phonology—Hindú Astronomy. Crown 8vo. cloth, pp. 446. 12*s.*

Whitney.—ATHARVA VEDA PRÁTIÇÁKHYA; or, Çáunakíyá Caturádhyáyiká (The). Text, Translation, and Notes. By WILLIAM D. WHITNEY, Professor of Sanskrit in Yale College. 8vo. pp. 286, boards. £1 11*s.* 6*d.*

Whitney.—LANGUAGE AND THE STUDY OF LANGUAGE: Twelve Lectures on the Principles of Linguistic Science. By W. D. WHITNEY. Third Edition, augmented by an Analysis. Crown 8vo. cloth, pp. xii. and 504. 10*s.* 6*d.*

Whitney.—LANGUAGE AND ITS STUDY, with especial reference to the Indo-European Family of Languages. Seven Lectures by W. D. WHITNEY, Professor of Sanskrit, and Instructor in Modern Languages in Yale College. Edited with Introduction, Notes, Tables of Declension and Conjugation, Grimm's Law with Illustration, and an Index, by the Rev. R. MORRIS, M.A., LL.D. Cr. 8vo. cl., pp. xxii. and 318. 5*s.*

Whitney.—SURYA-SIDDHANTA (Translation of the): A Text-book of Hindu Astronomy, with Notes and an Appendix, containing additional Notes and Tables, Calculations of Eclipses, a Stellar Map, and Indexes. By W. D. WHITNEY. 8vo. pp. iv. and 354, boards. £1 11*s.* 6*d.*

Whitney.—TÁITTIRÍYA-PRÁTIÇÁKHYA, with its Commentary, the Tribhâshyaratna: Text, Translation, and Notes. By W. D. WHITNEY, Prof. of Sanskrit in Yale College, New Haven. 8vo. pp. 469. 1871. £1 5*s.*

Williams.—A DICTIONARY, ENGLISH AND SANSCRIT. By MONIER WILLIAMS, M.A. Published under the Patronage of the Honourable East India Company. 4to. pp. xii. 862, cloth. 1851. £3 3*s.*

Williams.—A SANSKRIT-ENGLISH DICTIONARY, Etymologically and Philologically arranged, with special reference to Greek, Latin, German, Anglo-Saxon, English, and other cognate Indo-European Languages. By MONIER WILLIAMS, M.A., Boden Professor of Sanskrit. 4to. cloth, pp. xxv. and 1186. £4 14*s.* 6*d.*

Williams.—A PRACTICAL GRAMMAR OF THE SANSKRIT LANGUAGE, arranged with reference to the Classical Languages of Europe, for the use of English Students, by MONIER WILLIAMS, M.A. 1877. Fourth Edition, Revised. 8vo. cloth. 15*s.*

Williams.—A SYLLABIC DICTIONARY OF THE CHINESE LANGUAGE, arranged according to the Wu-Fang Yuen Yin, with the pronunciation of the Characters as heard in Peking, Canton, Amoy, and Shanghai. By S. WELLS WILLIAMS. 4to. cloth, pp. lxxxiv. and 1252. 1874. £5 5*s.*

Williams.—FIRST LESSONS IN THE MAORI LANGUAGE. With a Short Vocabulary. By W. L. WILLIAMS, B.A. Fcap. 8vo. pp. 98, cloth. 5*s.*

Williams.—MODERN INDIA AND THE INDIANS. Being a Series of Impressions, Notes, and Essays. By MONIER WILLIAMS, D.C.L. Second Edition. Post 8vo. cloth, pp. 244. 1878. 7*s.* 6*d.*

Wilson.—Works of the late HORACE HAYMAN WILSON, M.A., F.R.S., Member of the Royal Asiatic Societies of Calcutta and Paris, and of the Oriental Soc. of Germany, etc., and Boden Prof. of Sanskrit in the University of Oxford.

Vols I. and II. ESSAYS AND LECTURES chiefly on the Religion of the Hindus, by the late H. H. WILSON, M.A., F.R.S., etc. Collected and edited by Dr. REINHOLD ROST. 2 vols. cloth, pp. xiii. and 399, vi. and 416. 21*s.*

Vols. III, IV. and V. ESSAYS ANALYTICAL, CRITICAL, AND PHILOLOGICAL, ON SUBJECTS CONNECTED WITH SANSKRIT LITERATURE. Collected and Edited by Dr. REINHOLD ROST. 3 vols. 8vo. pp. 408, 406, and 390, cloth. Price 36*s.*

Vols. VI., VII., VIII, IX. and X., Part I. VISHNU PURÁNÁ, A SYSTEM OF HINDU MYTHOLOGY AND TRADITION. Vols. I. to V. Translated from the original Sanskrit, and Illustrated by Notes derived chiefly from other Purāṇás. By the late H. H. WILSON, Edited by FITZEDWARD HALL, M.A., D.C.L., Oxon. 8vo., pp. cxl. and 200; 344; 344; 346, cloth. 2*l.* 12*s.* 6*d.*

Vol. X., Part 2, containing the Index to, and completing the Vishnu Puráná, compiled by Fitzedward Hall. 8vo. cloth. pp. 268. 12*s.*

Vols. XI. and XII. SELECT SPECIMENS OF THE THEATRE OF THE HINDUS. Translated from the Original Sanskrit. By the late HORACE HAYMAN WILSON, M.A., F.R.S. 3rd corrected Ed. 2 vols. 8vo. pp. lxi. and 384; and iv. and 418, cl. 21*s.*

Wilson.—SELECT SPECIMENS OF THE THEATRE OF THE HINDUS. Translated from the Original Sanskrit. By the late HORACE HAYMAN WILSON, M.A., F.R.S. Third corrected edition. 2 vols. 8vo., pp. lxxi. and 384; iv. and 418, cloth. 21*s.*

CONTENTS.

Vol. I.—Preface—Treatise on the Dramatic System of the Hindus—Dramas translated from the Original Sanskrit—The Mrichchakati, or the Toy Cart—Vikram aand Urvasi, or the Hero and the Nymph—Uttara Káma Charitra, or continuation of the History of Káma.

Vol. II.—Dramas translated from the Original Sanskrit—Malâti and Mádhava, or the Stolen Marriage—Mudrá Rakshasa, or the Signet of the Minister—Ratnávalí, or the Necklace—Appendix, containing short accounts of different Dramas.

Wilson.—THE PRESENT STATE OF THE CULTIVATION OF ORIENTAL LITERATURE. A Lecture delivered at the Meeting of the Royal Asiatic Society. By the Director, Professor H. H. WILSON. 8vo. pp. 26, sewed. London, 1852. 6*d.*

Wilson.—A DICTIONARY IN SANSKRIT AND ENGLISH. Translated, amended, and enlarged from an original compilation prepared by learned Natives for the College of Fort William by H. H. WILSON. The Third Edition edited by Jagunmohana Tarkalankara and Khettramohana Mookerjee. Published by Gyanendrachandra Rayachoudhuri and Brothers. 4to. pp. 1008. Calcutta, 1874. £3 3*s.*

Wilson (H. H.).—See also Megha Duta, Rig-Veda, and Vishnu-Puráná.

Wise.—COMMENTARY ON THE HINDU SYSTEM OF MEDICINE. By T. A. WISE, M.D., Bengal Medical Service. 8vo., pp. xx. and 432, cloth. 7*s.* 6*d.*

Wise.—REVIEW OF THE HISTORY OF MEDICINE. By THOMAS A. WISE, M.D. 2 vols. 8vo. cloth. Vol. I., pp. xcviii. and 397; Vol. II., pp. 574. 10*s.*

Withers.—THE ENGLISH LANGUAGE SPELLED AS PRONOUNCED, with enlarged Alphabet of Forty Letters. With Specimen. By GEORGE WITHERS. Royal 8vo. sewed, pp. 84. 1*s.*

Wordsworth.—THE CHURCH OF THIBET, and the Historical Analogies of Buddhism and Christianity. A Lecture delivered at Bombay by W. WORDSWORTH, B.A., Principal of Elphinstone College. 1877. 8vo. pp. 51. 2*s.* 6*d.*

Wright.—FEUDAL MANUALS OF ENGLISH HISTORY. A Series of Popular Sketches of our National History, compiled at different periods, from the Thirteenth Century to the Fifteenth, for the use of the Feudal Gentry and Nobility. Now first edited from the Original Manuscripts. By THOMAS WRIGHT, Esq., M.A. Small 4to. cloth, pp. xxiv. and 184. 1872. 15*s.*

Wright.—THE HOMES OF OTHER DAYS. A History of Domestic Manners and Sentiments during the Middle Ages. By THOMAS WRIGHT, Esq., M.A., F.S.A. With Illustrations from the Illuminations in contemporary Manuscripts and other Sources, drawn and engraved by F. W. Fairholt, Esq., F.S.A. 1 Vol. medium 8vo. handsomely bound in cloth, pp. xv. and 512. 350 Woodcuts. £1 1*s.*

Wright.—THE CELT, THE ROMAN, AND THE SAXON; a History of the Early Inhabitants of Britain down to the Conversion of the Anglo-Saxons to Christianity. Illustrated by the Ancient Remains brought to Light by Recent Research. By THOMAS WRIGHT, Esq., M.A., F.S.A., etc., etc. Third Corrected and Enlarged Edition. Numerous Illustrations. Crown 8vo. cloth, pp. xiv. and 562. 14*s.*

Wright.—ANGLO-SAXON AND OLD-ENGLISH VOCABULARIES, Illustrating the Condition and Manners of our Forefathers, as well as the History of the Forms of Elementary Education, and of the Languages spoken in this Island from the Tenth Century to the Fifteenth. Edited by THOMAS WRIGHT, Esq., M.A., F.S.A., etc. Second Edition, edited, collated, and corrected by RICHARD WULCKER. [*In the press.*

Wylie.—NOTES ON CHINESE LITERATURE; with introductory Remarks on the Progressive Advancement of the Art; and a list of translations from the Chinese, into various European Languages. By A. WYLIE, Agent of the British and Foreign Bible Society in China. 4to. pp. 296, cloth. Price, £1 16*s.*

Yajurveda.—THE WHITE YAJURVEDA IN THE MADHYANDINA RECENSION. With the Commentary of Mahidhara. Complete in 36 parts. Large square 8vo. pp. 571. £4 10*s.*

Yates.—A BENGÁLÍ GRAMMAR. By the late Rev. W. YATES, D.D. Reprinted, with improvements, from his Introduction to the Bengáli Language Edited by I. WENGER. Fcap. 8vo., pp. iv. and 150, bds. Calcutta, 1864. 3*s.* 6*d.*